D1604322

Nixon's Back Channel to Moscow

NIXON'S
BACK CHANNEL TO
MOSCOW

CONFIDENTIAL DIPLOMACY
AND DÉTENTE

Richard A. Moss

Foreword by
Admiral James Stavridis, USN (Ret.)

UNIVERSITY PRESS OF KENTUCKY

Scholarly publisher for the Commonwealth,
serving Bellarmine University, Berea College, Centre College of Kentucky, Eastern
Kentucky University, The Filson Historical Society, Georgetown College, Kentucky
Historical Society, Kentucky State University, Morehead State University, Murray
State University, Northern Kentucky University, Transylvania University, University of
Kentucky, University of Louisville, and Western Kentucky University.
All rights reserved.

Editorial and Sales Offices: The University Press of Kentucky
663 South Limestone Street, Lexington, Kentucky 40508-4008
www.kentuckypress.com

The statements of fact, opinion, or analysis expressed in the manuscript are the author's and
do not reflect the official policy or position of the U.S. Government, the Department of
Defense, or any of its components. Review of the material does not imply Department of
Defense or U.S. Government verification or endorsement of factual accuracy or opinion.

Library of Congress Cataloging-in-Publication Data

Names: Moss, Richard A., author.
Title: Nixon's back channel to Moscow : confidential diplomacy and detente /
    Richard A. Moss ; foreword by Admiral James Stavridis, USN (Ret.).
Description: Lexington, Kentucky : University Press of Kentucky, 2016. |
    Series: Studies in conflict, diplomacy, and peace | Includes
    bibliographical references and index.
Identifiers: LCCN 2016043340| ISBN 9780813167879 (hardcover : alk. paper) |
    ISBN 9780813167886 (pdf) | ISBN 9780813167893 (epub)
Subjects: LCSH: United States—Foreign relations—Soviet Union. | Soviet
    Union—Foreign relations—United States. | United States—Foreign
    relations—1969–1974. | Nixon, Richard M. (Richard Milhous),
    1913-1994—Influence. | Kissinger, Henry, 1923–   —Influence. | Detente.
Classification: LCC E183.8.S65 M68 2016 | DDC 327.73047—dc23
LC record available at https://lccn.loc.gov/2016043340

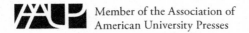

The introduction of caffeinated drinks and chocolate to Europe
may have sparked the Industrial Revolution;
their consumption certainly contributed to this book.
This book is dedicated to my wife, Amy, and son, Samuel,
who share my weaknesses for caffeine and chocolate,
and to my son, Daniel, who arrived as I was
finishing this book, and who has completed my family.

Contents

Foreword

The similarities abound between the Nixon era and our current time, with the caveat that much of the record of the earlier administration has since been declassified and is publicly available to anybody who wants to listen in on presidential conversations or read once-classified memos of the issues of the day. By contrast, the materials on WikiLeaks comprise a small percentage of the overall output by policymakers and derive only from certain agencies, such as the State Department. Richard Moss's study of back-channel diplomacy draws on rich, revealing sources such as the Nixon tapes, which journalist Bob Woodward called the "gift that keeps on giving."[1] Moss also relies on more than one hundred thousand pages of U.S. documents and the nearly complete record of U.S.-Soviet exchanges between Henry Kissinger and Anatoly Dobrynin, in addition to Russian, European, and other sources.

Moss presents some important lessons related to the conduct of back-channel diplomacy, in addition to describing in great detail the evolution of the relationship between Kissinger and Dobrynin. He presents ample evidence that back channels work best when they supplement rather than supplant more traditional diplomacy. Additionally, back channels can shelter sensitive negotiations from political pressure and compartmentalize information against leaks. Although they may function as a weapon in bureaucratic rivalries, such as that between Kissinger and Secretary of State William P. Rogers, back channels may also inadvertently telegraph anxiety or weakness on certain issues.

These lessons remain important as back-channel diplomacy persists today. For example, recent back channels probably have played a role in brokering the agreement to curb Iran's nuclear program in exchange for the relief of international sanctions,[2] and also in the reestablished diplomatic relations between the United States and Cuba.[3] President Barack Obama's back-channel diplomacy has had effects on today's U.S. foreign policy machinery similar to those that resulted from the back-channel diplomacy of the Nixon era. The opening to Cuba echoes Nixon's opening to China with the surprise it generated inside the Beltway, among foreign-policy watchers, the government bureaucracy, and the military, which has viewed Havana as a potential adversary for more than five decades.

National Security vs. Leaks

Leaks remain a perennial problem for the White House and diplomats,[4] and back channels are one way to shelter sensitive negotiations from outside factors like political pressure and interest groups. The advent of electronic materials, however, increases the impact far beyond the Pentagon Papers that plagued the Nixon administration and were viewed as justification to create the Plumbers. Interestingly, it was Secretary of State William Rogers, Henry Kissinger's bureaucratic nemesis in the conduct of foreign policy, who ordered the electronic storage of State Department cables.[5] Perhaps Rogers has the last laugh, despite Kissinger's apparent subscription to the maxim that you should outlive your enemies. The persistence of leaking also underlies political or bureaucratic rivalries today just as it did during Nixon's administration.

It was a slippery slope to Watergate from what could be seen as allowable national security measures by the Plumbers when probing how investigative journalist Jack Anderson acquired documents from the highest-level crisis management discussions to violations of the Constitution and American principles. That tension still exists as we deal with the fallout from and attempt to react appropriately as a society to what we have learned from WikiLeaks, Chelsea Manning, and Edward Snowden.

U.S.-Russian Relations

Despite the end of the Cold War and a true détente—the relaxation of tensions—during the 1990s and early 2000s, Vladimir Putin's Russia evokes memories of the Soviet Union under Leonid Brezhnev. While Russia has begun sending its aged fleet of Tu-95 "Bear" bombers to the warmer climes of Cuba and Venezuela and has recently been harassing NATO forces in the Baltic nations in ways reminiscent of the Cold War, the scale is substantially smaller. Russia's perceived national interests today also may be narrower than during the Nixon-Brezhnev era, just as the dividing lines between competing political-economic systems and alliances were much sharper.

Whereas Kissinger and Dobrynin could joke about "fomenting the maintenance of the status quo" and recognized the dividing lines between NATO and the Warsaw Pact, it seems that today's Russian leaders no longer enjoy such peace of mind and see what to their eyes appear to be U.S.-sponsored plots in the traditional Soviet sphere of influence. Vladimir Putin and other Russians cynically charge American interference in what used to be Moscow's backyard, likely trying to deflect attention from Russia's economic, social, and political problems.

That the conspiracy theories of Western machinations find an audience is troubling but explainable by the underlying tensions of Russia's geographical and intellectual position between East and West. The interpretation of Russia's past, its self-identity, character, and cultural worth, has hinged on many of the fundamental questions first raised during the Slavophile-Westernizer debates of the nineteenth century.[6] Should Russia adopt European customs and values or accept autocracy and Orthodoxy? Russia's history of being invaded, its renewed Orthodox faith, its view of itself as a conservative bastion against corrupt values, and its military punching weight make for a potentially volatile combination.[7] These factors make it even more important to have the types of candid, confidential exchanges that Kissinger and Dobrynin enjoyed. There also needs to be an understanding that the U.S.-Russian relations can be a force for progress in tackling the issues the world faces.

All of this adds up to a provocative and incisive book: read it.

Admiral James Stavridis, USN (Ret.),
Supreme Allied Commander, NATO, 2009–2013

Preface

"There have been more back-channel games played in this administration than any in history because we couldn't trust the goddamned State Department," President Richard Nixon fumed to several close associates in late December 1971.[1] Nixon's reference to "back-channel games" was verbal shorthand for the web of clandestine contacts that the Nixon White House used to conduct its foreign policy. This was diplomacy directed from 1600 Pennsylvania Avenue rather than the State Department through formal meetings with ambassadors and foreign ministers.

Nixon's surreptitious taping system captured discussion of an especially sensitive matter related to the back channels during the same December 1971 meeting in the Executive Office Building (EOB), now known as the Eisenhower Executive Office Building. Nixon used his hideaway office in the EOB, an imposing structure connected to the White House by tunnels, to escape the clamor and formality of the Oval Office.[2] Through the crackle, hiss, and buzz of the recorded conversation, Nixon and his associates reviewed how the White House Special Investigative Unit, more commonly known as the Plumbers, had discovered that the military had been spying on the White House and the National Security Council (NSC).

The investigation began in early December when investigative journalist Jack Anderson quoted classified documents in his syndicated columns to critique the Nixon administration's response to the Indo-Pakistani War. Chief domestic advisor John Ehrlichman and White House aide David Young reviewed the results of their inquiry for Nixon, Chief of Staff H. R. "Bob" Haldeman, and Attorney General John Mitchell. Ehrlichman and Young described how a navy stenographer attached to the NSC–Joint Chiefs of Staff (JCS) liaison office, Yeoman 1st Class Charles Radford, had stolen documents and passed them through the chain of command to JCS chairman Admiral Thomas Moorer.

How Anderson came into possession of the documents remains a mystery. The Nixon White House believed Yeoman Radford was the source of the leak, viewing Radford's social and religious ties to Anderson, in addition to possible sympathy for India, as motives and means to commit "a federal offense of the highest order."[3] Nixon viewed Anderson's and Radford's Mormonism with particular suspicion, and he speculated that the two had a homosexual relationship.[4] Radford admitted taking documents and passing them to the JCS, but he denied being the source of the leak under questioning, including polygraph examinations. Anderson went to his grave in 2005 without revealing his source, but he told one author: "You don't get those kind of secrets from enlisted men. You only get them from generals and admirals."[5]

Foreshadowing Watergate—the same dramatis personae were implicated in the scandal—Nixon decided to cover up what became known as the Moorer-Radford affair. Nixon may have realized that his penchant for secrecy had encouraged the JCS to spy on the White House: "I mean, Moorer, I have total confidence that he's on our side. I just wish he'd have asked, and we'd have given it to him in advance," Nixon conceded.[6] Nixon agreed with John Mitchell that exposure of the spy ring could implicate the entire JCS, damage the reputation of the military while the United States was still embroiled in Vietnam, and destroy the relationship between the commander in chief and the military.[7] "The thing that is very, very bad about this," Nixon admitted, was "that if this story got out, it would be used to destroy the services. . . . Here're the services setting up their own Gestapo and so forth, spying on the president."[8]

Covering up the spy ring—itself a response to the administration's secrecy—was the price Nixon felt he had to pay to implement his grand vision for a structure of peace and transcending the zero-sum game of the Cold War. Nixon's penchant for secrecy earned him a place in history as one of America's greatest strategists before it destroyed his presidency.

Abbreviations

ABM	Anti-Ballistic Missile
ACDA	Arms Control and Disarmament Agency
AL	Awami League
ALCM	Air-Launched Cruise Missile
ARVN	Army of the Republic of Vietnam (South Vietnam's army)
CAB	Cabinet Room (Nixon Tapes taping location)
CDHW	Camp David Hard Wire (Nixon Tapes taping location)
CDST	Camp David Study Table (Nixon Tapes taping location)
CIA	Central Intelligence Agency
CPSU	Communist Party of the Soviet Union
CRP or CREEP	Committee to Re-Elect the President
CWIHP	Cold War International History Project
DMZ	De-Militarized Zone
DNSA	Digital National Security Archive
DRV	Democratic Republic of Vietnam (a.k.a. North Vietnam)
EBB	(National Security Archive) Electronic Briefing Book
EOB	Executive Office Building
FBI	Federal Bureau of Investigation
FBS	Forward Base System
FOIA	Freedom of Information Act
FRG	Federal Republic of Germany (a.k.a. West Germany)
FRUS	*Foreign Relations of the United States,* documentary series produced by the U.S. Department of State

GDR	German Democratic Republic (a.k.a. East Germany)
HAK	Henry Alfred Kissinger
ICBM	Inter-Continental Ballistic Missile
JCS	Joint Chiefs of Staff
KGB	Soviet Committee for State Security (Komitet Gosudarstvennoy Bezopasnosti)
MBFR	Mutually Balanced Force Reductions
Memcon	Memorandum of Conversation
MIRV	Multiple Independently Targeted Reentry Vehicle
MRV	Multiple Reentry Vehicle
NARA	National Archives and Records Administration
NATO	North Atlantic Treaty Organization
NCA	National Command Authority
NEA	State Department Bureau of Near Eastern Affairs
NLF	National Liberation Front (a.k.a. Viet Cong)
NPMP	Nixon Presidential Materials Project
NPT or NNPT	Nuclear Non-Proliferation Treaty
NSAEBB	National Security Archive Electronic Briefing Book
NSC	National Security Council
NSSM	National Security Study Memorandums
NT	Nixon Tapes
OVAL	Oval Office (Nixon Tapes taping location)
PDD	President's Daily Diary
PFLP	Popular Front for the Liberation of Palestine
PLO	Palestinian Liberation Organization
PPP	Pakistani People's Party
PRC	People's Republic of China
RG	Record Group
RN	Richard Nixon, also the title of Nixon's memoir.
RNPLM	Richard Nixon Presidential Library and Museum
SALT	Strategic Arms Limitation Talks
SAM	Surface-to-Air Missile
SLBM	Submarine-Launched Ballistic Missile
SRG	Senior Review Group

TASS	Telegraphic Agency of the Soviet Union
Telcon	Telephone Conversation Transcript
UAR	United Arab Republic
ULMS	Under-sea Long-Range Missile System (a.k.a. Trident)
WHT	White House Telephone (Nixon Tapes taping location)
WHY	*White House Years,* first volume of Kissinger's memoirs
WSAG	Washington Special Action Group

Introduction

Khenry and Anatol

In short, the Channel was only the tip of the iceberg. Its underlying design was strategic, but often its manifestations were tactical.

—Henry A. Kissinger, 2007

Looking back, I can say with a fair degree of confidence that without that channel it would hardly have been possible to reach many key agreements in a timely manner or to eliminate dangerous tensions that arose periodically.

—Anatoly F. Dobrynin, 2007

On the evening of February 14, 1969, Henry Kissinger attended a reception at the Soviet embassy in honor of Georgi Arbatov, the founder and director of the Soviet Academy of Science's Institute of the U.S.A. and Canada. Kissinger had earlier dealings with Arbatov, but the new national security advisor to Nixon was not there to see the Soviet academic.[1] Ushered upstairs to the private apartment of the party's host and the person he really came to see, Kissinger found Soviet ambassador Anatoly Dobrynin "confined to bed with the flu." Kissinger and Dobrynin nevertheless had an "extremely forthcoming" conversation about the status of U.S.-Soviet relations and the hazards to peace. Kissinger reported back to Nixon that the Soviets wished "to conduct conversations with some person you designate who has your confidence, but who was not part of the diplomatic establishment."[2] Years later, Kissinger recalled, "[Dobrynin] suggested that since we would work closely we call each other by our first names. From then on, he was 'Anatol' and I was 'Henry' (or more often 'Khenry,' since the Russian language has no 'h' sound)." Poking fun at his own Teutonic baritone, Kissinger added: "We spoke in English. I did not make fun of him because he spoke with an accent."[3]

According to Dobrynin's contemporaneous account, however, it was Kissinger who suggested the creation of a confidential channel on President Nixon's behalf. Kissinger told Dobrynin: "The Soviet side . . . knows how to maintain confidentiality; but in our State Department, unfortunately, there are occasional leaks of information to the press." It was for these reasons that Nixon wanted to maintain a "most confidential exchange of views with the Soviet leadership." The president would meet with Dobrynin occasionally to facilitate the process but would also "actively utilize a confidential channel between Kissinger and the Soviet Ambassador." Kissinger professed his readiness to meet "any time, any place" with Dobrynin to discuss "several different problems *in parallel* and *simultaneously.*" Dobrynin told his superiors he was ready to work with Kissinger.[4]

Kissinger's bedside meeting with Dobrynin, several phone calls, and another visit to the Soviet embassy paved the way for a private meeting at the White House between Nixon and Dobrynin.[5] In a one-on-one session, Nixon endorsed the use of a back channel between Kissinger, as his personal representative, and Dobrynin, as the intermediary to the Soviet leadership. Over time, the relationship came to be known as "the Channel" and was the primary back channel in U.S.-Soviet relations during the Nixon administration. During the tête-à-tête, Nixon declared a goal of improving superpower relations, the relaxation of tensions more commonly known as détente. Following the private exchange, Kissinger and Acting Deputy Assistant Secretary of State for European Affairs Malcolm Toon entered the room. According to Nixon's chief of staff, H. R. Haldeman, the inclusion of Toon afterward was something of a compromise solution after Secretary of State William Rogers objected that "the P[resident] should never meet alone with an ambassador" and also because of Kissinger's concerns about State Department leaks. Nevertheless, the topics the men discussed would become the preliminary roadmap to détente: strategic arms limitations, a potential Middle East settlement, the future status of Germany and that perennial Cold War flashpoint, Berlin, and the U.S. withdrawal from Vietnam. Dobrynin reported back to Moscow that he sensed delay and that it would be at least a month before a more detailed agenda could be set for frank discussions in both open and private channels.[6]

After the president's endorsement directly to Dobrynin, Kissinger worked his connections to build rapport with the Soviet ambassador. Two days later, Kissinger consulted with Averell Harriman, the former U.S. ambassador to the Soviet Union (1943–1946) and an éminence grise on that nation. The new national security advisor knew that Harriman frequently met with Dobrynin. Without divulging plans for a special back channel, Kissinger told Harriman that anything he could do to "validate" him with Dobrynin would "be of tremendous help."[7] Kissinger's personal attention to his relationship with Dobrynin, and the efforts of major policy actors on both sides of the Cold War divide to reinforce the personal and confidential diplomacy, became a hallmark in achieving détente.

In later years, the three main back-channel interlocutors—Kissinger, Dobrynin, and Nixon—reflected on the private exchanges that had shaped superpower relations. Nixon credited Kissinger with the idea of developing a "private channel" in which Dobrynin and the Soviets "might be more forthcoming in strictly private and unpublicized meetings."[8] Likewise, in his memoir, Dobrynin recalled that the confidential channel's widespread use "turned out to be unprecedented in my experience and perhaps in the annals of diplomacy."[9] Kissinger, too, lauded the importance and explained the function of the Channel whereby he and Dobrynin "would, informally, clarify the basic purposes of our governments and when our talks gave hope of specific agreements, the subject was moved to conventional diplomatic channels." From a bird's-eye view, "it was a way to explore the terrain, to avoid major deadlocks." In cases where formal negotiations reached an impasse, "the Channel would open up again." The informal nature of the meetings meant that "neither side was precluded from raising [an] issue formally because of adverse reaction from the other," and "at least inadvertent confrontations were prevented."[10]

The use of back channels outside the foreign policy apparatus was hardly unprecedented, either in the annals of diplomacy or even specifically in U.S.-Soviet relations. Kissinger acknowledged that there were earlier precedents for advisors serving as intermediaries at presidential behest, such as "the relationship between Woodrow Wilson and Colonel House or between Franklin Roosevelt and his intimate, Harry Hopkins."[11] More broadly speaking, the use of special emissaries and personal intermediaries is almost as old as diplomacy itself, and many agreements in history have been worked out through secret channels bypassing established diplomatic institutions.

Long before Nixon became president, the executive branch had utilized private correspondence with foreign leaders, presidential emissaries, confidential channels, and other types of communication beyond the purview of the normal foreign policy bureaucracy. Earlier back channels had typically been used to resolve specific issues, such as establishing U.S.-Soviet diplomatic relations in 1933 and negotiating the withdrawal of American missiles from Turkey as part of the settlement of the Cuban Missile Crisis. In the latter example, Attorney General Robert Kennedy, at the behest of his brother President John F. Kennedy, had used back-channel approaches through a KGB operative, Georgi Bolshakov, and also through Ambassador Dobrynin, in the resolution of the 1962 crisis.[12] Dobrynin, therefore, was no stranger to back channels.

Nor was Kissinger a stranger to U.S.-Soviet back-channel diplomacy. Recently declassified documents corroborate a claim by Georgi Arbatov that Kissinger had been an envoy to Moscow in December 1967 for the Johnson administration, under cover of the Soviet-American Disarmament Study Group (SADS), more than a year before the Kissinger-Dobrynin channel was established.[13] According to Arbatov—the Soviet academic at whose party Kissinger later met Dobrynin—Kissinger's "real mission" in late 1967 was "to feel out the possibility of gaining Moscow's support in solving the [Vietnam] conflict."[14]

In essence, Kissinger went to Moscow in an attempt to revive Operation Pennsylvania, an unsuccessful peace proposal to Hanoi via two French intermediaries, Raymond Aubrac and Herbert Marcovich. Operation Pennsylvania paved the way for what would become known as the "San Antonio Formula," after a speech (in San Antonio) in which President Johnson said that the United States would stop all aerial and naval bombardment of North Vietnam in exchange for peace negotiations.[15] In the words of biographer Walter Isaacson, "Thus began Kissinger's first experience with secret diplomacy and his baptism into the difficulties of dealing with the North Vietnamese."[16] Kissinger's role in Operation Pennsylvania was publicly known in April 1968, but his attempt to revive the negotiations with the North Vietnamese was unknown until the publication of Arbatov's memoir.[17]

The proposals Kissinger put forward at SADS in 1967 resembled those he would promote as Nixon's national security advisor: a cease-fire, the withdrawal of both U.S and North Vietnamese troops from South

Vietnam, and a political settlement. Arbatov recalled that Kissinger's pro- posals "did not make a great impression on anyone [in the Soviet leader- ship]."[18] Nevertheless Kissinger's exercise clearly demonstrated his growing belief that the road to peace in Vietnam went through Moscow and pro- vided a blueprint of Johnson's bombing-halt-for-negotiations strategy.

Despite the earlier precedents, the Dobrynin-Kissinger channel was novel in its breadth, its sweeping exclusion of the State Department, and most significantly for its central role in shaping détente. Since the early 1970s, critics and supporters alike have acknowledged that the Nixon administration centralized foreign policy, bypassed more traditional diplomacy, and used back channels to set the course and tone of policy. Back-channel communication in U.S.-Soviet relations during the Nixon administration was by no means limited to the main Dobrynin-Kissinger channel and often included the president himself and a range of oth- ers—including State Department officials—who sidestepped normal dip- lomatic procedures.

Although there were occasional references in the press between 1969 and 1972 to meetings between Dobrynin, Kissinger, and Nixon, the first reference to a special "back-channel" relationship between the Soviet ambassador and the national security advisor probably did not occur until journalist John Newhouse published a series of articles in the *New Yorker* in 1973. These articles became the basis for *Cold Dawn: The Story of SALT,* also published in 1973. Newhouse painted a brief but sympathetic picture of the diplomacy used to break impasses in the Strategic Arms Limitations Talks (SALT), but he did not fully realize the extent of the back-channel relationship, which remained masked until years later.[19] Kissinger himself gave the fullest account of his confidential channels with the Soviets in his 1979 memoir, *White House Years,* and nearly every account—critical and favorable—that has mentioned the back channel has relied on Kissinger's memoirs. Dobrynin's memoir, *In Confidence,* published in 1995, gave the Soviet side of the story based on the long-serving Soviet ambassador's own accounts of his meetings with Kissinger. Fittingly, Dobrynin inscribed the copy he gave to Kissinger: "To Henry, opponent, partner, friend."[20]

Although the Kissinger-Dobrynin channel began in 1969, back-chan- nel diplomacy with the Soviets was not dominant until 1971, when the Channel became "operational," as Kissinger later wrote, to cover the Ber- lin negotiations, break an impasse in SALT, and begin tentative planning for a summit meeting.[21] Nixon and Kissinger consciously and actively expanded the use of back-channel diplomacy throughout 1971 to include discussions over a Middle East settlement and private correspondence between Nixon and Brezhnev, which was often sanitized before being circulated to Secretary of State Rogers and other cabinet officials. For Kissinger, back channels were a means to avoid controversy by preventing leaks, controlling policy, and avoiding entanglement with the State Department's supposedly sclerotic foreign policy bureaucracy.[22]

Scholars and journalists have offered a variety of alternative justifications for the establishment of the Channel, such as the Nixon administration's general obsession with secrecy, the president's desire to maximize personal credit for domestic political gain, and Kissinger's efforts to centralize power. Historian Jussi Hanhimäki, investigative journalist Seymour Hersh, Arms Control and Disarmament Agency (ACDA) head Ambassador Gerard Smith, and others have also highlighted the flaws of back-channel diplomacy on a range of specific topics to an indictment of the entire Nixon-Kissinger foreign policy.[23]

In the standard text on U.S.-Soviet relations, arms-control-expert and policymaker-turned-chronicler Raymond Garthoff cautioned that Kissinger's rise to prominence "developed unevenly over time" and contended that the Channel covered up a central shortcoming with regard to the Strategic Arms Limitations Talks (SALT). Despite its being cited as one of the main achievements of the Nixon-Kissinger détente policy, Garthoff saw some problems with the interim SALT agreement signed at the Moscow Summit in 1972: "Kissinger came to realize that he had not negotiated the substance of offensive limitations advantageously, or even satisfactorily, and sought to conceal this fact. It was all the more important for him to do so as he had allowed no participation or sharing of responsibility for those negotiations with the rest of the government."[24]

Despite the criticisms of the Nixon-Kissinger foreign policy and the use of back channels, many scholars agree that the use of confidential channels was inseparable from and essential to facilitating reduced U.S.-Soviet tensions. At a 2007 conference hosted by the State Department, historian Robert Schulzinger stated: "The Moscow Summit was the culmination of the process of détente. . . . I don't see that summit coming about without this channel." Jeremi Suri, the author of an intellectual biography of Kissinger, agreed. He explained that the confidential channel reinforced three elements of détente, namely: shielding negotiations on sensitive subjects from "complicating elements"; reinforcing agreement "in key areas of traditional Cold War conflict, especially Europe"; and "furthering the channel . . . to lock out new entrants into the channel or into negotiations who might complicate diplomacy." Russian-born scholar Vladislav Zubok likewise stressed that the Soviet leadership was ready to tackle issues on Europe, but "when you talk about the United States . . . you had to have a back channel and secret diplomacy to achieve what was achieved." Zubok continued that there was "a ninety percent chance . . . that there would not have been a summit in Moscow in '72, and such a productive summit that it was, without the back channel."[25]

Although much has been written about détente, this is the first study to focus on the central role of back-channel diplomacy in shaping the reduction in superpower tensions.[26] Semantically, "back channel" or "confidential channel" in this book refers to communication outside of the normal State Department purview, such as the Nixon-Brezhnev exchanges, while "the Channel" refers specifically to the Kissinger-Dobrynin meetings and communications. Nearly all depictions of U.S.-Soviet relations to date have relied upon retrospective (and occasionally self-serving) memoirs, interviews, and oral histories. Although such sources are valuable, the preponderance of declassified primary sources better clarifies the issues and reduces the dependency on the participants' after-the-fact viewpoints.

This book would not be possible without the nearly one-thousand-page record—jointly compiled, translated, annotated, and published by the U.S. Department of State and the Russian Foreign Ministry—in *U.S.-Soviet Relations in the Era of Détente, 1969–1972*. This unprecedented collection makes this work possible because it includes both the American and Soviet memoranda of conversations (memcons) of the back-channel meetings and phone calls, in addition to cables and other sources. Unfortunately, while most U.S. policy meetings during the period in question have been declassified, the Politburo minutes for the Soviet side remain largely unavailable.[27] To corroborate the published Soviet records of the back channel, this book relied on the documents available at the National Security Archive and the Cold War International History Project (CWIHP), in addition to the memoirs of former Soviet officials.[28]

It is ironic that one of the most secretive presidential administrations in U.S. history, with its cloak-and-dagger intrigues to plug leaks, is also possibly one of the best documented due to the Nixon tapes. The availability of more than 2,600 hours of Nixon's taped conversations, in addition to detailed memoranda of meetings, policy papers, transcripts of Kissinger's telephone conversations (telcons), Chief of Staff H. R. "Bob" Haldeman's daily diary, and a host of other rich resources makes it possible to explore the Kissinger-Dobrynin relationship over several years of interaction on the defining issues of superpower relations.[29] Historians are fortunate to have a unique opportunity to examine the real-time discussion, deliberation, decision, and implementation of Nixon's détente policy.

This work makes particular use of the Nixon tapes to go behind the back channel to uncover what Nixon and his foreign policy advisors discussed before, during, and after meetings with their Soviet counterparts. Kissinger did not keep detailed written records of every back-channel meeting, but he usually briefed the president in person or on the phone following his meetings with Ambassador Dobrynin or other Soviet back-channel interlocutors, such as Soviet embassy counselor minister Yuli Vorontsov. These discussions, more candid than polished written memos, would have been lost to history were it not for the Nixon tapes and the Kissinger telcons. This process has involved reviewing hundreds of hours of tapes for conversations that correlate to U.S.-Soviet back-channel exchanges.[30] While there are a number of potential pitfalls to using such a unique and challenging source as the tapes, every effort has been made to transcribe and integrate original and accurate transcripts into this study, especially when the recordings refer to meetings for which no paper records exist.[31]

In addition to declassified tapes and documents, the publication of a number of documentary collections, such as the *Foreign Relations of the United States* (*FRUS*) produced by the U.S. Department of State, have also enriched this study. When combined with an abundance of secondary sources, memoir accounts by most of the major participants (American and Soviet), press coverage at the time, and declassified archival materials, a thorough examination of crucial moments in U.S.-Soviet relations between 1968 and 1972 has finally become possible. Furthermore, the combination of sources can also illuminate the three-dimensional human beings who shaped, argued, schemed, and, in moments of pique, swore about policy.

This book documents and analyzes the function of the back channels in U.S.-Soviet relations from Nixon's inauguration through what has widely been heralded as the achievement of détente, the May 1972 Moscow Summit. This work argues that although back-channel diplomacy may have been useful in improving U.S.-Soviet relations in the short term by acting as a safety valve to relieve tensions and giving policy actors a personal stake in the improvement in relations, it provided a weak foundation for long-term détente. Incongruously, this focus on U.S.-Soviet back-channel diplomacy mitigates some of criticisms levied against Nixon and Kissinger in their secretive conduct of diplomacy, such as contextualizing that the administration did not act as recklessly during the 1971 Indo-Pakistani War as most accounts charge. The conduct of back-channel diplomacy was neither as positive as the administration figures made it out to be nor as egregious as the detractors have contended. The Nixon White House used back channels most successfully when they supplemented, rather than bypassed, traditional diplomacy. This is the history of what was fundamentally compromise and communication from both American and Soviet policymakers.

Organizationally, this book traces the evolution of confidential channels during the Nixon administration and examines certain flashpoints in U.S.-Soviet relations. Kissinger and Nixon moved to expand the back-channel relationship with the Soviets in late 1970 in the wake of the Cienfuegos crisis, a sort of light version of the 1962 Cuban Missile Crisis. Handling the mini-crisis via the Channel allowed the Soviet and U.S. leaderships to move to break impasses that had developed in negotiations over SALT and a Berlin access agreement.

Back channels served as a safety valve that allowed détente to proceed on a number of occasions. The 1971 South Asian crisis and war threatened to undermine détente before it could really begin as the United States backed Pakistan and the Soviet Union backed India during the short war. The U.S. involvement in Vietnam and Moscow's support for Hanoi remained constant irritants as Washington tried to enlist Moscow's assistance in its negotiations with North Vietnam. The Channel also served as a means by which the Nixon administration relayed to the North Vietnamese that aggressive action would be met with force. Both Washington and Moscow had their own internal crises over whether or not to cancel the Moscow summit when the Soviet-backed North Vietnamese Army launched its Easter Offensive against U.S.-backed South

Vietnam in late March 1972. The solution—agreeing to disagree—was handled largely through back-channel means.

Both sides also used back channels as an accelerator and as a brake to "link" key negotiations, and both sides displayed anxieties in back-channel dealings. While the Nixon administration tied offensive and defensive limitations together in SALT, the Soviets made a Berlin agreement into the price for a Soviet-American summit. Likewise, the Sino-American rapprochement that began in earnest with Kissinger's secret trip to China in July 1972 was a game changer that factored into U.S. and Soviet decision making on U.S.-Soviet détente and managing the Channel.

Although this study touches upon back-channel diplomacy in seeking a Middle East peace settlement, the peace process itself is beyond its chronological and thematic scope. The Nixon administration inherited a number of circumstances as a result of the 1967 Arab-Israeli War and initially favored multilateral negotiations in search of a Middle East settlement through the State Department. Secretary of State Rogers and Assistant Secretary of State for Near Eastern and South Asian Affairs Joseph Sisco achieved a cease-fire in 1970 that lasted, more or less, until Arab forces attacked Israel in October 1973. The Middle East did not really fall under the purview of the Channel until September 1971, and even thereafter, there was little constructive movement in the Channel or otherwise on the Middle East until the outbreak of war and Arab oil embargo markedly altered the situation.[32]

This examination of U.S.-Soviet back channels shows how back-channel diplomacy can be an extremely effective tool in achieving bold, popular policies that have the potential to reorient foreign policy. Confidential diplomacy can be used to overcome bureaucratic inertia, especially if the established foreign policy–making establishment opposes the policy aims or is seen as untrustworthy by the elected elites.

There are, however, certain drawbacks. No matter how monumental such masterstrokes may be, they cannot be maintained without an element of structure. People change, as do political fortunes. Nixon is a case in point. As the Watergate scandal unfolded, the president's ability to govern effectively declined, weakening his bargaining position with the Soviets. The Kremlin sympathized with Nixon but assessed the situation realistically. For example, in June 1974, on the eve of the third U.S.-Soviet summit, Brezhnev told East German leader Erich Honecker, "We don't want to take advantage of this [Watergate] factor, but we must consider Nixon's weaknesses."[33]

Nor did Kissinger remain static. Once it was disclosed that Kissinger had been the president's special envoy to China, had undertaken secret negotiations with the North Vietnamese in Paris, and had gone on a secret trip to Moscow in April 1972, Kissinger's public profile changed and his stature rose. This exposure, conversely, became a liability for a back-channel agent, as the press—and, no doubt, foreign powers—tried to track his every move.

The use of back channels also increased bureaucratic friction and created an environment where policymakers in the United States could neither speak candidly nor trust one another. Ironically, Kissinger had warned of such dangers in an earlier life. In an article he published about Otto von Bismarck shortly before joining the Nixon administration, Kissinger denigrated the Iron Chancellor's accomplishments by noting, "Statesmen who build lastingly transform the personal act of creation into institutions that can be maintained by an average standard of performance [that is, a bureaucracy]."[34] Back channels helped to ensure a successful summit meeting—and, for a time, détente flourished. The subsequent course of events would soon prove, however, that the back channel could not survive indefinitely as an institution.

1

Precedents and Back-Channel Games, 1968–1970

He, Nixon, was aware that I, the Soviet Ambassador, had "success-fully and without any publicity" maintained confidential ties that Presidents Kennedy and Johnson had had with the Soviet Govern-ment. . . . In that connection, he is designating his chief aide, Kis-singer, for such contacts with me.
                              —Anatoly Dobrynin to the Kremlin, February 1969

Aside from the Watergate scandal that led to the only presidential res-ignation in U.S. history, Richard Milhous Nixon is usually associated with three foreign policy initiatives: the opening to China, the end of American involvement in the Vietnam War, and détente with the Soviet Union. The fact that these three major foreign policy initiatives relied on back-channel diplomacy was a product not only of design but also an underlying philosophy about secrecy and the conduct of international relations. Nixon and his special advisor for national security affairs, and later secretary of state, Dr. Henry Kissinger, carefully managed and com-partmentalized confidential exchanges, often without the knowledge of the Departments of State and Defense. From the beginning of the admin-istration, these men consciously centralized the policymaking machinery in the White House–based National Security Council (NSC).[1]

U.S.-Soviet back channels suited both the Kremlin and the White House and had begun before Nixon assumed office in 1969. This chapter traces the development of the Nixon administration's foreign policy structure, early back-channel overtures to the Soviets, the evolution of bureaucratic rivalries within the administration, and the early development of the Channel between Kissinger and Dobrynin. Once in place, the new Nixon administration quickly established the foundation of back-channel dialogue and created mechanisms that would later become the central venue of U.S.-Soviet relations and the shaping of détente. Trends that became apparent in 1971 and 1972 had their origins as bureaucratic actors maneuvered and the Soviets and the new administration became more comfortable with each other.

Richard Nixon assumed the presidency on January 20, 1969, as arguably one of the best prepared of his predecessors when it came to foreign policy. Inside and outside public office, Nixon cultivated contacts with world leaders, traveled extensively, read widely, and wrote about the larger world for a sizeable audience.[2] Regardless of his own credentials, Nixon has been forever linked with Henry Kissinger. The Harvard-educated Jewish refugee from Nazi Germany, a naturalized American and professor at Harvard's prestigious School of Government, became Nixon's primary policy implementer.[3] If Nixon was the architect, Kissinger was the builder. Like any relationship, the one between the president and his national security advisor changed over time, with peaks and valleys shaping the landscape along the way.[4] In a White House where the chief of staff, H. R. "Bob" Haldeman, served as a gatekeeper to the president, Kissinger was among the few assistants who had regular and consistent access to Nixon.[5] Kissinger also served as Nixon's personal liaison in a web of back-channel negotiations and alternate diplomatic arrangements with friend and foe alike.

Many back channels existed—and not just with the Soviet Union. The Nixon administration regularly bypassed the State Department's cable system via the Situation Room in the White House basement, sending coded communications to foreign leaders and American ambassadors stationed abroad. For example, Kissinger communicated directly with the U.S. ambassador to Pakistan, Joseph Farland, who served as an emissary to Pakistan's military dictator, President Agha Mohammad Yahya Khan (hereafter referred to as Yahya). Kissinger also arranged a back channel through the U.S. ambassador to Bonn, Kenneth Rush, known as the "special channel," to communicate with West German state secretary Egon Bahr and West German chancellor Willy Brandt. In early 1971, Kis-

Republican presidential candidate Richard Nixon and President Lyndon Johnson face each other across the table of the White House Cabinet Room, July 1968. Once elected, Nixon used early back channels with the Soviets to kill the idea of an early summit meeting between the Soviet Union, the outgoing Johnson administration, and the incoming Nixon administration. (LBJ Library, WHPO. LBJ Library photo by Yoichi R. Okamoto)

The back-channel interlocutors, Anatoly Dobrynin and Henry Kissinger, in the White House Map Room, March 1972. Decades later, Dobrynin inscribed a copy of his memoir, *In Confidence*, to Kissinger: opponent, partner, friend. (RNPLM)

singer communicated with Bahr through a covert navy operation based in Frankfurt, complete with specially encrypted messages.[6] The "special channel" with the West Germans affected the Kissinger-Dobrynin channel as the United States responded to Willy Brandt's policy of improving relations with the Communist East (Ostpolitik), and in the negotiations over the Quadripartite Access Agreement on Berlin signed in September 1971.

Under Nixon's general guidance and agreement, Kissinger reformulated the foreign policy machinery and centralized power in the NSC system.[7] Kissinger worked vigorously to put Nixon's and his own imprint on the system. As the president's special assistant for national security affairs, Kissinger chaired a number of committees under the umbrella of the NSC, giving him an institutional-bureaucratic advantage over the secretaries of state and defense. Kissinger supervised the work of the Senior Review Group (SRG), an interagency group that discussed policy option papers, and the 40 Committee, which oversaw covert activities.[8] Kissinger also spearheaded the Washington Special Actions Group (WSAG), an NSC subcommittee for crisis management and the preparation of contingency plans, which was set up after the North Koreans shot down an American EC-121 reconnaissance plane in April 1969.[9] The NSC-based foreign policy was also a source of bureaucratic conflict.

Although he had been one of Nixon's few close personal friends since the 1940s, Secretary of State William P. Rogers was gradually relegated to irrelevance by the administration's conduct of foreign policy generally, and the use of back channels specifically. According to Kissinger, the use of back channels to circumvent Rogers began "the day after Inauguration."[10] Efforts to bypass the State Department had begun earlier, when Nixon set up early back channels with the Soviets during the 1968 presidential campaign and the postelection transition period through Robert Ellsworth and Henry Kissinger. Back channels and secret policy initiatives continued through Nixon's time in office, often without Rogers's knowledge. By the autumn of 1971, Rogers had been almost completely circumvented on détente, the opening to China, and even the Middle East. In May 1972, just days before the departure to the Moscow Summit, Nixon told Kissinger, "Be sure you warn Gromyko and obviously Brezhnev that they've got to be very careful not to talk about the special channel where Rogers is involved." The president cautioned, "Because then we'd have to explain what the hell it is to him."[11] Even at this late date, approaching the end of the first term, Nixon wanted to keep Rogers in the dark.

Rogers's diminished position became publicly known during Nixon's first term, and the press usually focused on Kissinger. In a multipage spread in the *New York Times Magazine* in 1972, for example, Milton Viorst wrote how morale at the State Department and the Foreign Service had declined as a result of the conduct of foreign policy from the White House instead of the State Department's headquarters on C Street. Although the headline read, "William Rogers Thinks Like Richard Nixon," the first picture was actually of Kissinger with the caption, "Nixon's national security adviser has been called 'the Secretary of State in everything but title.'"[12] As if to highlight the virtual insignificance of the State Department under Rogers, the Viorst article half-heartedly attempted to explain Rogers's justifications about State's diminished role in the foreign policy process. The article also devoted considerable space to Kissinger: "He is executive of the National Security Council and of the various interagency committees established under its aegis; the channel through which intelligence and memoranda are regularly conveyed to the president, and the president's daily briefer on foreign-policy problems. . . . Because of his proximity to the president and his unlimited access to information, he is in a position to be the most powerful man in the foreign-policy process. And—except, perhaps, for the president himself—he is just that."[13]

Viorst wrote before the extent of back-channel diplomacy became known. Behind the scenes, the back-channel modus operandi fanned the flames of a heated rivalry between Kissinger and Rogers, and by early 1971 Kissinger had the upper hand due to his indispensable role in the administration's foreign policies.

In the bureaucratic gamesmanship, Kissinger found a willing collaborator in the president. In his memoir, Kissinger wrote: "Inevitably, Rogers must have considered me an egotistical nitpicker who ruined his relations with the president; I tended to view him as an insensitive neophyte who threatened the careful design of our foreign policy. The relationship was bound to deteriorate."[14] It was Nixon—not Kissinger—who excluded Rogers from the first official meeting between the president and Dobrynin in February 1969. It was Nixon who agreed to have Malcolm Toon—not Rogers—represent the State Department after the short one-on-one session in which the president endorsed the Channel.[15] Rogers, a novice on foreign affairs, had ably served as the attorney general during the Eisenhower administration, and Nixon reportedly chose him for his lawyerly skills.[16]

In the White House, Rogers came to be seen as an occasionally useful bureaucrat and a front man, not a policymaker or even an implementer of policy. By contrast, Kissinger, with his deep German accent and scholarly credentials, lent an air of intellectual sophistication and structure to Nixon's more abstract conceptions and political image. After three years in office, Nixon bluntly reflected behind the closed doors of the Oval Office about Rogers's role. "[Rogers] made a big, old error in terms of his own place as Secretary of State and in history," Nixon stated matter-of-factly to George Shultz and John Ehrlichman. "[Rogers] has panted so much to be liked by his colleagues at the State Department, that the State Department runs him, rather than his running the State Department. He has panted so much to be liked by the press that covers the State Department, that the press run him, rather than [he] them." Rogers had failed, time and again, in Nixon's eyes, to step up to the critics and pundits who criticized the administration.[17]

Nixon typically shied away from personal confrontation, and in handling the Kissinger-Rogers rivalry, he usually relied on strong men to mediate or keep in check personality conflicts in his administration. Nixon primarily delegated dispute resolution to Chief of Staff Haldeman, a task upon which Haldeman regularly and revealingly reflected in his handwritten and later taped diary. With their Teutonic-sounding names, Haldeman and chief domestic advisor John Ehrlichman were known as "the two Germans" and also as the "Berlin Wall" for largely insulating Nixon from having to deal with staff squabbles.[18] In addition to "the two Germans," Attorney General John Mitchell, Nixon's former law partner and campaign chief, was another central player in smoothing ruffled feathers within the administration.[19]

When Nixon ordered Kissinger to handle discussions with the Soviets on a possible Middle East settlement in the summer of 1971, he willfully excluded Rogers from the loop and fueled a Kissinger-Rogers flare-up. Likely sensing a stall and backroom maneuvering by his bureaucratic nemesis, Kissinger, Rogers forced the issue by calling Haldeman at home on January 16, 1972. However, Rogers's gambit failed when Nixon dispatched Haldeman and Mitchell to develop a solution. Haldeman

Nixon's chief of staff, H. R. "Bob" Haldeman (above left), and chief domestic advisor, John Ehrlichman (above right). With their Teutonic-sounding names, Haldeman and Ehrlichman were known as "the two Germans" and also as the "Berlin Wall" for largely insulating Nixon from having to deal with staff squabbles. (RNPLM)

reported back to Nixon that Rogers had argued: "The theory here is that the president has announced his policy. State Department carries it out. The NSC is not supposed to be in operations, it's supposed to be a policy group." As for the Middle East discussions, Rogers told Haldeman, "[T]he NSC is not involved in the Mid East. . . . I am handling that. We've been doing it for three years and it's worked very well."[20] Instead of reaffirming Rogers's Middle East role, Nixon chastised the secretary's outmoded thinking about the role of the State Department, and he softened the blow to Rogers in a letter drafted by Haldeman.[21] Had not Kissinger's secret July 1971 trip to China and ongoing negotiations with the North Vietnamese hammered the point home to Rogers that the NSC, and its chief, were, in fact, "in operations"?

Bureaucratic maneuvering aside, back-channel diplomacy had other functions. Despite their different backgrounds, Nixon and Kissinger shared similar beliefs about the pursuit of national interests, the dangers of the thermonuclear age, and a philosophy of secrecy. Both men gravitated to the use of back channels. As Nixon scholar Joan Hoff, a proponent of the "Nixinger" foreign policy, has noted: "Both relished covert activity and liked making unilateral decisions; both distrusted bureaucracies; both resented any attempt by Congress to interfere with initiatives; and both agreed that the United States could impose order and stability on the world only if the White House controlled policy by appearing conciliatory but acting tough."[22] Back channels allowed public and private messages to diverge and provided a potential silver bullet to avoid the issue of leaks and the press.

Like the State Department, the Foreign Service, the amoebic "bureaucracy," academics, and the "Eastern Establishment," the Fourth Estate could not be trusted, Nixon believed. His enemies, perceived and real, could be fought with secrecy, and public opinion could be shaped or altogether circumvented by timely breakthroughs and bold plays concealed by confidential moves.[23] At one point, Nixon admonished Kissinger, "Now, Henry, remember, we're gonna be around to outlive our enemies." In a low voice, Nixon added: "And, also, never forget: The press is the enemy. The press is the enemy. The press is the enemy. The Establishment is the enemy. The professors are the enemy. . . . Write that on a blackboard a hundred times and never forget it."[24] Without resorting to armchair psychology, as seems fashionable in several biographies that have labeled Nixon paranoid or neurotic, it is worth noting that once in power, the Nixon administration had some reason to be suspicious.[25]

In a vicious and destructive cycle, leaks by officials of highly classified documents confirmed Nixon's hatred of the press, exacerbated his fears, and reaffirmed the use of back channels to shelter sensitive negotiations. Leaks about arms control efforts started two weeks into the administration as Nixon was caught off guard at a press conference on February 6, 1969—less than a month in office—by the revelation that Secretary of Defense Melvin Laird had halted the deployment of the Sentinel Anti-Ballistic Missile system. Laird had not discussed the matter at the NSC, according to Haldeman, and the facts had not been included in Nixon's briefing material.[26] In the first year, leaks continued with materials from high-level meetings about troop withdrawals from Vietnam, the reversion of Okinawa to Japan, the secret bombing of Cambodia, and even internal deliberations about Supreme Court nominations appearing in the press. Early in the administration, Kissinger endorsed wiretaps on NSC staffers and journalists to try to discover the sources of leaks.[27] The leaks only increased, and the administration took more active measures in response.

In June 1971, the *New York Times* began to publish excerpts from the Pentagon Papers, a top-secret study commissioned in 1967 by then secretary of defense Robert McNamara. The study documented American involvement in Vietnam from 1945 to 1967—before Nixon became president. Initially, Nixon reacted to the news calmly, but after consulting with Kissinger and Attorney General John Mitchell, he decided to pursue legal action against the *Times* to block further publication.[28] White House aides Egil "Bud" Krogh and David Young proposed the formation of the White House Special Investigative Unit to ferret out and stop the disclosures. The so-called Plumbers became entangled with the Committee to Re-Elect the president (CRP, or CREEP), and its illegal activities became the foundation of the "abuse of government power" charges brought against the president and a number of his top aides by 1974. Nevertheless, there were legitimate national security considerations behind the activities, at least initially.

Part of the rationale behind the Plumbers was to protect back channels. In 1995, Kissinger told journalist and author James Rosen, "We felt that if the government didn't protect its secrets, the whole apparatus would be in danger." Rosen explained, "The 'apparatus,' of course, was not merely the foreign policy process as it existed on organizational charts, but the elaborate work of secret back channels, in and out of government, that Nixon and Kissinger used to conduct war and diplomacy."[29] The sanctity of information was essential to the conduct of back-channel diplomacy, and Nixon and Kissinger carefully compartmentalized the records of the back channel, with few staff members privy to the level of discussions between Kissinger and Dobrynin.

As one of its first assignments, the president tasked the White House Special Investigations Unit with plugging a leak that had revealed the U.S. draft position on the Anti-Ballistic Missile (ABM) issue on the front page of the *New York Times*. The July 23, 1971, story by William Beecher also revealed the delegation's fallback position.[30] In 1980, Ambassador Gerard Smith, the head of the U.S. SALT delegation, wrote, "The Beecher leak now appears less prejudicial than it did in the heat of the negotiations."[31] At the time, however, Smith was livid. Kis-singer explained to the president the day after the article was published, "Well, Gerry Smith has written you a letter by cable saying he thinks you should institute criminal proceedings because he is really in a hell of a spot there." Nixon asked, "So, you don't think ACDA did this, do you? His people?" Kissinger replied, "I don't think so. . . . Oh, he's beside himself, because . . . he hadn't even presented it to the Russians yet." Earlier in the conversation, while discussing a different leak, Kissinger warned: "I think there is a traitor on the 7th floor of State. It used to be you could say the system is leaking. . . . It literally leaks now within 24 hours."[32] As part of the investigation by the Plumbers, Nixon ordered the widespread use of polygraphs on dozens of State Department and Department of Defense employees by CIA examiners.[33]

The cumulative effect of the leaking and the domestic political upheaval of the time contributed to a siege mentality in the White House. Raymond Price, Nixon's main speechwriter, recalled that in Nixon's first sixteen months in office, the FBI reported that there were forty thousand bomb threats or actual bombings: "It was the fashionable thing to burn whole sections of cities down and stage mass riots . . . [and] mass marches on Washington came into fashion." "Just as one example," Price explained, "on one of these marches to Washington, we had to ring the entire White House complex with buses to keep the mobs from storming the White House. . . . These were the 'idealistic demonstrators' being applauded by the news media. We didn't see it that way."[34] Price could have been referring to the security response to any number of protests, such as the November 15, 1969, protest against the Vietnam War or the May 4, 1970, protest in response to the Kent State shootings. Whether or not ringing the executive offices with buses, snipers, and barricades was actually necessary during these peaceful protests, the White House perceived the response to be necessary. The tumult of the time no doubt added to the siege mentality.

The Nixon administration was not alone in feeling under siege and forced to confront a generational rift. Historian Jeremi Suri has described détente itself as a conservative response—not just in the United States, but in France, Germany, and China as well—to the dislocation of the 1960s.[35] Détente could also be considered a search for stability in an international arena when American economic preeminence was being fractured and military strength was being sapped ten thousand miles away in Southeast Asia. Besieged at home by popular unrest, and with U.S. prestige tarnished by its continuing involvement in Vietnam, the Nixon administration sought détente with the Soviet Union and rapprochement with China. Back-channel diplomacy was a means to an end, and part of the rationale behind the use of secret diplomacy was compartmentalizing negotiations.

The Transition Period, 1968–1969: The Ellsworth and Kissinger-Sedov Channels

Before his narrow victory in the November 1968 election, Nixon used two back channels to message the Soviets. The first overture and the closest precedent to the Kissinger-Dobrynin channel developed during the presidential campaign and went active immediately after the election, when Nixon dispatched his longtime aide and personal friend Robert Ellsworth to make contact with Ambassador Dobrynin and Soviet chargé d'affaires Yuri Cherniakov. The second channel, between Kissinger and a KGB intelligence officer, Boris Sedov, functioned informally during the presidential campaign and petered out shortly after Nixon's inauguration. Both the Kissinger-Sedov and Ellsworth-Dobrynin-Cherniakov contacts served as feelers to assess the Soviet leadership's receptiveness to back-channel contacts in general, and as precedents for the Channel. The early back-channel forays also served immediate political concerns during the transition period between Nixon's election and inauguration.

In several meetings in late 1968, the Ellsworth-Dobrynin-Cherniakov channel established communication between the president-elect and the Soviet leadership and developed the language used to launch later back-channel relationships. On November 24, 1968, Ellsworth hosted Dobrynin for dinner and made the initial outreach about Nixon's readiness "for confidential contacts with Moscow." Ellsworth "rather solemnly" told the Soviet ambassador that "he, Ellsworth, was authorized to maintain informal contacts with the Soviet ambassador on problems of mutual interest to Nixon and the Soviet leaders."[36] With Dobrynin in Moscow for consultations about the new administration in December, Nixon sent Ellsworth to the Soviet embassy to meet with chargé d'affaires Yuri Cherniakov to "sound out the views of the Soviet leadership" on Vietnam, the Middle

East, arms control, and Czechoslovakia. Resembling the first Kissinger-Dobrynin meeting in February 1969, Ellsworth conveyed that Nixon wanted to "initiate a confidential exchange of views between Nixon and the Soviet leaders through verbal messages and correspondence."[37]

The Kissinger-Sedov contact added the dimension of Soviet intelligence seeking additional information about the main players in the incoming Nixon administration and corroborating the Ellsworth-Dobrynin-Cherniakov exchanges. The KGB deputy *rezident* at the Soviet embassy at the time, Oleg Kalugin, recollected that the Sedov-Kissinger contact became an "important relationship" and "a fruitful back channel between the leadership of our two countries." Kalugin boasted that the soon-to-be national security advisor "began to convey to us that Nixon was no anti-Communist ogre and that he wanted improved relations with the U.S.S.R."[38]

In contrast, Kissinger characterized Sedov as "a KGB operative who seemed to have had the Rockefeller assignment during the campaign," noting that the contact was "sporadic," hardly formalized, or of any great significance in U.S.-Soviet relations.[39] Officially, Sedov was stationed in Washington, D.C., as a reporter for the Novosti Press Agency, but his true function was well known to American counterintelligence.[40] Kissinger claimed he had used the Sedov contact simply to reinforce the message that Nixon had no desire to participate in a joint summit meeting between the Soviets, the outgoing Johnson administration, and the incoming Nixon administration. Nixon's predecessor, Lyndon Johnson, had pushed the idea of a summit meeting with the Soviets for some time, partially as a means by which to deflect criticism of the growing U.S. involvement in Vietnam, but also as a means to encourage the limitation of strategic armaments, such as the Nuclear Non-Proliferation Treaty (NNPT, or NPT) to halt the spread of nuclear weapons.[41] Nixon later posited that he saw "no solid basis" at the time that in a last-minute summit with Johnson the Soviets would "negotiate seriously on any critical issue. Nor did I want to be boxed in by any decisions that were made before I took office."[42]

Although it is plausible that Kalugin overstated the importance of the contact of his subordinate, Sedov, with such a high-profile actor, the truth probably lies somewhere between Kissinger's dismissal and Kalugin's braggadocio. Kissinger and Sedov met several times at the posh Pierre

Hotel in New York City in December 1968 and January 1969. The two men had wide-ranging discussions on the Soviet and American views on the major issues in superpower relations and established that both sides were sincere in seeking communication.

In a memorandum to the president-elect, Kissinger reported the results of a December 18, 1969, meeting with Sedov in New York. As Kalugin hinted, Kissinger noted that he had reiterated Nixon's desire for "an era of negotiation" and expressed hope that the Soviets would "find that the president-elect is open minded, precise, and interested in lasting settlements based on the real interests of both countries." Kissinger also believed that the joint Johnson-Nixon summit idea would be a "crucial test" because "the only purpose of a summit meeting now can be propaganda to embarrass the new Administration."[43] The Soviets got the message, because Cherniakov handed a note to Ellsworth that same day stating that the situation had been "clarified." Kissinger wrote, "It was the end of the summit idea."[44]

Kissinger told Sedov, "On the strategic missile talks, Mr. Nixon is intent upon an assessment of our strategic position before moving into the negotiation stage." "Our analysis of the issue, however," he warned, would "be influenced by Soviet willingness to negotiate seriously on other questions—particularly Vietnam and the Middle East." Although the NPT was signed in 1968, it had yet to be ratified by the Senate, and the Nixon administration's handling of the ratification would also be seen as a litmus test of its commitment to arms control. Picking up the idea of arms control, Kissinger told Sedov that issues in Soviet-American relations would be linked, which was the first time the new administration had acted on a concept of "linkage."[45]

After a working trip to the president-elect's Key Biscayne vacation home, Kissinger met again with Sedov on January 2, 1969. Kissinger repeated that the new administration viewed progress on arms control as tied to progress in the Vietnam peace negotiations and constructive discussion about the Middle East. Sedov replied that the Soviet Union would do its part to ensure ratification of the NPT and remained committed to arms limitation. The KGB officer then raised a proposal Cherniakov had delivered to both Ellsworth and to outgoing secretary of state Dean Rusk on December 30, which outlined a Soviet proposal for a Middle East settlement. The proposal suggested Soviet influence with the Arab states, perhaps due to Soviet foreign minister Andrei Gromyko's recent trip to the region, but made progress contingent on Israel returning to its pre-1967 borders.[46] Sedov asked if the proposal *"could be seen as a sign of good faith"* in the spirit of his earlier meeting with Kissinger. Kissinger replied non-committally that the new administration was studying the proposition.[47]

Sedov also inquired if Kissinger's recent article in *Foreign Affairs,* widely considered a mouthpiece of official U.S. diplomacy, reflected the thinking of the incoming administration. In the article, Kissinger argued for a mutual withdrawal of military forces—American and North Vietnamese—from South Vietnam, while delaying a political restructuring of South Vietnam as long as possible.[48] Kissinger replied to Sedov that "all realistic options" remained on the table for Vietnam. Sedov inquired as to the time frame Kissinger envisioned for the American withdrawal from Vietnam; Kissinger answered that the process would take three to five years, with the expectation that there be no "violent upheaval" during the interval. Both sides could withdraw, and elections could be held if both sides refrained from offensive actions. Sedov then concluded the discussion by stating that the Soviet leadership "was very interested that the inaugural speech contain some reference to open channels of communication to Moscow." Kissinger replied, "This would be easier if Moscow showed some cooperativeness on Vietnam."[49]

Although Sedov had refused to commit his government on Vietnam, Kissinger nevertheless recommended to the president that the phrase be included in the inaugural address. In a memorandum of January 4, Nixon initialed his agreement.[50] "I was never clear whether this request reflected an attempt by Sedov to demonstrate his influence to Moscow," Kissinger wondered years later, "or whether it was a serious policy approach by the Politburo. In any event I saw no harm in it."[51] The gesture cost nothing in the grand scheme but almost certainly established goodwill between the new administration and the Soviet leadership. The move also demonstrated the utility of back channels for both sides. In his inaugural address, the new president gave a nod to the Kissinger-Sedov channel when he proclaimed, "Our lines of communication will be open."[52]

After assuming office, Nixon immediately promoted the "linkage" concept Kissinger had used in the Sedov channel. Nixon wrote Secretary of State Rogers and Secretary of Defense Melvin Laird to make sure the new administration would stay on message. In a letter to Rogers, the president expressed his conviction that "the great issues are fundamentally interrelated." Nixon proclaimed: "I do not mean by this to establish artificial linkages between specific elements of one or another issue or between tactical steps that we may elect to take. But I do believe that crisis or confrontation in one place and real cooperation in another cannot long be sustained simultaneously."[53] Nixon explained to Laird that although the Soviet Union remained the "central security problem" for American policymakers, the decision to proceed with SALT could not "depend exclusively on our review of purely military and technical issues." Rather, Nixon wrote, "This decision should also be taken in the light of the prevailing political context and, in particular, in light of progress toward stabilizing the explosive Middle East situation, and in light of the Paris talks."[54] Giving the concept intellectual credibility and polish, Kissinger believed that linkage could bypass bureaucratic inertia, and as a method for "an integrated conceptual framework" over the long term.[55] Linkage eventually proved to be a double-edged sword in the diplomatic arsenals of both Washington and Moscow.

After these tentative steps with Sedov, Kissinger began to erect a structure of linkage, tying the improvement in one area of relations to another, seemingly unrelated area, in particular, tying détente to Moscow's assistance in facilitating fruitful negotiations with Hanoi. The concept became a pillar of the Nixon-Kissinger foreign policy that would be conveyed to the Soviets time and again through back channels and conventional diplomacy.

The Kissinger-Sedov and Ellsworth channels proved short-lived once Nixon took office and set up "the Channel" with Dobrynin. Nixon's formal assumption of office obviated the need to communicate through Ellsworth, the semi-official point of contact during the presidential campaign and the transition period. Soon after taking office, Nixon appointed Ellsworth as his ambassador to the North Atlantic Treaty Organization (NATO).

With Nixon's endorsement on February 17, 1969, the Kissinger-Dobrynin channel quickly supplanted the Kissinger-Sedov contact and became the preeminent U.S.-Soviet back channel. For all intents and purposes, the Sedov channel had dissipated by early March 1969, if not earlier. Kalugin argued that Dobrynin was jealous of the KGB's success and moved to exercise bureaucratic control over U.S.-Soviet relations through the Soviet embassy in Washington.[56] U.S. documents show that there may have been some truth to Kalugin's argument but also that the Sedov back channel had outlived its usefulness besides showing a willingness by both sides for confidential contacts between Nixon and the Soviet leadership. American sources also suggest that the Sedov channel switched to Dobrynin on January 31, 1969, when the KGB officer told Kissinger that Dobrynin would bring a note from the Soviet leadership in mid-February.[57]

According to Kalugin, Brezhnev personally made the decision to abandon the Sedov-Kissinger channel at Ambassador Dobrynin's insistence. Dobrynin had accepted the contact during the election because it would have been "improper" for the Soviet Union—through its official ambassador—to have direct contact with a presidential candidate. In addition to the known exchanges, Kalugin contended: "Even before sending an official message of congratulations, Brezhnev forwarded a confidential congratulatory note to Nixon through Sedov. . . . For more than a month afterward the Soviet regime and the president-elect communicated through the Sedov-Kissinger back channel." After the inauguration, however, Dobrynin pushed the issue, and Brezhnev accepted the logic that "all contact with the new administration should go through the Foreign Ministry and the embassy in Washington."

Most of Kalugin's assertions can be verified by memoranda of conversation and Kissinger's painstakingly detailed memoir account, *White House Years.* One gets the sense, however, that Kalugin may have overstated the prominence of the Kissinger-Sedov channel in light of the fact that he did not mention the contacts between Ellsworth, Cherniakov, and Dobrynin. In fact, Kalugin implies that the Kissinger-Sedov contact was the only channel in U.S.-Soviet relations until Dobrynin asserted his authority. Adding further credence to an overstatement of Sedov's prominence, Kalugin recalled how Sedov continued to meet with one of Kissinger's top aides, Richard Allen, later President Ronald Reagan's national security advisor. Sedov, apparently a risk-taker, even suggested trying to recruit Allen as an intelligence asset. Kalugin wrote that he dismissed Sedov's idea.[58]

American sources suggest that Sedov had made problems for himself that undermined his utility as a back-channel agent with Kissinger. For example, Kissinger learned from the FBI that Sedov had "informed a Lebanese-American citizen with ties to the KGB of his contact [with Kissinger]." On June 11, 1969, Kissinger wrote a letter to Under Secretary of State Elliott Richardson suggesting, "In view of [Sedov's] continuing activity, I believe it would be appropriate, through discussions with the Soviet Ambassador, to request that Sedov be returned to the Soviet Union." Failing private discussions, Kissinger warned, Sedov might have to be declared persona non grata.[59] Thus, an early U.S.-Soviet back channel also had an element of colorful characters and smoke-and-mirrors spy craft. In April 1970, Sedov called to tell Kissinger he was leaving and offered an opportunity to "say good bye and if you want me to say anything in Moscow we have a chance tomorrow." Sedov seemed to be asking if there might be one more back-channel message he could convey to the Kremlin. Kissinger replied: "We are in good shape. I wish you a good trip back and we will miss you." Sedov added, "Come to Moscow and we will be glad to show you around."[60]

Building "the Channel"

Over the course of 1969, Kissinger and Dobrynin moved to formalize the back channel and assiduously guarded its sanctity. Both men were still building rapport and establishing protocol. The two often met for meals in the privacy of the White House Map Room or at the Soviet embassy, and occasionally they met at Kissinger's residence. They spoke on the phone frequently. Based on a review of the declassified Kissinger telcon collection—which includes only the conversations that were transcribed at the time—Kissinger and Dobrynin spoke on the phone approximately 450 times between the beginning of the administration in January 1969 and the May 1972 Moscow Summit. According to Dobrynin, "Later, as our contacts became more frequent and we met almost daily, the president ordered the installation of a direct and secure telephone line between the White House and the Soviet embassy for the exclusive use of Kissinger and me." When he visited Kissinger at the White House, Dobrynin typically traveled incognito from the Soviet embassy on Sixteenth Street and used the East Wing diplomatic entrance to avoid the prying eyes of journalists.[61]

In the course of contacts over many years, Kissinger and Dobrynin formed a friendship based on mutual respect for each other's talents and the realization that each represented governments that did not always see eye to eye. A decade after the creation of the Channel, Kissinger praised Dobrynin: "He understood that a reputation for reliability is an important asset in foreign policy. Subtle and disciplined, warm in his demeanor while wary in his conduct, Dobrynin moved through the upper echelons of Washington with consummate skill. His personal role within the margin available to ambassadors was almost certainly beneficial to U.S.-Soviet relations."[62]

Likewise, Dobrynin said that his relationship with Kissinger made it possible to improve U.S.-Soviet relations. "We both knew," Dobrynin wrote, "that we could frankly and in complete confidence explore the possibility of resolving our troubles and always tried to play them down, not play them up." Dobrynin added: "[Kissinger] was businesslike and did not resort to ambiguities to avoid specific problems. When we later entered into serious negotiations, I learned that he could give you a big headache, but he was clever and highly professional, and never dull or bureaucratic."[63]

Kissinger and Dobrynin had their first one-on-one meeting over lunch at the Soviet embassy on February 21. Before the meeting, Kissinger had analyzed the message from the Soviet leadership to President Nixon that Dobrynin had delivered four days earlier. Kissinger wrote to Nixon that the Soviets "are prepared to move forward on a whole range of topics. . . . In other words, we have the 'linkage.' Our problem is how to play it."[64] Surprisingly, Kissinger did not leave a record and did not mention the first meeting of "the Channel" in his memoir. Fortunately for posterity, Dobrynin wrote a detailed memcon of the meeting.

According to the Soviet ambassador, he and Kissinger discussed the Soviet note to Nixon point by point, sketching an outline of the issues in U.S.-Soviet relations. Kissinger "took out of his pocket an English translation of the text of [Soviet] views and presented the president's views, checking from time to time against our text, in the margins of which he had notes for the conversations with me." They further discussed the Middle East. Specifically, both sides expressed a willingness to have a bilateral exchange of views, but the question arose as to where: New York, Moscow, or Washington? Kissinger hoped he could get an answer from the Soviets after President Nixon's first trip abroad, a weeklong trip to Europe to meet with French president Charles de Gaulle, British prime minister Harold Wilson, and German chancellor Kurt Georg Kiesinger.

The conversation also touched on a number of concerns in Soviet-American relations, and Kissinger used the opportunity to reinforce the Channel with his Soviet counterpart. On behalf of the president, Kissinger suggested that "the most fundamental issues requiring a high degree of confidentiality . . . be addressed . . . through the confidential Kissinger/Soviet Ambassador Channel." Nixon agreed with the Soviet government that "the foundations of the postwar order in Europe should not be changed," and he did not have "the slightest intention of intervening in the affairs of Eastern Europe." Only over the status of West Berlin did there exist "an appreciable difference of opinion between us." On Nixon's behalf, Kissinger essentially endorsed the status quo, that is, the division between Eastern and Western Europe.

After mentioning that Paris would be the most "difficult place" on Nixon's first official state visit, Kissinger brought up Vietnam. The Channel became a vehicle to convey domestic political concerns, and Kissinger warned, "Progress must be made at the Paris talks . . . [because] Nixon 'simply cannot wait a year for Hanoi to decide to take some new step and take a more flexible position.'" The United States also would not accept "outright military defeat" or "a settlement that would be followed immediately [Kissinger stressed the word 'immediately'] by a replacement of the South Vietnamese government." Dobrynin wrote, "One could conclude from Kissinger's remarks that Nixon is primarily concerned about his own political reputation and how the settlement in Vietnam might affect his political future."

Regarding possible contact with the PRC, Kissinger told Dobrynin that the Nixon administration was "keeping the doors open," perhaps an allusion to turn-of-the-twentieth-century U.S. "Open Door" diplomacy to prevent the dissolution of China into competing spheres of influence by foreign powers. Dobrynin asked about the timetable for strategic arms limitation negotiations and noted "observed inconsistency in the statements of U.S. Government officials." Kissinger replied "disagreements within the government" that boiled down to "the connection between the beginning of the talks and the deployment of the U.S. Sentinel ABM system" caused this confusion. Kissinger opined that talks should begin in five to six months, meaning the summer of 1969. Nixon had raised the subject of a summit meeting with the Soviets on February 17; Kissinger raised it again, and Dobrynin again replied: "The question of such a meeting" would "naturally have to be resolved by the two sides on the basis of the specific situation." For now, the prospect of a superpower summit had been tabled.[65]

Setting the Agenda: 1969–1970

Over the following twenty-two months, Kissinger met privately with Dobrynin or the Soviet counselor-minister Yuli Vorontsov nearly forty times.[66] The confidential exchanges touched on the full range of Soviet-American relations, and both sides moved to strengthen and expand the role of the Channel. By the end of 1969, they discussed the start of arms limitations talks and the joint ratification of the Nuclear Non-Proliferation Treaty, U.S. involvement in Vietnam and the status of the Paris peace negotiations, the establishment of four-power talks to handle West Berlin, the prospect of a superpower summit meeting at the highest levels, Sino-Soviet disputes and U.S. policy toward the PRC, and the Middle East. The Nixon administration used the Channel to reinforce linkage between progress in the Paris talks with the North Vietnamese and additional arms control negotiations with the Soviets. The Soviets used the back channel to downplay or dismiss the application of linkage. While a great deal of repetition occurred, Kissinger and Dobrynin essentially built the foundation upon which détente was later constructed.

It is a sociological phenomenon that institutions tend to perpetuate themselves; like an institution, the back channel self-perpetuated. During the first two years of the Nixon administration, both the White House and the Kremlin moved early and often to promote the Kissinger-Dobrynin channel. After their second meeting on March 3, 1969, Kissinger reported that Moscow wanted to engage in a "strictly confidential exchange on delicate and important matters" via the Channel.[67] On another occasion, when Dobrynin was meeting with Kissinger at the White House, the president interrupted and asked that Dobrynin be brought to the Lincoln Sitting Room. Nixon told Dobrynin he intended "to continue utilizing this 'channel,' which is operating successfully and has proven its effectiveness."[68] By the end of 1969, Kissinger and Dobrynin agreed to "meet regularly to discuss specific topics."[69] Dobrynin later noted, "Thanks to the confidential channel the Soviet leadership has a sure and reliable connection with the president."[70] The constant reinforcement of the Channel, which continued over the course of years, served as reassurance for both the Soviet leadership and the White House that they had a dependable channel where it mattered most.

Although the Soviets quickly recognized the utility of the Channel, they also tried to capitalize on bureaucratic divisions in the Nixon administration. Most pointedly, Dobrynin noted in March 1969, "The fact that Kissinger, with the president's approval, in effect disavowed Secretary of State Rogers should be noted; it clearly shows that a clash of opinions and a struggle for influence with the president continue within the Administration as it works out its foreign policy."[71] Two days later, Dobrynin told Moscow that the back channel with Kissinger represented "the most effective practical channels for us to influence the president" but noted that Rogers and his deputies, specifically Elliott Richardson, were "still learning the ropes" and their influence would increase.[72] Dobrynin stressed the role of broad contacts on a personal level to read the new administration's intentions. Dobrynin continued to meet with Rogers and other State Department officials, especially Joseph Sisco, on the Middle East, but Kissinger's back-channel disavowals of Rogers's viewpoints became increasingly strident.

Although he had met with Kissinger several times over the preceding months, it was not until June 1969 that Dobrynin endorsed expanding the Channel. Dobrynin called Kissinger "an intelligent and erudite person" but also described him as "quite vain." The Soviet ambassador noted his "fairly good personal rapport" with Kissinger and advised, "In the future it would, presumably, be advisable to develop and utilize the Kissinger channel even more actively in order to exert influence and communicate our views on various important issues through him to President Nixon personally."[73] Dobrynin saw the Channel as an indispensable means to candidly exchange views and attempt to influence the Nixon administration. The personal stake in improved relations would become an influential component of the Kissinger-Dobrynin channel for both interlocutors.

The Channel and Vietnam

Discussion of Vietnam remained a continual theme in the Channel, and American attempts to link Vietnam to détente remained an undercurrent in confidential exchanges. Nixon and Kissinger constantly stressed that progress in negotiations on arms control and the Middle East would be aided by the resultant improvement in the international environment if the irritant of war could be removed without a South Vietnamese collapse. They contended that U.S.-Soviet relations could not improve until or unless the Soviets pressured their ally, the North Vietnamese, to come to the bargaining table and cease offensive action. In the Channel, Kissinger often kept the Soviets better apprised than the South Vietnamese of his secret negotiations with Democratic Republic of Vietnam (DRV, a.k.a. North Vietnam) officials in Paris that began in August 1969, in the hope that Moscow would pressure Hanoi to negotiate. Until the final settlement in 1973, the secret back-channel negotiations in Paris complemented the formal talks begun in May 1968 by the Johnson administration.[74] Over the course of the first year in office, the Nixon administration continued to pursue a negotiated settlement while responding to an enemy offensive. Nixon also developed a policy to "Vietnamize" the war, the strategy being that South Vietnamese troops would stand up as American troops stood down and gradually withdrew, minimizing U.S. casualties. On Midway Island on June 8, 1969, Nixon met with South Vietnamese president Nguyen Van Thieu and announced his Vietnamization plan and a withdrawal of twenty-five thousand troops.

In 1969, less than a month after his meeting with Nixon and establishing the channel with Kissinger, Dobrynin presented his initial impressions of the new administration and suggested strategies to achieve Soviet aims. "Nixon and those around him are convinced that we are chiefly interested in reaching an agreement with the U.S. on limiting the strategic arms race (for economic reasons) and in getting West Germany to ratify the nuclear non-proliferation treaty," Dobrynin reported. "But for the new administration the subject of greatest interest is the Vietnam issue." The White House wanted to "alleviate somewhat" domestic pressures, and to take "measures to strengthen the Saigon regime." According to Dobrynin, Nixon emphasized "the great importance . . . that the Soviet Union already provided at the time the negotiations on a Vietnam peace settlement were initiated, and especially to Soviet help in ensuring the future success of these negotiations."

Because the Americans lacked a "specific and well-developed program for negotiations with us," Dobrynin told the Foreign Ministry, Moscow should stall and allow political pressures to build on the White House.

Dobrynin advised that Moscow refrain from showing "particular interest in officially raising the issue of beginning negotiations, but rather bide our time for a while until the U.S. side finds itself compelled to approach us."[75] The waiting game had begun, especially on arms control, and in the interim the new administration formulated plans to extricate itself from the Vietnam quagmire "with honor."

The North Vietnamese, meanwhile, had launched an offensive less than a month after Nixon took office. Kissinger reflected, "Nearly half of all the casualties of the Nixon period were suffered in the first six months, 60 percent the first year, as a result of a Communist offensive whose planning clearly antedated Nixon's inauguration."[76] Moreover, Nixon decided to secretly bomb infiltration routes and North Vietnamese sanctuaries in Cambodia. The administration carried out the bombing campaign, initially known as Operation Menu (complete with targets Breakfast, Lunch, Snack, Dinner, Dessert, etc.), in secret, but stories appeared in the American news media soon after it began. The public disclosure of the secret strikes provoked an angry reaction from the White House and led to the wiretap program Nixon and Kissinger ordered on the NSC, Department of Defense, and State Department staff members, in addition to several journalists.[77] The back-channel exchanges, however, are striking for their silence on the bombing strikes.

On April 10, 1969, Kissinger phoned and invited Dobrynin to his Georgetown residence to speak "in confidence about Vietnam." When the two men met four days later, Kissinger told Dobrynin that the president had reviewed domestic and foreign policy relating to U.S. involvement in Southeast Asia. According to Dobrynin's urgent telegram to the Soviet Foreign Ministry, Nixon and Kissinger were "convinced" that Hanoi and the National Liberation Front (NLF) were "clearly employing delaying tactics . . . counting on the fact that U.S. public opinion [would] ultimately grow weary and [would] force Nixon to capitulate." The opinions expressed in the *New York Times,* Kissinger stressed, could not be taken as the administration's views, and Nixon would sooner escalate the situation militarily and turn rightward politically to appeal to supporters of 1968 third-party candidate George Wallace rather than accept defeat in Vietnam. Using the meeting to reinforce linkage, Kissinger issued a nondenial denial to Dobrynin: "He, the president, is fully aware that such a (military) course of events would inevitably affect Soviet-U.S. relations, although he himself would not want to establish some sort of linkage or dependence between the Vietnam War and the pursuit of agreements with the Soviet Union on other issues and in other regions. However, at the same time, it would be unrealistic to assert that what is happening or might happen in Vietnam has no impact at all on Soviet-U.S. relations, and this too is of concern to the president."

The president's plan to break the negotiating deadlock with Hanoi included a significant concession: the United States agreed to allow the NLF to join a South Vietnamese coalition government by electoral rather than military means. Although he refused to countenance the overthrow of South Vietnamese president Nguyen Van Thieu, Nixon was willing to change the South Vietnamese constitution to allow participation by a peaceful NLF-turned-political-party. In essence, Kissinger asked the Soviet government to pass along the proposals to Hanoi and warned that the administration would disavow any of the proposals if they were made public or divulged to the South Vietnamese.[78]

Apart from Vietnam, Kissinger reported to the president that "the Soviet leaders were eager to continue talking." Moscow refused to cut aid to or otherwise coerce Hanoi, but Kissinger warned Dobrynin that the Nixon administration would end the war by "unilateral means," a signal that it would escalate militarily.[79] After another meeting a week later, Dobrynin wrote, "On the whole, one gets the impression that, in addition to diplomatic pressure on the DRV and the NLF, the Administration is also preparing to exert additional military pressure."[80] The Nixon administration had inherited a bad situation, and continued North Vietnamese action had further pressured the new administration even before it had the opportunity to form a coherent response. Four hundred American soldiers died each week, while the Army of the Republic of Vietnam (ARVN) suffered an even higher casualty rate during the offensive.[81]

Kissinger and Nixon carefully stage-managed the next back-channel meeting with Dobrynin on the morning of May 14, 1969. In what became standard practice, Kissinger invited the Soviet ambassador to the White House to give him a preview of a major policy address affecting U.S.-Soviet relations, a "new" approach on Vietnam. Kissinger met alone with Dobrynin for the first part of the meeting, and, according to Dobrynin, Kissinger stressed Nixon's pragmatic, "realistic approach" to dealing with the war in Vietnam. Nixon recognized the NLF "as a reality that exists and operates in South Vietnam" and was willing to accept South Vietnamese neutrality, "whatever the South Vietnamese themselves agree on." "In the final analysis," Dobrynin concluded, "he is even prepared to accept any political system in South Vietnam, 'provided there is a fairly reasonable interval between conclusion of an agreement and [the establishment of] such a system.'"[82]

Proponents of the "decent interval" hypothesis have argued that Nixon and Kissinger sought a "reasonable," "decent," or "healthy" interval between the U.S. exit from Vietnam and South Vietnam being left to its own fate.[83] Dobrynin's report of the conversation with Kissinger does not support the "decent interval" theory in this instance, however. The Soviet ambassador's report that the United States would accept "any political system" in South Vietnam after "a fairly reasonable interval" clearly referred to a *political* solution contingent on the renunciation of force. For the NLF to participate in South Vietnam's political life in an electoral process, Kissinger consistently insisted to Dobrynin, it must transform itself into a political party and forgo the use of arms.

After roughly half an hour between Kissinger and Dobrynin, Nixon made a prearranged call to interrupt the meeting and received Dobrynin in the Lincoln Sitting Room.[84] The president asked the Soviets to play a "constructive role" with the North Vietnamese. Dobrynin noted that the speech seemed a "sincere attempt" to break "the current impasse with regard to a Vietnam peace settlement." According to Dobrynin, Nixon reiterated that the United States did not seek military bases in South Vietnam, nor did it envision future military ties. Echoing Kissinger's remarks several weeks earlier, he reported that Nixon said that Hanoi had not engaged "in any serious negotiations in Paris, anticipating that time will work against him, i.e. against Nixon, and that he will ultimately have to give in, mainly owing to pressure from public opinion in his own country." Nixon called Hanoi's approach a serious miscalculation.[85]

That evening, Nixon went on television from the White House Theater with a message that the United States would not attempt to impose a military solution on the battlefield, but neither would it withdraw unilaterally. American credibility was on the line, he declared. Nixon described the "basic terms" of the peace plan: "mutual withdrawal of non–South Vietnamese forces from South Vietnam and free choice for the people of South Vietnam." The president also offered up his flexibility and warned,

"Nobody has anything to gain by delay."[86] Essentially, Nixon had used the back-channel meeting with Dobrynin to clarify both his willingness to negotiate with the NLF as a party to the talks and to reinforce threats of force in the face of continued delay.

On the eve of Dobrynin's return to Moscow for consultations, in June 1969, Kissinger amplified the appeal to the Soviets and again attempted to link progress on Vietnam with improved Soviet-American relations. Kissinger recorded that he told Dobrynin that "the Soviet Union supplied 85% of the military equipment" to Hanoi, which "was attempting to break down the president's public support." Dobrynin dismissively replied that the United States "always seems to link things."[87] Dobrynin noted that Kissinger had made a *more direct appeal to us* to assist in overcoming the current impasse in Paris," where the formal talks remained deadlocked. Kissinger, according to Dobrynin's account, "speaking frankly [said that] . . . in recent months Moscow has been less actively involved." The Soviet ambassador warned that there could not be "any alternatives to peace talks and a peaceful settlement, unless the current administration wants to repeat the previous administration's mistakes." Dobrynin concluded, "The conversation left the definite impression that, for Nixon, foreign policy problem number one remains how to find a way out of the Vietnam War on terms that would be acceptable to him and that would ensure his re-election."[88]

Kissinger and Dobrynin did not meet for three months. When they did, on September 27, 1969, the Middle East and Vietnam dominated the conversation. "To us Vietnam was the critical issue," Kissinger reported. "We were quite prepared to discuss other subjects, but the Soviet Union should not expect any special treatment until Vietnam was solved." Dobrynin raised the subject of a South Vietnamese coalition government, and Kissinger replied that the back-channel discussions had already "covered the subject at great length previously" and that he "could add nothing." Kissinger dejectedly remarked, "It was a pity that all our efforts to negotiate had failed," and bemoaned the fact that there had been no response to the back-channel exchanges in April and May about American willingness to negotiate with the North Vietnamese and the NLF.

With an element of theater and the various actors playing roles and coming in on cue, Nixon called Kissinger in the middle of the discussion. The president told his national security advisor to convey to the Soviet ambassador that "the train had just left the station and was now headed down the track." According to Kissinger, "Dobrynin responded that he hoped it was an airplane and not a train and would leave some maneuvering room." Kissinger reported his response: "I said the president chooses his words very carefully and that I was sure he meant train. . . . We could not negotiate in a forum of ultimatums."[89] The veiled threat of escalation against North Vietnam was inherent in Nixon's and Kissinger's statements. Soviet-American détente would be held up until the situation in Vietnam improved—either through negotiations or through unilateral U.S. actions, such as military strikes, troop withdrawals, and aid to South Vietnam.

In a conversation with the president soon after the meeting with Dobrynin, Kissinger said he had been "very tough" and "didn't give an inch." When Dobrynin raised the possibility that if the White House extended an invitation, Gromyko would see the president before he returned to the Soviet Union, Kissinger reported that there were "no incentives" for such a meeting. Kissinger told Dobrynin that the Soviet leadership would need to request a meeting—which they did not do— effectively killing the idea for 1969. Gromyko did not meet with Nixon until September 1970.

The back-channel discussion also touched on Kissinger's first secret negotiations with the North Vietnamese in Paris.[90] Jean Sainteny, Kissinger's friend and a well-connected figure who had been a senior official in French Indochina, had served as an intermediary with the North Vietnamese to facilitate both a private correspondence between Nixon and Ho Chi Minh and to establish private sessions with Kissinger in Paris. In early August, Kissinger met with his old negotiating counterpart, Hanoi's delegate-general, Mai Van Bo, and plenipotentiary at the plenary peace talks, Xuan Thuy. In retrospect, Kissinger wrote that the private meeting, the only one in 1969, "achieved little except to restate established positions in a less contentious manner."[91] A month after the Paris session, Dobrynin— perhaps appealing to Kissinger's vanity—told Kissinger, "Hanoi had told Moscow that they had been very impressed by [Kissinger's] presentation and thought [he] understood Vietnamese conditions very well."[92] As Kissinger made clear in his discussion with the president and in his memorandum of the meeting with Dobrynin, the United States had put the ball into Hanoi's court and expected movement.

On October 9, Dobrynin relayed his impression that the Nixon administration had become "increasingly convinced" that the Soviet leadership had "lost interest in a quick settlement in Vietnam." Dobrynin believed that the problem remained the "stubborn unwillingness of the U.S. side to agree to establish a coalition government in South Vietnam." Although Kissinger repeatedly denied that progress on arms control and the Middle East were tied to Vietnam, Dobrynin had the impression that "one nonetheless sensed that the policy of the White House towards us is in fact based on the concept of linkage between the issues."[93] In a telegram the next day, the Soviet ambassador proposed giving the administration the Kremlin's "assessment" of the Paris talks, "with a touch of constructiveness," to give Nixon and Kissinger the appearance of Soviet assistance in facilitating the negotiations. Let linkage work against the Americans, Dobrynin insisted. He argued that the White House might then accept the situation in Southeast Asia and adopt a more "flexible" response in other areas like arms control.[94] In other words, although both sides continued to deny the existence of linkage in public, in private they continued to use it wherever they believed their own interests were at stake.

On October 17, Dobrynin requested a meeting with the president to deliver Moscow's "reply on SALT" and arranged to meet three days later with Nixon and Kissinger at the White House.[95] First, he delivered an aide-mémoire from the Soviet leadership, which lamented the lack of progress in bilateral Soviet-American relations.[96] The diplomatic note reflected Dobrynin's suggestions that Moscow take a harder line with the United States.

According to Kissinger's record of the meeting, Nixon responded candidly, "almost uninterruptedly for half an hour." The president focused on the first anniversary of the bombing halt ordered by President Johnson and said that the Soviet Union had "done nothing" toward a settlement. North Vietnamese delays, allegedly encouraged by Moscow, were an attack on the presidency. Nixon stated that "he did not believe much in personal diplomacy, and he recognized that the Ambassador was a strong defender of the interests of his own country." National interests, not personal diplomacy, were central—an ironic statement for such an advocate of back-channel diplomacy. Nixon then promoted linkage again and "pointed out that if the Soviet Union found it possible to do something in Vietnam, and the Vietnam War ended, the U.S. might do something dramatic to improve Soviet-U.S. relations, indeed something more dramatic than they could now imagine." "But until then," he warned, "real progress would be difficult."[97]

Dobrynin's account was significantly more detailed than Kissinger's and painted the conversation in a totally different light. According to Dobrynin, Nixon twice emphasized that he would "*never . . .* accept a humiliating defeat or humiliating terms." Nixon would use "other measures" to avoid defeat, and chastised the Soviet note. Nixon also gave a primer on his philosophy of diplomacy and the proper use of back channels: "While I wish to maintain personal, confidential contacts with the Soviet leadership, I fail to understand it when Moscow bypasses diplomatic channels and directly sends me a message in which there is absolutely nothing new, just reiteration, in particular, of the long-familiar Soviet expression of full support for North Vietnam. That could be also done through the State Department if the U.S.S.R. absolutely has to say that again. In any case, I don't favor that sort of personal diplomacy."

According to Dobrynin, Nixon affirmed:

> I must state plainly, and in all candor, that the war in Vietnam is the main obstacle to enhancing and developing Soviet-U.S. relations. I am not saying we cannot or should not seek ways to resolve other issues. That has to be done, but through normal diplomatic channels with their attendant procedures, which will take a great deal of time and effort. Progress here is not out of the question, but it is fundamentally limited by the framework and capabilities of such channels. Until the war is over, those are, in fact, the only channels that can be used (the implication being that it is hard to count on a quick agreement, which is possible only at a high level).

Dobrynin contrasted his own "calm" tone with the president's initial outburst in response to the aide-mémoire. Dobrynin asserted that Nixon's behavior and "emotional coloration" made it "perfectly clear . . . that events surrounding the Vietnam crisis now wholly preoccupy the U.S. President, and that to all appearances the fate of his predecessor, Lyndon Johnson, is beginning to really worry him."[98] Three days later, Dobrynin cabled the Kremlin, "The vehemence of [Nixon's] remarks testified to his growing emotionalism and lack of balance with respect to events related to Vietnam, rather than to a firm conviction that he will in fact be able to get the U.S.S.R. to influence the D.R.V. in the direction that he, Nixon, needs."[99]

The depths to which U.S.-Soviet relations had sunk became evident when the Nixon administration decided to conduct a worldwide secret nuclear alert in October 1969, and planned massive bombing-mining operations against North Vietnam, known as Operation Duck Hook. Recent scholarship has shown that the administration designed the secret nuclear alert to coerce the Soviets into helping end the Vietnam War.[100] Duck Hook never materialized, and the nuclear alert failed to have the desired effect.[101] An examination of the back-channel exchanges reinforces the centrality of the Vietnam issue but indicates, too, that the alert may also have been intended to convey the administration's more general displeasure about the broad state of U.S.-Soviet relations.

The administration sent other signals. In his meetings with Dobrynin in September and October 1969, Kissinger described several unproductive attempts to negotiate with the North Vietnamese, including private correspondence between Nixon and Ho Chi Minh and his own secret August negotiating session in Paris.[102] The White House also decided to make the Soviets ask for an invitation for Gromyko to meet with Nixon. In meetings with Dobrynin, Nixon and Kissinger complained that the Soviets were not doing anything to rein in their intransigent North Vietnamese allies. Kissinger hinted at the top-secret military alert in talking points he sent to the president before the meeting on October 20. Kissinger advised: "Should Dobrynin refer to our current readiness measures, you should simply tell him that these are carefully controlled exercises which in view of the uncertainties of the future you feel it incumbent on you to undertake. They involve no threat."[103]

In his own "copious notes," Dobrynin described Nixon's response when it came to more detailed discussions about the state of the Vietnam peace negotiations.[104] The Soviet ambassador reported the president's contemptuous comments:

The U.S. Government took this step and stopped the bombing. A year has gone by, and what has happened? The Soviet Union has not done a thing. Of course, Nixon said with a tinge of sarcasm, we now have an oblong negotiating table in Paris, to which the Soviet Union contributed to a certain extent. . . . Instead, what we have is a total impasse and the other side's unwillingness to even talk until its peremptory demands are accepted.

The Soviet Union, Nixon continued, also prefers to remain silent, even though its leaders have been sent several personal confidential messages from him, the president, in a spirit of goodwill. However, the Soviet Union continues to support Hanoi 100 percent in all of its demands and to provide North Vietnam very substantial assistance.

All this, Nixon went on, has led him to conclude that to all appearances, the Soviet Union does not want the war in Vietnam to end. I know the Soviet leaders tell me the opposite. I don't question their sincerity. But if they were in my shoes, they too would probably come to the same conclusion.[105]

Constrained by domestic political opinion, Nixon and Kissinger still tried to link Vietnam to an improvement in Soviet-American relations. The fact that the White House chose to abandon Duck Hook and remained vague about the nuclear alert showed that they had sent a garbled rather than a strong signal to the Soviets, back-channel or otherwise. The Channel simply signaled general displeasure on both ends at the end of 1969.

A year after his election to the presidency, oblong table in Paris aside, Nixon had precious little to show by way of foreign policy accomplishments. The desire for peace with honor in Vietnam continued to elude the administration, while Nixon and Kissinger's steadfast commitment to linkage precluded any meaningful improvement in U.S.-Soviet relations. Throughout 1969, Kissinger and Dobrynin had talked past each other on Vietnam. The administration's insistence on linkage as a precondition for consideration of matters dear to the Soviets had done little to promote the prospects for détente. Linkage's deterrent effect had been nullified by the fact that the Soviets had so far gained nothing from détente and had much to lose if they abandoned Hanoi. Furthermore, as Dobrynin later admitted, the Soviet leadership was prepared to wait out Nixon.[106] A series of crises would brew in 1970 and force a reassessment of the back channel.

2

At a Crossroads

Cienfuegos, SALT, and Germany-Berlin

Say, for example, we were to go up and report to the Senate every month as to what progress [in SALT has been made]. That is why it didn't happen in Vienna, you see. It's no reflection on [Gerard] Smith and his boys. They were doing great, but the point is that with the Soviet [Union] things have to be done sometimes at the highest level. And it has to be done with the highest secrecy. Once it's done, then it can all be public.

—President Richard M. Nixon, May 19, 1971

At noon on May 20, 1971, President Nixon made a surprise announcement to a television and radio audience from the White House. The president succinctly explained that a yearlong deadlock in the Strategic Arms Limitation Talks (SALT) had been broken "as a result of negotiations involving the highest level of both governments."[1] On the surface, the "highest level" had been an exchange of letters between the president and Soviet premier Alexei Kosygin. Unsurprisingly, Nixon neglected to mention the fact that the United States and the Soviet Union had used the Kissinger-Dobrynin channel to overcome the SALT impasse and that both the secretary of state and the head of the SALT delegation, Ambassador Gerard Smith, had been categorically excluded from the private machinations. As the president explained to his cabinet before the announcement, "We did not inform anybody because we thought it was very important that there be no leaks."[2]

Kissinger recalled that the bureaucratic machinery for reviewing SALT issues was "extremely time-consuming," and, in an election year,

Nixon shaking hands with West German chancellor Willy Brandt. Secretary of State William Rogers stands to Nixon's left, March 1970. (RNPLM)

"Nixon was determined that the credit for SALT go to him and not to Smith."[3] In addition to Kissinger's rationalizations for the resort to back channels on SALT, both the White House and the Kremlin used the confidential channel to reinforce linkage between the major issues in U.S.-Soviet relations, including arms control, negotiations over the perennial Cold War flashpoint, Berlin, and the prospect of a superpower summit.

Nixon and Kissinger used back channels as both an accelerator and as a brake to modulate progress on negotiations central to building détente. In the case of SALT, the two nations initially used the Kissinger-Dobrynin channel to break the impasse that had developed by the end of 1970 and to fast-track the agreement announced in May 1971 to freeze the construction of offensive missiles and lay the groundwork for a defensive limitation. The confidential channel again went into play in April 1972 to include Submarine-Launched Ballistic Missiles (SLBMs) in the offensive freeze and culminated with the Interim Agreement on the Limitation of Strategic Offensive Arms and the Anti-Ballistic Missile (ABM) treaty signed at the Moscow Summit. Recognizing the Kremlin's desire to ease

A 1972 Herblock Cartoon.
(© The Herb Block Foundation)

**"IT LOOKS LIKE MORE
NON-MUSHROOM WEATHER TO ME."**

tensions on its western flank, the White House also used the back channel to delay the negotiation and ratification of the Four Power (Quadripartite) Agreement on Berlin.

The U.S. holdup over the Four Power Agreement in turn delayed the West German ratification of the "Eastern treaties," namely, the 1970 Moscow and Warsaw treaties. West German chancellor Willy Brandt's astute secretary of the prime minister's office, Egon Bahr, linked the ratification of the Eastern treaties to a satisfactory settlement for Berlin. In fact, Brandt and Bahr tied their "new Ostpolitik" policy of improved relations between the West and the Communist East, including the settlement of borders and exchanges between East and West Germany. After the United States, the Soviet Union, Great Britain, and France signed the Quadripartite Agreement in September 1971, Nixon and Kissinger continued to use the Kissinger-Dobrynin channel to convey subtle threats to the Soviets that the United States could upset ratification of the Eastern treaties by West Germany's parliament, or Bundestag.

The Soviets used the Channel to dangle the prospect of a superpower summit before the Nixon administration. Although he had dismissed the idea of a joint summit with Lyndon Johnson before assuming the presidency, Nixon expressed an early interest in a summit meeting with the Soviet leaders during his first term. Through the back-channel exchanges, the Soviets recognized that Nixon wanted a summit meeting in order to boost his standing in U.S. domestic politics. According to Dobrynin, by the end of 1970 the Soviet leadership decided to "drive a hard bargain" with the Nixon administration based on the "belief that Nixon wanted a summit meeting to enhance his political fortunes for his reelection campaign the following year."[4] The hard bargain was apparent to the White House. Kissinger explained in his memoirs, "Clearly, if I linked Berlin to SALT the Soviets linked Berlin to a summit."[5]

This chapter examines the moribund state of U.S.-Soviet relations during 1970 and how the White House used back channels to break the SALT impasse, delay the negotiations and ratification of the Quadripartite Agreement, and push for a summit meeting in 1970–1971. Both the United States and the Soviet Union used linkage in the back channel, and domestic political considerations increasingly affected the White House policy calculus. In 1970, the back channel was only one means of communications with the Soviet leadership in addition to regular diplomacy through Foggy Bottom. As Kissinger outmaneuvered Rogers in bureaucratic struggles within the Nixon administration, however, the Channel became the primary mechanism for U.S.-Soviet relations and in shaping superpower détente by resolving matters of concern for both sides.

1970: From Drift, Doubt, and Turmoil to Back-Channel Breakthroughs

Both Kissinger and Dobrynin have declared that the Channel did not become fully operational until early 1971, an assertion corroborated by a statistical analysis of the official back-channel record.[6] However, the national security advisor and the Soviet ambassador disagreed sharply over why the back channel did not become *fully* operational until 1971. Dobrynin blamed the Nixon administration, which, in his opinion, "was not yet genuinely interested in making Soviet-American relations a major foreign policy priority in 1970." He correctly claimed that the

United States' leadership primarily wanted "to end the Vietnam War" but disingenuously added that "1970 did not see a single major crisis in Soviet-American relations."[7] Kissinger presented a diametrically contrasting viewpoint in *White House Years*. "Inconclusive exchanges in 1969," the national security advisor noted, "degenerated into a series of confrontations."[8]

Kissinger explained that Soviet-American relations had faced a number of shocks in 1970: the Soviet dispatch of troops and an advanced Surface-to-Air Missile (SAM) system to Egypt in March; the U.S. incursion into Cambodia to destroy Communist sanctuaries from May through June; the Soviet-backed Syrian attack on Jordan in September; the Soviet attempt to construct a nuclear submarine base in Cienfuegos Bay, Cuba, in September–October; and, finally, the election of Socialist Salvador Allende in Chile in November.[9] U.S.-Soviet exchanges on SALT, trade, Germany-Berlin, and a summit meeting took place against the backdrop of the series of crises, and little substantive progress occurred. Above all, however, the Channel was only a part of the larger superpower relationship, which was still being conducted largely through regular diplomatic channels.

Although the Channel touched upon most areas of U.S.-Soviet relations, policy choices and simple logistics also held back its expansion until 1971. The State Department handled the crisis over the Soviet deployment to Egypt, although there were several noteworthy back-channel exchanges after American intelligence detected Soviet moves. In the case of the Jordan crisis in August–September 1970, the Kissinger-Dobrynin channel had been on hiatus because Dobrynin was in Moscow for extended consultations. More generally, the Middle East was the primary bone of contention in superpower relations in 1970. From the beginning of his administration, Nixon directed the State Department to play the lead role on the sensitive Middle East negotiations with the Soviets. The State Department's efforts focused largely through the United Nations, although Assistant Secretary of State for Near Eastern and South Asian Affairs Joseph Sisco primarily handled the communication with the Soviets through Ambassador Dobrynin.

There are several reasons why Kissinger and the Channel remained secondary on the Middle East until the summer of 1971. First, Sisco had over a decade of experience as a Foreign Service officer and had been the

chief U.S. mediator on the Arab-Israeli dispute since the Johnson administration. In comparison, Kissinger had never visited any Arab countries
and had only limited experience with the Middle East prior to becoming
national security advisor. Nixon also expressed concerns about Kissinger's objectivity because of his Jewish heritage.[10] Kissinger later admitted
as much: "[Nixon] had his doubts as to whether my Jewish faith might
warp my judgment. Normally I would have shaped his strategic options
and given tactical guidance to the departments. But I was precluded from
doing this in the Middle East."[11] As Kissinger was effectively locked out of
Middle East policy—at least until late 1971—so was the Channel.

The Egyptian crisis in early 1970 hinted at the expansion of the Channel but was largely handled via conventional diplomatic exchanges. In a
letter of January 31, 1970, to President Nixon, Premier Alexei Kosygin justified Soviet support for the Arab states, although he ignored the fedayeen
attacks on Israel that had provoked the so-called War of Attrition. Rather,
the Soviet leaders focused on Israeli retaliatory "deep penetration" raids
on Egypt using advanced American jets.[12] Kosygin threatened that if
Israeli "adventurism" continued, the Soviet Union would be "forced to
see to it that the Arab states have means at their disposal" against Israel.[13]
Although the letter was delivered via Kissinger, the Soviets also delivered
the same letter to both British prime minister Harold Wilson and French
president Georges Pompidou.[14]

Starting in January 1970, the Soviets dispatched troops to man the
sophisticated, low-altitude SA-3 SAM system the Kremlin leaders had
agreed to provide to Egyptian president Gamal Abdul Nasser. Contrary to
earlier accounts that claimed the Soviets agreed to provide the SA-3 system
during Nasser's trip to Moscow in January 1970, historian Isabella Ginor
has convincingly argued that the deployment was already being implemented by the time of the meeting. Ginor reasoned that Nasser sought
greater Soviet commitment and that an entire Soviet Air Force group had
already been stationed in Egypt by the end of the month. Soviet troops
traveled to Egypt incognito, and the first low-altitude SA-3 missiles went
online toward the end of March 1970, reflecting months of preparation.
U.S. and Israeli intelligence detected the missile installations in March.[15]

After a back-channel meeting on March 10, before he learned of the
Soviet SA-3 deployment, Kissinger believed that Dobrynin had offered
"significant concessions." In his memo of the conversation, he noted

that the Soviets, in effect, "offered a ceasefire along the Suez Canal, thus enabling us to show the Israelis that we have achieved something for them with our policy on the Kosygin letter." Kissinger gleaned another lesson from the encounter: "In the negotiations on Egypt our policy of relative firmness has paid off on all contested issues." Although the Kremlin had made the "first move" with the Kosygin letter, "holding firm and offering no concessions was the right course."[16] The Soviets could be convinced, but only if the United States stuck to its guns and drove a hard bargain.

Before the meeting with Dobrynin, Kissinger discussed with the president the politically sensitive topic of American military aid to Israel. Nixon insisted that the United States would provide only replacements for Israeli planes lost in combat, and that it would not expand Israeli capabilities lest it provoke the Soviets. "We are not going along on a massive Israeli request," the president stated. "It would force the Soviets into a massive reaction including men into the UAR [United Arab Republic, an Egyptian and Syrian political union between 1958 and 1961; Egypt went by this name until 1971]." Kissinger agreed: "They have held back and now we must see what they are doing."[17] Kissinger began to draft a cease-fire plan and develop a strategy to bring the Israelis on board. Unfortunately, the Soviets had already begun surreptitiously sending men to Egypt.

Dobrynin's account suggested the March 10 meeting focused on SALT, although he stressed that *he* had been tough with Kissinger on the Middle East. "The main thing is that the U.S. side, if it truly wants progress on a settlement," Dobrynin told Moscow, "must abandon its one-sided approach to resolving the main issues of a Middle East settlement: the withdrawal of troops and establishment of borders."[18] Both Kissinger and Dobrynin continued to report their tough postures toward each other, Kissinger to his single constituent—Nixon—and Dobrynin to a larger audience.

The discovery of the Soviet deployment to Egypt only hardened the White House's resolve. The back-channel exchanges demonstrated to Nixon and Kissinger that the Soviets had sent, at best, mixed signals; at worst, they were being duplicitous. The president was inclined to believe that the Soviets acted out of a strategic design. "The Soviets wanted to maintain their presence in the Middle East," Nixon explained, "not because of ideological support for the cause of Arab unity but because it was through Egypt and the other Arab countries that the Soviets could gain access to what the Russians had always wanted—land, oil, power, and the warm waters of the Mediterranean."[19] In a theme repeated throughout his presidency, Nixon saw Moscow as an enabler of aggression. Soviet weapons and materiel provided the means by which countries like Egypt, Syria, India, and North Vietnam could launch attacks and upset the balance of power.

Kissinger's attempt to draft a cease-fire with the Israelis came to an abrupt halt. The national security advisor called the Soviet ambassador to the White House on March 20. "We had, in fact, begun discussions with the Israelis about a ceasefire and had obtained Israeli approval," Kissinger told Dobrynin. "But within 24 hours of calling them in to make it final and to establish definite time limits, we learned about the introduction of Soviet SA-3 missiles and Soviet combat personnel." The deployment reminded Kissinger of the Soviet dispatch of weapons to Cuba that precipitated the Cuban Missile Crisis. He recorded that, as a consequence, "the president had canceled his request to the Israelis for a ceasefire, and the matter was now off." According to Kissinger, Dobrynin replied that he would need to consult his government.[20]

Dobrynin added detail in his own contemporaneous account of the exchange. According to the ambassador, Kissinger made very clear that the White House was upset by the Soviet move, which had introduced "a qualitatively new factor into the overall situation." The ambassador listed his own response as significantly more strident than Kissinger had reported:

> The U.S. ignores the fact that Israel, acting as the aggressor, has not only occupied large amounts of Arab territory, which the Arab peoples are fighting to liberate, but it is also continuing barbarous air raids into regions deep inside the UAR and other Arab countries. Air defense systems in the UAR, regardless of their type or designations, do not threaten Israel itself, because they are purely defensive weapons. To equate this issue with the piratical raids by Israeli aircraft is like portraying burglars who systematically rob other people's homes as the injured parties when the homeowner decides to install a lock to keep the burglars out.[21]

The back-channel discussions on the Middle East continued in a secondary capacity, as the State Department worked to establish a fragile cease-fire between Israel and Egypt. As Kissinger and Dobrynin talked past each other and postured themselves as tough brokers in their own memoranda, Soviet troops and missiles bolstered the effectiveness of Egypt's air defenses and hampered Israeli air strikes. Before the issue came to a head over the SA-3s, Kissinger had recommended the use of the Channel to quietly handle the Middle East concerns, but the Soviets did not respond.[22] When Israel and Egypt accepted "an uneasy cease-fire" in August 1970, Nixon called it a "major accomplishment for Rogers and Sisco." Still, the president realized that "even though the cease-fire was violated by Egypt almost before the ink was dry, it established the United States as the honest broker accepted by both sides."[23] Nixon, however, overlooked the sizable Soviet presence along the Suez Canal and through-out Egypt. When the president pushed for the Middle East discussions with the Soviets in the back channel a year later, the Soviets agreed. In the interim, however, there would be additional hurdles to overcome. During the "Autumn of Crises," as Kissinger termed it, the Soviets again attempted to expand their influence in the Middle East and the Caribbean.

After assassination attempts on his life and several hijackings by the Popular Front for the Liberation of Palestine (PFLP) to fedayeen-controlled areas of Jordan, the pro-Western Hashemite king, Hussein bin Talal, evicted the Palestinian Liberation Organization (PLO) from his country during "Black September" 1970. The Soviet-supported Syrians backed the PLO and massed forces to threaten an attack on Jordan. Although the king's forces beat back the attack, the risk of superpower conflict seemed high. The White House quietly deployed the USS *Independence* carrier and six destroyers to the coast of Lebanon. Kissinger wrote: "These steps were to be taken without announcement. . . . Our silence would give them an ominous quality."[24]

The back channel during "Black September" was also silent because Dobrynin was out of town for seven weeks, and thus exchanges were via regular diplomatic channels. The U.S. ambassador to the Soviet Union, Jacob Beam, met with Soviet deputy foreign minister Sergei Vinogradov, and the Kremlin likewise communicated with the White House through their counselor minister in Washington, Yuli Vorontsov. Kissinger called Vorontsov "clever, amiable, and discreet but quite powerless."[25] Reflect-ing both Dobrynin's absence and the later expansion of the Channel, the Jordan crisis produced relatively few U.S.-Soviet exchanges, especially in comparison to later events like the Indo-Pakistani War of 1971, and

Soviet-backed North Vietnam's spring 1972 offensive. After the United States backed the possibility of Israeli air strikes and the deployment of ground troops in support of King Hussein, the Soviets encouraged the Syrians to withdraw from Jordan. Working with Sisco and Rogers, Kissinger coordinated the U.S. response through the Washington Special Actions Group (WSAG) and communicated with Tel Aviv, Amman, Cairo, London, Paris, and Moscow largely through diplomatic channels. The back channel, however, expanded in response to another crisis when Dobrynin returned in late September 1970.

Cienfuegos

"Bob, look at this," Henry Kissinger said as he slammed a thick file onto H. R. Haldeman's desk on September 18, 1970. Moments after showing the chief of staff reconnaissance photos, Kissinger described their content: "It's a Cuban seaport, Haldeman, and these pictures show the Cubans are building soccer fields. . . . Those soccer fields could mean war." After the no-nonsense, crew-cut Haldeman gave him a quizzical look, Kissinger explained, "Cubans play *baseball,* Russians play *soccer.*"[26] In addition to soccer fields for recreation, the Soviets were building a naval base on Cienfuegos Bay, complete with SAM sites, communications towers, barracks, and other facilities that could be used to service nuclear (armed and powered) submarines.[27] Even before the Jordan crisis had been settled, American reconnaissance flights over Cuba detected the construction activity.[28] Kissinger notified the president of the situation, noted that he would receive a CIA briefing later that day, and said he had scheduled an emergency SRG session for the next morning.[29]

After the earlier troop deployment to Egypt and Soviet support for Syria's action against Jordan, Kissinger told Haldeman that the Soviet plan in Cuba was a "real plot" and that Nixon's "credibility with the Soviets" was at stake.[30] Kissinger retrospectively explained, "I saw the Soviet move as going beyond its military implications; it was part of a process of testing under way in different parts of the world." The national security advisor advocated "facing the challenge immediately lest the Soviets misunderstand our permissiveness and escalate their involvement to a point where only a major crisis could remove the base."[31] On the advice of Llewellyn "Tommy" Thompson, a leading Soviet expert and former U.S.

ambassador to the Soviet Union, the State Department suggested "quiet talk" a month later between Secretary Rogers and Soviet foreign minister Gromyko at the annual United Nations General Assembly session. Kissinger relied on the assessment of JCS chairman Admiral Thomas Moorer and insisted the matter could not wait five weeks.[32] Kissinger's eventual success in bypassing Rogers and using a confidential exchange to resolve the Cienfuegos crisis enhanced the Kissinger-Dobrynin channel and gave it a renewed sense of purpose.

Initially, Nixon sided with Rogers's option in handling the crisis. Kissinger called Cuba a "neuralgic problem for Nixon" and added that a "potential Cuban crisis during an election struck a raw nerve."[33] Nixon always believed that the "rally around the flag" effect of the Cuban Missile Crisis had contributed to his loss in the 1962 California gubernatorial race. In September 1970, the midterm congressional ballot was less than two months away, and Kissinger recalled: "Nixon's preferred strategy was to confront the Soviets right after the election. He accepted my analysis, but for the interim he chose Rogers's policy of soothing delay." A master of bureaucratic intrigue, Kissinger knew a way to convince the president of the urgency of the situation. In Nixon parlance, Kissinger pulled out his hole card: chief of staff Bob Haldeman.

"It was risky to approach Haldeman," Kissinger recalled, "since he was likely to interpret any substantive concern as a signal of emotional instability. . . . But he was sure to communicate my uneasiness to Nixon."[34] Kissinger proved correct on both counts. Haldeman's diary entry for September 20, 1970, initially heavily redacted when published in 1994, has now been fully declassified and describes Kissinger's candid assessment of the Cienfuegos crisis. The national security advisor feared that a Soviet submarine base in Cuba would bolster Soviet offensive capabilities. The possibility of a summit meeting hid Moscow's true aim, Kissinger surmised: to cover "for their Cuban operation following the same pattern as in '62." Kissinger told Haldeman that the administration needed to put up a united front with the Soviets generally and Dobrynin specifically. According to Haldeman's notes, the Kissinger-Rogers dispute had some serious implications:

K[issinger] fears R[ogers's] softness will mislead them—as [Dean] Rusk did in '62. Thinks this will surface in ten days–two weeks.

Can't hold until after elections, which is what [the] P[resident] wants. *Fears if R goes ahead with Dobrynin mtgs. etc. Soviets will lose all their fear of RN—then P will have to go violently the other way. Last thing we want is crisis w/ Russians now—esp. w/ this new strategic advantage.*[35] Is now beyond point of just indulging Rogers, could project a two-year series of crises.[36]

Kissinger suggested to Haldeman that Dobrynin's long consultations in Moscow had a sinister motivation; that the White House would "have no one to talk to." The submarine base and the boost to Soviet strategic capabilities would be a fait accompli. Recognizing Nixon's own worries about Cuba and the midterm elections just weeks away, Kissinger called it a *"real kick in teeth to RN."* Kissinger wanted to redouble his efforts with Haldeman "to handle all this, especially with [the] P[resident] and vis-à-vis Rogers."[37]

The approach to Haldeman worked in Kissinger's favor when Nixon decided to send a signal to the Soviets about Cienfuegos before departing for a two-week trip to Europe. Since only a narrow window of opportunity existed between Dobrynin's return to Washington and Nixon's departure, Kissinger managed to convince the president to communicate a tough-but-sensible line with the Soviets through the back channel. They also kept Rogers in the dark.

As was customary after consultations in Moscow, the Soviet ambassador called Kissinger to arrange a meeting. On September 24, Dobrynin asked to see the president about "the summit and things about Jordan." Kissinger was coy about Dobrynin's request. "I have no particular need to talk with you," Kissinger told his interlocutor. "I have to see if the president has time and if not, you may have to talk with me."[38] Several hours later, Kissinger told Nixon, "I was very cool to [Dobrynin], and said I didn't know if your schedule permitted you to see him." Nixon replied: "I will not see him. If he wants to give a message, he can see you. . . . I don't think we want to appear that everytime [*sic*] he comes back I am going to slobber over him." "Tell him if there is something substantive that would justify my seeing him, I will," Nixon ordered, "but if it is just routine I can't do it."[39] Kissinger diplomatically conveyed Nixon's response to Dobrynin twenty minutes later. The Soviet ambassador, using similar tactics, replied that he would have to "check with Moscow" if he could meet with the national security advisor instead of the president to transmit the message.[40]

Kissinger and Dobrynin met twice on September 25, 1970; the first time at Dobrynin's request in the morning; the second at Kissinger's request in the late afternoon. In the morning meeting, Dobrynin delivered a note that the Soviet leadership was ready to proceed with a summit meeting "in principle" and that the Channel would be the forum for "exploratory conversations." On the Jordan crisis, Dobrynin said that the White House had never responded to an earlier démarche. Kissinger pithily responded, "Certainly we were willing to discuss them with Moscow but it seemed to us that over a period of weeks every Soviet démarche had been followed by the contrary action and we simply wanted to wait to see what would happen." According to Kissinger's memorandum of the meeting, Dobrynin "said we might not believe it but the Soviet Union had not known of the invasion of Jordan by Syria and that in any event Soviet advisors had dropped off Syrian tanks prior to crossing the frontier." Kissinger noted that he "let this somewhat contradictory statement go" and said he would need to consult with Nixon on Middle East issues. He refused to discuss any other matters until they had dealt with the Cuban problem.[41]

In the late-afternoon meeting, Kissinger focused almost exclusively on the situation in Cuba and stressed that he wanted to use the back channel "unofficially" to leave the Soviets a way out. A White House announcement that the United States "did not yet know whether there was actually a submarine base in Cuba" was made "deliberately in order to give the Soviet Union an opportunity to withdraw without a public confrontation." Kissinger elaborated that the United States was under "no illusions" and had confirmed the construction of the base. He warned, "we would view it with the utmost gravity if construction continued and the base remained," and stressed that the administration did not want a public confrontation but "would not shrink from other measures including public ones if forced into it." The White House considered Vorontsov's August 4 démarche upholding the Cuban Missile Crisis "understanding"—that the Soviets would not station offensive weapons in Cuba—as an "act of bad faith." A solution existed, however. "If the ships—especially the tender—left Cienfuegos," Kissinger elucidated, "we would consider the whole matter a training exercise."[42]

Dobrynin promised to report to his government and said he would quickly have an answer.

Dobrynin recorded the two meetings in a single memorandum. Regardless of the differences in their reporting styles, Kissinger and Dobrynin agreed on the importance of the back-channel means of the communication. "Kissinger, on his initiative and citing instructions from Nixon," Dobrynin cabled, "requested that an oral communication from the president be transmitted to the Soviet Government." The president was "very seriously concerned" about the construction of a nuclear submarine base in the port of Cienfuegos. The U.S. government would "treat this as a violation of the understanding that was reached between the two governments back in 1962 and that in effect was again secretly reaffirmed in August [1970]." "Such a precipitate violation of this recently reaffirmed understanding," Kissinger explained, "if it is taking place, would make an extremely negative impression." The issue had become a matter of "national security," which could not "be ignored by any American president, who is obligated to take all measures to ensure the security of his country." Tellingly, "Kissinger said that the president requests that this message not be regarded as some kind of official representation or protest, but rather as his strictly confidential and important appeal to the Soviet leaders in the hope that it will receive the attention it deserves."[43]

Before Nixon departed for Europe, and Kissinger to Paris for secret negotiations with the North Vietnamese, the White House used other signals to the Soviets that it would not tolerate the base at Cienfuegos. A Pentagon press briefing on September 24 that mistakenly disclosed the details of the Soviet construction efforts led to a spate of news stories the next morning. Kissinger was initially outraged when he saw the morning papers but later claimed "the Pentagon bloopers were actually our salvation." The disclosure, which was partly prompted by Secretary of Defense Laird, pushed Nixon toward handling the situation quickly, against the State Department's advice.[44] Nixon ordered additional destroyers to patrol the Caribbean and endorsed Kissinger's approach to the Soviets through Dobrynin. Kissinger gave a press briefing reaffirming the American understanding of the 1962 agreement in between his meetings with Dobrynin on September 25.[45] Meanwhile, the situation in Jordan resolved itself when Syrian tanks and troops departed, and the prospect of Israeli intervention dimmed.

When Nixon and Kissinger returned from Europe, Kissinger again met with Dobrynin on October 6. The Soviets essentially backed away from the base construction, reaffirmed (again) the 1962 understanding, and presented a few "clarifying questions" such as the definition of what constituted a "base."[46] Kissinger consulted the NSC-JCS liaison officer, Capt. Rembrandt Robinson, and explained the semantic distinctions to Dobrynin on October 9 during a conversation that focused primarily on the Egyptian-Israeli cease-fire.[47] In a meeting between Nixon and Gromyko later that month, Nixon skirted the topic of the Cienfuegos base because, according to Kissinger, "he did not wish to get into the sensitive Kissinger-Dobrynin exchanges in the presence of his Secretary of State."[48] Although the story fizzled in the press, the resolution of the crisis led to both hidden costs and benefits.

For Kissinger, the quiet resolution of the Cienfuegos crisis and subsequent visits by Soviet submarines to Cuba, testing the Nixon administration's resolve, showed how successful the back channel could be: "All this, it must be remembered, was handled almost entirely by private diplomacy. The process was essentially a series of messages in the presidential Channel, backstopped by interagency coordination in the WSAG. Rather than a dramatic confrontation on the order of 1962, we considered that quiet diplomacy was best suited to giving the USSR an opportunity to withdraw without humiliation."[49]

As for lessons learned, Kissinger wrote: "We could not forget, of course, the deception that had been attempted. Nor would we be oblivious to the reality that Soviet restraint when it was achieved, resulted only from our forcing of the issue and determined persistence."[50] Kissinger established a contrast between dealing with the Soviets through the State Department versus communicating via back channels. In Kissinger's estimation, Secretary Rogers, and, by extension, the State Department, prevaricated and encouraged aggressive Communist action by their weakness. In contrast, the back channel was sophisticated and direct, allowing the administration to play it tough with the Soviets and earning their restraint through respect. Cienfuegos boosted the back channel and marked a turning point for the Nixon administration's handling of U.S.-Soviet relations. Nixon and Kissinger would return again and again to the theme that the Soviets needed to be dealt with firmly—although not necessarily publicly—and the back channel eventually overshadowed the State Department as the main means of U.S.-Soviet relations.

The waters of Cienfuegos also diluted Rogers's authority and gave Kissinger an upper hand in their rivalry. Again, the ubiquitous Haldeman provided a window into the Kissinger-Rogers dispute and the handling of the Soviet submarine base. On September 26, Haldeman reported: "P gave Haig his whole theory about how to handle crisis, said we couldn't let K-Rogers battles get in the way of dealing with substance. Recognizes both were tired and strained but that will always be the case in a major crisis. Simply have to get them both to quit acting like little children, trying to nail the other and prove him wrong. Since P sees exactly what they're doing, it's obvious neither will get away with it."

Haldeman told the president that Kissinger had raised the idea that he should leave the administration. "To shake [Kissinger] a little," Haldeman reported that he had "agreed with [Kissinger] that maybe he should think of leaving." Nixon said he would put Kissinger's deputy, Alexander Haig, "in the spot" if Kissinger departed, but this "would really be a major loss, and then State and Rogers would run rampant which would be very bad."[51] Haig knew of the back channel with Dobrynin, and Nixon knew that the increasingly pragmatic forum could disappear if Kissinger decided to leave the administration.

After the Europe trip, the Kissinger-Rogers "flap" again flared up when Kissinger failed to inform Rogers that the Cienfuegos crisis had been resolved in talks with the Soviet ambassador. Rogers complained to Haldeman after an NSC meeting on October 14 that Kissinger "was meeting with Dobrynin about Cuba without telling him." As a result, when Rogers talked to Dobrynin he "looked foolish because he didn't know." Rogers suspected that Kissinger was "doing this under P's orders and want[ed] to know why."[52] Although Nixon considered disclosing the back channel to Rogers at the end of 1970, he never followed through.[53] Shying away from conflict with his old friend Rogers, Nixon tacitly endorsed Kissinger. The former professor reinforced Nixon's own inclination to play it tough with the Soviets, a refrain heard repeatedly behind the closed doors of the executive offices.

Of the crises in 1970, only the resolution of the Cienfuegos crisis in September-October had a real back-channel element and became more important in the evolution of the Kissinger-Rogers dispute and the decision to expand the channel. From December 1970, the Kissinger-Dobrynin contact became increasingly active to address Germany-Berlin,

SALT, and a possible superpower summit. The machinery in place since early 1969 finally went active.

SALT: From Origins to Deadlock

Richard Nixon's epitaph is taken from his inaugural address and reads: "The greatest honor history can bestow is the title of peacemaker."[54] Although the thirty-seventh president is a case study in contradictions— the man of Quaker upbringing who cursed and talked with relish about "bombing the bejeezus" out of North Vietnam—the high-minded talk about "peace" was more than lip service. Nixon partially defined himself by a commitment to the abstract concept of peace, and arms control became one of the centerpieces of his administration.

The ABM treaty and SALT agreement concluded at the Moscow Summit in May 1972 have been heralded as the centerpiece of détente and as the foundation of arms control based on the limitation and eventual reduction of strategic armaments. ABM and SALT did not, however, develop in isolation, and the Nixon administration pursued a variety of additional arms control measures inside and outside back channels. Earlier agreements, including the Limited Test Ban Treaty (1963) that banned atmospheric testing of nuclear weapons, and the Outer Space Treaty (1967) that banned the testing or deployment of weapons in space, demonstrated that the United States and the Soviet Union could reach arms control agreements.

Nixon inherited the Nuclear Non-Proliferation Treaty (NPT) from his predecessor, which prohibited the sharing of military nuclear technology to non-nuclear powers. President Johnson had submitted the NPT for ratification, but the Senate canceled the vote following the August 1968 Soviet-led Warsaw Pact invasion of Czechoslovakia. The incoming Nixon administration decided to pursue ratification of the NPT, bypassing concerns about nuclear-sharing arrangements with the Federal Republic of Germany (FRG, or West Germany) and European allies through NATO.[55] The White House pursued joint ratification and deposit of the treaty with the Soviet Union via the back channel on June 12, 1969, while Secretary of State Rogers pressed Soviet foreign minister Gromyko on the issue in September.[56] The Senate ratified the treaty by a vote of 83 to 15 on March 13, 1969, and the United States and the

Soviet Union jointly filed their ratification instruments on November 24.[57]

After taking office, the Nixon administration embarked on a number of arms control programs that primarily focused on the Soviet Union. After picking up the torch on NPT, Nixon unilaterally terminated the U.S. biological weapons program in 1969 and promoted the Biological and Toxin Weapons Convention in April 1972. In his memoir, Dobrynin noted with pride that he signed the treaty on behalf of the Soviet Union and still had the pen from the ceremony in Washington. It is unfortunate that although the Soviet Union had a major role in drafting the agreement, it consistently violated the treaty and produced ever-deadlier bio-weapons.[58] The Nixon administration also signed a treaty prohibiting the testing or deployment of nuclear weapons on the seabeds in 1971.

The strategic weapons balance, however, was in a state of flux when Nixon assumed office, and the Soviet Union was quickly approaching parity or surpassing the United States in a number of weapons categories. During the Johnson administration, the United States had settled on a "triad" force of 1,054 Inter-Continental Ballistic Missiles (ICBMs), 650 Submarine Launched Ballistic Missiles (SLBMs), and hundreds of bombers such as the B-52 Stratofortress stationed at airbases or forward-based systems (FBS) ringing the Soviet Union. Although the United States did not have any programs in place to build major new weapons systems, it enjoyed a technological lead in missile accuracy and the development of Multiple Independently Targeted Reentry Vehicles (MIRVs). At its simplest, MIRVs would allow one missile to carry multiple warheads that could strike different targets. MIRVs were seen as a "force multiplier" and a potentially destabilizing factor in the arms race, since one missile could destroy a number of the opposing side's missiles. After assuming office, Nixon learned that the continued MIRV testing and deployment could give the United States an advantage in the face of the Soviet buildup of large missiles known as SS-9s, with their single multimegaton warheads—each more than one hundred times more powerful than the bomb the United States dropped on Hiroshima.[59]

American and Soviet strategic forces were not analogous, either quantitatively or qualitatively, and each side possessed certain advantages and disadvantages. Although American missiles were more precise, Soviet missiles were generally larger and could carry a heavier payload, or "throw weight." Heavy throw weight could, hypothetically, mean the capacity to include more MIRVs or decoys, and/or use overwhelmingly powerful, multimegaton warheads. The asymmetrical force structures stemmed from several factors, some the result of basic geography. The landmass of the Soviet Union was substantially larger than that of the United States, favoring ICBMs, while the United States initially had an advantage in SLBMs and an overwhelming advantage in forward-based bombers. Although the U.S. landmass was smaller, the United States had nuclear-armed allies like Great Britain and France. How could the SALT tackle the myriad of technical issues that were always arising, like the development of bomber-carried cruise missiles (Air-Launched Cruise Missiles, or ALCMs), which could fly below radar? How could negotiators account for "hardened" or "super-hardened" silos, which could survive anything but a direct hit? Meaningful arms control negotiations faced an array of questions that defied easy solutions. As Haldeman told Nixon at one point, "People don't understand SALT." The president replied: "SALT is way over their heads. They haven't the slightest idea what SALT is. It's too goddamned complicated."[60] In another conversation, Nixon referred to "land-based submarines," probably confusing land-based ICBMs with SLBMs.[61]

The Strategic Arms Limitation Talks ostensibly dealt only with "offensive" weapons systems, but by the late 1960s "defensive" weapons had entered into the arms control equation. Both the United States and the Soviet Union had developed and begun deploying early Anti-Ballistic Missile (ABM) systems by the time of the Nixon administration. The United States had begun testing the "Nike-X" system during the Eisenhower administration, which developed into the more sophisticated Sentinel system during the Johnson administration. On March 14, 1969, Nixon announced his decision for an ABM program that included a Safeguard system, a modified version of the Sentinel system, designed to provide area defense—such as ICBM fields in the Midwest, or the capital city (National Command Authority, or NCA)—against a relatively small nuclear attack by China or an accidental, irrational, or unsophisticated attack by the Soviet Union. The Soviets had started deploying an ABM system known as the Galosh around Moscow in the mid-1960s and kept improving their system incrementally with technological advances in radar and computer control systems.[62]

Discussions over "defensive" weapons systems had their own complex of technical issues. Although the United States enjoyed a substantive lead in terms of radar development, computerized command and control programs, and guidance systems for an ABM system, the Soviets were making progress with their Galosh system and had several breakthroughs of their own in radar technology. Like the discussions about "offensive" weapons, technical issues compounded the problems for arms control negotiators, such as defining the narrow distinctions between ABMs and SAMs. The original Galosh deployment, for example, provoked fears that the separate SA-5 "Tallinn" SAMs guarding approaches to Leningrad against strategic bombers was actually an ABM system.[63]

Beneath its esoteric veneer, often impenetrable to outsiders, the SALT impasse boiled down to one central issue: whether or not to link negotiations on offensive and defensive weapons systems. The United States steadfastly insisted that both offensive and defensive weapons systems be linked. American policymakers feared that the Soviet buildup in offensive weapons posed a special risk because the eventual numerical superiority combined with their greater potential destructive capacity would blunt American technological superiority; for example, the greater yield of Soviet warheads could compensate for any possible inferiority of their guidance systems. Decoupling would effectively ensure that no meaningful progress would be made on offensive limitation. Conversely, the Soviets desired an ABM agreement because, even as they concentrated on their offensive buildup, they realized that they lacked the ability to match the Americans in the sophistication of their defensive weapons. Hence, it became essential for the Soviets to decouple negotiations so they could concentrate on one area of interest to them without making meaningful concessions on the other.[64]

Nixon and Kissinger deduced that the Soviet desire for progress on the limitation of defensive weapons outweighed their desire to continue their offensive buildup. Furthermore, to add pressure on the Soviet bargaining position, the White House and the Defense Department insisted on not only the development and deployment of an American ABM system but also continued R&D and production of new offensive systems. As Nixon explained to Sen. John McClellan (D, AR) in 1971: "We've got to have something to give, and what we've got to give is the fact that we are building an ABM system, all right? We give on that, then they have to give on something on the offensive side. Otherwise we can't make a deal. Put yourself in their position."[65] The back channel made compromise possible and gave both sides something to give.

The back channel factored into U.S. arms control efforts from the beginning of the Nixon administration. Both the Kremlin and the White House used the back channel to set the timetable and the arrangements for the start of SALT and thereafter kept tabs on the issues discussed by the formal delegations. The Channel became the preferred medium by which Nixon and Kissinger first delayed the start of SALT in order to develop a consensus position on the talks. At Dobrynin's suggestion, the Soviets followed suit with their own delay, sensing that they could gain leverage by waiting for political pressures to build on a divided U.S. bureaucracy. The back channel also proved to be the means by which the United States and the Soviet Union agreed to alternate meeting spots between Helsinki and Vienna. Finally, with the SALT negotiating rounds in deadlock over whether or not to link offensive and defensive weapons in a comprehensive agreement, the back channel broke the impasse. In a very awkward fashion, Nixon and Kissinger fabricated a cover story about an exchange of letters between the president and Soviet premier Alexei Kosygin to hide the central role of the Kissinger-Dobrynin channel from Secretary Rogers, Ambassador Smith, and the U.S. SALT delegation. The head of the Soviet SALT delegation, Vladimir Semenov, knew of the back channel—likely without authorization—and later caused some problems in the Channel as a result.

Both sides used the back channel as both a brake and an accelerator as it suited their interests. At the first back-channel meeting between Kissinger and Dobrynin, on February 21, 1969, Dobrynin reported that he had "called Kissinger's attention to the recently observed inconsistency in the statements of the U.S. Government officials (Rogers and Laird) with respect to the time frame for beginning the talks." Kissinger told the Soviet ambassador about a divergence of views in the U.S. bureaucracy and that it could take five to six months for the new administration to develop a strategy on SALT. Kissinger added that "certain disagreements within the government" revolved "around the connection between the beginning of the talks and the deployment of the U.S. Sentinel ABM."[66] As Kissinger later lamented, "By April [1969] . . . a series of lower-level public statements and leaks not authorized in the White House had pre-

cipitated a commitment to start SALT talks by 'late spring or early summer.'"[67] Kissinger told Dobrynin on several occasions that the leaks were
not administration policy and stressed that the two sides should adhere to
the timetable enunciated in the back channel.

The astute Soviet ambassador saw opportunity in the dichotomy
between what he read in the newspapers and the private line in the Channel, in addition to Kissinger's admission of bureaucratic divisions. Seeking to exploit a tactical advantage, Dobrynin recommended delaying the
start of serious negotiations and not displaying any "particular interest" to
the White House.[68] When the national security advisor finally informed
Dobrynin in June 1969 that the White House was ready to begin the
talks, as had been stated in the first meetings of the Channel, the Kremlin
stalled for four months. Kissinger later assumed that the Soviets wanted
to wait for "the end of the Senate's ABM debate and not spoil the argument of our critics that our ABM program was incompatible with arms
control negotiations."[69] In August 1969, after much debate and a stren-
uous lobbying effort by Secretary of Defense Melvin Laird, the Senate
voted to fund ABM by a margin of one vote.[70] Contrary to Kissinger's
assessment, Dobrynin hardly mentioned news reports about arms control
in his reporting to Moscow. The Soviet ambassador did, however, make
frequent mention of the divisions in the Nixon administration between
the White House, the State Department, and the Defense Department.[71]
The Soviet delay could be attributed to Dobrynin's accurate recognition
of the divided U.S. position on SALT rather than the Senate ABM vote,
which had concluded two months before Dobrynin delivered the Soviet
SALT position. Evidently, the back channel could and did occasionally
backfire.

The decision to have alternating SALT rounds in Helsinki and Vienna
resulted from discussions in the Channel. Kissinger and Dobrynin had
discussed potential sites for SALT over the preceding months with a number of host options, including Washington and Moscow. When Nixon
refused to meet with Soviet foreign minister Andrei Gromyko in September 1969, the task fell to Secretary Rogers to introduce Ambassador Smith
as the head of the U.S. SALT delegation. Rogers told the long-serving
Soviet foreign minister that Helsinki "would be difficult" and expressed
a willingness to conduct sessions at alternating sites. Gromyko, living up
to his reputation as "Grim Grom," said the Soviet Union did not wish "to

be prodded into replying to the U.S. proposal."[72] The location remained unresolved until Dobrynin met with Nixon and Kissinger at the White House on October 20, when he delivered the Soviet SALT position, and Nixon agreed to start the talks in Helsinki on November 17, 1969. Somewhat perplexed by and dissatisfied with the choice of the Finnish capital, Nixon stated that Rogers was "under instructions to point out the difficulties of Helsinki." Perhaps jokingly, Dobrynin said that the only thing Rogers had said to Gromyko about the subject was "to hell with 'Sinki." In a more serious manner, the Soviet ambassador suggested a compromise by starting sessions in Helsinki before moving to Vienna. Kissinger opined that the United States would have "to consult some Allies, but that there seemed to be no insuperable difficulties."[73] And so SALT began, the details developed in the back channel.

The first series of the Strategic Arms Limitation Talks commenced in Helsinki between November and December 1969. Kissinger thought it wise to treat the first session as "exploratory," and both sides began a dialogue on the technical terminology to be used in the discussions. Moreover, the first series of talks became a means to test the waters with the Soviets and to define the agenda for future talks.[74]

From an institutional and bureaucratic standpoint, the U.S. SALT delegation suffered from a number of disadvantages vis-à-vis their Soviet counterparts. In the first detailed account of SALT, *Cold Dawn,* journalist John Newhouse wrote that the institutional composition of the U.S. delegation, headed by Ambassador Gerard Smith, led to a great deal of friction between the State Department and the Arms Control and Disarmament Agency (ACDA) on one hand, and the Pentagon, the military, and the White House on the other. Newhouse explained that "Smith's role was one of several reasons that the delegation was regarded with suspicion, and occasionally with open hostility." Smith's "only apparent weakness," however, was that he directed *both* ACDA and the SALT delegation:

> However unfairly, Smith was seen as ACDA's man at SALT, chiefly concerned with extending the range of what might be negotiable. As such, he lacked the full confidence of the White House (and the Pentagon). . . . Moreover, in a system designed to permit the president and his senior advisor to control the action on security, perhaps nobody of stature could have gained the con-

fidence and authority for which Smith must have longed. Because he was persistently denied the responsibility he thought he should have, Smith quit at the start of Nixon's second term.[75]

Smith did himself no favors by arguing against MIRV testing and pushing for the "zero ABM" option even after a narrow Senate vote in August 1969 to fund Safeguard. In a meeting between Smith, ACDA deputy director Philip Farley, Ambassador Dobrynin, and Soviet counselor minister Vorontsov on February 9, 1970, the Soviets "kept coming back to the ABM matter," although they were fairly silent on the MIRV issue.[76] Against the backdrop of the earlier meeting with Smith, Dobrynin would have a similar discussion about SALT with Kissinger.

On February 18, 1970, Dobrynin and Kissinger had lunch together in the downstairs library at the White House "both to avoid the press' seeing Dobrynin coming in and to avoid staff members' asking questions," Kissinger noted. "Another reason was to show Dobrynin that we were paying some special attention." In what became a regular event, the Soviets took exception to some of the points raised in the president's annual foreign policy report, which Nixon and Kissinger had inaugurated to showcase the administration's foreign policy achievements to Congress.[77] According to Kissinger, Dobrynin thought the report "well-balanced" but objected that the mention of South Vietnam's President Thieu and Romania's Ceauşescu but no other foreign leaders "would rub people the wrong way." Kissinger surmised the "people" who might object were "likely the audience sitting in the Kremlin." Dobrynin also worried aloud that "there would be "great exception taken in the Soviet Union" to a published list of countries "where the Red Army had been used since 1945." Kissinger responded that the report was "not written primarily for Moscow audiences" and that there "was no particular intention attached to" the mentions of Thieu and Ceauşescu.

Dobrynin then inquired about the organization of the report, the Nixon administration's foreign policy structure, and a line in the report that "the only status quo in the world today is the fact of change." Specifically, Dobrynin worried that the United States "no longer recognized the existing dividing lines in Europe." Using humor to disarm his interlocutor, Kissinger said, "It was odd for a Marxist to argue that such a phrase produced any difficulties." Dobrynin understood the joke, "smiled and said that in Europe we are fomenting the maintenance of the status quo." Foreign policy reports and Marxist philosophy aside, the meeting actually focused on SALT.

According to Kissinger, Dobrynin raised the subject of the Nixon administration's strategic doctrine of "sufficiency" and how the developing Safeguard ABM fit into the picture. Kissinger explained that Defense Secretary Laird's statements that the United States would speed up and expand ABM deployment were simply part of the "regular budgetary cycle." After Kissinger differentiated between "area defense" and "point defense" for Dobrynin, he suggested that he let one of his technical experts explain the system in greater detail at a later date.[78]

Dobrynin then read a "little note" to Kissinger, which the national security advisor reproduced verbatim in his memorandum of the conversation. Dobrynin said that the note "did not . . . represent a formal communication but some tentative instructions." Significantly, the backchannel note informally protested leaks, ostensibly from the American SALT delegation. Dobrynin read aloud, "We do not understand, in particular, what was that that guided the American side when despite agreement about the confidential nature of the talks it in fact released to the press through its various spokesmen many elements of the contents of the Helsinki negotiations." "Such an approach," the Soviet leaders protested, "can hardly make a favorable impact on the atmosphere of the talks in the future." The Kissinger-Dobrynin channel would continue to serve as a two-way channel to delicately and informally protest leaks, and arms control remained a frequent source of such protests.

The Soviets also expressed their puzzlement at Secretary of Defense Laird's "demanding" the speedup of ABM deployment, in addition to development of new weapons systems such as the B-1 supersonic heavy bomber program, the Under-sea Long-Range Missile System (ULMS), and the development of a "a new ground-based," that is, mobile, ICBM system.[79] Although Kissinger did not say so to Dobrynin, Laird's advocacy for ABM and new offensive systems likely resulted from the fact that the Soviet Union had surpassed the United States in terms of land-based launchers.[80]

In toto, by raising the issues of both offensive and defensive weapons, the Kremlin had questioned the Nixon administration's desire for continued SALT negotiations. Kissinger reiterated that he and Dobrynin should "schedule another conversation devoted primarily to SALT." The back channel could, after all, be part of the solution. "I told Dobrynin that we should have a full discussion, and that we might set up two channels," Kissinger recorded, "one for the formal negotiations and one between him and me to deal with general principles."[81] The back channel could thus shelter the sensitive issues from the problems of leaks and domestic politics.

Dobrynin's account of the February 18 meeting largely overlapped with Kissinger's, although it is notable because he detailed an impromptu and candid U.S. civics lesson by Kissinger. If the former professor gave a good lecture, then Dobrynin took excellent notes that highlighted the importance of the back channel. "Kissinger said that on behalf of the president, he could state firmly that their position had not changed," Dobrynin wrote. Kissinger frankly explained that there were "two sides to the same coin" on arms control: "One is the substance of the position itself. The second is the purely domestic aspect, namely, how to get some program or other 'through Congress' in order to obtain the necessary appropriations—something the administration has to do every year."

If the Soviets were curious about the "actual position" of the U.S. government rather than the "propaganda intended for Congress," it need look no further than the confidential channel, Kissinger reassured. Dobrynin described how Kissinger went through U.S. plans on ABM and new weapons systems and explained American worries about the continuing Soviet buildup. Only two of six planned complexes were then under construction, in Montana and North Dakota, to protect Minuteman ICBM fields. Due to funding and different phases of construction, Kissinger assured Dobrynin, the sites were unlikely to become operational for five or six years. Kissinger also stressed that regardless of what the press or politicians said, the back channel had become the preferred means "for transmission to Moscow."

Kissinger asserted that Nixon continued to "link" the deployment of the Safeguard ABM system to "progress on Soviet-U.S. negotiations." The U.S. government, Dobrynin reported, was prepared to discuss ABM development, "including the possibility of limiting ABM systems in both our countries," at the April 1970 SALT round in Vienna. At the second round, the United States was "considering two possible approaches to seeking an accord: a limited agreement that would make it possible to achieve real results somewhat more quickly, or a broader approach to the problem and an effort to agree on some kind of comprehensive solution."

Kissinger told Dobrynin that the development of MIRVs could change the strategic balance and solicited input on Soviet views, which would be "studied most carefully by President Nixon and could have a substantial influence on his consideration of various projects in the area of strategic arms." The Soviets chose to ignore the MIRV issue in subsequent sessions and the agreement on offensive limitations signed at the May 1972 Moscow Summit failed to address the topic. Kissinger did not note his mention of MIRVs in his own memorandum of conversation, although, to be fair, Dobrynin wrote that the topic was not the primary issue of their discussion. "It was evident, however, from all of Kissinger's remarks," Dobrynin recorded, "that what mainly interests them is the deployment of the SS–9s and our strategic military doctrine in relation to these missiles." The two diplomats therefore had missed an opportunity to bring MIRVs into the arms control equation.[82] It is also possible that both sides had made sufficient technical progress in developing (and, for the United States, deploying) MIRVs to give them up.

Months before the sessions in Vienna began, Kissinger and Nixon proposed the use of the back channel to "bypass" the SALT negotiations and ABM concerns. Dobrynin wrote that the White House believed the Kissinger-Dobrynin "confidential link" could be utilized to exchange views at the highest levels for "fundamental issues pertaining to the subsequent course of the negotiations, for selecting the most promising issue, etc., so that afterwards, without detailed explanations to the delegations themselves, they would simultaneously be sent instructions which had been agreed upon through this channel." The solution could address Soviet complaints about leaks coming out of the U.S. SALT delegation for which, Kissinger admitted, "there was some justification—that certain information from the negotiations in Helsinki had become known to the press." Kissinger tried to restore confidence in the commitment to SALT and ABM negotiations and guaranteed that the White House was "not responsible for such leaks." The problem lay with Congress, Kissinger told Dobrynin. After Ambassador Smith had given "a closed-door discussion with members of Congress who deal with disarmament and armed forces issues, some information started leaking to the press." Arms control leaks were not isolated incidents. This had "also happened before with other issues," Kissinger told Dobrynin, and Nixon pledged "all possible additional measures to maintain the confidentiality of the Vienna talks."[83]

As Kissinger had promised in their meeting on February 18, he brought along his NSC expert on SALT, Laurence Lynn, when he met with Dobrynin in the military aide's office on March 10. John Newhouse wrote that, "excepting Kissinger, [Lynn was] the most important White House influence on SALT," and that he "had Kissinger's confidence to a degree possibly never matched by any colleague or successor."[84] Although the three men "briefly" discussed the finer points of area defense, point defense, and missile types, Kissinger wrote that Dobrynin "was not interested" and "wanted to talk to [Kissinger] alone." Dobrynin had apparently studied up on the technical issues after his earlier discussions with Smith and Kissinger.

On behalf of the Soviet government, the ambassador reiterated the Kremlin's "doubts about the seriousness" of the White House approach to SALT but raised three points. First, the Kremlin agreed with Kissinger's earlier proposal that the Channel be used for "an exchange of views both before and during the SALT talks with a view to coming to a conclusion between us on some of the principal outstanding issues." Second, the Soviets "wanted the president to know" that they were "approaching the Vienna discussions very seriously and would try to find an area of agreement." Lastly, "the Soviets were prepared to discuss either comprehensive or separate agreement." Echoing the White House line, the Kremlin, too, "believed that a comprehensive agreement would be better because it would lead also to a solution of other political problems." If a comprehensive offensive-defense agreement could not be reached, however, it "would not preclude coming eventually to a comprehensive agreement."[85]

Dobrynin summarized that "it could be understood" that the U.S. government believed "the issue of anti-ballistic missile defense could become the subject of a separate agreement within the framework of the problem under discussion." Again, Dobrynin criticized Laird's statements about the expansion of the Safeguard ABM system. Kissinger replied that the plans were long-term and were not immutable. Hinting at the Soviet strategic buildup, Kissinger asserted that neither side was suspending "implementation of plans it had made earlier to develop strategic forces simply because the initial negotiations had taken place in Helsinki." Verification remained a stumbling block in the U.S. arms control community, although the president "privately" believed that the linchpin of any agreement could be accomplished via "national technical means" like satellite reconnaissance.[86]

The Kissinger-Dobrynin contact did not have a meaningful role in establishing the direction of the second round of talks, which began in Vienna on April 16, 1970. Although the Soviets continued to endorse the use of the contact, Dobrynin conveyed the Kremlin's position that the negotiating teams in Vienna would have to hash out a possible agreement. On April 7, Dobrynin told Kissinger that the American suggestion to "settle the matter in our channel presented a difficulty." Dobrynin explained that the lead Soviet SALT negotiator, Vladimir Semenov, "was a Deputy Foreign Minister and it was hard for a mere Ambassador to interject himself." Kissinger pointed out that the Channel could be the forum for "a more limited agreement."[87] Essentially, the Soviets were wary of the back channel as the means to settle SALT and deferred to Semenov's authority—for the time being. As the back channel grew in importance, so did Dobrynin's influence. The differences in rank between the "mere" ambassador and the deputy foreign minister soon narrowed.

Dobrynin returned to Moscow before the second round of SALT began, but on the eve of his departure, April 9, he met Kissinger for dinner. Kissinger reported that the U.S. SALT delegation "would present a very comprehensive proposal at Vienna, including qualitative as well as quantitative restrictions." Kissinger again pushed for the back channel to determine a limited, or simple agreement that could be possible by the end of 1970. "The best way to handle it," Kissinger told Dobrynin, "would be for the Vienna talks to concentrate on comprehensive measures, while he and I would try to work out a limited agreement in the interval."[88] Dobrynin recorded Kissinger's disclaimer that the U.S. SALT delegation was "totally out of the loop regarding this aspect of the issue."[89]

While he was in the Soviet Union for consultations, Dobrynin missed the small crisis caused by the American incursion into Cambodia in April–June 1970. In the ambassador's absence, Kissinger had delivered a note on Cambodia to Vorontsov, which, Dobrynin reported in June, had caused some consternation back in Moscow. On June 10, Dobrynin reported that Kissinger told him that the United States would not accept a "limited agreement that would affect only ABM systems" for both political and military reasons. Kissinger countered that "a possible first agreement between our countries on strategic arms could be based on the establishment of some specific agreed ceilings simultaneously for offensive and defensive weapons." Once again, Kissinger stressed the sensitive nature of communication in the back channel and reiterated Nixon's preference for an exchange of views "on a strictly confidential basis."[90]

Kissinger and Dobrynin met two weeks later, knowing that SALT had ground to a halt and confirming what Ambassador Smith had been saying for a month. After an NSC meeting on April 8, Nixon signed off on National Security Decision Memorandum (NSDM) 51 and directed the U.S. SALT delegation to pursue two options with the Soviets in Vienna: the so-called Option C, which would ban MIRVs; and, as a fallback, Option D, which would ban both MIRVs and ABMs.[91] The Soviets quickly rejected both options because the Nixon administration had, at the last minute, linked the ban on MIRVs to on-site inspections rather than national technical means. In the meeting with Dobrynin on June 23, Kissinger reviewed the background of the situation. He noted that Semenov had suggested an early end to the round in Vienna and that Smith "was pressing for new instructions authorizing him to offer a more limited option." Significantly, Kissinger stated that "the president did not want the settlement to be arrived at in Vienna but, if possible, at a summit meeting." The link was clear: Nixon preferred to break any deadlock in Vienna at a summit meeting. Dobrynin replied that he did not have instructions on the matter but would make inquiries. When Dobrynin asked if a separate ABM agreement could be possible, Kissinger replied that the U.S. position had not changed.[92]

In response to the initial Soviet rejection of Options C and D, Nixon approved a new SALT proposal for discussion in Vienna: Option E. In summary, this option proposed a single, comprehensive agreement for both offensive and defensive limitations. In the numbers game of launchers, Option E called for a combined total of 1,710 strategic missiles divided between ICBM and SLBM forces, with a sublimit on "heavy" ICBMs like the Soviet SS-9. On the defensive side, the proposal called for either a single National Command Authority ABM site or a complete ban on ABM systems, Smith's preferred "zero" option. The proposal did not address MIRVs or forward-based bombers, both areas of American superiority. In land-based missiles, however, the Soviets had finally surpassed the United States, as Laird had announced months earlier, and the Soviets were fast-tracking the program to build SLBM-equipped submarines. Limiting the total number of launchers, therefore, was a priority for the U.S. delegation.[93]

Despite the best Option E efforts, SALT became deadlocked by the autumn of 1970. When Gromyko met with Nixon, Kissinger, and Rogers in October 1970, they discussed SALT only in passing. Both sides agreed to continue negotiations in a businesslike "spirit" at the third round of SALT in Helsinki, set to begin on November 2. Nixon expressed the American goal of a comprehensive agreement covering both offensive and defensive limitations. "If the agreement dealt only with ABM we could not accept it," Nixon said. "If it dealt only with offensive missiles, the Soviet Union would not accept it."[94] A Soviet counterproposal in Helsinki in December, however, insisted on decoupling offensive and defensive limitations. The Soviets once more made an ABM agreement into a precondition for offensive limitations, and the Nixon administration refused to bite.

The virtual deadlock in SALT and the improvement in U.S.-Soviet relations came to a head when Kissinger and Dobrynin met for a three-hour lunch on December 22, 1970. Reading the accounts both men wrote, however, makes one wonder whether Kissinger and Dobrynin attended the same meeting.

According to Kissinger, the meeting "took place in an extremely cordial atmosphere" and covered "the general state of U.S.-Soviet relations as well as a number of specific topics." Kissinger noted that bilateral relations had "worsened in the past couple of months" due to misperceptions and faulty coordination by both sides. He suggested "frank exchanges" to remove "imagined differences based on misunderstanding as well as to make progress on real issues." Dobrynin then raised the issue of SALT. Kissinger recorded that Dobrynin said that "the Soviet Union had made an offer on ABM, and the impression had been created that direct White House intervention stopped it." Dobrynin then suggested that the United States could offer "some compromise" since an ABM agreement would be easier to conclude and could pave the way for progress on offensive limitations. "I pointed out that it was essential, however, that we keep our channels straight," Kissinger contended, and that a "Summit meeting in September [1971] would make sense."[95]

Although Kissinger depicted himself as a tough, composed negotiator, Dobrynin described his counterpart as "clearly on the defensive during the conversation." The Soviet ambassador wrote, "I gave a highly critical analysis of the current state of U.S.-Soviet relations, which had arisen through the fault of the Nixon Administration." Dobrynin recorded that Kissinger "defended the well-known U.S. position [and] he was about to go on speaking in the same vein regarding conclusion of a separate, narrower agreement on ABM defense (i.e., in opposition to such a separate agreement)," when Dobrynin interrupted Kissinger's soliloquy. "I was getting the impression," Dobrynin wrote, "that the main obstacle to such an [ABM] agreement . . . was Kissinger himself with his beloved global linkage theory." In response to Dobrynin giving voice to this suspicion, "Kissinger began to make all sorts of excuses" and "stated that even now he himself is considering whether it would not in fact be possible to enter into such an agreement." Kissinger remained noncommittal.

Dobrynin wrote that Kissinger became "noticeably agitated" during the conversation. Surprisingly, Kissinger neglected to record the source of his dismay in his own memcon, even though it was substantially longer and more detailed than Dobrynin's account. The Soviet ambassador, however, described Kissinger's ire. According to Dobrynin, Kissinger said he had received a "coded message" describing a private exchange between Ambassador Smith and his Soviet opposite, Semenov. Apparently, Semenov told Smith that "they, the heads of the delegations, should not count on getting any work done during that period [the summer of 1971], because that will be the very time when the leaders of both governments will be actively preparing for a summit meeting, which is planned for precisely that time." Excluded from the narrow circle that knew of the proposed summit meeting—not even Secretary Rogers knew of any serious discussions—Smith "transmitted these comments by the Soviet representative directly to the White House and to President Nixon personally as some earth-shaking news." The White House shifted to damage control, "attempted to keep [the news] from falling into anyone else's hands," and sent "appropriate strict orders . . . to Smith to keep quiet about this matter." Kissinger chastised the Soviets for failing to keep the strictest secrecy about the summit. "I decided to inform you of this," Kissinger apparently said, "because I recalled Moscow's strict warning which said that besides the leaders themselves, only three other people know about the summit meeting: on the Soviet side— the Minister and the Ambassador, on the U.S. side—only Kissinger."[96]

Semenov's slipup about a summit to Smith was not the last time the

Soviet deputy foreign minister revealed discussions from the Kissinger-Dobrynin channel. On several occasions, Semenov provoked Kissinger's consternation by bringing back-channel discussions into SALT. Kissinger recorded two incidents in his memoirs and indicated that Semenov had tried "to play our two channels against each other."[97] Without the internal Foreign Ministry or Politburo files, however, it is impossible to determine whether or not the Kremlin was intentionally crossing channels between Washington and Helsinki-Vienna. One possibility is that Semenov was privy to some of the back-channel exchanges and used his knowledge and personal initiative to boost his own position. Routing information on a number of Dobrynin's reporting cables to Moscow suggests that Gromyko disseminated the telegrams.[98] As a deputy foreign minister reporting directly to Gromyko, Semenov could have seen Dobrynin's cables.

Another possibility is that the Soviet Foreign Ministry, which knew that Smith was out of the loop and had witnessed Kissinger's attempts to bypass the talks in Helsinki and Vienna, tried to capitalize on the divisions in the American position. Gromyko's assistant at the time, Arkady Shevchenko, wrote, "When Dobrynin's reports arrived in Moscow, Gromyko was the first to receive them, he decided to whom they should be shown, and his proposals served as the basis for decisions on Soviet-American affairs."[99] It is conceivable that Semenov was acting on instructions, as Kissinger believed. The irony was that the back-channel reporting had significantly broader dissemination in the Soviet Union, a closed society, in comparison to the open society of the United States.

Whatever the differences between Kissinger's and Dobrynin's records of the December 22, 1970, meeting, the two tried in January 1971 to remove the obstacles blocking the path to détente. The Soviets pushed for movement toward resolving the perennial Cold War problem of Berlin and the settlement of German borders. Nixon and Kissinger shifted gears on SALT and actively linked arms control issues—offensive and defensive weapons—to a summit meeting. The back channel proved to be the avenue for resolution for both sides.

Breaking the Impasse: Germany-Berlin and SALT

New opportunities and perils in the Soviet-American relationship came with the start of a new year, 1971. During the first two years of the Nixon administration, Kissinger had repeatedly pressed the Soviets to resolve issues via the back channel. However, U.S.-Soviet tensions in the Middle East, the continued U.S. war in Southeast Asia, Soviet adventurism in the Caribbean, and Dobrynin's having been out of Washington during the series of crises in 1970 had hampered the further development of the Channel. In a sense, the Channel had been reactive rather than proactive, responding to events rather than shaping them. Forward movement on SALT had stalled with the Soviet rejection of Option E, in addition to their continued insistence on having an ABM agreement before committing to an offensive freeze. The November-December 1970 SALT round lasted only forty-six days. As John Newhouse wrote: "The two sides were never so far apart. . . . In tone and substance, the biweekly meetings were about as inspiriting as Helsinki's brumous sky."[100] Although both sides blamed each other for difficulties, the leadership in the Kremlin and the White House, respectively, moved in 1971 to bridge their differences.

Frustration about the lack of progress in improving relations was not the only reason Soviet and American leaders decided to act in early 1971. Periods of "good" or friendly relations were the exception to the Cold War rule of superpower animosity; business as usual could have continued as usual. The success of West German chancellor Willy Brandt's "new Ostpolitik" policy, however, catalyzed the improvement of U.S.-Soviet relations. Brandt's trusted advisor and state secretary, Egon Bahr, tied ratification of the August 12, 1970, Moscow Treaty and the December 7, 1970, Warsaw Treaty to the conclusion of a four-power agreement on Berlin. As Nixon had Kissinger, Brandt had the eminently skillful Bahr to develop the link between the Eastern treaties and the Berlin access agreement. Separate from Washington, Bonn had blazed a new trail toward pan-European détente. As historian Hope Harrison wrote, as a result of Ostpolitik, "West Germany exercised significant influence over U.S. policymaking . . . [and] acted to push the U.S. into serious negotiations with the Soviets."[101]

Far apart from the back channel, the division of Germany and the status of Berlin had been a focal point since the inception of the Cold War. As a result of the July 1945 Potsdam Conference, the allied powers—the United States, the Soviet Union, Great Britain, and France—divided the city into four occupation zones. The Western allies combined their occupation zones and introduced a new currency in 1948, which the Soviets promptly rejected. Moscow then blocked rail and road access to the city of West Berlin, located deep inside what the following year would become East Germany (German Democratic Republic, or GDR). The United States responded with the Berlin Airlift, and the Soviets backed down in 1949. Access to West Berlin and the legal status of the city remained thorny political problems that affected the lives of everyday Germans. Periodic crises arose through the 1950s, and by 1960 and the election of President John F. Kennedy, the GDR faced an exodus of skilled professionals escaping to West Germany (the Federal Republic of Germany, or FRG) via West Berlin. The construction of the Berlin Wall in 1961 alleviated some of the tension by stemming the flow of refugees but did not settle the legal issues or address concerns for Germans on both sides of the divide.[102]

Not content to remain dependent on the whims of the Western allies, West Germans of different political backgrounds approached better relations with their Eastern neighbors. As the former mayor of West Berlin, Willy Brandt brought personal experience of the divide when he became chancellor in September 1969 as the leader of the Social Democratic Party (SPD). Brandt's path to détente also had a number of precedents, such as the French pursuit of better relations with both the Soviets and the Communist Chinese during the 1960s. The net result of the two Eastern treaties settled Germany's borders on the Oder-Neisse Line, committed Germany to the peaceful resolution of international disputes, and legalized the division between East and West Germany that remained until Reunification in 1991.[103]

The Soviet pursuit of Westpolitik and the underlying rationale for the Kremlin's desire to improve relations with West Germany should not be discounted. The Soviet leadership had experienced firsthand the hardships of the Second World War and had a deeply ingrained fear of German "revanchism," the resurrection of German power, nationalism, and militarism. Germany had twice invaded the Russian motherland during the first half of the twentieth century, and Russian history was defined by foreign invasions. Geopolitical concerns, in addition to psychological and historical, also factored into the Soviet policy. Having experienced a handful of bloody incidents with the Chinese in 1969 on their far eastern borders, Soviet decision makers wanted to secure their western frontier.[104]

More than two decades after the end of the Second World War, the

Kremlin also began to rethink its relationship with the West, especially the FRG. In an unpublished section of his memoirs, Soviet deputy foreign minister Anatoly Kovalev described Brezhnev's decision to pursue a treaty with West Germany. At the end of 1969, in the winter garden at the luxurious Zavidovo estate, Brezhnev discussed cigarette preferences and how to deal with West Germany:

> "What do you smoke?" he asked me. I offered him a pack of 'Marlboro.'" He inhaled several times and then grimaced.
> "'The News' is better. I am used to them," he said lighting up one of his favorite cigarettes [made especially for the general secretary]. "You are familiar with German matters. Tell me, is it worth signing a treaty with the FRG; in general, what is the attitude of the West Germans?"
> In my response to Brezhnev, I accentuated the fact that a considerable misconception exist[ed] in the Soviet Union regarding Western Germany, a country believed to be full of militarists and revenge seekers. As an indicator of the general mindset, I pointed out the anti-fascist, humanitarian direction adopted by the postwar West German literature, theater, and film. I provided appropriate examples. Brezhnev appeared to be interested and asked clarifying questions. Approximately half an hour later when he left the winter garden, I was left with the impression that Brezhnev made a personal decision regarding the pact between the Soviet Union and Western Germany—the pact was necessary.[105]

Eight time zones away from the hunting grounds of Zavidovo, Nixon looked at Brandt's Ostpolitik with suspicion and skepticism. Assistant Secretary of State for European Affairs Martin Hillenbrand, who was intimately involved in the Quadripartite Agreement, recalled that the "White House reaction to the whole business was distinctly unenthusiastic—a reaction that was to turn even more negative as other elements of *Ostpolitik* unfolded."[106] As presidential historian Robert Dallek has argued: "Brandt outfoxed and frustrated Nixon and Kissinger. He stole the headlines from them without, in their judgment, advancing toward reliable improvements in East-West relations."[107] Nevertheless, Ostpolitik became a model for U.S.-Soviet détente because Brandt demonstrated that the

Soviets were amenable to agreements. Separate from the four-power talks, the Kissinger-Dobrynin channel set the stage for the agreement and reinforced linkage for *both* the United States and the Soviet Union. Nixon wanted SALT to conclude at a meaningful summit meeting, while the Soviets, specifically Foreign Minister Gromyko, linked the summit to progress on Germany-Berlin.

In the beginning of 1971, Soviet efforts to push the Germany-Berlin issue with the United States entered into the back channel. Nixon and Kissinger initially used the Channel to promote four-power discussions to deal with the Berlin question, but the ambassadorial talks on Berlin, like those on SALT, had stalled over the course of 1970. In the interim, Brandt and Bahr had pressed forward with their diplomatic initiatives with Moscow and Warsaw. After the conclusion of the Warsaw Treaty in December, Brandt wrote Nixon, French president Georges Pompidou, and British prime minister Edward Heath explaining that the next step toward détente should be a quadripartite agreement on Berlin. The Warsaw Treaty, Brandt wrote, was "intended to help ensure, without prejudice to the rights of the Four Powers in relation to Germany as a whole, that the problem of the Oder-Neisse Line will no longer be a political burden on the relationship between the Federal Republic of Germany and Poland, and an impediment to an East-West détente in Europe." Brandt recommended a "conference-like character in the coming year."[108] Contrary to U.S. discussions that short-lived riots in Gdansk, Poland, in December 1970 might derail the Soviet acceptance of West German Ostpolitik, the Kremlin joined Brandt's lobbying effort to promote a settlement on Berlin in the new year.[109]

On January 4, 1971, Gromyko sent Dobrynin an "extremely urgent" telegram instructing the ambassador that it was "imperative" to meet with Kissinger, "bearing in mind" that the U.S. leaders were preparing "new instructions" for the U.S. ambassador to West Germany, Kenneth Rush. Gromyko wrote that his discussions with President Nixon in October created "the impression that there is a sufficient degree of accord between our sides as to the necessity to remove tension in and around West Berlin." The time was ripe for negotiation on the "whole range of subjects," but, the Soviet foreign minister lamented, "the meetings of the four Ambassadors did not actually proceed in this direction." With the principles established, the Soviet leadership hoped the four-power negotiations on

West Berlin, set to resume in mid-January, could be focused on "formulating possible decisions, to work out the texts which are to constitute an accord." Although the multiplicity of parties involved created an element of confusion and potential for disagreement, Gromyko noted: "Accord on West Berlin is contemplated as a kind of package. This is not a unique case in international practice." Progress on West Berlin, the foreign minister contended, would be a "test of good will" for both the U.S. and the Soviets. Significantly, Gromyko instructed Dobrynin to sound out Kissinger's willingness to work out positions and draft text through the Channel before the four ambassadors discussed the matter. Gromyko caveated, "Of course, this idea should not be cast as a specific proposal, lest U.S. opponents of the agreement with us make use of it to influence French and British positions in a negative manner."[110]

Kissinger, at the Western White House in San Clemente, California, working on Nixon's annual "State of the World" report, suddenly received an urgent phone call from Ambassador Dobrynin. Poking fun at the national security advisor, Dobrynin chided, "You sleep too late Henry." After Kissinger explained that he was in California, Dobrynin continued, "I asked Vorontsov to call to Mr. [David] Young and give him a special message to you . . . in terms of our confidential channel." Dobrynin was, of course, referring to the note Gromyko had instructed to be conveyed to the White House. Stressing the back-channel aspects and importance of the note, Dobrynin carried on: "I thought it would be all right because the message is in an envelope so that only the two of us would know what it was. It is from the top to top." Kissinger asked if the answer could wait until Monday, January 11, when the two men were scheduled to meet.[111] "I have not read the message so I cannot tell you what I think," Kissinger reasoned. Dobrynin explained that the note was "a continuation of the talk between the president and Gromyko," circuitously referring to Germany-Berlin. The ambassador reiterated, "This is in our channel. It is not going anyplace else. . . . I will see you on Monday."[112]

Kissinger called Dobrynin several hours later and reassured, "I have just talked about that document with the president and I will be prepared to discuss it with you on Monday." Dobrynin piqued Kissinger's interest and proffered some additional, tantalizing details about the expansion of the Channel. "I have instructions which I did not want to put in writing in that message," Dobrynin stated. "If President OKs we could have some talks between you and I." The ambassador added: "It probably can be taken care of in 2 or 3 meetings. . . . Not how to solve but [it's the] direction where we go . . . speeding up two major points."[113] The back channel had now become a tool to link different parts of the U.S.-Soviet relationship.

The next day, January 7, Dobrynin notified Kissinger that Moscow had instructed him "rather urgently to come to Moscow for consultations," and the two agreed to move up their meeting. Kissinger said he could meet "first thing on Saturday morning" if Dobrynin could put off his departure. Dobrynin emphasized the importance of the Soviet proposal on Berlin and inquired if Kissinger could give a more immediate response. With the time pressure, Kissinger agreed that the U.S. response was important and that he had "very concrete propositions to make."[114] The two men discussed logistics, and Kissinger called Dobrynin again "to mention one thing on a semi-personal basis." If Dobrynin could not delay his departure and meet with Kissinger, the national security advisor awkwardly admonished, "I think it would be very hard to be understood by the president if you were pulled out in light of the communication of yesterday without waiting for an answer." Dobrynin agreed and promised to "check with Moscow."[115]

The Soviet note on Germany-Berlin became the vehicle by which Germany-Berlin entered into the Kissinger-Dobrynin channel, and also the means by which the back channel broke the SALT impasse. William Hyland, an NSC staffer helping Kissinger with the "State of the World" report, analyzed the Soviet note and observed the considerable pressures on the Kremlin to accelerate a Berlin access agreement:

Since the [December 1970] Polish riots and purge, the Soviets must have come under fire from the East Germans, and perhaps within the Politburo for investing too heavily in *Ostpolitik* and accepting Western precondition of a Berlin settlement. This note seems to be a sort of appeal at the highest level for a show of responsiveness. The Soviets may have some considerable concern that they cannot go into a Party Congress in March with their Western policy in a shambles—no Berlin progress, no move to ratify the treaties, no prospect for economic assistance from the West Germans—but that we hold the key.[116]

In his memoir, Hyland wrote that Kissinger "indicated he thought that we had reached a turning point with the Soviets." According to Hyland, Kissinger "plotted a strategy . . . to bring matters to a conclusion in the German-Berlin negotiations, which he now took into his private channel with the Soviet Ambassador." As Hyland remembered, Kissinger saw a back-channel opportunity for linkage between Berlin and SALT.[117] To accelerate the Berlin negotiations, Kissinger wrote that he had "recommended to Nixon that we return guarantees of access and a clearly defined legal status for West Berlin." Berlin would not, however, be dealt with in isolation. As Kissinger later explained: "I proposed linking the Berlin negotiations to progress in SALT; SALT, in turn, we would make depend on Soviet willingness to freeze its offensive buildup. Nixon approved."[118]

Both Kissinger and Dobrynin altered their travel arrangements so they could meet on the morning of Saturday, January 9, 1971; Kissinger flew back to Washington from San Clemente for one day, and Dobrynin had delayed his departure to Moscow. On the German question, Kissinger recorded, "The president said that he would be well disposed towards the negotiations if they did not cut the umbilical cord between West Berlin and the Federal Republic." Kissinger suggested a quid pro quo: "If the Soviet Union could give some content to the transit procedures and if the Soviet Union could find a way by which it could make itself responsible, together with the four allies, for access, we would, in turn, attempt to work out some approach which took cognizance of the concerns of the East German regime." He also promised to discuss with Dobrynin the concerns "in substance," and "if we could see an agreement was possible, we could then feed it into regular channels." The back channel could therefore be used to preview the Berlin agreement.

The two then turned to SALT and Nixon's decision to "make an ABM agreement only, provided it was coupled with an undertaking to continue working on offensive limitations and provided it was coupled with an undertaking that there would be a freeze on new starts of offensive land-based missiles during the period of these negotiations." The offensive-defensive link would remain, although the United States would no longer insist on a comprehensive agreement. As with Germany-Berlin, the Channel could also be used to resolve SALT, ideally before the formal talks resumed in Vienna in March 1971. Kissinger suggested an exchange of letters or public statements. On the question of submarines, Kissinger—

and this later became a source of some controversy—stated that he had "no specific proposal to make." SLBMs would ostensibly be dealt with later, and Dobrynin promised to have an answer when he returned from consultations.[119]

In his memoir, Nixon wrote, "On January 9, 1971, I sent a personal message to Brezhnev stressing the necessity of linking offensive and defensive weapons if an agreement were to be reached."[120] Although Kissinger floated the idea of an exchange of letters or a joint public statement on January 9, Nixon and Kosygin—not Brezhnev—did not exchange letters on SALT until two months later. Both the White House and the Kremlin shared letter drafts via the confidential channel, while Kissinger and Dobrynin settled on an ABM-only agreement coupled with both the commitment to conduct negotiations on offensive weapons and a freeze on additional construction. In fact, the letter Nixon described in his memoirs was imaginary, a cover story for the real, back-channel discussions on SALT and Berlin. The former president fell prey to his own myth, an untruth told to the State Department and the American SALT delegation at the time to mask the Kissinger-Dobrynin channel.

After two weeks of consultations, Dobrynin returned to Washington and met with Kissinger on January 23. The back-channel agents agreed to meet regularly, and the Soviets also accepted Kissinger's modified offensive-defensive noncomprehensive SALT deal. Dobrynin emphasized the "most extensive US-Soviet relations review that he could remember," with both Brezhnev and Gromyko. The ambassador offered a summit meeting in the "second half of the summer," an offer from which the Soviet leadership would later backtrack. The Kremlin found the U.S. proposed agenda of discussion on Europe, Berlin, SALT, a possible Middle East settlement, and the war in Vietnam, "acceptable." On Berlin, in the more immediate time frame, Dobrynin raised the possibility of bringing "an expert from Moscow . . . without, however, necessarily telling the expert what he was here for." Kissinger counseled delay until he could work out an arrangement with Ambassador Rush and Egon Bahr.[121]

Kissinger had already set in motion a surreptitious system coordinating discussions in the Channel with the "special channel" then being established with Rush, Brandt, and Bahr. As Walter Isaacson summarized, "The plan Kissinger worked out was that Bahr and Rush would come up with ideas to solve the Berlin impasse, Kissinger would negotiate them with Dobrynin, and then Rush and Bahr would put whatever was worked out back into the formal machinery." On January 27, Kissinger dispatched one of his personal assistants, James Fazio, to Bonn to recall Ambassador Rush and request that Bahr visit Washington on short notice.[122]

The next day, in another back-channel meeting, Kissinger told Dobrynin how the arrangement should function. Kissinger said "that the president was prepared to proceed along the line that we had discussed; that is to say, that Dobrynin and I would discuss the outstanding issues, and after some agreement in principle, move our conclusions into the Four-Power discussions on Berlin." Kissinger assured Dobrynin that he would "speak to Bahr on an early occasion, and that we were also bringing Ambassador Rush back to make certain that he would be in on these arrangements." Once again, Kissinger used the opportunity to stress the sanctity of the Channel. "I reiterated the need for total secrecy of this channel," Kissinger reported, "and that if the channel became public or was leaked to people other than those authorized to know, we would simply break it off." Dobrynin replied that the Soviet side "had always respected the privacy of this channel; moreover, it was very much in their interest to preserve its secrecy, and I could therefore be sure." Dobrynin said that although the Soviet ambassador to the four-power talks, Valentin Falin, "had told Bahr that there might be a separate channel," he had not "told him its nature and, except for that, no other person had been told."[123] Using the cover of a plane flight from New York to Cape Canaveral to watch the moon launch of Apollo 14 on January 31, Kissinger advised, and Bahr agreed, to handle the details of the Berlin agreement with Rush outside of the West German Foreign Ministry and the U.S. Department of State.[124] Kissinger omitted the finer points about his secret channel with Dobrynin, other than telling Bahr he would be kept informed of any meetings with Dobrynin on Berlin.[125]

Between February and March 1971, the back-channel discussions on SALT and Berlin had a start-stop character, especially as the White House inaugurated a new communications channel to Rush through a U.S. naval officer stationed in Frankfurt. Kissinger used it to brief Rush with information from Dobrynin and updated the Soviet ambassador. Drafts of a potential quadripartite agreement entered into the Channel almost immediately, which laid groundwork for a mutually acceptable agreement. In addition to focusing the agenda of the four-power talks behind the scenes and accelerating negotiations, the Channel became a moderator and a tool to reinforce linkage. Although the back-channel discussion of SALT initially looked promising, it took both sides time to formalize the agreement. As Kissinger wrote, "Whereas I held out on Berlin to speed progress on SALT, Gromyko slowed up SALT to accelerate the discussions on Berlin."[126] At meetings with Kissinger on February 4 and 10, Dobrynin confirmed Moscow's willingness to conclude a formal agreement on ABM, coupled with a tacit offensive freeze.[127] In his memoir, Kissinger wrote that the Soviets later backpedaled on this point and hypothesized that the Soviets were buying time on congressional debates to scale back the Safeguard ABM program. In addition, Kissinger speculated that the Kremlin wanted to focus on Berlin.[128]

The meeting on February 10 later became something of a controversy after the May 20 announcement because Kissinger allegedly failed to include SLBMs in the freeze.[129] In his memo of the February 10 meeting, Kissinger wrote, "Dobrynin . . . asked whether we included land-based systems only or sea-based ones as well." Kissinger replied, "We were prepared to do *either.*" Later in the conversation, Dobrynin said that the Soviet side was "prepared to discuss sea-based systems, but they preferred not to do so at this point."[130] Dobrynin did not make the distinction between land- and sea-based systems in his own record and vaguely iterated that "the Soviet side's position on limiting strategic arms [was] well known to the U.S. Government." The ambassador defined the strategic offensive weapons as "all nuclear arms of the parties which, regardless of their geographical location, are capable of reaching the other party's national territory," and restated that the FBS would need to be addressed before an agreement could be reached.[131]

On February 14, Dobrynin sent a telegram to the Foreign Ministry with initial observations about the recently expanded discussions in the confidential channel. Dobrynin surmised that Nixon wanted the political credit that would presumably come along with a summit announcement. The ambassador observed that Nixon "clearly fears that word of his confidential dialogue with us on strategic arms, West Berlin, and primarily the Middle East might leak out early." The ambassador advocated exploiting the fact that the complicated negotiations were being conducted from the White House without the benefit of expert knowledge. From a practical standpoint, Dobrynin pointed out that it could be advantageous to shape the debates earlier, before the circle of knowledge expanded to include

State Department people, and to push the drafting of agreements forward to the four-power talks and the upcoming SALT round in Vienna.[132]

As progress was developing on SALT and after a short trip to Key Biscayne, Kissinger called Dobrynin to the White House on February 16 to protest the arrival of a Soviet submarine tender in Cienfuegos Bay. In his memcon, Kissinger portrayed the meeting as reading the riot act to Dobrynin, and focused on the tension of the meeting, playing the hard line with his counterpart, and the "chilly atmosphere." According to Dobrynin's account, Kissinger came across as much more diplomatic, unable to talk about anything other than Cuba on the president's orders. Kissinger depicted himself as a "bad cop" for the president's consumption, whereas he was the "good cop" to Nixon's "bad cop" in Dobrynin's memcon.[133]

The tender quickly departed from Cuba, and Kissinger delivered a draft letter on SALT on February 22. That evening, Kissinger informed Nixon that he had delivered the letter and "some of [Dobrynin's] suggestions were most constructive. . . . He fell all over himself. He offered again to talk about the Middle East and I ducked that question. On Berlin, I gave him some of the stuff I had from Rush and Bahr."[134] Several days later, Kissinger commented: "That Dobrynin is as sharp as a tack. The way that he edited that letter of yours . . . actually strengthened it."[135] As the back-channel exchange of letters began, changes were also taking place in the White House with far-reaching consequences.

On the morning of February 16, 1971, Nixon met alone with his aide Alexander Butterfield in the Oval Office. Butterfield described the details of the sophisticated sound-activated taping system the Secret Service had just installed for the president. Because the system operated by "voice activation," Butterfield explained, "you don't need to turn it on and off." Nixon inquired if it would be possible to expand the system, and, echoing the rationale he would express years later in his memoir account, Nixon stressed his own reason behind the decision to tape: "You see, the purpose of this is to have the whole thing on the file for professional reasons." Butterfield told the president that he had gone over the potential use of the tapes for note taking with Haldeman, and appealed to the president's desire for the strictest secrecy: "Only five people . . . know about it, outside of Haldeman, then you and me."[136] In addition to the American-backed South Vietnamese incursion into Laos in the spring of 1971, the back-

channel breakthrough on SALT and maneuvering on the Berlin agreement were among the first foreign policy events documented by the secret
taping system.

The reels had been rolling for less than two days when Kissinger raised
the back channel on February 18, 1971, in an exchange that exempli-
fied the perennial problem of leaks. That morning, syndicated columnist
Joseph Kraft had published an article that said that Kissinger had found
himself "in the thick of a furious internal fight about the next American move in arms control negotiation." The article also said, "Many arms
control enthusiasts in the State Department and the [Arms Control and]
Disarmament Agency would like to build on the Russian offer" delinking
offensive and defensive weapons but allowing NCA ABM sites.[137] NCA-
only would necessitate dismantling ABM sites then under construction
in the Midwest. In the middle of a morning meeting with the president,
Kissinger fumed, "The ACDA people . . . leaked a column to Kraft, which
I'm afraid is going to blow up my negotiation with Dobrynin because
they put in there . . . the whole debate on the arms control section [of
the World Report]." Without knowledge of the back channel, Kissinger
feared, the bureaucracy had undermined the confidential discussions:
"Rogers and Smith want to give them . . . an ABM-only agreement. Now
here, the Russians have already accepted your proposal." He added, "I
would bet they are going to back off now, to see whether they can't get
more." As Dobrynin's telegram of February 14 demonstrated, the Soviets
were, indeed, "trying to get more" by capitalizing on Nixon's fear of leaks
and his desire for a summit meeting.

Kissinger saw the leak as a personal affront, and he pointed out that
he was in the same boat as the president. "I thought, frankly, Mr. President," Kissinger confided, "it was an issue of pure vanity, that they wanted
to get credit and they didn't want you to get credit." Striking a political
nerve, Kissinger added, "What is so revolting to me is that last August,
when we could have had an ABM-only agreement, and when it could
have helped you at the elections, they fought it, saying it was an election
stunt."[138] As could be predicted, Nixon was less than pleased by the leak.

Although Rogers remained in the dark about the details of the back-
channel moves on SALT, Nixon told him a week later, "I don't believe
[Smith], I don't have any confidence in him . . . and, particularly, his shop,
naturally." Smith, a holdover from the Johnson administration, had pro-

verbially gone native, his team had leaked, and Nixon feared that Smith wanted only to protect his institutional prerogatives instead of following the president's orders. "As anybody who would be involved in long negotiations," Nixon told Rogers, Smith looked at the issues "sometimes in miniscule terms, and also that he just has too much of a tendency . . . [that] he doesn't want to fight with his own people." The bureaucracy was protecting itself, following the institutional imperative to perpetuate itself. Alluding to White House control of SALT, the president emphatically added that for any "big play" and "any agreement with the Russians" on SALT, "*we've got to get the credit here.*" "On the SALT thing," Nixon ordered, "let us develop our own strategy. Let Smith continue to work on table support."[139] Although Rogers seemingly could not get a word in edgewise, such conversations suggested behind-the-scenes maneuvers by his bureaucratic rival, Kissinger.

As the discussions continued, Nixon and Kissinger became legitimately concerned that the Soviets were trying to play the front channel, Smith and the SALT delegation, against the Kissinger-Dobrynin channel. On March 10, Dobrynin met with Ambassador Smith and tried to see if Smith would accept an ABM-only agreement in 1971. Smith knew vaguely of the Channel after the December 1970 Semenov slipup about a summit meeting, but he remained completely in the dark about the exchange of letters Kissinger had arranged with Dobrynin. Kissinger told the president on March 11, a day before Dobrynin delivered the Soviet reply on SALT, that Dobrynin, "that son-of-a-bitch[, was] just taking your letter, without telling Smith he's got it, and feeling out whether Smith is willing to give more." Kissinger added: "Smith's nearly dropped his teeth, because Dobrynin had always said the Russians will never accept trading . . . the Washington system in for [zero] ABM. Here, Dobrynin offered it to him yesterday for nothing." There was a silver lining in Dobrynin's move, Kissinger surmised, "because if they do come back now with the letter, it doesn't look like an arbitrary decision of yours."[140]

Dobrynin delivered the Soviet response on SALT at 8:00 a.m. on March 12, which Nixon later characterized as a "return to earlier hard-line insistence on ABM-only terms." The Soviets were again demanding that an ABM agreement be concluded before any offensive limitation. The president reflected, "After having made what appeared to be considerable progress in our relations, it looked as if we were in for another period of testing by the Soviets."[141] The offending phrase in the Soviet note expressed the desire to "concentrate in the current year on solving the questions related to the limitation of ABM systems, in order to conduct, *after* [the] conclusion of a separate agreement on ABM limitation, active talks aimed at limiting strategic offensive weapons."[142] With the necessary caveat that he would need to consult with the president, Kissinger shared his "first reaction" with Dobrynin. The reply was "merely a restatement of the maximum Soviet position," not a serious position. Kissinger insisted: "We could not agree to an ABM-only agreement. We could also not agree to discuss a 'freeze' only after an agreement had been made."[143] At Dobrynin's suggestion, Kissinger redrafted the American proposal while Dobrynin reworked the Soviet letter for their next meeting. Kissinger figured that Dobrynin had been sent with two sets of instructions since "he would never have offered redrafts on his own authority."[144]

Minutes after his meeting with Dobrynin had concluded, the national security advisor was in the Oval Office reporting to the president. "They, of course, are driving their usual hard bargain," Kissinger explained. "They say, 'Let's negotiate in detail the defensive first, and then we will discuss the freezing.' I told him I didn't know your thinking." Kissinger continued: "I think what we have to ask them is this, Mr. President: that they agree to the principle of freezing of deployments, then we will authorize Smith to discuss ABM with them. And then, before the whole thing gets wrapped up, we will agree to the specifics of the freezing." While the Congress cut the U.S. defense budget, Kissinger advised, "I don't think with this new Soviet missile buildup we can afford to sign an ABM agreement . . . that isn't very specific." Nixon underscored the sense of urgency "to get something done before Smith gets out there."[145] SALT would resume only three days later in Vienna, and, as Kissinger remembered, "We had to formulate new instructions that were at a minimum not incompatible with what was going on in the special Channel."[146]

Kissinger and Dobrynin met on March 15 to discuss respective revised drafts, and again the next day to work out an understanding that essentially became an "amalgam" of the two notes.[147] Simply put, the Soviet draft of March 15 continued to insist that the ABM agreement be agreed upon as a first step "to facilitate more favorable conditions for finding ways to reach an agreement on strategic offensive weapons."[148] Kissinger's modified draft maintained the commitment to conclude an ABM agreement within the year that included "an obligation" to reach an agreement on limiting strategic systems. The draft also spelled out the definition of a "freeze" of "offensive strategic missile launchers," presumably including ICBMs, such as the Soviet SS-9s, and SLBMs. Kissinger wrote "no additional offensive strategic missile launchers would be brought to completion after a fixed date to be agreed," and "such a 'freeze' would not affect replacement or modernization of offensive launchers." In a memorandum to the president explaining the back-channel discussions on SALT, Kissinger noted that although the United States had yet to receive a formal reply from the Soviets, "the text, as it now stands, is of course only an agreement in principle. . . . But the present text meets our essential requirement for coupling an offensive freeze with any ABM agreement."[149]

Dobrynin's memcon contradicted Kissinger's in one key area—the noninclusion of SLBMs. According to Dobrynin: "The word 'freeze,' Kissinger once again explained, affects land-based weapons, but they are willing, as they have said before, to extend this to both sea-based weapons and aircraft."[150] Kissinger would be repeatedly criticized after the announcement of the interim SALT agreement in May 1971 for allegedly failing to include SLBMs in the freeze, a back-channel failing of sorts. Between the interim agreement and the Moscow Summit, Kissinger worked tirelessly to clarify the issue and eventually included SLBMs. After the Moscow Summit, Kissinger was criticized for having given the Soviets a theoretically numerical superiority in SLBMs.

As usual, Kissinger met with the president right after Dobrynin departed the premises on March 16. "I think we may have better than a 50–50 chance," Kissinger said with pride. "I have the impression that they want an agreement." Explaining the public perceptions on the negotiations, Kissinger cited a *New York Times* editorial, "not that that matters, but in which they say we're being obstinate by linking offensive and defensive weapons." The mere mention of "The Gray Lady" was enough to upset the president. "They want it [ABM-only] because that's the drive of everybody who's opposed to ABMs, is simply to go back and be done with it. Correct?" Nixon retorted. Kissinger replied that the administration was "doing better than what *The New York Times* recommended." The back-channel deal could have an effect on public opinion, and even win over that enemy, the press. "They accept it because we're getting an offensive freeze, also," Kissinger said. "You'll get an ABM limitation with a good chance of one different from what they want, which is Washington." Later in the discussion, Kissinger assured the president that the summit-SALT link could be a form of political insurance: "The advantage of a summit, even if it gets a sort of half-baked SALT agreement, whatever the SALT agreement is, it's a lot better than a nuclear test ban." Kissinger added, "It would defuse people. They can't very well attack their president when he's getting ready for a summit meeting."[151]

With SALT effectively set in motion by the amalgam draft, Kissinger and Dobrynin returned to the Berlin issue on March 18. The Soviets were moving on multiple fronts in the Channel, and Dobrynin delivered a complete Soviet draft agreement on Berlin. In a cover memo with Russian- and English-language versions of the draft, Dobrynin wrote, "If in the opinion of the American side, the Soviet proposals could form a basis for further four-power talks and for drawing up final formulations, the Soviet Union could officially table them." In a separate, handwritten note, Dobrynin questioned whether the back channel and the special channel were functioning properly together:

> You will also recall that you mention the intention to instruct Ambassador Rush to conduct [a] confidential exchange of opinion with [Soviet] Ambassador [to the GDR Pyotr] Abrasimov on working out of an "appropriate foundation" concerning a "serious limitation" of the Federal Republic's political activity in West Berlin. Although the Soviet side has agreed on this proposal of the United States, Ambassador Rush has not yet contacted Ambassador Abrasimov on this subject. Moscow wouldn't like to make conclusions from these and some other facts that the channel Ambassador—Dr. Kissinger does not function effectively when matters concern practical steps. But at the same time these facts do attract attention.[152]

Haldeman was with the president when Kissinger described his meeting with Dobrynin and the Soviet proposal later that afternoon. Kissinger told Nixon and Haldeman that the agreement "on first reading [was] acceptable." The national security advisor continued: "I'll send it to Rush on my private channel to him for his analytical comment. . . . There're some major concessions." Kissinger explained that Dobrynin hoped for "a preliminary response from me," within a few days and that the Soviets were "very anxious to move ahead."[153] In his diaries, Haldeman recorded that the "long proposal" was "getting much closer apparently." Haldeman added that Kissinger was optimistic and thought "maybe there's something workable that can be developed from it."[154]

Both the Berlin and SALT negotiations continued after the back-channel exchange of draft letters on SALT and the Soviet draft agreement on Berlin. Kissinger continued to push for progress on SALT, while Dobrynin pushed for progress on Berlin.

To the Interim SALT Agreement

On March 26, 1971, Dobrynin delivered the Soviet reply to the amalgam draft that had been worked out in the back-channel meeting nine days earlier. The Soviets agreed to freeze strategic offensive weapons, but only "*after* an agreement on ABM systems limitation has been reached."[155] A day earlier, at a meeting primarily devoted to the Berlin negotiations, Kissinger had delivered an oral note, "a written but unsigned communication whose status is that of the spoken word and which can therefore more easily be disavowed."[156] Kissinger's oral note conveyed that the negotiators would "elaborate the full text of an ABM agreement" but would simultaneously work out the terms of a phrasing for freezing offensive strategic weapons that would be an "obligation to come to an agreement." The gulf between the Soviet and American positions was narrowing. Contrary to Nixon's recollection that "the SALT talks in Vienna . . . and the secret exchanges of messages through Kissinger and Dobrynin immediately became more intense and serious,"[157] the SALT-related discussions temporarily lulled.

The Soviets applied a back-channel brake for several weeks on SALT. As Kissinger later explained, "Moscow was slowing down negotiations further by the simple device of removing its negotiator."[158] To be fair, Dobrynin had been recalled to attend the Twenty-Fourth Communist Party of the Soviet Union (CPSU) Congress in Moscow. Before Dobrynin departed for Moscow, Kissinger called from San Clemente and joked: "You and I are going steady. We should exchange telephone numbers." Dobrynin accordingly gave his personal phone number in Moscow, and Kissinger turned to clarifying the SALT-ABM positions. The Soviet ambassador repeated the formula from Kissinger's oral note to be sure he understood the American position correctly. After some back-and-forth, Dobrynin promised to convey to Moscow that the United States would accept a separate defensive agreement with a simultaneous offensive freeze and the commitment to reach an offensive limitation.[159] Still, with these issues left unresolved in the back channel, the Vienna round of SALT likewise stalled by the end of March.[160]

Other than temporarily delaying further back-channel discussions on SALT and Berlin, the Twenty-Fourth CPSU Congress had other significance more broadly related to détente. The Congress, which started on March 30 and went on for ten days, signified the ascendance of Brezhnev and a policy of improved relations with the United States. Moreover, as Arkady Shevchenko remembered, Brezhnev "had come to see himself as the prime mover behind the European security campaign," which included the Moscow Treaty and would come to encompass Mutual Balanced Force Reductions (MBFR) in Europe and the Helsinki process.[161] Significantly for the back channel, Ambassador Dobrynin was elevated to the Central Committee of the CPSU during the Party Congress. After the Congress convened, Kissinger called Dobrynin, "just to see whether the line to Moscow [was] real." Kissinger added: "Congratulations on your election. . . . It gives all of us here a feeling of greater confidence in you." About SALT, Kissinger noted: "On the exchange of letters, [we're] hoping you have an answer. It is on the suggestion you and I have already discussed." Dobrynin signaled his understanding.[162]

Nixon and Kissinger perceived domestic politics related to defense spending—especially on ABM and the MIRV deployment—as a threat to the back-channel negotiations with the Soviets. Nixon wrote, "The major problem, as I saw it, was going to be the American negotiating position. Congressional doves were treating the Soviet ABM-only proposal as a way to chalk up a belated victory over the administration on the ABM issue and urged that I accept immediately."[163] Congress and the press grew skeptical about the necessity of funding expensive projects like Safeguard in order to provide a bargaining chip in arms control negotiations when publicly known SALT negotiations seemed to be making little forward movement. The fact that Congress, the press, and even the official SALT delegation knew nothing about the back-channel dealings did not help matters. Kissinger later admitted as much: "In fairness, our secret style of negotiations left us vulnerable to these pressures; our critics did not know that we could do better." Immediately qualifying the statement, Kissinger added, "On the other hand, had they know they would have pressed us to accept the current Soviet proposals, which we were seeking to improve."[164]

At the height of the continuing debate about funding Safeguard in 1971, which ultimately scaled ABM sites from six down to four, Nixon confided the real situation to George Shultz, the director of the Office of Management and Budget. Although he did not mention the back channel, Nixon stated: "Here's what the situation is, in a nutshell, in case you never heard it: By the end of this summer—and we will know then, yes or no—by the end of this summer, probably we will have an ABM agreement." The president explained to Shultz that the U.S. position required both offensive and defensive limitations. "And also, we should know whether we will have coupled with that . . . a freeze on their [Soviet] offensive deployment. See, the two have to go together," Nixon explained. The president highlighted that the move could have an enormous "psychological effect" in the country, as well has having enormous implications for defense spending.[165]

Nixon continued the same line two weeks later with a group of Senate Republicans in the Cabinet Room. According to his memoir, the president told the senators, "If SALT is to have a chance, we cannot give away in the Senate things we might want to negotiate with the Soviets." After all, the Soviets were tough negotiators. Nixon continued, "The Soviets have strong reasons to have an agreement, but we know for a fact that they will only deal from strength and that they only respect those who have strength; otherwise they have historically moved into the power vacuums."[166]

Separate from the discussion of domestic politics, Kissinger wanted to press the SALT issue with Dobrynin after the latter's return from the party congress. If the Soviets dragged their heels on the exchange of letters, Kissinger threatened to discontinue the Channel. The national security advisor told the president: "I'm not going to let him diddle me. . . . My judgment, Mr. President, if you agree, is that we should go for broke with this fellow now. And then—" Nixon interrupted, "Oh, hell, yes." Kissinger continued: "I'll just tell him this is [it]. I'll break the contact. I won't see him anymore, because if we can't settle a simple exchange of letters, then let him work with the State Department. . . . I mean, that's a daring ploy, but they want this contact."[167]

After returning to Washington, D.C., Dobrynin met with Kissinger on April 23, with a note on SALT. There was a sense of anticipation in the Oval Office after nearly four weeks of waiting when Kissinger entered to report the results to Nixon and Haldeman. Kissinger had barely entered the room when Haldeman asked, "Who won?" Kissinger explained at length that Dobrynin had compromised somewhat but had tried to keep the link between SALT, the summit, and Berlin:

> It was a draw. To sum it up, Mr. President, they've, to all practical purposes, given in on this SALT thing. They've come back with a letter from Kosygin, and they're willing to have the exchange of letters published. Up to now they wanted it secret. . . . On the summit, they reaffirm the invitation and they want it in September. . . . They do not want an announcement now. And they say there has to be some progress in Berlin. . . . When he said that, I blew my top, I mean deliberately. I said "Now . . . You're making a terrible mistake. . . . If we have a goal, then the president will never play for little stakes, would recognize that it has to fit into this framework. If you're trying to hold him up with Berlin as a means to get to the summit, you don't understand him. I'm not even sure if he'll let me continue talking to you on Berlin under these circumstances." . . . This was the only way of doing it, because we really cannot promise to be able to deliver on Berlin.[168]

Kissinger later wrote that, "in the glacially deliberate style of Soviet negotiators," the note accepted the U.S. proposal "that offensive limitations could be completed; it was a good definition of simultaneity."[169] According to Haldeman's contemporaneous account, Kissinger had the SALT agreement "at least 90 percent okay," but Nixon was concerned about how to present the breakthrough both to the public and to his own administration. Rogers and Smith remained unaware of the back-channel maneuvering, and the president was inclined "to announce this quickly while Rogers [was] away" on a trip to the Middle East.[170]

The Soviet position had moved closer to the one the White House desired, but it was not a complete victory because, Kissinger explained, "the Soviets took away a previous concession: The agreement was to be dependent on our accepting an ABM system limited to national capitals."[171] Both the SALT delegation and Kissinger had offered the NCA option a year earlier, but the defense funding situation had changed, and with it so had plans for Safeguard. The Soviet Galosh system around Moscow already protected a number of ICBMs, whereas construction on the American Safeguard system had started in North Dakota and Montana. An NCA-only ABM treaty would mean that the United States would have to dismantle what it had already begun building and go through another funding debate in Congress to build a system around Washington, D.C., while the Soviets could keep their own system.[172] On April 26, Kissinger offered a compromise solution in the form of another oral note by allowing the specifics of ABM sites to be "deferred to subsequent negotiations."[173]

In early May 1971, Semenov became a thorn in Henry Kissinger's side and threatened to unravel the back channel with several approaches to Smith. Kissinger described one "bizarre incident," on May 2, in which Semenov "suddenly broached to Smith over a private dinner the very proposal for an ABM agreement limited to capitals, followed by a freeze on ICBMs to be discussed *after* the ABM agreement was concluded, which had been rejected by me six weeks before." Smith immediately cabled Kissinger and urged acceptance of what appeared to be a major Soviet concession. Kissinger was livid and blamed Gromyko for trying to give Semenov "a part of the action" on the breakthrough. Semenov took a different tack on May 9, "to demonstrate his addiction to bypassing the Channel." This time, he suggested an ABM agreement within a year and a freeze on ICBMs—not including SLBMs—and suggested consecutive negotiations. Kissinger was "blunt" with Dobrynin on May 11, when he related the shock in the White House to Smith's report that Semenov had paved the way to an agreement.[174]

Dobrynin's detailed memorandum of his conversations with Kissinger on May 11, 1971, demonstrated how utterly incensed the national security advisor became at Semenov's serious slipups with Smith, to the point of threatening to discontinue the confidential channel. In addition to demonstrating the extent of Kissinger's outburst, the material also highlighted Dobrynin's observations about Kissinger's personal investment in the Channel and partially explained why the Kremlin acquiesced to the American position in the exchange of letters the next day. Dobrynin wrote: "To the 'great surprise' of the president, Kissinger continued, the ideas of the head of the Soviet delegation, as they are set forth in Smith's memorandum, cover all the points on which the president himself was secretly negotiating with the Soviet Government through the confidential channel on ABM issues. . . . Smith's memorandum created a 'sensation' among the State Department leadership and the Disarmament Agency, which, including Rogers, do not know anything about the negotiations through the confidential channel."

Kissinger told Dobrynin that the president was "furious" and saw Semenov's bypassing of the Channel as "'the Soviet leadership's unwillingness' to resolve important matters directly with the president, through the confidential channel." Kissinger asked, "Otherwise what does one make of the fact that he, the president, has been waiting for a reply for two weeks now to his simple proposal to delete temporarily from the official text the reference to the capitals, leaving this matter for future discussion, during which a compromise can be found?"

Dobrynin said Kissinger appeared unnerved by the event, when he "blurted out all this in a rather irate manner (and he said all this over an ordinary city telephone line)." Kissinger even read from coded cables he had received from the SALT delegation to make his point. Dobrynin claimed, "I calmly replied that I did not understand what he was angry about, much less the far-reaching conclusions they are drawing on the basis of one conversation between the heads of the two delegations."

Dobrynin also saw something more "personal" behind Nixon's and Kissinger's outrage. Kissinger "eagerly conducted confidential negotiations on ABM defense in hopes of success, which would elevate him in the president's eyes." The Soviet ambassador continued, "Now, however, especially with this snag, he has become nervous, fearful both of a failure through the confidential channel and the possible exposure of his behind-the-scenes role in conducting negotiations with the other side, bypassing the State Department." "But that is not the main thing," Dobrynin contended. "Nixon himself, as is well known, in terms of his personal traits is a very petty and distrustful man with a huge ego, who carries grudges." Combined with "his long-standing anticommunist ideology" and "the heightened suspiciousness (which is characteristic of him in general) regarding the Soviet Union's motives and actions," no wonder Nixon saw malice in Semenov's misstep. With a distasteful rhetorical flourish, Dobrynin opined that Nixon's suspiciousness was "encouraged in every way by his inner circle, as well as by the Zionists and other anti-Soviets," and had "now reached pathological proportions."[175]

Two decades later in his memoir, Dobrynin offered a different, toned-down explanation for the Semenov slipup that justified some of the outrage in the White House. Dobrynin explained, "It turned out that Semenov . . . had learned from his friends in Moscow about the confidential channel and its work, and decided to take an initiative along the same lines, without of course revealing to anyone that he knew about the channel." As for a motive, Dobrynin surmised that Semenov "hoped to give Moscow a pleasant surprise with his improvisation and obtain permission to continue negotiations along those lines." In addition to enraging Kissinger, Semenov's plan backfired with Gromyko. The Soviet foreign minister "launched a secret investigation in Moscow to find the source of his information but did not succeed in uncovering it." Regardless, Moscow curtailed Semenov's freedom to pursue his own initiatives. He remained the head of the Soviet SALT delegation, "but without information on what was passing through the confidential channel."[176] Dobrynin's position as Kissinger's back-channel interlocutor gave the Kremlin a window into the highest circles of American policymaking, something that Gromyko clearly did not want to lose. Semenov's maneuvering had threatened the continuation of the back channel for the last time. The ambassador finally eclipsed the deputy foreign minister when Gromyko preserved the sanctity of the Channel.

On May 12, 1971, a day after Kissinger's outburst, Dobrynin delivered the latest Soviet proposal on SALT. The Soviets had desisted from insisting on ABM systems limited to the two capital cities and had agreed to conduct simultaneous negotiations on both offensive and defensive weapons. Nixon triumphantly wrote, "Now we had our breakthrough."[177] On May 15, Kissinger and Dobrynin arranged the joint announcement of the breakthrough and set the date for the actual exchange of letters between Nixon and Kosygin for May 20. The back channel had achieved its first major success.

The breakthrough had other implications, such as the delicate matter of informing Smith and Rogers that they had been completely bypassed and trying to develop a plan to address the issues—MIRVs and SLBMs—that the back channel had not addressed. Kissinger met with Smith for breakfast on the morning of May 19 to break the news, while Nixon met with Rogers. Kissinger wrote that the task of briefing Smith "was not a pleasant assignment," and "I showed Smith all the exchanges with the Soviets and a summary of my conversations." "Though he later privately expressed understandable bitterness," Kissinger noted, "when such conduct could have detracted from the first major achievement of the Nixon Administration in East-West relations he put national unity before his own feelings."[178]

Meanwhile, in the Oval Office, Nixon listened intently to Rogers's report about his recent trip to the Middle East and his impressions of Egyptian president Anwar Sadat. Nixon switched roles about twenty minutes into the conversation and awkwardly told his secretary of state about "an exchange of letters" that had allegedly been worked out "quickly" after the CPSU Twenty-Fourth Party Congress. Rogers sat silently and made few remarks as Nixon emphasized the importance of secrecy and his plans to hold a Cabinet meeting.[179]

Haldeman recorded that Nixon was worried because "Rogers' reaction was really almost no reaction at all." On instructions from the president "to be frank" and "tough," Haldeman went to the State Department to meet with Rogers. Rogers, "clearly very upset," asked: "Why didn't you tell me that you were doing this? There's no need for me to be involved, but I do have to be informed." The secretary complained "that both K[issinger] and the P[resident] had promised him that they would not have any other further meetings with any Ambassadors, and particularly Dobrynin, without letting him know." He felt it "would make him into a laughingstock again" and that it destroyed "his effectiveness and credibility." Rogers even offered to resign if the president was "sending him a signal." Like a loyal trooper, Rogers wanted to make sure he had the story right, so Haldeman continued the thankless task of describing the imaginary letter in January, Nixon's real admission to Rogers in February that he did not trust Smith, and the rapid chain of events after the party congress and while Rogers was in the Middle East.[180] No matter what spin the White House put on the breakthrough, Rogers correctly inferred that he was a victim of the back-channel machinations.

With the interim SALT agreement approaching a dénouement, Nixon became extremely concerned about political credit and shielding the back-channel part of the breakthrough from public scrutiny. Having received an invitation to send an American emissary to the People's Republic of

China on April 27, Nixon was also very concerned about the effect of the
evolving Sino-American rapprochement and the back-channel movement
on SALT. In Kissinger's absence, the president used Kissinger's deputy, Al
Haig, as a sounding board on May 6:

> NIXON: Let me tell you, what we're going to play it like, though.
> We're going to have a hell of a time explaining it to Rogers,
> but that's all right. I'll do it. I'm just going to tell him that
> Dobrynin came in with a message. I'm not going to tell him
> I saw him. . . . Dobrynin may come in with that National
> Command Authority again, and I'm just going to turn it
> down. To hell with it. Don't you agree?
> HAIG: . . . I was encouraged by what Semenov said yesterday. I
> think what he was saying was, in effect, they will take the
> Moscow package; you can have ABM anyplace you want it;
> but, you'll have a ceiling on the number of missiles. . . . It
> could be either, but I think they're going to come back to it.
> NIXON: Well, on the other hand, why does Semenov tell it to
> that asshole Smith? I mean, Henry's always so jealous of his
> channel . . . and there are good reasons for it—
> HAIG: Well, I think the reasons for that are just as simple, sir. To
> the degree they can keep you from getting the credit, they're
> going to do it. They don't want you to be reelected—not one
> goddamn bit.

The White House would receive credit—not the SALT delegation—
Nixon boasted, because, "they don't know how much I control it." Haig
replied that the Soviets wanted a summit and the opening with the Chinese could become a lever on Soviet behavior. Nevertheless, Haig insisted,
"We can't move too quickly with the Chinese." Nixon saw his foreign
policy plans coming together. "You understand," the president explained,
"I'm not saying we're going to move to the Chinese or the Russians. And
on ABM, I'll delay that goddamn thing 'til hell freezes over, if necessary. . . . SALT will help if it comes. . . . We either have to have a summit
announcement with the Russians, or an announcement of some kind of
a visit with the Chinese, a public announcement of progress on the Chinese front, a significant thing." Later in the conversation Haig praised

the president and noted that a succession of announcements—an interim SALT agreement, an opening to China, and a meeting with South Vietnamese president Thieu—would be "tight, because it's going to be tough." He assured the president: "But you're going to have right on your side. Then, when you follow that with a summit . . . and a high-level Chinese meeting—one or the other, or perhaps both if we do it very well—I think we've got it. . . . Your foreign policy would have been absolutely revolutionary."[181] As Dobrynin observed, an element of vanity certainly existed in the Nixon White House.

The issue of SLBMs and the details of the final agreement would keep the official SALT delegations busy for months and would occasionally enter into the back channel. In a January 2, 1972, phone conversation, for example, Kissinger told Nixon that he and Dobrynin had worked out a preliminary "technical point" on the way to the final SALT agreement: "We had stated the limits on submarine missiles in terms of numbers of submarines and he would like to do it in terms of the total number of missiles, regardless of how many each submarine carries. . . . In other words, rather than say the limit is 41 submarines we would say 600 missiles, or whatever the figure is." The eventual total number of SLBM launchers would be much higher. "And if he can make that concession," Kissinger continued, "he should say . . . that the ABM thing should be a treaty, and the other [offensive limitation] an executive agreement." Nixon agreed.[182] Because of—and occasionally in spite of—the back channel, the first offensive limitation, SALT I, and a treaty limiting defensive systems to two ABM sites were both concluded at the Moscow Summit in May 1972.

The Back-Channel Brake and the Quadripartite Agreement

Before and after the interim SALT agreement announced on May 20, 1971, the Soviets continued to clamor for a Berlin settlement. Recognizing the linkage between a Berlin settlement and the ratification of the Moscow Treaty, which he had personally negotiated with FRG State Secretary Egon Bahr and Foreign Minister Walter Scheel, Gromyko decided to make the Berlin agreement into the price for a summit.[183] According to Dobrynin, at a Politburo meeting following the Twenty-Fourth Party Congress, Gromyko insisted the Soviet Union should "take advantage of

Nixon's eagerness for a summit by first solving the problem of West Berlin." The Kremlin's tactic of delay on a U.S.-Soviet summit "only helped precipitate Nixon's visit to China, something we were of course unaware of at that time and did not in the least expect."[184] Gromyko got his Berlin agreement, but Nixon and Kissinger's back-channel brake, applied on a number of occasions, raised the price and delayed the agreement.

In the candid environment of the Channel, Dobrynin acknowledged Soviet eagerness for the Berlin agreement on a number of occasions. Just as the Kremlin exploited American weaknesses through the back channel (for example, delaying the start of SALT to allow political pressures to build on the Nixon administration), the White House took advantage of Soviet anxieties on Berlin. For example, on April 27, 1971, Kissinger told Dobrynin that the United States was "struck by the rapidity of their responses on Berlin and the slowness of their responses on SALT." When Kissinger downplayed the U.S. "interest as a nation" on Berlin, Dobrynin retorted that "this was true," but the Kremlin nevertheless saw "some progress on Berlin," as a "sign of . . . good will."[185] Later, to exploit the Soviet's linkage between a Berlin agreement and the summit, Kissinger told the president he was "slowing it down a little . . . just to get the summit."[186] The Soviets could have their agreement, but not too quickly.

As the national security advisor and back-channel agent, Kissinger could see the larger U.S.-Soviet relationship, coordinate between different negotiations, and modulate progress on individual initiatives. The opening to China became one major event when Kissinger applied the back-channel brake to prolong negotiations and delay an agreement. According to a State Department historian: "For three weeks, the White House sent messages to the Ambassador in Bonn, urging him to delay the talks. . . . Rush followed these instructions carefully, managing, in particular, to defer consideration of two major issues—West German representation and Soviet presence—until the end of July."[187] Kissinger's ability to modulate negotiations—accelerating or decelerating, as necessary—to work with the larger strategic picture became one of the major strengths (and weaknesses) and defining features of the back channel with the Soviets.

Although the Kissinger-Dobrynin channel certainly factored into the Berlin negotiations—initiating them in the four-power format in 1969, providing a venue to exchange drafts and to quietly work out contentious points, and providing a mechanism to move items into formal negotiations—the real action took place in Bonn between Rush, Bahr, and Valentin Falin. Falin replaced the original Soviet delegate to the four-power talks, Pyotr Abrasimov, an abrasive Communist Party functionary and the Soviet ambassador to the GDR, because Kissinger conveyed complaints about Abrasimov to Dobrynin in the back channel.[188]

Simply put, the Kissinger-Dobrynin back channel supplemented rather than overruled the Berlin negotiations. From a logistical standpoint, the American end of the "special channel," Ambassador Kenneth Rush, choreographed the diplomatic dance between the White House, the Soviets, the West Germans, the French, and the British. Kissinger effusively praised Rush in his memoirs as the "linchpin": "He kept me briefed for my negotiations with Dobrynin; he kept in close touch with the other Western allies to make sure that the allied positions remained compatible; he also had to curb Bahr's propensity for solitary efforts and for claiming credit with the Soviets for all the concessions made. And Rush had to accomplish all this without the knowledge of his own State Department. It was an odd way to run a government. The miracle is that it worked, due in large measure to Rush's unflappable skill."[189]

Most importantly, Nixon trusted Rush. In 1936, Duke University assistant professor of law Kenneth Rush had met an enterprising law student named Richard Nixon, and the two became lifelong friends. Ambassador Rush came not from the Foreign Service or the government bureaucracy, but as the president of Union Carbide Corporation. Rush followed the ever-changing timetable set by the White House, bypassed the State Department when required, kept Nixon and Kissinger apprised, added meaningful policy guidance into the Kissinger-Dobrynin channel, and headed the negotiations. After a speedup and slowdown over the summer, the United States, the United Kingdom, France, and the Soviet Union signed the Quadripartite Agreement on September 3, 1971. Although Nixon devoted only little more than a paragraph in his one-thousand-page memoirs to the achievement, he summarized that "the agreement contained provisions that would prevent harassment of travelers and visitors from West Berlin to East Berlin and East Germany, make available to West Berliners passports to the Communist-controlled section, and ensure West Berlin's representation abroad by the Bonn government." "By removing at least one of these obstacles," Nixon added, "we were able to clear the way for a summit meeting."[190]

For better or worse, the Channel provided a mechanism for high-level intervention on both SALT and Germany-Berlin. It would be counterfactual to argue that both issues could have been settled through more traditional negotiations conducted through the State Department. It might have been possible but would have been extremely unlikely considering the personalities and the preferences not only of Nixon and Kissinger but also of the Soviet leadership. Leaving the big breakthroughs to the Arms Control and Disarmament Agency (ACDA), the State Department, or anywhere else ran counter to the operating procedures with which Nixon felt comfortable and effective. The documents and tapes demonstrate an administration plagued by leaks and worried that the bureaucracy could deny political capital to the politically sensitive White House. The back-channel maneuvers in the wake of the Cienfuegos crisis signaled the bureaucratic ascendance of Kissinger vis-à-vis Rogers and the traditional foreign policy bureaucracy. The Kremlin also had vested interests in the use of the back channel and allowed Brezhnev and Gromyko to pursue a détente policy with the United States. As the Channel grew in importance, both Kissinger and Dobrynin rose in stature.

A comparison between the "front channel" SALT and Berlin negotiations, in addition to the contrast between the lead negotiators and their knowledge—or lack thereof—of the Kissinger-Dobrynin channel reveals strengths and weaknesses of U.S.-Soviet back-channel negotiations. Both negotiations were ultimately successful in that the United States and the Soviet Union accepted and ratified the agreements, and both agreements survived the test of time. The Berlin agreement lasted until the end of the Cold War and German Reunification. SALT expanded over time to include actual reductions in nuclear armaments, and the ABM Treaty that grew out of SALT became one of the foundations of arms control policy until George W. Bush abrogated the treaty three decades later.

Bureaucratic and institutional structures also differentiated the agreements. The Berlin negotiations were more complicated by their multilateral nature but were more straightforward in a purely bureaucratic sense for the United States. The White House had to contend only with the State Department when it came to the Quadripartite Agreement. Although the strategic arms limitation talks were, in effect, bilateral, they were bureau-cratically complicated because they involved a broad spectrum of groups with often conflicting aims, namely the White House, the State Depart-ment, ACDA, Department of Defense, and the military. Kissinger chaired the Verification Panel under the umbrella of the NSC in order to seek a consensus on the resolution to individual technical issues and to set the broader agenda. Domestic politics and congressional funding debates also influenced the U.S. SALT position. Although less complicated, the Soviet Foreign Ministry had to contend with the Soviet military on SALT-ABM.

Personalities also mattered. Nixon and Kissinger trusted Ambassador Rush and admired his discretion. Instead of using the Channel to bypass Rush, Nixon and Kissinger confided in him. Instead of circumventing the four-power talks, the back channel supplemented the official talks and was informed by Rush. Rush represented the president, not the bureaucracy. In comparison, and as his colorful language shows, Nixon did not hold Ambassador Smith, or the bureaucracy he represented, in high regard. On the contrary, Nixon stated on many occasions that Smith wanted only to protect himself and the ACDA/State positions. The perennial problem of leaks eroded whatever sympathies Nixon might have had for ACDA and State, and fed his suspicions. On the flip side, Nixon seemed obsessed with "getting credit," and the back-channel bypass allowed credit to go to the White House. Secretary Rogers was also left out of the loop—not because Nixon distrusted his longtime friend but because of the tensions that existed between Kissinger and Rogers. The sensitive negotiations, political stakes, and press play also contributed to the conflict. In the case of SALT, the back channel bypassed the official delegation to achieve a breakthrough.

Back channels also had a number of drawbacks and could exacer-bate bureaucratic tensions and present opportunities for the other side to play back channels against front-channel negotiations. Semenov's slipups were a case in point. Whether Semenov acted alone in his slipups, on instructions from above, or whether he acted for himself with unauthor-ized knowledge of the back channel, the events provoked charges of bad faith. As could be expected, at times both Kissinger and Dobrynin threat-ened to break the Channel. Additionally, back channels were not neces-sarily immune to outside pressures, be it congressional votes or separate diplomatic initiatives.

Yet, the back channel had a number of strengths, too. With Nixon's blessings, Kissinger effectively wielded the back channel to alternately slow down and speed up the Berlin negotiations. The back-channel brake and accelerator worked effectively. The Channel forced the fundamental issue of whether or not to pursue détente, and set the agenda for super-power discussions that came to define improved relations between the two adversaries. Leaks had been a problem, especially on arms control issues, from before Nixon could even conduct a policy review after taking office. In addition to using some unsavory and illegal methods that came to haunt the administration, it is undeniable that U.S.-Soviet back channels effectively controlled and compartmentalized information. The Channel gave a basic window into the decision-making process in the United States and the Soviet Union, on negotiating assets and vulnerabilities.

Despite the inherent drawbacks of such centralized foreign policy and a deluge of details for Kissinger, confidential channels were useful tools in the diplomatic arsenal to reinforce linkage—for both the White House and the Kremlin. The back-channel exchanges allowed SALT to evolve. The White House compromised by shifting from a single, comprehensive agreement covering both offensive and defensive limitations to a two-site ABM agreement, plus an offensive freeze. Although the defensive weap-ons limitations developed into a formal treaty, the offensive limitations were addressed. SALT, despite its shortcomings, such as failing to address MIRVs, set a new arms control precedent. As Vladimir Semenov suc-cinctly said in a toast after the first SALT sessions in Helsinki: "You give something, you take something. . . . That is the meaning of agreement."[191]

3

"Playing a Game," Finding a "Lever"

Back Channels and Sino-American Rapprochement

We are playing a game—without being too melodramatic—whatever happens with the election . . . is going to change the face of the world. . . . Now, the China move I've made not because of any concern about China, because I have none, not for fifteen years. But I think we need to do something about the Russians and to have another specter over 'em.

—President Richard M. Nixon

In his 1967 *Foreign Affairs* article "Asia after Vietnam," Republican presidential hopeful Richard Nixon wrote, "Taking the long view, we simply cannot afford to leave China forever outside the family of nations, there to nurture its fantasies, cherish its hates and threaten its neighbors." Nixon continued, "There is no place on this small planet for a billion of its potentially most able people to live in angry isolation." *Foreign Affairs* had been something of a bellwether of official opinion since the advent of the Cold War, when George Kennan outlined his theory of containment.[1] Originally oriented to stop Soviet expansionism, the containment policy adopted during the Truman administration evolved to include blocking the growth of "Red China," the People's Republic of China (PRC), after the Communist victory on the mainland in 1949. The United States supported the Chinese Nationalist regime of Jiang Jieshi on the island of Taiwan and found itself on the opposite side of the PRC on important international issues

throughout the 1950s and 1960s: the Korean War, the 1954 Geneva negotiations on Indochina, two crises over the Taiwan Straits, Chinese support
for Third World revolutionary movements, and the Vietnam War. When
Nixon became president, he began to reevaluate U.S. foreign policy interests, which included the possibility of making overtures to reestablish relations with the PRC after twenty years of nonrecognition.[2]

As national security advisor, Kissinger was initially skeptical about
Nixon's overtures to Communist China but later defined himself by his
role in "opening" China to the United States. As an advisor for Nelson
Rockefeller, the New York governor and one of Nixon's challengers for the
1968 Republican presidential primary, Kissinger had written a July 26,
1968, speech for his earlier benefactor that contained the germ of triangular diplomacy: "I would begin a dialogue with Communist China. In
a subtle triangle of relations between Washington, Peking and Moscow
we improve the possibilities of accommodation with each as we increase
our options towards both."[3] Turning a nascent idea into a practical policy
became, of course, an entirely different matter, one for which confidential
channels were ideally suited.

Sino-American rapprochement as a case study in back-channel diplomacy has been ably recounted and documented in detail elsewhere.[4]
Starting with his inauguration, Nixon publicly and privately signaled Beijing that he wanted to open lines of communication with the PRC. In
addition to acquiescing to the Soviet request conveyed by Boris Sedov
to include a phrase about open lines of communication in his inaugural
address, Nixon directed the next sentence to the Chinese. Alluding to his
1967 *Foreign Affairs* article, Nixon said, "We seek an open world—open
to ideas, open to the exchange of goods and people—a world in which no
people, great or small, will live in angry isolation."[5] Additional channels
included intermittent ambassadorial talks in Warsaw, contacts with the
Chinese embassy in Paris, and private discussions with third parties. During the autumn of 1969, Nixon laid the foundation for future confidential
contacts with the Chinese through Romanian leader Nicolae Ceauşescu
and Pakistani ruler Mohammed Agha Yahya Khan. Ultimately, Washington and Beijing settled on the Pakistani channel, which would have its
own repercussions in 1971.[6]

Agency for Sino-American rapprochement cannot be ascribed only to
Nixon and Kissinger; Chairman Mao played an "American card" every

bit as much as the White House played a "China card," and improved relations would have gone nowhere without his approval. For the most part, American policymakers and the intelligence community missed the gestures, but the long-serving chairman took personal charge of opening relations with the United States and sent a number of signals from the start of the Nixon administration. For example, the chairman personally instructed the *People's Daily* to take the unprecedented step of publishing Nixon's inaugural address. Behind the scenes, Mao reinstated the "Four Marshals," who had been removed from power during the upheaval of the Cultural Revolution, to conduct a study on options with the United States. The chairman urged the marshals to "think outside the box," and in September 1969, one of the marshals, Ye Jianying, recommended "playing the American card."[7] Of course, Ye's recommendations did not occur in isolation.

The Sino-Soviet conflict, which first surfaced in the late 1950s and degenerated into armed border clashes in 1969, proved to be the main catalyst for Sino-American rapprochement. A classic dictum in international relations—*the enemy of my enemy is my friend*—underscored a basic fear among Soviet leaders of a Sino-American, anti-Soviet entente. Although the PRC had signed a formal alliance with the Soviet Union in 1950 and had massively intervened with Soviet aid in the Korean War, the relationship had begun to splinter by the late 1950s over a number of disagreements on international policies. The split was bad enough that the Soviets withdrew technical advisors and reneged on an agreement to provide the Chinese with a prototype nuclear weapon in 1959. Increasingly sharp rhetorical skirmishes characterized the 1960 and 1964 Communist Party congresses. The 1964 exchanges were also tempered by the 1962 war between China and India, which Moscow did not anticipate. Increasingly radical at home, the Chinese also determined to pursue their own nuclear deterrent. The Chinese Cultural Revolution, which began in 1966, led to a further erosion of Sino-Soviet relations, and Soviet leaders feared anarchy in their eastern neighbor.

By the late 1950s, a group of CIA analysts had recognized the basic incompatibilities between the Soviet Union and Communist China, arguing that the two poles of the Communist world were separated by ideological divergence and deep-seated animosity.[8] The vehemence of propaganda emanating from both the Soviet Union and the People's

Republic of China throughout the 1960s showed that little hope for reconciliation existed between the two powers, even though the Communist giants shared common interests, such as support for North Vietnam against the United States (aid to North Vietnam became a competition between which power truly supported socialist revolution).[9]

The war of words nearly developed into an actual war in 1969 after a series of clashes between Chinese and Soviet troops occurred along the Sino-Soviet border. Escalating skirmishes caused a war scare in Beijing as the Soviet Red Army deployed thousands of troops to the border regions. The Soviet-led Warsaw Pact invasion of Czechoslovakia in 1968 to crush the Prague Spring, and the subsequent proclamation that became known as the "Brezhnev Doctrine," also concerned Chinese policymakers. The Brezhnev Doctrine retroactively justified earlier crackdowns in Hungary in 1956 and East Germany in 1953, and stated that the Soviet Union would intervene anywhere Communist rule was threatened. Although that threat seemed ostensibly confined to the Eastern Bloc countries, the Chinese believed it could be directed at them and their Cultural Revolution.[10]

The China question almost immediately entered into the dialogue of the Kissinger-Dobrynin channel. The Nixon administration's public line and the message to the Soviets differed from what it said behind the closed doors of executive offices. Publicly, the Nixon administration said it would pursue relationships with both the Soviet Union and the People's Republic of China. Privately, Nixon and Kissinger hoped to play the Soviets and the Chinese off each other—the concept of triangular diplomacy.

In retrospect, it seems that triangular diplomacy had less to do with the concrete and crude move of playing the powers off each other than it did with trying to influence the perceptions and emotions of Communist leaders. The possibility of triangular diplomacy, whether theoretical or practical, did not exist until the Chinese made it possible. The documentary record suggests that it was only after Sino-American rapprochement had been set in motion in April–May 1971, with the Chinese Ping-Pong diplomacy and the secret traffic through the Pakistani channel, when U.S. policymakers began to talk of playing the Communist powers off one another for American advantage. Nixon took a very realpolitik view when he later explained his rationale to his chief domestic advisor, John Ehrlichman:

NIXON: The Russians are going to throw the summit, throw
   it [away]? Not on your life. They've gone exactly the other
   direction. They want theirs [even more, even though we
   hadn't heard from] the Chinese. The Chinese want theirs
   because of the Russians. Now, this is a good thing.
EHRLICHMAN: Yeah.
NIXON: As long as you play it even-handed. Now, this, therefore,
   can put us in a very powerful position. It's the sort of
   position the British were in in the 19th century when among
   the great powers of Europe, they'd always play the weaker
   against the stronger. That's what we're doing with the
   Chinese. See?[11]

Similarly, Kissinger told Nixon right after the successful Beijing summit in February 1972: "We are playing an absolutely cold-blooded game.
. . . We need it for the Russians and if it serves our purpose we'll go against
the Chinese. Right now the Chinese are making our policy go."[12]
   Soviet back-channel injunctions to the White House against collusion with the PRC actually had the opposite effect, convincing Nixon
and Kissinger that an opening to China could be used to moderate Soviet
behavior. The Soviets unintentionally and repeatedly telegraphed their
apprehensions about China to the White House through the back channel. Dobrynin wrote in his memoirs, "Personally, I believed that we were
making a mistake from the start by displaying our anxiety over China
to the new administration."[13] Instead of enlisting U.S. sympathy against
purported Chinese aggression or forming a "condominium" against the
Chinese, the Soviets inadvertently gave the Nixon administration a "back-
channel button" that could be employed, both subtly and not so subtly,
whenever Nixon and Kissinger wanted to play on Soviet fears.
   Although leading Nixon administration officials had long hinted that
the United States would welcome better relations with the world's most
populous nation, the preeminence of the "China card" as a factor driving U.S.-Soviet relations began in earnest with Nixon's announcement on
July 15, 1971, that he would visit the People's Republic of China the following year. Even though Nixon had effectively torpedoed a joint summit
with President Johnson and the Soviets in 1968, he and Kissinger reiterated via the back channel that he would welcome a high-level meeting

during his first term to deal with concrete issues in Soviet-American relations. Kissinger pushed the summit idea from 1969 to the eve of his secret trip to China in 1971 to get the Soviets to agree in principle and to set a tentative agenda. As described in chapter 2, the Kremlin stalled and made the summit contingent on a Berlin settlement.

Despite progress on the Berlin agreement, Kissinger could not convince the Soviets to commit to the summit until after the China announcement. China changed everything. Aleksandrov-Agentov, the general-secretary's foreign policy advisor who has been described as "Brezhnev's Kissinger," wrote that as a result of Sino-American "probing regarding a possible meeting between the leaders of the two countries . . . they found the desired lever that would allow them to put pressure on Moscow regarding the possibility of a [Soviet-American] summit meeting. And this was an effective lever."[14] More bluntly, the Soviets had overplayed their hand on the summit. As Raymond Garthoff summarized, the Soviets began "pressing with alacrity for a Moscow meeting before the president's visit to Beijing. Thus the United States, which had initially been the *demandeur* or supplicant for a summit, had reversed roles with the introduction of the China factor."[15]

Although the Nixon administration stressed that better relations with China would not be sought at the expense of any third nation, Nixon and Kissinger turned the proverbial China screw when they wanted a Soviet response. The Moscow summit became the ultimate stakes in a geopolitical poker match of triangular diplomacy.

Telegraphing Anxiety: From the Ussuri River to "Polo I"

President Nixon's first state visit to cosmopolitan Paris and Rome in March 1969 contrasted sharply with the remote wilderness border along the Ussuri River, where Chinese and Soviet forces fought each other on Damansky Island, as the Russians call it, or Zhenbao Island by its Chinese name.[16] The State Department's Bureau of Intelligence and Research saw the clash as an outgrowth of tensions over the preceding decade and predicted "similar incidents . . . from time to time."[17] Later in the month, two CIA summaries noted that Beijing had likely instigated the attacks and that after repeated incidents the situation had "stabilized" by March

19.[18] The White House cautiously responded and refrained from making detailed statements. Kissinger later wrote: "While I favored establishing a triangular relationship as a matter of theory, both Nixon and I still considered the People's Republic of China the more aggressive of the Communist powers. We thought it more than likely that Peking had started the fighting."[19] In addition to contemporaneous American intelligence analysis, recent scholarship has confirmed that the Chinese precipitated the incident on Damansky Island, although border incidents and violence had occurred on both sides over the preceding decade. Using Chinese sources, Yang Kuisong wrote, "the [1969] military clashes were primarily the result of Mao Zedong's domestic mobilization strategies, connected to his worries about the development of the 'Cultural Revolution.' The situation at the border quickly got out of hand and created, for Beijing, a perceived danger of war that Mao had never intended."[20] The clashes had other unintended consequences and provided the viable rationale for Sino-American rapprochement.

Less than two weeks later, Kissinger and Dobrynin discussed the altercation during a late dinner meeting on March 11. The conflicting accounts both men left for posterity suggest a tense mood during the candid exchanges. According to Kissinger, Dobrynin raised the topic and "became very emotional" when the national security advisor said that the Nixon administration regarded the dispute "primarily as a problem for China and the Soviet Union and we did not propose to get involved." Rather, Dobrynin insisted, China was "everybody's problem."[21]

Dobrynin's record of the March 11 dinner suggests that he played it cool with his counterpart, and that Kissinger, "on his own initiative, and without any questioning," actually brought up the subject. Dobrynin reported that he had explained the clash "per existing instructions." In response, Kissinger said that American analysts believed there would "be no normalization in Sino-Soviet relations" as long as Mao was alive. Dobrynin added the soothing explanation that "Kissinger began to assert that the Nixon Administration 'does not intend to somehow capitalize' on friction in Sino-Soviet relations." Echoing the public line, Kissinger explained that the new administration simply sought to "to improve relations both with the Soviet Union and with China, while simultaneously avoiding entanglement in their quarrels."[22] Outwardly, at least, the Nixon administration promoted the concept of parallel relationships. In retrospect, however, it appears that Dobrynin made the contentious topic more palatable to his bosses in the Kremlin.

Kissinger remembered the meeting of March 11, 1969, as a strategic break and suggested "heavy-handed Soviet diplomacy . . . made us think about our opportunities."[23] When he described the meeting to President Nixon later that evening on the phone, Kissinger said that Dobrynin had "asked how we evaluated the Chinese clash." Kissinger told the president: "I told him we think it is their problem. We don't presume to give them advice. We won't play any little games. . . . Obviously, this is much on their minds." Nixon replied, "Sometimes events which we could not have foreseen may have some helpful effect—who knows?"[24] The back-channel discussion with Dobrynin had planted a seed that eventually sprouted into triangular diplomacy, although other signs corroborated the U.S. policy of opening to China.

Two days later, on March 13, the Soviet ambassador reported his "preliminary conclusions" about the Nixon administration and estimated that Sino-American rapprochement was not beyond the realm of possibility. Based on official statements by administration officials and private exchanges with Nixon, Kissinger, and Rogers, Dobrynin predicted that the administration would "pursue a pragmatic course that envisages negotiations with the Soviet Union in cases where it serves U.S. interests and where it is possible to reach a compromise." Nevertheless, the administration could endeavor "to establish a relationship with Peking that would make it possible to more effectively exploit Soviet-Chinese differences and reduce Chinese pressure on South and Southeast Asia." The White House might redirect "Chinese militancy more to the north, but not at the expense of an appreciable deterioration in Soviet-U.S. relations." Dobrynin hypothesized that the administration would use "the idea of 'containment' of the Soviet Union" to apply "pressure on it from two flanks—the West German (NATO) and the Chinese." The Soviet ambassador immediately qualified his statement, writing, "publicly and in their dealings with us they [the Nixon administration] exhibit a certain caution."[25]

When Kissinger met with Dobrynin on April 3, the NSC had begun discussions on U.S. policy toward China, and the Soviets and Chinese had clashed again on Damansky/Zhenbao. The skirmishes produced more casualties and involved tanks, artillery, armored cars, and large numbers

of troops but had temporarily subsided by the time the Soviet ambassador and the national security advisor met at the White House. Kissinger
succinctly described how Dobrynin "turned to China" and "referred to a
news story that I was in charge of a policy review of Communist China
and asked what conclusions we had reached." Kissinger replied that the
administration "had reached no conclusions." The national security advisor posited, "from a sheer political point of view, I thought China would
be a major security concern of the Soviet Union no matter who governed
it." When Dobrynin raised the possibility that Taiwan "could well be an
independent state," Kissinger wrote he "did not respond."[26] In contrast to
the sole paragraph Kissinger devoted to the discussion of China, Dobrynin
reported page after page of quotations and details. If the level of detail in
reporting reflected each power's concerns about China, then Kissinger's
brevity compared to Dobrynin's meticulousness showed that the Kremlin
may have been suffering from Sino-neuralgia and the White House was
just beginning to understand the viability of triangular diplomacy.

Dobrynin acknowledged that he wanted to confirm press reports that
Kissinger had formed a special committee to review U.S. policy toward
China. The ambassador was likely referring to a column printed the day
before, on April 2, by veteran *New York Times* reporter Peter Grose. Grose
wrote that Washington anticipated that the results of the Ninth Chinese
Communist Party Congress in Beijing (April 1–24, 1971) could conceiv-
ably allow the Chinese leadership to "establish enough stability to permit the start of a substantive dialogue with the United States." Unnamed
"United States officials" divulged that the NSC staff "was canvassing
appropriate executive departments about steps that might be taken to end
the estrangement of two decades between the United States and mainland
China." Grose also reported that Secretary Rogers expressed a willingness
to begin a dialogue with the Chinese in his testimony before the Senate
Foreign Relations Committee on April 1, and that leading Democrats,
especially Senator Edward Kennedy (D, MA), were pushing the administration to remove the ban on travel to the PRC, relax the trade embargo
that had been in force since 1949, reduce the U.S. military presence on
Taiwan, and establish U.S. "consulates on the mainland as a prelude to
diplomatic relations."[27]

An inveterate news consumer (and news maker), Kissinger knew what
Dobrynin was talking about when the ambassador raised the question

about the policy review group, and he saw an opportunity to bring U.S. domestic politics into the Channel and campaign on the administration's behalf. Kissinger likely recalled an opinion piece published several days earlier by Democratic image-crafter Theodore Sorenson, contrasting the viewpoints of "Liberals," "academics," and "leading Democrats" with those of the Nixon administration. In an opinion piece published on March 30, Sorenson, the speechwriter and advisor to President Kennedy, admonished that the United States "should not take sides in this [Sino-Soviet] dispute, to appear to take sides, to permit ourselves to be used by either side, or to give either nation grounds for charging that we have taken sides." Sorenson adjoined, "It is true that Peking's words have been more hostile than Moscow's . . . [b]ut Moscow's deeds have been more threatening." Regardless, the United States should have "separate but equal" policies with regard to both China and the Soviet Union.[28] Coincidentally, on the same date, Grose reported Senator Kennedy's views "at a thousand-plate banquet and before the television cameras" that the United States should end the twenty-year trade embargo with the PRC, withdraw U.S. troops from Taiwan, take "steps toward diplomatic recognition—whether Peking would respond favorably or not," and abandon "opposition to letting Communist China take a seat at the United Nations."[29]

Dobrynin recorded that Kissinger said the calls for a new China policy by "our liberals, especially those from the Democratic Party like the young Kennedy, Sorensen and others," could "only cause uneasiness in Moscow." Kissinger reassured his counterpart that it was fortunate for the Soviets that the Nixon administration did "not share all these views," and that the policy was "nothing unusual." Dobrynin posited that Kissinger's remarks demonstrated "that considerations related to the struggle between the parties in anticipation of the next election are already beginning to have some impact on the foreign policy activities of the Administration, and the Administration is evidently not averse to portraying itself to us in a more favorable light than its rivals, the Democrats, on the China question."

Kissinger repeated the White House line that the United States could not indefinitely ignore China but considered relations with the Soviet Union more important. The national security advisor repeated what Nixon had told Soviet deputy foreign minister Vasily Kuznetsov on March 31, at President Eisenhower's funeral: "There are currently two great powers in the world . . . but in 20 or 25 years the situation could change because another great power could emerge—China; that is why it is important for the USSR and the U.S. to use every opportunity . . . that serve[s] the objectives of maintaining peace." Kissinger conceded that U.S. policy on China depended on China's policy after the PRC Ninth Communist Party Congress and admitted, "We are . . . also employing the services of some of our friends from Western Europe to sound out Peking's intentions and identify for ourselves possible areas for improving relations with China (through trade, exchange of representatives of the press, cultural ties, etc.)." The United States would never trade Taiwan to the PRC, Kissinger asserted, and a real divergence of positions on important issues between the United States and the PRC remained major obstacles.

Just as Mao would likely hinder an improvement in Sino-Soviet relations, Kissinger told the ambassador, American experts agreed "that as long as Mao is alive, it is unlikely that U.S.-Chinese relations will develop to any extent." With shades of Nixon's 1967 *Foreign Affairs* article, Kissinger pointed out the realist viewpoint that the world's most populous nation could not be ignored indefinitely and the United States should "do some 'groundwork' in this area for the future." Moreover, Kissinger "stressed" that the Nixon administration did "not intend to play on Soviet-Chinese disagreements." The Soviet Union was the administration's "No. 1 priority," and any attempt to "play on the disagreements could embroil the United States itself and even further alienate both the U.S.S.R. and the P.R.C."

On the China question, Dobrynin concluded that the Nixon administration had adopted "a wait-and-see attitude." The administration would follow events and pursue opportunities but without causing "undue difficulties in the relations with us," the ambassador confidently reported. Naturally, the approach did "not eliminate the question of the inevitable U.S. attempts—albeit gradual at this point—to use the differences between the USSR and the PRC to its own advantage." The ambassador remarked that Kissinger had minimized the China question and said the U.S. attempt to improve relations with China could not be characterized as "building bridges . . . because bridges are still a long way off." He believed the United States would undoubtedly try to exploit Sino-Soviet differences, but the practical implications would be in the distant future.[30]

During the first few months of the Nixon administration, the back-channel dialogue on the China question developed into a pattern that continued throughout Nixon's first term in office. Starting with the first clashes along the Ussuri River in March 1969, the Kremlin displayed its anxieties about China in the Channel. The White House could not fail to see the signals. Soviet moves in the Caribbean and the Middle East, coupled with slow progress in discussions of concern to the White House, such as SALT and a Soviet-American summit, inadvertently pushed the White House to recognize the possibility of Sino-American rapprochement and the viability of triangular diplomacy.

A back-channel meeting on June 11, 1969, continued the pattern. Before returning to Moscow for consultations, Kissinger reported that Dobrynin had told him that the Soviet Union "had no problem with any of their allies." Kissinger replied, probably needling his opposite, that "China was still a Soviet ally." Dobrynin replied "emphatically" and corrected Kissinger, stating "China is not an ally; it is our chief security problem."[31]

Dobrynin did not mention the exchange, but he reported, as usual, with more detail and in a disarming manner. According to Dobrynin, Kissinger brought up the topic and reaffirmed that the Nixon administration did "not intend to interfere in any way in the current Sino-Soviet conflict." It was "a matter of principle and will not change," Kissinger assured Dobrynin, explaining that "a careful analysis" after the Ninth Party Congress did not give "any evidence at all that the Peking leadership is prepared to take a somewhat more conciliatory line toward the U.S." He continued "half ironically" that the Soviet Union had replaced the United States "as the main target of Chinese criticism." Nevertheless, the PRC remained implacable on the issue of Taiwan. Taipei and Beijing could negotiate between themselves, but Taiwan remained "an important link in the chain of [American] bases to deter Peking's expansionist tendencies." Détente with Moscow remained Washington's main priority, even if the United States had become "greatly distressed" by growing Sino-Soviet "differences." As an increasingly global power, the Soviet Union naturally enjoyed a more important role in securing world peace, so, Kissinger asserted, "the Soviet Union must now play a more active role in reaching a [Vietnam] settlement." According to Dobrynin, both he and Kissinger agreed that the war in Vietnam "mainly" served "the interests of China."[32]

The back channel served as a two-way street for information and to reinforce or challenge intelligence gathered elsewhere. Dobrynin's assertions about the border clashes along the Ussuri River could be confirmed by U.S. intelligence collection, just as the Soviets could evaluate what Kissinger told Dobrynin about Sino-American ambassadorial talks in Warsaw. The location of the talks in Poland made it easy for the Soviets to snoop, so Kissinger did not tell Dobrynin anything the Soviets did not already know.[33] In the first back-channel meeting on February 21, 1969, Kissinger told Dobrynin that the Chinese had canceled the Warsaw session that had been scheduled to take place the day before. Kissinger said the Chinese had acted "on the pretext that the U.S. had been involved in the case of a Chinese diplomat who had defected," but he believed the real reason was "due to the fact that Mao and his colleagues [were] not prepared . . . to enter into a dialogue with the Nixon Administration."[34] Dobrynin continued to keep tabs on the talks through the back channel.

Meanwhile, consistent with what Kissinger told Dobrynin, the administration sent a number of public and private signals that Washington wanted better relations with Beijing. For example, in July 1969, the State Department eased restrictions on travel and trade. In addition to attempting to jump-start the Warsaw Talks, Nixon and Kissinger quietly sent out tentative feelers for back-channel contacts with the Chinese via both Pakistan and Romania during a "round-the-world tour" in the summer of 1969. The administration also sent subtle signals by referring to the "People's Republic of China" instead of calling it "Communist China."[35]

In August 1969, Soviet forces attacked a Chinese squadron on the border of Xinjiang Province, hundreds of miles to the southwest from the earlier clashes along the Ussuri. The Soviets' overwhelming use of force, combined with the fact that the Chinese had their main nuclear test facility in the same province, at Lop Nur, suggested that the Sino-Soviet conflict had taken a turn for the worse. During August and September 1969, the Soviets signaled to American policymakers that Moscow was considering a preemptive strike against Chinese nuclear facilities.[36]

The idea was not a new one. During the Kennedy and Johnson administrations, U.S. planners had considered a preemptive strike on Chinese nuclear facilities before Beijing successfully tested a fission weapon in 1964 and became the world's fourth nuclear power.[37] Georgi Arbatov noted that the United States had put "out cautious, unofficial feelers" to probe for the Soviet reaction to a strike on Chinese nuclear facilities. He wrote that the Kremlin ignored the idea because "such feelers could have been a deliberate provocation. Had we shown any interest in the idea, the United States could immediately have used it against us to create even greater friction in our relations with the People's Republic."[38] Arbatov's assertions aside, preemptive action was always a contingency, even if it was unethical or impractical.

Naturally, the Soviets feared Chinese strategic capabilities since Beijing had tested a hydrogen (fusion) weapon in 1967 and was developing missiles that could reach European Russia. The Kremlin may have used its own midlevel approaches to the United States to litmus-test the idea of a preemptive strike and/or to sow discord between the United States and the PRC. Either way, Soviet accounts dismissed the possibility that Moscow even considered such options.

Aleksandrov-Agentov later mocked Kissinger's recollection of Soviet feelers for preemptive action. He called Kissinger's comment a "slanderous maneuver . . . to scare the Chinese leaders, to force them to form closer ties with America." He added, "On the threshold of Nixon's visit to Peking Nixon needed to deepen the quarrel between China and Moscow, to push them towards a closer alliance with the U.S.A."[39] Aleksandrov-Agentov was being disingenuous on several points. The events in question not only occurred two-and-a-half years before Nixon's visit to China, but months before any discernible progress in Sino-American relations had been made, and in direct response to the escalating Sino-Soviet border clashes. Nor did the United States have to incite the Chinese to fear the Soviets; the Soviets did that themselves by actions rather than words. Regardless, the Soviet feelers certainly provoked a response in American policy circles.[40]

In terms of the Channel, the idea of a Soviet strike on Chinese nuclear facilities came up, but only in a hypothetical manner, after the tensions on the Sino-Soviet border had somewhat stabilized. Following the funeral of Ho Chi Minh in Hanoi, on September 11, 1969, Soviet prime minister Alexei Kosygin diverted his return flight to meet with Chinese prime minister Zhou Enlai at the Beijing airport. The meeting restarted stalled border talks and alleviated some of the tension, although it left the underlying problems unresolved. The border talks continued without real progress for some time.[41]

Nearly a month after the Zhou-Kosygin meeting and nearly two months after these Soviet feelers, Dobrynin met with Kissinger on October 9. Dobrynin recorded that Kissinger raised the subject of China "half-jokingly . . . (but essentially in a serious vein)" by stating that the Soviet delay in starting SALT was "due to the recently opened dialogue between the USSR and the People's Republic of China." "Echoing Kissinger's tone," Dobrynin told his opposite that Moscow based its foreign policy "not on any considerations of the moment but on well-known principles." Any attempt by Washington to exploit Sino-Soviet differences—"and there are certain indications of this," Dobrynin warned—"might lead to a very serious miscalculation." He added, "Kissinger said that to judge from the information at their disposal, the PRC leadership, in the period just before the above-mentioned [Kosygin-Zhou] meeting, began seriously taking into account the possibility of a preemptive strike by the Soviet side, particularly against Chinese nuclear centers." Surprisingly, when Dobrynin inquired "as to what the U.S. Government itself really thinks about this matter," Kissinger replied "that had it not been for the unexpected march of Soviet troops into Czechoslovakia last year, their response would have been negative. In the light of the Czechoslovak events, however, Washington no longer questions the determination of the Soviet Government [to act] if it believes there is a genuine threat to the supreme national interests of the USSR." Dobrynin did not offer comment.[42]

When Dobrynin met with Nixon and Kissinger on October 20, 1969, he delivered a message from the Soviet leadership to the White House that repeated the warning that any attempt to "make a profit from Soviet-Chinese relations at the Soviet Union's expense . . . can lead to a very grave miscalculation and is in no way consistent with the goal of better relations between the U.S. and the U.S.S.R." Earlier "assurances by American leaders" that the United States "was not interested in any aggravation of conflict" showed a "sign of sober realization," although the Kremlin pointed out its dissatisfaction with the state of Soviet-American relations.[43] The clearly articulated Soviet apprehensions about American triangular diplomacy later reinforced Nixon's determination to pursue better relations with Beijing, especially when Sino-American rapprochement became more of a reality.

At Nixon's behest, the veteran diplomat and U.S. ambassador to Poland Walter Stoessel arranged additional Warsaw sessions with the Chinese scheduled for January and February 1970.[44] In a memo to Kissinger, NSC staffer Helmut Sonnenfeldt informed Kissinger that Ambassador Smith and Ambassador Llewellyn Thompson had recommended giving Dobrynin advanced notice that the Warsaw Talks would resume. Sonnenfeldt wrote, "In the last Administration it was standard practice for the State Department to provide Dobrynin with detailed records of the Warsaw." Sonnenfeldt believed that "this practice of the last Administration should not be resumed in this one."[45] Kissinger agreed. In a phone conversation on December 13, 1969, Nixon told Kissinger to handle any discussion of the Warsaw Talks "on a confidential basis" with Dobrynin.[46] Any informing of the Soviets would be done in the back channel, adding a sense of gravitas to the proceedings.

As was typical on the sensitive topic of Sino-American contacts, the memcons Kissinger and Dobrynin wrote reflected a kind of "he said, she said" scenario—maybe more of a "he said, he said" scenario—when the two met on January 20, 1970; coincidentally, the same day the talks resumed in Warsaw. Kissinger claimed that the ambassador "began the conversation by asking what had happened in Warsaw" and "said that China was a neuralgic point with them." Although China could not pose a realistic military threat, that is, deploying nuclear-armed ICBMs, for several years, Dobrynin told Kissinger "people were not very rational on that issue," and "he just wanted to convey the intensity of feeling in Moscow."[47] Dobrynin's admission about Soviet neuralgia would have been a very direct display of insecurity that Kissinger could not have missed.

Dobrynin wrote that Kissinger raised the topic "on his own initiative," and the Warsaw discussions "did not introduce 'anything new' into the Sino-American equation." Kissinger "went to great lengths to emphasize" that the United States wanted to normalize relations with China "not out of anti-Soviet sentiment, but out of a "natural desire" on the part of the United States to improve relations with all the major powers."[48] Curiously, the back-channel discussions missed significant movement at the February 20 talks in Warsaw, when the Chinese issued an invitation for the United States to dispatch an envoy to Beijing for talks. Regardless, the Chinese canceled additional Warsaw talks in response to the U.S. incursion into Cambodia during the spring of 1970.[49] The White House regrouped after the canceled Warsaw talks and thereupon redirected its

efforts through the Romanian and Pakistani channels. So began the waiting game for Sino-American rapprochement.

In line with the lack of substantive progress in Sino-American rapprochement (the first tentative steps in the Pakistani channel did not begin
until November–December 1970), there were few mentions of China in
the back-channel discussions between 1970 and the spring of 1971. For
example, when Kissinger raised the prospect of improving Soviet-American relations at a June 10, 1970, meeting aboard the presidential yacht
Sequoia, it "led Dobrynin to ask . . . how we were getting on in our
relationship with China." Kissinger replied by pressing the back-channel
button: "I said that it was very interesting that China was vitriolic in its
public attacks but very polite in its private conversations. Dobrynin said
that he suspected as much. He said, 'Are you going to try to get on better terms with Communist China?' I responded that we would continue
talking but their own experience must teach them that progress would not
be very rapid."

Dobrynin tried, unsuccessfully, to use China to pressure the United
States, stating he "believed China would try to lead a crusade against
us [the United States]." Kissinger nonchalantly replied, "I said that we
were relaxed about this and would probably try to stay in contact with
them."[50] Dobrynin, however, scarcely mentioned China in his record of
the meeting.[51]

A month later, the Soviet ambassador described another encounter
with Kissinger linking China and SALT: "Kissinger either intentionally
or unintentionally left the impression (although he never said so outright)
that their current approach to this issue is based chiefly on the political
aspect, in the area of relations with China." U.S.-Soviet agreement on
strategic weapons could help the Soviet Union in its relations with China,
because Beijing "would essentially be faced with a united front (or at least
the potential for such a front) of the two main nuclear powers." SALT
could have other effects: "As a result of such an agreement with us, the
Americans themselves would largely be deprived of the basis for the game
that currently constitutes an important part of their present China policy,
namely playing on the friction between the USSR and China." Dobrynin
hypothesized that the United States was stalling on SALT, "forced to
rethink its previous approach to the relevant separate agreement with us
at this time." "They are now approaching this matter primarily from a

political standpoint," Dobrynin added, "in terms of grand, global strategy and in close linkage with the whole complex of Soviet-U.S. relations." The United States was awaiting "further developments . . . since, to all appearances, *they now believe we are raising this issue chiefly in pursuit of our political objectives vis-à-vis China.*"[52] The United States awaited movement on the China front, which started anew at the end of 1970, just as the United States began to press anew for a summit meeting with the Soviets.

Role Reversals and the Soviet-American Summit

The idea of a Soviet-American summit had been a topic of frequent discussion in U.S.-Soviet back channels since the start of the Nixon administration. Washington quickly displayed its desires for a politically profitable summit, and the Soviets decided to use that desire to its advantage. The Soviets overplayed their hand, however, by delaying and raising the price of the summit to the point when, unbeknownst to the Kremlin, Washington and Beijing began a dialogue toward a Sino-American summit.

U.S.-Soviet back-channel talk of a prospective summit meeting began almost as soon as Kissinger and Dobrynin started meeting privately. Kissinger and Nixon stuck to the talking point that the United States would welcome a "constructive" summit meeting after the proper "preparatory work."[53] In the record of the first back-channel meeting, Dobrynin recorded that Kissinger had raised the summit question but that he had played the role of the reluctant partner, "not to emphasize any special interest of ours," and therefore limited himself to a noncommittal reply.[54] Likewise, on March 13, 1969, Dobrynin reported that Nixon was not yet ready for a summit but had "committed himself quite strongly vis-à-vis both the American people and the international community." The summit issue would serve as the Soviet's own back-channel button to apply pressure on the Nixon administration.[55]

Many years later, Dobrynin wrote, "The question of a summit cropped up time and again during my contacts with Kissinger during the Administration's first two years, but it became a live issue only during the following year, in the middle of 1971." Dobrynin questioned Kissinger's claim that "the Soviet side overplayed its hand by making its price for a summit during 1970 a de facto alliance by Moscow and Washington against China, a European security conference, and a SALT agreement on Soviet terms." The Soviet ambassador did "not remember any such demands. . . . The leadership of the Soviet Union was not that naive." He argued that neither side was ready for a summit before the middle of 1971, partially due to Soviet domestic politics—whether Brezhnev or Kosygin would assume the preeminent spot—and due to the Nixon administration's supposedly "ambivalent and confusing" approach.[56] As is common with memoir accounts, however, Dobrynin's is not entirely accurate.

Similar to Dobrynin's explanation, Raymond Garthoff wrote that Kissinger had "a colossal misunderstanding" out of Soviet-American discussions at the Strategic Arms Limitation Talks working groups about a so-called "accidental war" agreement and a joint Soviet-American response to a third-party nuclear "provocative attack." Without having access to the records of the Kissinger-Dobrynin exchanges, Garthoff systematically deconstructed Kissinger's memoir and described how the national security advisor made a mountain out of a molehill, equating the natural arms control discussions with a Soviet desire to form an anti-Chinese condominium with the United States as a price for a summit meeting. Garthoff pointed out that the United States had actually made a similar proposal in arms control negotiations and that he, Garthoff, had suggested to his counterpart, Vladimir Semenov, that the matter be raised informally with SALT lead Gerard Smith. Kissinger saw the raising of the "provocative war" matter as a violation of the understanding of how the back channel operated and focused on its "spy novel" tradition and "jumped to the conclusion that 'collusion against China was to be the real Soviet price for a summit.'" Garthoff argued that Kissinger missed "an attempt on the Soviet side to advance, not slow down, agreement and a summit." He continued, "This major error by Kissinger in confusing the accidental war and provocative attack proposals at the very least deprived the U.S. government of an indication that the Soviets were interested in moving toward an early summit."[57]

Although Kissinger may have misinterpreted the way the Soviets raised the "provocative attack" proposal through Semenov with Smith instead of using the back channel, the Soviets clearly delayed the summit and tried to raise the price. (Soviet-American collusion against China was not, however, the price demanded or accepted.) In 1971, the NSC staff prepared a "Top Secret/Sensitive/Eyes Only" timeline that detailed the twists and turns on the summit in the back-channel exchanges. The timeline and Dobrynin's own records corroborate that the Nixon administration actively pursued a summit meeting through 1969 and 1970, but that the Kremlin followed Dobrynin's earlier advice to drive a hard bargain. For example, at a June 23, 1970, back-channel meeting, Dobrynin told Kissinger that the Soviets wanted to have a SALT agreement but were "without instructions on [the] question of breaking [a] deadlock via [a] summit." In July 1970, Dobrynin promised to "seek guidance" on the summit from Moscow. In September 1970, a month after Vorontsov told Kissinger the summit was "under very active discussion in Moscow," Dobrynin returned from extensive consultations and said the Soviet leadership was willing to agree to the summit only "in principle."[58]

Moscow and Washington finally announced a summit on October 12, 1971, set for May 1972. Condensing a long, convoluted narrative about the trials and tribulations of planning a summit meeting, it appears that the Soviets inadvertently pushed the United States toward rapprochement with the Chinese not only by displaying their anxieties but also by inaction and delay on a Soviet-American summit meeting. Ironically, the Soviets dragged their heels on the summit just as the Pakistani channel was beginning to go online.

After an October state visit to the United States, Pakistani president Mohammed Agha Yahya Khan flew to Beijing in November 1970. Without informing his own foreign minister, Yahya conveyed a message from Richard Nixon to Chinese premier Zhou Enlai. The United States sought a secret channel with the Chinese. Zhou remarked, "We have had messages from the United States from different sources in the past, but this is the first time that a proposal has come from a Head (of State/Gov't), through a Head, to a Head!" The Pakistani channel had just gone live, and after some back-and-forth, Sino-American rapprochement began in earnest.[59] In the age of encrypted flash telegrams, electric typewriters, and burgeoning satellite communication, the handwritten dispatches delivered by courier used in the Pakistani channel seem rather quaint, but they ensured the utmost secrecy. Such methods also allowed Kissinger to catch Dobrynin unaware when he disclosed in July 1971 that he had just visited China. First, however, the Soviets would raise the stakes on a superpower summit.

As the Channel actively sought to break the SALT and Berlin impasses in 1971, the discussions on the summit initially progressed until

Gromyko linked it to Berlin during the Twenty-Fourth Party Congress in April. Again, the two men focused on issues other than China, such as the Middle East, SALT, Berlin, the summit, trade, and other matters. A brief exchange occurred in response to the March 15, 1971, State Department announcement that the United States had suspended restrictions on travel to China using American passports. According to Kissinger, the next day, "Dobrynin then asked me what was intended by the lifting of the travel restrictions to Communist China." Kissinger called the decision "routine." When Dobrynin "said he noticed that travel restrictions were lifted towards Communist China, but not towards Cuba," Kissinger replied, "This must be because we are trying to drive a wedge between Cuba and China." In response, "Dobrynin smiled sourly."[60] Otherwise, the Channel remained focused elsewhere.

After Dobrynin returned from the party congress with instructions to make the summit contingent on a Berlin accord, Nixon and Kissinger grew increasingly impatient with being the victims of Soviet linkage. On April 26, Kissinger emphasized to Dobrynin that the Kremlin should be prepared to announce a summit the next time they raised the issue.[61] Right after he met with Dobrynin, Kissinger reported to Nixon what he firmly told his counterpart:

> "You must suffer from a misapprehension. The summit must reflect mutual interests or it isn't worth doing. So, we've talked to you about it for a year. . . . Your Foreign Minister said, 'Let's not have fencing matches.' We seem to be having a fencing match. So the president has said he's . . . making his plans. When you are ready to have a summit, you let us know, but don't come to me unless you are ready to set a date, and announce it quickly." He said, "Oh no, no, we're planning on it. September, of course. We're planning on it."[62]

The next day, Kissinger and Dobrynin met in the White House in the office of one of the president's military assistants at 3:30 p.m. to discuss the evolving Berlin agreement. Although he did not know it at the time, in the middle of his meeting with Dobrynin, Kissinger received an important phone call from Pakistani ambassador Agha Hilaly requesting an urgent meeting. When Hilaly met with Kissinger in the White House later that evening, he gave Kissinger a handwritten note, forwarded by Yahya, from Zhou, which included an invitation to publicly receive "a special envoy of the president of the U.S. (for instance, Mr. Kissinger) or the U.S. Secretary of State or even the president of the U.S. himself for direct meeting and discussions."[63] The China breakthrough had finally arrived.

With the knowledge of hindsight, it appears that Kissinger wrote his memcon of the April 27 meeting with Dobrynin influenced by the great step forward on the path of Sino-American rapprochement. Kissinger, somewhat uncharacteristically, wrote in depth that the Soviets would not stand any American attempts at "blackmail" by playing China and the Soviet Union off each other:

> Dobrynin then raised the issue of China policy. He said he hoped we were not trying to blackmail the Soviet Union by the moves we were making on China. The reaction in the Soviet Union would be very violent. I said to Dobrynin that, first of all, we had not initiated the moves. Secondly, we were too realistic to believe that we could blackmail the Soviet Union. We had stated publicly on innumerable occasions that we were prepared to normalize relations with the People's Republic of China. We did not see how that could constitute any threat to the Soviet Union. Moreover, as Dobrynin well knew, there were a number of issues outstanding between us and the Soviet Union which, if resolved, would produce such an enormous improvement in our relationship that the whole issue of who was blackmailing whom would become academic.[64]

Bolstering the assertion that events may have influenced Kissinger's reporting, Dobrynin made no mention of China in his own report.[65]

Later that evening, Nixon called Kissinger with "a couple of thoughts" on whom to send as an envoy. After rattling off a list (and probably playing a mind game with Kissinger by mentioning his earlier benefactor, Nelson Rockefeller, as a potential envoy), Nixon said, "We have played a game, and we've gotten a little break here." Kissinger replied, "But we set up this . . . whole intricate web. . . . When we talked about 'linkage,' everyone was sneering. . . . But we've done it now. . . . We've got it all hooked together."

Kissinger corrected himself, "I mean, we've got Berlin hooked to SALT." After going back to the subject of envoys (again), Kissinger compared the Soviets and the Chinese. "The difference between them [the Chinese] and the Russians," Kissinger explained, "is that if you drop some loose change and try to pick it up the Russians step on your fingers and fight you for it. . . . The Chinese don't do that." The Chinese communicated on "a high level," and, Kissinger added, "if you look at the summit exchange, they haven't horsed around like the Russians."[66]

The White House mood was ebullient as Nixon and Kissinger saw three policies—détente with the Soviets, rapprochement with the Chinese, and ending American involvement in the Vietnam War—beginning to come together. In the words of Robert Dallek, "Improved relations with China were a large part of the diplomatic revolution [Nixon and Kissinger] envisioned."[67] The breakthrough with the Chinese allowed a transition for hypothetical discussions of playing the Russians and the Chinese off of each other to more concrete talk of competing summits and Nixon's first summit destination, Beijing or Moscow.

In another interesting twist, the Kissinger-Dobrynin channel lagged nearly a month behind a very public sign of improving Sino-American relations: so-called "Ping-Pong diplomacy." Early in April at the World Table Tennis Championship in Japan, the Chinese invited the U.S. team to visit China. With a great deal of media attention and public fanfare, the American team accepted, traveled to China on April 12, and met with Zhou in the Great Hall of the People on April 15.[68]

According to Dobrynin, Kissinger "noted that he would like to briefly address the issue of China" at a meeting on May 10, 1971. Kissinger believed that the U.S. media had speculated that the improvement in U.S.-Chinese relations had "anti-Soviet motives on the Administration's part." Kissinger said that Nixon had made a "special point" during a press conference in April 29 and had dismissed conjecture that "one purpose of our normalizing our relations or attempting to normalize our relations with Mainland China is to some way irritate the Soviet Union," saying, "Nothing could be further from the truth."[69]

Throwing out what turned out to be a red herring, Kissinger conceded the "possibility" that "the Ping-Pong episode and [Zhou] Enlai's reception of the American team . . . could have been prompted by the Chinese leadership's continuing rivalry with Moscow." After all, the "invitation came on the heels of the Soviet party congress. Developing a "'constructive dialogue' with Peking," he reassured Dobrynin, did not signify that the administration was in any way "hostile to the Soviet Union." The United States had important issues to address with both China and the Soviet Union. Parallel relationships would suffice. Dobrynin replied he wished to avoid "a detailed discussion of the whole subject of China." Dobrynin reported, "I went on to stress that if the U.S. nevertheless felt tempted to extract some benefit for itself in this process, at the expense of the U.S.S.R.—and there are certain indications of this—I would like to frankly warn [them] in advance that this line of conduct, if it is followed, could result in a very serious miscalculation." The veteran ambassador wrote, "On the whole, one could sense in Kissinger's statements a certain wariness and a desire on the part of the White House to somehow balance the potential impact of the latest flirtation between Washington and Peking on Soviet-U.S. relations." Either Kissinger was a good actor, or Dobrynin misread Kissinger's cues; perhaps both occurred.

Over the summer of 1971, Kissinger and Dobrynin discussed the U.S. commitment to its "two China" policy at the United Nations and began fleeting movement toward a Soviet-American summit. The China factor remained beneath the surface of the exchanges as Kissinger played his cards close to the vest and conducted his own kind of disinformation campaign with the Soviets through the back channel.[70] Nixon and Kissinger looked at the China enterprise as self-styled realists. In an Oval Office conversation on May 27, Kissinger determined to give the Soviets one month to act on the summit, before he planned to go to China on his secret mission. Nixon raised the topic:

NIXON: We have a situation here with them [the Soviets], and with the Chinese. We are still dealing with governments that are basically hostile to us.
KISSINGER: Oh, no question.
NIXON: So hostile to us that we, therefore, have got to do those things that are in our interests. And here it's cold turkey. If the sons-of-bitches don't play, fine.
KISSINGER: And, actually, I think the Russians are really, basically, gangsters as types. . . . The Chinese are a little more civilized.

NIXON: That's about all. Those Chinese are out to whip me.

KISSINGER: Oh, they're both out to get us. The difference is that the Chinese will probably go for a big knockout, while the Russians will try to bleed us to death. . . .

NIXON: If they want to play that kind of game, then all bets are off. And I think you've got to get to the summit thing faster. . . .

KISSINGER: I can do it next week.

NIXON: And, I'd put it right to 'em, hard. What the hell are they going to do?

KISSINGER: That's right. I'll tell him. But, the threat has to be there: If they can't accept it now, we won't go in September no matter what they do. . . . That's the threat we have to [make]. Otherwise it's bleeding us.[71]

Later that afternoon, Nixon and Kissinger returned to the contrast between the Chinese and the Soviets and how Moscow wanted to drive a hard bargain on the summit. Kissinger reported, "Dobrynin again this morning talked about that trade deal, that $500 million trade deal [for the Kama River Project]." Nixon replied: "Well, but he didn't raise the summit? He never raises it, does he?" Kissinger explained: "No . . . Well, no. They are very cute. They figure you're very eager, so they figure they're first going to make you pay on Berlin. Then they're going to make you pay on trade and after that they give you the summit." Nixon worried that the profusion of agreements would detract from a summit agenda: "What the hell are we going to talk about there?" Kissinger responded: "We need the summit for a number of reasons. It will discipline them during SALT."

The Soviets appeared to be backpedaling on the recently announced interim SALT agreement. "So what I think we should do is," Kissinger suggested, "it's playing dangerously, it's living dangerously, but that's how you've got where you are in foreign policy and in other things, too. . . . The thing to do is to tell, in my view, is to tell Dobrynin in early June, 'We reviewed our state of relations. Things are now moving on a number of fronts. Either you can commit yourself now for a summit in September, or we won't have one this year.'" Nixon, however, believed this posture could make the United States "appear too eager." If the Soviets did not move on the summit, Kissinger responded, "And then if they turn us down,

Mr. President, then I would drag our feet on trade on Berlin. . . . I'd certainly on trade drag our feet. Otherwise we'll have given them almost everything they need and they don't need the summit any more." Nixon liked the idea. "Hell, I'd never sign another goddamn thing for them if there isn't a summit," Nixon stated. If the Soviets did not deliver a summit, Nixon hoped the Chinese would come through, adding additional insult to the Soviets. "If we don't have a summit at all with the Russians, to hell with them. You got a deal with the Chinese? We'll go to China earlier. Why not?" Kissinger replied, "It also has the advantage that then we know where we stand."[72]

At another back-channel *tour d'horizon,* this time at Camp David on June 8, Kissinger pushed the Soviets for a response on the summit, as he had discussed with Nixon two weeks earlier. Kissinger disclosed to Dobrynin the failure of the Romanian channel with the Chinese, perhaps to throw the Soviets off the scent of improving Sino-American relations through the Pakistani channel. "In their talks to Moscow," Dobrynin stated, "the Chinese were taking a very tough line about the United States, accusing the U.S. of being the hotbed of imperialism." When Dobrynin asked if the United States had "sent a message through Ceausescu," Kissinger wrote, "I replied that there were limits to the messages third parties could carry."[73] Dobrynin described the exchange in greater detail and continued to allay the Kremlin's fears of Sino-American collusion:

> According to Kissinger, they currently have no steady contacts with Peking through any kind of intermediary. For now the contacts are only sporadic. "Ceausescu was not, at this point, carrying out any kind of special assignment for President Nixon during his recently concluded visit to the PRC." When Ceausescu had come to Washington [in October 1970], Nixon had told him in general terms of his desire to gradually normalize relations with Peking and said that he, Ceausescu, could, if he wished, inform the Chinese leadership about these sentiments of his [Nixon's]. In connection with Ceausescu's current [June 1971] trip to Peking, however, no special requests of any kind were made of him at this time.[74]

Kissinger had mixed truth, that the United States had abandoned the Romanian channel, with a lie, that the United States had "no steady contacts with Peking." Kissinger presented his ultimatum to Dobrynin and pressed him for the Soviet answer on the summit "by the end of June, or else no summit this year."[75]

The personal touch and ultimatum to Dobrynin failed to get the Soviets to reply on the summit before the end of June, but not for lack of trying on the ambassador's part. After the Camp David meeting, Dobrynin sent an extremely urgent telegram to Moscow that focused on the summit, an issue that commanded "a great deal of President Nixon's personal attention." Dobrynin reviewed his back-channel dealings with Kissinger and Gromyko's decision to link the summit to progress in the Berlin negotiations. The summit would be a political boost for Nixon "although it will scarcely be a decisive factor in the actual election," Dobrynin estimated. A summit could boost Soviet-American trade and lead to the conclusion of the ABM treaty. Vis-à-vis the Chinese, a summit could help Moscow by making it "difficult for the Chinese to launch a propaganda assault on the meeting after their celebrated 'ping-pong' flirtation with the U.S." "Such an assault," Dobrynin continued, "will inevitably affect the flirtation between Peking and Washington and slow down the normalization of Sino-U.S. relations." Dobrynin requested guidance and summarized the problem for the Soviet leadership: "The issue we now face is whether to make an actual final decision on this matter, taking into account the current situation and the possible future state of our relations with the Nixon Administration."[76] Despite Dobrynin's urging for a resolution and additional warnings from Kissinger, the Soviets failed to deliver a definitive response before July 1971. Perhaps the Soviet leadership still wanted a sealed Berlin agreement before it would acquiesce to hosting a summit.

On July 1, Kissinger met with Nixon. As Kissinger remembered: "A great deal of time was spent on the order in which the prospective summits with China and the Soviet Union might be held; we still had not heard from Moscow about a September meeting. We decided that whatever the response, the China summit would now come first."[77] That evening Kissinger departed for Islamabad via Saigon, Bangkok, and New Delhi.

On July 5, when Kissinger was in Bangkok, Haig cabled that Vorontsov had delivered the Soviet reply on the summit. Instead of affirming the summit for September 1971, the Soviets postponed the meeting. Kissinger saw this as a blessing in disguise. "The Soviets had unwittingly

Kissinger and Winston Lord, July 1971. (RNPLM)

done us an enormous favor," Kissinger later wrote. "They had outfoxed themselves. The Kremlin's reply freed us from the complexity of managing two parallel summits. Moscow could not blame us for opening first to Peking." Kissinger immediately cabled Haig to have Rush apply a back-channel brake on the Berlin negotiations.[78]

After faking a case of "Delhi belly," the dysentery not unknown in South Asia, Kissinger and two aides, John Holdridge and Winston Lord, secretly departed for Beijing on a Pakistani International Airline Boeing 707 jetliner on the evening of July 8. Kissinger met with Zhou Enlai several times during July 9–11, beginning the process of Sino-American rapprochement and paving the way for a summit and a joint announcement. The Sino-American summit details would be worked out at a later date by a special envoy (who turned out to be Kissinger). Kissinger arrived in San Clemente on July 13 and immediately briefed the president. Nixon and Kissinger then gave Secretary of State Rogers a sanitized account and assigned him the unenviable task of informing American allies about the paradigm shift.[79]

On the evening of July 15, from San Clemente, Kissinger called Dobrynin in Washington. In a smoke-and-mirrors maneuver, the White

A 1971 Herblock Cartoon.
(© The Herb Block Foundation)

GREAT LEAP FORWARD

House had summoned the ambassador to take a phone call from Kissinger on a secure line. At the prearranged time, Kissinger called Dobrynin and said: "The President asked me to call you personally. We have an oral note for your government when I am through." Giving Dobrynin a few minutes advance notice before Nixon went on national television, Kissinger read the short announcement to Dobrynin:

> Premier [Zhou Enlai] and Dr. Henry Kissinger, President Nixon's Assistant for National Security Affairs, held talks in Peking from July 9 to 11, 1971. Knowing of President Nixon's expressed desire to visit the People's Republic of China, Premier [Zhou Enlai], on behalf of the Government of the People's Republic of China, has extended an invitation to President Nixon to visit China at an appropriate date before May 1972. President Nixon has accepted this invitation with pleasure. The meeting between the leaders of China and the United States is to seek the normalization of relations between the two countries and also to exchange views on questions of concern to the two sides.

The president's military aide, Col. Richard Kennedy, then handed Dobrynin an oral note, that stated that the United States was "willing to continue, and indeed to speed up, the process" toward a Soviet-American summit. The China announcement was "not directed against any countries." It continued, "The President very much hopes that the Government of the Soviet Union will choose to join with the United States in a policy of furthering and accelerating the positive developments in their relations." Kissinger then applied the back-channel button, beyond the oral note:

> Your recent decision to delay [the date for such a summit] has caused us to proceed [first with the announcement the president is making this evening]. . . . This announcement changes nothing in U.S.-Soviet relations. We can take [one of] two routes— We can proceed promptly with the various subjects you and I have discussed and which we are hereby reaffirming, or we can both undertake agonizing reappraisal. We are prepared for either course, though we prefer to proceed on our present course.[80]

Two days later, Dobrynin sent the Kremlin his analysis of the Sino-American breakthrough, an event "unquestionably of major international significance, with potentially broad consequences for regions such as Southeast Asia and the Far East, as well as for relationships within the USSR–PRC–U.S. triangle." Dobrynin then described the motivating factors behind Nixon's approach to the PRC. First, the ambassador surmised, the president desired "to exploit Soviet-Chinese differences to the maximum and to deepen and intensify them whenever possible." Second, he called Nixon an "unscrupulous" political animal, who had a "tremendous desire to be re-elected president in 1972." Vietnam, of course, remained central. The opening to China would allow Nixon to "greatly reduce pressure from his own public opinion for a prompt solution of the Vietnam issue and withdrawal of U.S. troops." In response, Dobrynin recommended that Moscow use Nixon's political desires for reelection to moderate American behavior, veil Soviet anxieties about Sino-American relations, and stick to Soviet interests in dealings with the administration. Soviet-American relations, Dobrynin contended, transcended others because they were increasingly global in nature while the Chinese were only a regional force.[81]

After meeting with Dobrynin on the morning of July 19, Kissinger told Nixon: "Well, I told Dobrynin I was beginning to doubt that there is a God, because I lied to him. I'm sure that if there were one, I would have been punished." Nixon laughed. Kissinger noted that when Dobrynin had raised the timing of a U.S.-Soviet summit: "I said to him, 'I told you 6 months ago that we couldn't do it in November and December. So when you said you wanted it in November and December, well, the president had to assume that this was a nice way out of turning him down.' He said, 'No, no, no, no we want it. We very much want it.'" Later in the conversation, Kissinger added: "[Dobrynin] said, 'Would you be willing to come before going to Peking?' I said, 'Anatol, it's not dignified.'" Kissinger continued, "I said, 'We have to go now in the order in which we announce it.' He said, 'Would you be willing to announce it before you go to Peking?' I said, 'Well, I've got to show it to the president.'" Kissinger concluded, "I think they're going to come to us. I think we can announce the Moscow summit before you go to Peking, and that would actually help."

Nixon and Kissinger also discussed how to firm up the dates with both the Chinese and the Soviets and when to make specific announcements for the two summits. "And the sequence that I now see is that I might go to Peking at the end of September," Kissinger stated. "Get the damn thing locked up—" Nixon interrupted, "then announce it." Kissinger continued, "—then announce the summit for Peking. Then, while I'm in Peking, tell them that you're going to announce the summit for Moscow. And then, at the end of October, announce the summit for Moscow for the end of March." The announcement of a Beijing summit would reinforce the Soviet desire for a Moscow summit, just as the announcement of the Moscow summit would reinforce the Chinese desire for a Beijing summit. Neither Communist power wished to be the odd man out.

Kissinger commented that the prospect of holding summits in both Beijing and Moscow would be "one spectacular after another" for domestic and foreign audiences. He explained, "I think they [the North Vietnamese] have got to settle now." Returning to the introduction of Chinese pressure on the Soviets, Kissinger recounted: "[Dobrynin] asked, 'What can you really settle with the Chinese?' He said, 'I thought we were your natural partners in Southeast Asia. We're both trying to avoid Chinese expansion in Southeast Asia.'"

Kissinger indicated that Dobrynin's demeanor had changed with the Sino-American opening: "He talked to me with a respect that I hadn't encountered before." Nixon asked, "Was he shaken?" Kissinger replied, "A

A 1971 Herblock Cartoon.
(© The Herb Block Foundation)

bit shaken." In addition to his changed tone, Dobrynin gave an optimistic assessment of the state of U.S.-Soviet negotiations. Kissinger reported: "Oh, he said, 'SALT is going along fine. Berlin is going along fine.'" Kissinger thought that Dobrynin's optimism was a marked departure from before the secret trip, when, Kissinger now told Nixon, "He just thought he had you on the run."[82]

Dobrynin, however, produced a contemporaneous account of his July 19 meeting with Kissinger that differs significantly from Kissinger's. According to Dobrynin, Kissinger was the one "impatiently waiting" to raise the subject of his secret trip, while he also negatively assessed the state of U.S.-Soviet relations. Dobrynin recounted that "Kissinger greatly lamented the serious difficulties that have existed and continue to exist 'at the psychological level' in establishing between the president and the Soviet leadership the necessary personal mutual understanding and unbiased assessment of each other's motives," though he did hope to "overcome this psychological barrier."[83]

Kissinger later remembered that the "authentic Soviet response was diplomatic, not propagandistic. . . . Other negotiations deadlocked for months began magically to unfreeze: Berlin, for example, and the talks to guard against accidental nuclear war . . . both these negotiations moved rapidly to completion within weeks of the Peking announcement."[84] The opening to China did not just result in Soviet moves toward cooperation with the Nixon administration; the administration itself became more accommodating, recognizing that the new pressure on the Soviets could result in improved relations with both Beijing and Moscow.

As the Soviets regrouped to improve relations with the United States in the wake of the China announcement, back channels continued and expanded in importance. First, Nixon began a personal correspondence with Brezhnev in August 1971, to discuss the major areas of concern in Soviet-American relations. Meanwhile, the back-channel discussions between Kissinger and Dobrynin became more strident and worked out a joint announcement for a summit meeting in Moscow. Unforeseen consequences of the China announcement also occurred when the Soviet Union and India bolstered diplomatic and military ties almost immediately. The increasing back-channel communication between the United States and the Soviet Union came just as stirrings of war in South Asia threatened to become a watershed in superpower relations.

Kissinger as a Special Emissary to Moscow

Kissinger used the opening to China as a springboard to enhance his own prestige; building off the newfound fame, Kissinger also cemented the role of the Channel with the Soviets. The back-channel exchanges relating to China and pushing for a summit were also connected to the idea of having Kissinger go to Moscow as a special emissary to set up a summit or communicate directly with the Soviet leadership. Kissinger's and Dobrynin's accounts sharply contrast on the idea. The divergence is also noteworthy because it started so early in the back channel. The record suggests that Kissinger put himself forward to increase his own prominence within the administration and to centralize the conduct of Soviet-American relations in 1969.

On June 11, 1969, Kissinger wrote to Nixon, off-handedly mentioning the idea at the end of a memo reporting his latest meeting with Dobrynin. Kissinger explained: "Dobrynin . . . asked whether I might be willing to come to Moscow sometime very quietly to explain your thinking to Kosygin and Brezhnev. I told Dobrynin that this would have to be discussed with you but that if it were for the right issue, you would almost certainly entertain the proposition." Dobrynin's account made no mention of the unusual and early suggestion of having Kissinger go to Moscow to talk to the Soviet leadership.[85]

Two years later, after he had gone to China as the president's personal emissary and the Moscow summit had been announced, Kissinger wrote that Dobrynin had approached him again on the idea of an advance trip to Moscow. "Gromyko had been very much impressed by his conversation with me," Kissinger reported on November 18, 1971, "and he felt that it would advance the Summit significantly if I go there." The secretary of state "had already asked twice to be invited" so "the issue was all the more urgent." Kissinger then downplayed the idea, saying "a secret visit would . . . leave an impression of collusion."[86]

Dobrynin, on the other hand, wrote that Kissinger "intimated that he would very much like to visit Moscow." "After emphasizing the extreme sensitivity of this matter several times," Dobrynin noted, "Kissinger asked, in the event of our possible response in this connection that it be conveyed directly to him alone, bypassing all diplomatic channels. He also urged that his interest in making a trip to Moscow not be mentioned anywhere."[87] Was the insistence on the highest secrecy and that the "possible response" be "conveyed directly to him" bureaucratic maneuvering on Kissinger's part? It is impossible to know for certain, but the consistency and back-channel angle suggest that Kissinger used the Channel as a tool to maneuver through the byzantine halls of power in Washington, and he wielded it very effectively.

Sino-American rapprochement continued to affect Soviet-American back channels. Despite Dobrynin's counsel to avoid displaying concern about the American opening to China, the Kremlin continued to keep tabs on progress in Washington's moves toward Beijing. Some matters of controversy arose, such as U.S. intelligence sharing with the Chinese about the disposition of Soviet forces along their borders to the North and West. When Soviet intelligence discovered that the United States had shared satellite reconnaissance with the Chinese during the Beijing Summit, Dobrynin raised the issue with Kissinger. Kissinger, of course, denied that it had taken place.[88]

Americans hardly had to provoke the Russians with their overtures toward the Chinese; the Soviets repeatedly demonstrated the linkage themselves. For example, in a briefing on March 1, 1972, which Dobrynin requested in order to discuss Nixon's February 1972 trip to China, he could not hide Soviet insecurities. Kissinger told Nixon that Dobrynin "asked a number of specific questions about the Chinese attitudes toward the Soviet Union." Following discussion about the China trip, the Middle East, and SALT, "Dobrynin then reaffirmed the Soviet Union's extreme interest in having a successful summit in Moscow."[89]

The back channel became the primary medium by which the United States and the Soviet Union telegraphed their anxieties and motivations. Dobrynin early recognized Nixon's desire for a summit meeting, especially as a boost in American domestic politics, and suggested that the Kremlin exploit that desire by driving a hard bargain. The tactic worked for over two years but backfired when Gromyko set the Berlin settlement as the price for a summit meeting. The Soviet desire to raise the price for a summit became an inadvertent push factor in Sino-American rapprochement, in addition to natural reasons for Washington and Beijing to seek improved relations with each other. In fact, the Soviet position reaffirmed Nixon's natural inclination to take a "tough" line with them and reinforced the wisdom of pursuing a Chinese summit first—an option made viable by the Chinese.

Likewise, the Soviets telegraphed their anxieties about China and alerted the Nixon administration that triangular diplomacy could be more than theoretical. There were hints as early as 1969, but not through American actions. Rather, it was Chinese agency that allowed the Nixon administration to recognize that there was a realistic option with the Chinese. After all, it was Chinese miscalculation that provoked the first clash with the Soviets along the Ussuri River and caused Soviet anxiety. The net effect was one of the rationales behind the improvement in Sino-American relations. Aside from dueling summit meetings with Beijing and Moscow, however, triangular diplomacy was more about playing off Soviet and Chinese perceptions rather than competing interests. Following the advent of Ping-Pong diplomacy and the activation of the Pakistani channel, Nixon and Kissinger began to turn abstract theoretical ideas into a more sophisticated concept of triangular diplomacy, playing the stronger power off the weaker.

Ironically, the U.S. opening to China became one of the driving forces in the move toward the Moscow summit. First, however, there would be complications that nearly derailed détente.

4

Divergent Channels

A "Watershed" on the Subcontinent

> Mr. President, by next October people will say: "What India-Paki-
> stan crisis?" if the Democrats want to make an issue of it. . . . When
> the history is written, this will look like one of our better maneuvers.
> —Henry Kissinger, March 31, 1972

India and Pakistan already had a generation of conflict between them by
the time Richard Nixon assumed the presidency in January 1969. Tensions had abounded following the British withdrawal from the Subcontinent in 1947 and its subsequent partition. The partition resulted in two
countries defined largely by religion: the Muslim-majority country of
Pakistan, and the larger, Hindu-majority country of India. Pakistan was
in a geographically tenuous position from its inception, being divided into
western and eastern wings, separated by more than one thousand miles
astride India. Other than Islam, little united the two wings, with ethnic
Punjabis dominating West Pakistan, and Bengalis making up the majority of East Pakistan. Enmity between India and Pakistan arising from
a variety of religious, political, and territorial disputes, particularly over
Kashmir province, had resulted in two wars; one in 1947, another in 1965.
Further complicating matters, India had standing disputes with China
that had resulted in a Sino-Indian war in 1962.

Lack of enthusiasm for a South Asian "complication" notwithstanding, the Nixon administration faced a crisis on the Subcontinent due to a
collision of natural disaster and human miscalculation that resulted in a
third war between India and Pakistan, in addition to the birth of Bangladesh from what had been Pakistan's eastern wing.[1] In his 1978 memoirs,

President Nixon framed the U.S. response in Cold War terms as a success: "By using diplomatic signals and behind-the-scenes pressures we had been able to save West Pakistan from the imminent threat of Indian aggression and domination. We had also once again avoided a major confrontation with the Soviet Union."[2]

Kissinger's far more detailed chapter on the U.S. "tilt" to Pakistan in the first volume of his memoirs, *White House Years,* complements and largely corroborates Nixon's account. Kissinger argued that Nixon did not want to "squeeze" Pakistani president Agha "Yahya" Khan and tried to put forward a neutral posture to the bloodshed in East Pakistan that was initially triggered by a severe flooding and a cyclone, the worst natural disasters of the twentieth century. Nixon did not want to encourage secessionist elements in Pakistan, a Cold War ally, but above all, before his secret trip to China in July 1971, Kissinger wanted to preserve the special channel to the PRC. Kissinger saw three obstacles to handling the situation in South Asia: "the policy of India, our own public debate, and the indiscipline of our bureaucracy." Kissinger stressed that the United States attempted to restrain India by making clear American opposition to Indo-Pakistani conflict and attempting to enlist Soviet assistance with their ally, India, toward the same goal.

The August 1971 Indo-Soviet Treaty of Peace, Friendship, and Cooperation on the heels of Kissinger's groundbreaking trip to China was, in Kissinger's view, a particular cause for alarm because it "deliberately steered nonaligned India toward a de facto alliance with the Soviet Union" and enabled India to take an uncompromising stance against the instability in Pakistan. Kissinger faulted Indian intransigence, interference in East Pakistan, and a refusal to negotiate on substantive matters, rather than Pakistani provocations, as the precipitating causes of the Indo-Pakistani War of 1971. Kissinger also believed the crisis had been solved at the edge of an abyss by the various messages sent through confidential channels (including the White House–Kremlin "Hot Line") and diplomatic channels to the Soviet Union, which allegedly led to the Indian acceptance of a cease-fire and the preservation of West Pakistan. Kissinger maintained that Indian restraint on attacking West Pakistan was, without a doubt, due to "a reluctant decision resulting from Soviet pressure, which in turn grew out of American insistence, including the fleet movement and the willingness to risk the [May 1972 Moscow] summit."[3]

Nearly every other account has faulted the Nixon administration's handling of the crisis, for its tilt to the dictatorial and arguably genocidal regime of Pakistani president Yahya Khan, its anti-Indian bias, its distorted reading of intelligence, and its claim that the United States "saved" West Pakistan by challenging democratic India and the Soviet Union. Critics have further charged that Nixon acted recklessly by sending Task Force 74, a flotilla led by the nuclear-powered aircraft carrier USS *Enterprise,* to the Indian Ocean at the height of the war, thereby exacerbating tensions and risking broader conflict between competing alliances, with India and the Soviet Union on one side, the United States, PRC, and Pakistan on the other.[4]

The charges levied by critics trace their origin to investigative journalist Jack Anderson's Pulitzer Prize–winning syndicated columns in December 1971–January 1972 that documented the Nixon administration's "tilt" toward Pakistan. Anderson's exposé was based on a selection of sensitive, high-level, leaked documents he had obtained from the White House. The most damaging sources Anderson obtained came from the Washington Special Action Group (WSAG), the National Security Council–based policy body that addressed the South Asian crisis. In his 1973 book *The Anderson Papers,* which further expanded the critique of the Nixon-Kissinger South Asia policy, the journalist charged: "Richard Nixon brought the United States to the edge of another world war. His actions were deliberate; he operated in secret; and he lied to the American people about his actions."[5]

Those critical of Nixon's policy have dominated the historiography of the episode on the Subcontinent and have largely followed Anderson's groundbreaking work, adding new insights based on documentary evidence as it became available over the last four decades. The critics range from former State Department officials such as Christopher Van Hollen and William Bundy, to memoirists like Dobrynin and Indian foreign secretary T. N. Kaul, to journalists, biographers, and historians. Kissinger biographers number among the critics and include investigative reporter Seymour Hersh, former *Time* magazine editor Walter Isaacson, and Finnish scholar Jussi Hanhimäki. In 2007, two volumes of the official documentary series *Foreign Relations of the United States,* produced by the State Department, joined excellent, earlier volumes produced by F. S. Aijazuddin and Roedad Khan.[6]

Documentary materials released since the early 2000s corroborate details of both sides and suggest that the Nixon administration's handling of the crisis on the Subcontinent was neither the abject failure depicted by critics nor the success that Nixon and Kissinger presented in their memoirs. Although Nixon and Kissinger superimposed a Cold War distortion on a regional situation, tried to spin stories in the media, and allowed personal biases to flavor their responses, they responded logically and perhaps justifiably when seen in the broader context of U.S.-Soviet relations. The Nixon administration steadily escalated diplomatic signals, and the top policymakers sincerely believed that India—not Pakistan—had launched external aggression with its support for Mukti Bahini (literally, "liberation force") raids into what was then East Pakistan.

Several additional themes run through Nixon and Kissinger's response to the Indo-Pakistan War, many of which were also reflected in U.S.-Soviet back-channel communications and in the taped conversations. Not surprisingly, Nixon and Kissinger's policy perceptions were clearly colored by their personal experiences with Indira Gandhi and Yahya Khan. The White House was unwilling to dismiss Yahya's role as an honest broker in Sino-American rapprochement and likewise saw duplicity on the part of Indira Gandhi after she visited Washington, D.C., in early November 1971 and claimed that India had no desire for war with Pakistan. In addition, the surreptitiously recorded conversations between the president and his advisors are rife with gendered speech and appeals to masculine "toughness" that colored Nixon's actions. Significantly, the frequent contact with the Soviets during the war mitigates some of the criticism of recklessness.

The tapes and communications with the Soviets also demonstrate that Nixon and Kissinger believed that the war started on November 21, 1971, in contrast to the date most often cited, December 3, 1971, when Pakistan struck forward Indian airbases. The tapes and back-channel records show that Nixon and Kissinger believed in November–December 1971 that an Indian attack could result in the "dismemberment" and Balkanization of West Pakistan. The Nixon administration attempted to spin the stories on the war to downplay American involvement on Pakistan's behalf, and due to the reliance on back-channel diplomacy, it is understandable that the administration's actions were criticized at the time for the sharp dichotomy between the public and private lines. Lastly, the experience

Nixon met with Indian prime minister Indira Gandhi on November 4–5, 1971. The Indians and Soviets had signed a twenty-five-year Treaty of Peace, Friendship, and Cooperation in August, on the heels on Kissinger's secret July 1971 trip to the People's Republic of China. When she met with Nixon, Gandhi assured the president that India wanted to avoid another war with Pakistan. The Indo-Pakistani War of 1971 was a litmus test for détente that pitted the United States, Pakistan, and China on one side against India and the Soviet Union on the other. The White House and the Kremlin kept in close touch via confidential channels. (RNPLM)

of the Nixon White House during the South Asian crisis reinforced earlier lessons of the Jordanian and Cienfuegos crises of 1970 that the Soviets would attempt to gain at American expense wherever they could and encouraged the Nixon administration to take a hard line with the Soviets.

Although the examination of the episode allows a more nuanced understanding of U.S policy and the important role of back-channel diplomacy, it cannot comprehensively address the multifaceted 1971 South Asian crisis and war because the situation on the ground outpaced Washington's and Moscow's efforts to manage the crisis at the time. Until high-level Indian materials, Indo-Soviet exchanges, Soviet Politburo meetings, and other sources become available—if ever—the complete story will remain out of reach. In addition, the larger moral issues in the Nixon administration's failure to condemn Pakistani atrocities, and the hypocrisy of most of the actors involved in the South Asian crisis and war, are beyond the scope of this study on U.S.-Soviet back-channel diplomacy. Fortunately, Princeton professor Gary Bass has addressed these ethical issues with clarity in *The Blood Telegram: Nixon, Kissinger, and a Forgotten Genocide.*[7]

In response to the crisis on the Subcontinent, starting in March 1971, Kissinger initially used his channel with Dobrynin to telegraph the theme that the United States and Soviet Union had "parallel interests" in trying to dissuade Pakistan and India from conflict. Following the announcement of Kissinger's "Polo I" trip to China in July 1971, and the signing of the Indo-Soviet Treaty of Peace, Friendship, and Cooperation less than a month later, the Channel shifted to urging the Soviets to restrain their Indian ally. The U.S.-Soviet dialogue on India increasingly echoed the U.S.-Soviet dialogue on Vietnam, in which the United States urged the Soviet Union to restrain North Vietnam from launching an offensive against South Vietnam. The general pronouncements about restraint became specific when the administration pushed Yahya to accept a mutual withdrawal of forces from Pakistani-Indian borders (in both East and West Pakistan) so as to minimize the possibilities of provocation by either side.

With Ambassador Dobrynin absent from Washington during the peak of the crisis and throughout the duration of the war (November 21–December 16), the primary interlocutor of U.S.-Soviet communication shifted to Soviet charge d'affaires Yuli Vorontsov. From the outset of the war, the Nixon administration decided that it would handle the

public American response primarily through the United Nations, in concert with the recently admitted People's Republic of China, while using
back channels to the Soviets, the Chinese, the Pakistanis, and the Indians
behind the scenes. Following the outbreak of hostilities between India
and Pakistan on November 21, Nixon and Kissinger shifted to the issue
of preserving West Pakistan, since the two men had reason to believe that
India sought to destroy both West and East Pakistan.

As the war proceeded, with disastrous results for Pakistan, the White
House made largely symbolic gestures in its frequent exchanges with the
Soviets. On December 9, Nixon and Kissinger invited the highest-ranking
Soviet personage available in the United States, Soviet agriculture minister Vladimir Matskevich, to the White House to convey the seriousness
with which the United States would view an Indian attack on West Pakistan, citing an informal security agreement made during the Kennedy
administration. Nixon upped the ante by dispatching the USS *Enterprise*
task group to the Indian Ocean, activated the Washington-Moscow hotline, and sent increasingly strident warnings to Brezhnev. Kissinger simultaneously hinted that an unsatisfactory Soviet response on India-Pakistan
would imperil the upcoming Moscow summit, to which the Soviets had
committed. The efforts to achieve a cease-fire in the United Nations
ground to a halt, and the dispute was ultimately settled by force of arms
when India accepted Pakistan's surrender on December 16.

The Indo-Pakistani War called into question the burgeoning U.S.-
Soviet détente. Additionally, a confluence of events brought into question
Kissinger's emotional stability and the viability of Nixon's reliance on the
national security advisor as his primary agent in the web of back channels. The reasons for this are fourfold: the long-standing friction between
Kissinger and the State Department; a growing sense that the United
States had not acted forcefully enough with the Soviets or the Indians to
avert the war; the Anderson leaks and the resultant press criticism; and the
discovery of the Anderson leak by the White House "Plumbers" investigation, which revealed that the Joint Chiefs of Staff (JCS) had been spying on Kissinger and the NSC through a navy yeoman, Charles Radford,
assigned to the JCS-NSC liaison office.

In the closing days of 1971, Nixon also worried aloud about Kissinger
suffering an emotional collapse, but he was determined to press ahead
with détente. Nixon told Haldeman and his chief domestic advisor, John

Ehrlichman, during a dramatic Christmas Eve conversation: "[Kissinger] is extremely valuable to us. He is indispensable at this point because of the China trip . . . and to a lesser extent the Russia trip. Rogers is not. But the point is that we cannot have Henry having an emotional collapse."[8] He further explained that the situation on the Subcontinent involved "unwashed heathen . . . picking away at each other over there" and that Kissinger need not overreact to the press criticism. Two hours later, Nixon asked Kissinger's former benefactor, Nelson Rockefeller, to reassure Kissinger: "Tell him to pay no attention to this nitpicking by people how we handled it. . . . Hell, India-Pakistan[,] there's no way it's ever going to come out and thank God we didn't get involved in the war. . . . And thank God we saved West Pakistan, which we did."[9]

Ultimately, rather than question the back-channel dealings that had failed to stave off the India-Pakistan conflict in the first place, Nixon further entrenched the use of back channels, his reliance on Kissinger as the primary implementer of policy, and bypassing the State Department on détente. Nixon saw Kissinger as indispensable and minimized the significance of alleged failures as the price to pay to conduct secret diplomacy and achieve breakthroughs.

In 1969, the Pakistani military removed Ayub Khan from power in a bloodless coup and installed the army chief of staff, Gen. Agha Yahya Khan (Yahya), as the chief martial law administrator. Yahya promised to restore democracy in Pakistan by scheduling elections for October 1970, and he began preparing the country for the election with a series of administrative reforms and regulations under the aegis of martial law. Yahya simultaneously created a dubious legal framework to retain power if the election did not turn out favorably.[10]

In addition to the enormous human suffering, massive flooding in August 1970 and a devastating cyclone in November, both disasters in East Pakistan, put the two wings on a trajectory of dissolution as Yahya postponed the elections until December 7, and East Pakistani discontent against the central government grew.[11] The rescheduled elections proved beyond a shadow of doubt that East and West Pakistan were divided by more than the thousand-mile distance between them. The uneven distribution of resources, tax burdens, ethnic differences, and a growing secessionist movement in East Pakistan had complicated the existence of Pakistan since partition.[12] Yahya's plan to democratize worked all too well because it shifted the election from rules based on parity, which had favored the geographically larger but less populated West Pakistan, to a system of direct elections based on population. The actual election results accurately reflected Kissinger's famous dining room quip to Yahya that, "for a dictator you run a lousy election."[13]

Voters returned an overwhelming victory for the nominally secession-ist Awami League (AL) under Sheikh Mujibur Rahman (Mujib) in East Pakistan.[14] Due to the comparatively large population of East Pakistan, Yahya's earlier structural reforms and the overwhelming electoral victory of 167 out of 169 seats in East Pakistan, the Awami League actually had a majority of seats for *both* East and West Pakistan. In West Pakistan, the Pakistani People's Party (PPP), led by Zulfikar Ali Bhutto, emerged as the strongest faction and proclaimed its support for the military and a united Pakistan.

By March 1971, the situation had degenerated in East Pakistan, and civil war loomed on the horizon after negotiations between Yahya, Bhutto, and Mujib broke down over power sharing and the federal structure for a new Pakistani constitution. There is some disagreement over who deserves blame, but in the end Yahya twice postponed and ultimately refused to seat the newly elected assembly charged with drafting a new constitu-tion.[15] In response to the second postponement, Mujib called a general strike across East Pakistan, and, in the words of scholar Sumit Ganguly: "The response to his call was overwhelming: it paralyzed the economy of the East. Mujib had started, what he had described as, a 'non-violent, non-cooperation movement,' but this movement quickly became violent."[16] Despite initial progress in negotiations between Yahya and Mujib in mid-March, by March 24 Bhutto refused to cooperate with the AL and the stage was set for confrontation.

After the breakdown in negotiations and moves toward East Paki-stani independence, Yahya initiated Operation Searchlight on March 25, 1971, and ordered Mujib's arrest. Although indigenous violence occurred in East Pakistan after Yahya's refusal to seat the new legislators and restore civilian control of the government, on Yahya's orders the Pakistani Army began a brutal crackdown to control the 75 million inhabitants in East Pakistan in what some have described as a policy of genocide.

The "Blood telegram"—which took its name from its author, the

U.S. consulate general in Dacca, Archer Blood—to the State Department on April 6, 1971, registered "strong dissent" against the lack of a U.S. response to the brutality of Operation Searchlight. Blood wrote: "Our government has failed to denounce the suppression of democracy. Our government has failed to denounce atrocities. . . . Our government has evidenced what many will consider moral bankruptcy. . . . But we have chosen not to intervene, even morally, on the grounds that the Awami conflict, in which unfortunately the overworked term genocide is applicable, is purely internal matter of sovereign state."[17]

The same day, Secretary of State Rogers informed Kissinger: "Our people in Dacca . . . bitched about our policy and have given it lots of distribution so it will probably leak. It's inexcusable." Kissinger repeated the charge in his memoir that the "Blood telegram" was deliberately given a low classification so that it would leak, and he depicted the telegram as bureaucratic dissent from established White House policy.[18] There was no discussion that the concerns Blood raised were valid, nor was there a reconsideration of U.S. policy.[19]

Kissinger reported the results of Operation Searchlight in a telephone conversation with the president on March 29, 1971: "The use of power against seeming odds pays off. 'Cause all the experts were saying that 30,000 people can't get control of 75 million. Well, this may still turn out to be true, but as of this moment it seems to be quiet." Nixon replied: "Well maybe things have changed. But hell, when you look over the history of nations 30,000 well-disciplined people can take 75 million any time. . . . Look what the British did when they took India."[20] American policymaking circles assessed that while the Pakistani military had gained control in the short term, force alone could not indefinitely stabilize the situation. Whether or not Operation Searchlight actually demonstrated the suitability of a smaller "well disciplined" force to quash civil unrest, the massive dislocation, including murder and rape, sent millions of refugees streaming across the border to India and threatened regional instability.

Throughout March 1971, Kissinger discussed the problems on the Subcontinent with Ambassador Dobrynin, who, in turn, dutifully reported the exchanges back to Moscow.[21] According to Dobrynin, after a March 15, 1971, meeting, Kissinger had informed him that the White House was concerned about Pakistan breaking apart and the United States was concerned about the "overall balance of power" in the region. Although Dobrynin did not describe his own response during the discussion, he reported that the Nixon White House wanted to preserve "a united Pakistan."[22] In a meeting the following week, Dobrynin noted Kissinger's fear that if Pakistan "were to split apart, West Pakistan would end up in the hands of Bhutto and his supporters, i.e., it would fall squarely into China's sphere of influence, and this would run counter to U.S. interests."[23] Kissinger continued to push the back-channel button on China, trying to enlist Soviet assistance to preserve a united Pakistan.

The refugee crisis that grew out of the repression in East Pakistan precipitated another Indo-Pakistani war in the winter of 1971 and internationalized the crisis. The massive influx of refugees from East Pakistan added enormous political and economic pressure on the Indian state of West Bengal and was almost immediately seen as a threat to India's internal stability.[24] Before the refugee problem turned into a major humanitarian crisis, however, Bengalis in East Pakistan proclaimed independence for the new nation of Bangladesh on March 26.

Indira Gandhi, bolstered by a decisive electoral victory for her Congress Party that March, was determined to address the growing refugee problem by supporting Bangladesh independence for a number of reasons. The publicly stated motivation was humanitarian and pragmatic, due to the millions of refugees who had fled repression in East Pakistan by June 1971.[25] By fanning the flames of Bangladeshi independence, however, she no doubt hoped to solve the two-decade-long security dilemma of a two-front conflict with the two Pakistani wings. Complicating matters and increasing the risk of war, India helped establish a Bangladeshi government-in-exile on April 13, 1971, and began training and providing covert support of pro-independence guerrillas known as the Mukti Bahini in cross-border reprisals against the Pakistani Army.[26] In the words of one scholar, Gandhi hoped "to exploit a window of opportunity" against Pakistan.[27] Despite appeals to the international community and after accepting foreign assistance packages, the largest from the United States, India refused to allow independent observers on-site. Adding to its own share of the conflict, West Pakistan refused to release Mujib and remained determined to prevent even a modicum of independence for East Pakistan. The long-standing Indo-Pakistani dispute over Kashmir and the fear of ethnic fragmentation of West Pakistan exacerbated the fears and compounded the problems for all interested parties.

In the case of the Indo-Pakistani War, the tangled web of a regional conflict between hostile neighbors was projected onto the backdrop of perceived superpower conflict. The episode on the Subcontinent highlights a number of back-channel relationships simultaneously in play during the crisis and war and occasionally with divergent aims. U.S.-Soviet exchanges on the deteriorating situation and war in South Asia demonstrated the Nixon administration's marked preference for the back channels to communicate policy goals with the Soviet Union. Records made available in the last decade show that Nixon and Kissinger directed policy from the White House during the crisis but used the State Department to send messages through official channels and to build a public relations case for action in the United Nations.[28] Moreover, Nixon and Kissinger distrusted the "bureaucracy" at the State Department, a view reinforced by actions such as the Blood telegram and a perceived pro-Indian bias, but they still relied on higher-level Department officials, such as Secretary of State Rogers and Assistant Secretary of State for Near Eastern and South Asian Affairs Joseph Sisco. Although the U.S. response was more complex than either supporters or detractors have argued, it is clear that the administration used back channels to convey their desire to use Soviet influence to contain the Indians, and to contain the potential risks of the regional conflict expanding into a superpower conflict due to entangling alliances and obligations.

The White House initially believed that India wanted to avoid conflict and argued for several months that the United States and the Soviet Union had "parallel interests" in trying to prevent an Indo-Pakistani war. At the same time, American policymakers realistically recognized that the refugee crisis could be the first step down the road to conflict. In May 1971, Samuel Hoskinson and Richard Kennedy of the National Security Council Staff summarized the situation for Kissinger: "In the short run at least we share a strong interest with the Soviets in avoiding another Indo-Pak war." On the basis of "a so-called 'special relationship' with New Delhi," the NSC staffers asked: "Is it possible and desirable to encourage the Soviets to play a peacemaking role? Or would some sort of consultation and joint, or at least parallel, action with the Soviets be more in our interests?"[29]

The theme of "parallel interests" also entered into the Kissinger-Dobrynin channel. At Nixon's request, Kissinger invited Dobrynin to Camp David on June 10, for a *tour d'horizon* of U.S.-Soviet relations.[30] After the June 8, 1971, meeting, Dobrynin reported back to Moscow that with regard to the brewing Indo-Pakistani crisis, Kissinger claimed that Washington had "reliable information" that India "has still not rejected the idea of providing armed assistance to East Pakistan." To counter the threat of an Indian attack, "the U.S. Government made a serious, confidential representation to Indira Gandhi when Delhi 'was on the verge of making a fateful decision.'" Dobrynin cabled, "Apparently, this had an effect and removed the immediate threat of an armed conflict between India and Pakistan." Kissinger hoped to convey that "President Nixon assumes that the Soviet Union is guided by similar, parallel interests in preventing such an armed conflict."[31]

Several weeks before departing on his secret trip to China, Kissinger informed Dobrynin that he had been instructed by President Nixon to "visit Delhi and confidentially, but in the strongest terms, call Indira Gandhi's attention to the fact that the U.S. takes a very serious view of this dangerous Indian course of action and the serious consequences associated with it." In the event of an Indo-Pakistani war, Kissinger warned that the United States would "cut off all future economic aid to India." Dobrynin reported back to the Kremlin: "In short, Kissinger summarized, the U.S. Government is for maintaining the territorial status quo between India and Pakistan while at the same time seeking a political solution to the problems that have arisen." Once again, Kissinger had stressed the parallel interests of the United States and the Soviet Union and "made it clear that the president [considered] the confidential exchange of views on this matter between him and the Soviet leadership to be useful," noting that it would "revisit this issue" after Kissinger's return from Asia.[32]

Dobrynin was one of the first people Kissinger met with following the startling revelation that he had visited Communist China and had secured a summit meeting with the world's most populous nation. Among many other topics in their July 19, 1971, meeting, the two men candidly discussed the continuing crisis in South Asia. Kissinger began his report to the president with the line: "Dobrynin was at his oily best and, for the first time in my experience with him, totally insecure." On India-Pakistan, Kissinger charged that he "had heard some reports that the

Soviet Union might encourage military adventures by India." Kissinger said, "Dobrynin answered that the Soviet Union was giving them political support but was strongly trying to discourage military adventures." Kissinger then explained that "a war between India and Pakistan could not be localized to East Pakistan." Dobrynin acknowledged this concern and noted, "Of course, the Pakistanis consider East Pakistan an integral part of their country, just as the Soviets consider the Ukraine or [the United States] consider[s] Alaska." Due to the risks of a conflict expanding, Dobrynin claimed that the Soviets were also "trying to localize it."[33]

In response to the U.S. opening to China, India took the diplomatic initiative by tilting toward the Soviet Union, taking out an insurance policy of sorts.[34] Dusting off a treaty that had been negotiated but never concluded, D. P. Dhar, Indian ambassador to the Soviet Union and a close associate of Indira Gandhi, traveled to Moscow in late July 1971 and quickly concluded the Indo-Soviet Treaty of Peace, Friendship, and Cooperation on August 9.[35] This development signified the first shift in the Soviet position on the crisis away from U.S.-Soviet "parallel interests." Indo-Soviet collusion expanded and was, perhaps, an unintended consequence of U.S. geopolitical paradigm shift toward China, in addition to being a brilliant Indian realpolitik counterpunch to the Pakistani channels Nixon and Kissinger had used to open China.

On the morning of August 9, 1971, in a larger conversation about China and the war in Vietnam, Kissinger and Haldeman informed the president about the Indo-Soviet treaty. Nixon inadvertently raised the subject by noting that in his morning news summary he had seen that "Gromyko was down there talking to that damned Indian Foreign Minister [Swaran Singh]." Nixon called Singh "that little son-of-a-bitch" and opined he was "insufferable."[36] Kissinger replied that the Soviet Union and India had just signed a twenty-five-year Treaty of Peace, Friendship, and Cooperation. Haldeman wryly noted that it had missed the morning news summary since it had just been announced on the radio. Kissinger explained the significance of the treaty: The Indians and the Soviets would "consult with each other in case of aggression of other countries against one of the parties." With unmistakable bravado, Kissinger promised "to give that Indian Ambassador [L. K. Jha] unshirted hell."[37] Angry about the development, Nixon said, "And the thing is, though, they [the Indians] should well understand if they're going to choose to go with the

Russians, they're choosing not to go with us." The president added: "Now, Goddamnit, they've got to know this. . . . Goddamnit, who's giving them a billion dollars a year? Shit, the Russians aren't giving them a billion dollars a year, Henry." Kissinger suggested that the response to India and the Soviet Union be handled from the White House via private channels, not the State Department.

As the conversation progressed, Kissinger elucidated the practice of triangular diplomacy and directly linked the policy of improved relations with the Soviet Union through a potential summit meeting to the U.S. opening to China, the simmering Arab-Israeli dispute, and the situation on the Subcontinent. Kissinger argued that the fear of Sino-American collusion would keep the Soviets in line, and the prospect of a summit meeting and the concurrent agreements that would be signed in Moscow could help delay another war in the Middle East and force the Soviets to restrain the Indians and avert war on the Subcontinent:

> KISSINGER: But their major reason is they're afraid of what you
> will do in Peking if they're in a posture of hostility to you. So
> they would like to have the visit hanging over Peking. They
> would like that you have the visit in the pocket . . . so that
> you will be restrained in Peking. We, in turn, want it because
> it's helpful to us to have Moscow hanging over Peking.

Shifting gears to the summit, the conversation continued:

> KISSINGER: When I handed your letter to Dobrynin, I didn't
> even mention the summit. He said, "Does the fact that
> there is no summit in there mean the president has lost
> interest?" He said, "Because I can tell you unofficially
> they are considering it now at the highest level in Moscow
> and there'll be an answer." And he said . . . speaking for
> himself—"they're not letting me go on vacation . . . because
> they want me to transmit that answer, that proposal."
> NIXON: Hmm. Well, either way, we shall see.[38]

When Soviet foreign minister Andrei Gromyko visited Washington in early September, the situation in South Asia, although important, still took a back seat to the long-standing problems in the Middle East and to greater bilateral U.S.-Soviet concerns—namely SALT details. In a background memorandum for the president, Kissinger listed the Subcontinent toward the bottom, but above Vietnam.

Kissinger's first priority was to insist on preserving the sanctity of back channels with the Soviet Union, specifically the Dobrynin-Kissinger channel and the direct Brezhnev-Nixon exchanges. Kissinger reminded Nixon to "avoid referring to the recent exchange of letters with Brezhnev, in order to preserve the strict confidentiality of this channel," during group meetings.[39] Despite "encouraging movement" in superpower relations, such as the May 20 SALT breakthrough, he contended, "We still do not know whether the Soviet leaders have been engaged in some tactical maneuvers to regulate their Western flanks while they prepare to deal with their dissident allies and with China, or whether a deeper trend in East-West relations is evolving." Noting the Indo-Soviet friendship treaty signed in August, Kissinger warned that the Soviet leadership was being opportunistic:

[They] seem to have taken advantage of the situation to consolidate their position in India, but without seriously trying to lessen basic dangers. The U.S.S.R. reportedly restrained India from recognizing the exile government from East Pakistan then. But it may be giving tacit support to the Indian help for the East Bengali guerrillas. Although they too might face difficult decisions if China intervened, they could reason that India would win easily and both China and the U.S., as friends of Pakistan, would suffer a setback.[40]

In another memorandum, Kissinger predicted that Gromyko would meet the president privately and convey "a personal message from Brezhnev." Kissinger advocated using the meeting with Gromyko to reinforce the utility of the Dobrynin-Kissinger channel's making "good progress" toward a summit meeting in the spring. Kissinger said that Dobrynin "foreshadowed that Gromyko would raise the Middle East . . . [to] be handled in the same framework as Berlin."[41] The memo also described the progress on Berlin and the Soviet role in the Vietnam peace negotiations but neglected the situation in South Asia.[42]

In a discussion several hours before Nixon met with Gromyko, Kissinger expanded the talking points and set the scene for the president. Interspersed with a discussion about SALT, Kissinger mentioned South Asia only in passing. The real gist of the planning meeting, however, was how to move the discussion of the Middle East from Foreign-Ministry-to-State-Department talks directly to the back channel. The two men carefully choreographed the handling of the preplanned private meeting between the president and the Soviet foreign minister while attempting to avoid an affront to Secretary of State Rogers. Rogers had been completely left out of the details on the private channel and summit planning, and, once again, Nixon used the Channel to bypass his own State Department.

Kissinger anticipated that Gromyko would raise the Mideast as the major item of discussion in the private meeting and saw the predicted discussion as a forum to reaffirm and expand the role of the back channels in U.S.-Soviet relations:

KISSINGER: Then [Gromyko] will raise the Middle East. And he will say something to the effect that last year I had mentioned—he won't mention my name—to them that if any real progress is to be made in the Middle East, the Soviet Union and the United States have to agree on their basic presence there. . . . And they're ready to talk in that framework to us now, until there's a comprehensive Middle East deal—

NIXON: If there's any progress on the Middle East, they have to agree to our presence there?

KISSINGER: No, no. They are willing in effect to limit their presence.

NIXON: Oh. All right.

KISSINGER: . . . And I think he's going to say that this should be in the same sort of channel that handled Berlin. My recommendation is, Mr. President, that you say, "This is a very complex subject," that you recommend that Dobrynin and I have some preliminary conversations to find out just how it could be done, after which you'll make a decision. This doesn't commit you to anything—

NIXON: That's right.

KISSINGER:—but keeps the carrot dangling. You might also,
    at the private meeting, reaffirm again this channel; it's just
    good for them to hear.
NIXON: Oh, don't worry.[43]

When Nixon met privately with Gromyko and interpreters, the conversation largely followed the preordained script the president had discussed earlier with Kissinger. The discussion focused primarily on SALT
and the Middle East, although South Asia came up toward the end of the
meeting. Nixon privately told Gromyko that he feared the situation in the
Subcontinent could "explode into war in the area." Gromyko responded
that "it was Soviet policy to do everything possible to prevent a confrontation and the Soviet Government had said so in its conversations with
Mrs. Gandhi." Despite Indian protestations to the Kremlin that it wanted
to avoid war, Gromyko noted that "the Soviets did not have as much
confidence as in the case of the Indian leadership." Furthermore, Gromyko "was gratified to know that the U.S. was interested in averting a war
between those two countries and that it stood on the position of counseling both sides to exercise restraint." Before the discussion turned to a
brief overview of trade interests and then to its conclusion, Nixon told the
Soviet foreign minister that the two would keep each other apprised.[44]

Following the longer discussion, the interpreters departed, and Nixon
had a twenty-minute tête-à-tête with Gromyko. After general pronouncements about the special role of the two superpowers in maintaining
international order, Nixon candidly described the importance of the Kissinger-Dobrynin channel and expressed his desire to move Middle East
discussions to the Channel. Nixon hewed to the talking points Kissinger
had gone over with him earlier that day:

NIXON: Kissinger's meetings with Dobrynin are very important.
    . . . Tomorrow, I have asked Kissinger to meet with you. . . .
    He has a message . . . that he would like to convey that's
    from me on a technical matter. It has to do with Vietnam.
    . . . The other thing that I didn't want to go into in the
    circle here is on the Mideast. Now it may be that working
    very, very quietly, Kissinger and Dobrynin, you see, that we
    can explore something on the Mideast. . . . It may be that

> the Mideast is too complicated to handle at the . . . foreign
> secretary level, see. It may be we have to work very privately.
> . . . State has the ambassadorial level and the Secretary
> of State and the rest. But the more we can have in this
> channel then I will personally take charge, which is what is
> important. And Brezhnev, of course, must do the same.

Emphasizing the role of the Channel, Nixon told Gromyko: "I do not take charge of things that don't matter. Where they matter, like between our countries, then I make the decisions." Nixon underscored, "We couldn't have done it without that channel.[45] Although the Nixon-Gromyko meetings in late September 1971 reaffirmed the utility of the back channels in U.S.-Soviet relations and expanded the topical coverage to the Middle East negotiations, they did not focus on the South Asia problems.

For all purposes, the Subcontinent remained the status quo, and nothing was done, practically, to move toward a resolution. By late October, as a result of the Indo-Soviet treaty and several high-level trips between Soviet and Indian diplomatic, political, and military officials, Soviet attitudes began to change from agreement with American pronouncements about restraint and averting war toward a sharper criticism of Pakistani actions. Contrary to the prognostication in the White House, the Soviets also moved to support of India through consultation and massive economic and military aid packages. As Richard Sisson and Leo Rose note, however, "the total shift in Moscow's position on 'Bangladesh' occurred only after Mrs. Gandhi's visit to Moscow from 27 to 29 September."[46]

The change in Soviet attitude did not go unnoticed in American policymaking circles and entered into the various U.S.-Soviet channels. In particular, the White House increasingly saw the Soviet Union as an enabler of Indian aggression, a pattern that also fit with the perceptions of the Soviet Union enabling North Vietnamese intransigence by supplying materiel for a potential offensive. As the pattern became clear, Nixon and Kissinger felt that the United States would have to risk détente, and mild protests gradually gave way to vigorous protests that the Soviet response to American wishes during the Indo-Pakistani war could be a "watershed" in U.S.-Soviet relations.

In the run-up to the outbreak of hostilities in late November 1971, the United States almost exclusively used the main Kissinger-Dobrynin channel to urge that the Soviets "restrain" their Indian ally and push for a political settlement that would, hypothetically, lead to a return of the refugees. Throughout the summer and fall, the White House urged a peaceful resolution to the fomenting crisis and managed to extract concessions from Yahya to keep the imprisoned Mujib alive and to accept an American proposal for a joint pullback of troops from the Indo-Pakistani borders.[47] The U.S. policy aimed at averting a war seemed to fall on deaf Indian ears, and the Soviets paid only lip service in the various channels, back channel or otherwise.

At an October 9 meeting held at Kissinger's request, the national security advisor "reinforced the president's comment about the India-Pakistan situation" to Dobrynin. Kissinger mentioned the cables urging restraint that the administration had sent to both India and Pakistan: "It was our information that the Indians were going to infiltrate 40,000 guerrillas into Pakistan and at the same time keep the army right at the frontier, in order to force a deployment of the Pakistan army and prevent it from suppressing the guerrillas." Kissinger told Dobrynin that President Nixon "attached the most urgent importance to the prevention of an India-Pakistan war, and was hoping that the Soviet Union would act in the same way." Dobrynin replied "that the Soviet Union had already sent demarches to both sides, but that the Indians were getting extremely difficult." Kissinger suggested "that if the Soviet Union ever could think of a joint step," the United States "would be prepared to undertake it and in a manner that would not take advantage of the Soviet Union's special sensitivities in the Subcontinent."[48]

While Kissinger visited China in October to plan for the upcoming Beijing summit, his deputy, Brig. Gen. Alexander Haig, became the temporary point man in the Channel. In a morning phone conversation on October 19, Haig told the Soviet ambassador that the United States was "exercising maximum restraint on the Pakistanis to pull back their forces." Alluding to the American proposal that both Pakistan and India pull their deployed troops back from their respective borders, Haig told Dobrynin that Kissinger was "fearful this situation could develop despite our best intentions." Nevertheless, the back-channel stand-in asked the Soviets to "exercise maximum restraint on the Indians." Dobrynin replied that both the Kremlin and the White House were working "along those lines" and promised to express Nixon's continuing concerns over the situation.[49] Four days later, Dobrynin called Haig with an oral reply from the Kremlin, but not before questioning why Haig was working on Saturday and playfully admonishing him to "just sit next to the fireplace and have a nice drink."[50] By early November, U.S. intelligence had largely corroborated back-channel exchanges that the Soviet Union and the United States were working toward parallel interests. For example, Gen. Robert Cushman delivered a CIA assessment on November 12, noting that "the Soviet Union was still urging moderation on India and that China was not likely to help Pakistan very actively if it came to war."[51]

Having little to do with the U.S.-Soviet back channels, but of significance in the narrative of the conflict on the Subcontinent, Prime Minister Gandhi visited Washington to press India's case against Pakistan and explain the dire nature of the refugee crisis. Presidential scholar Robert Dallek correctly called Gandhi's conversations with Nixon on November 4 and 5 "case studies in heads of state speaking past each other."[52] The failure to communicate almost certainly resulted from the fact that both Nixon and Gandhi had already made up their minds long before they met in the Oval Office that autumn. Nixon believed that India wanted to confront Pakistan and underlined the potential consequences—American aid to India would be cut off and the American people would not understand aggressive action. Gandhi knew that Nixon would not take India's side and had already calculated that the consequences would be short-lived.

On November 15, Kissinger called Dobrynin primarily to discuss the private Brezhnev-Nixon meetings at the Moscow summit, and the extension of a Soviet invitation to Mrs. Nixon to attend the event with the president. Kissinger warned Dobrynin that the United States was "extremely concerned" about the India-Pakistan situation. "We will not put it as rudely as this in diplomatic cables," Kissinger confided, "[but] we think India is determined to have a showdown." Kissinger continued, "In our view, sending arms into India is adding fuel." Dobrynin dismissed Soviet arms shipments as "publicity."[53] Dobrynin elaborated in his report to Moscow that Kissinger had cited "an absolutely reliable source" who had informed the United States that India was "on the verge of entering the 'decisive phase' of the conflict, and in fact assumes a 'denouement' right now is inevitable and even desirable."[54]

In the last back-channel meeting before war broke out on the Subcontinent, Kissinger attended a farewell dinner meeting for Dobrynin at the Soviet embassy on November 18.[55] The dinner conversation was a *tour d'horizon* covering the range of U.S.-Soviet relations, but toward the end of the evening the two men had a "brief discussion" on India-Pakistan. According to his account, Kissinger again raised the issue of Soviet arms shipments to India, and Dobrynin replied that the Soviet Union was "urging restraint on India" and that "the shipments had been kept at very low levels." Kissinger retorted, "it would make a very bad impression if Soviet actions produced a war." Dobrynin tried to reassure Kissinger, claiming that "there was no danger of that," although "there were many elements in India which wanted war." As seemed to be the norm in the records of the Kissinger-Dobrynin channel, Dobrynin's record of the meeting was more extensive. The Soviet ambassador reported back to the Kremlin that the Nixon administration was "seriously concerned" about a war on the Indian Subcontinent and had again called for U.S. and Soviet "parallel actions . . . to prevent this."[56]

Most accounts of the Indo-Pakistani conflict, particularly those which have examined the American response, have either ignored or downplayed the events of late November 1971 and have dated the start of the Indo-Pakistani War of 1971 to the Pakistani Air Force's December 3, 1971, raid on airbases in northwestern India.[57] Despite the logistical difficulties in acquiring accurate intelligence over a broad and porous border, American policymakers were kept well apprised of events on the ground by their connections to the Pakistani leadership, and knew of Mukti Bahini raids into East Pakistan with the support of Indian armor, artillery, and infantry.[58] Kissinger biographer Walter Isaacson wrote: "On November 22, when India conducted a cross-border operation into East Pakistan in support of Bengali separatists, Kissinger was one of the few (then or in retrospect) who considered this incident the start of full-scale war. . . . The State Department, on the other hand, downplayed the seriousness of these skirmishes; even Pakistan's President Yahya Khan cabled the next day to say he still hoped a war could be avoided."[59]

Although the point about "full-scale" war may be accurate, Isaacson's broader argument missed several important factors: the State Department was receiving contradictory reports from both Pakistan and India; per several secretly taped conversations, Nixon and Kissinger genuinely believed that India had started the war by supporting Mukti Bahini forces with regular Indian troops on Pakistani territory; and, most importantly, the simple fact of the situation on the ground—Indian regular forces had violated Pakistan's border in support of insurgents who were both trained and supplied by India.[60] As Sisson and Rose noted in their landmark study of the conflict, *War and Secession*, "In more realistic, rather than formal, terms, however, the war began on 21 November, when Indian military units occupied Pakistani territory as part of the preliminary phase to the offensive directed at capturing and liberating Dhaka."[61]

As reports of the number and severity of border skirmishes increased, Kissinger convened the WSAG to develop a response. Kissinger's planned response of going to the United Nations—minus the factor of the U.S.-Soviet back channels, which was unbeknownst to most of the group's members—developed largely out of the assessment by the State Department's Joseph Sisco, who told Kissinger:

In the present circumstances, where we do not have an all-out war but do have a significant increase in the numbers of incidents, we could try to get some form of restraining order from the Security Council which hopefully would arrest or slow down further deterioration of the situation. . . . We obviously need facts. But I think we know enough about the nature of the insurgency to believe it would be a good thing to begin to move our efforts somewhat more into the public domain and to begin to place some of the responsibility on the shoulders of the U.N.[62]

On November 22, 1971, American policymakers believed that there had been a large-scale incursion into East Pakistan backed by Indian forces. Kissinger called Nixon at 12:45 p.m. on November 22 and said there was "no doubt" there was "a large encroachment taking place . . . heavily backed by the Indians."[63] In a memo later that day, Kissinger relayed Pakistani radio broadcasts of an Indian offensive and added, "we have no independent evidence but it seems apparent that there has been a major incident."[64] In the Oval Office that afternoon, after continued reports came in through regular cable traffic and via back channels, Kissinger told Nixon that the Pakistanis said, "it's war," and opined that the situation was "a naked case of aggression." "Goddamnit, maybe we ought to say that," Nixon retorted.

Commenting that Mrs. Gandhi had just completed her tour to the capitals of the major powers, Kissinger suggested that she had made the decision to use force before going on her multicountry tour, despite her protestations to the contrary. Kissinger told the president: "They have been back exactly one week. . . . You told her we were going to try to move [the Pakistanis] politically. . . . She doesn't even know yet what the answers to these various proposals are that you made to them, that we said we were going to take up with Yahya." Kissinger, who still hoped that full-scale war could be averted, despite the "naked case of Indian aggression," suggested: "The thing to do, Mr. President, in my view, is to send a very sharp note to the Indians reminding them of all the things we've done . . . repeating what you've said that it simply will not be understood in this country. . . . Two, we should get a note to the Soviets along the same lines." Kissinger emphasized that the messages should be sent "immediately."

As an overall strategy, Kissinger endorsed the idea of coordinated action with the PRC in the United Nations Security Council. Kissinger suggested using his "first secret meeting" with PRC permanent representative to the United Nations Huang Hua on the evening of November 23 to raise the India-Pakistan issue.[65] Kissinger had prearranged secret "contact on U.N. matters or for emergency messages" with China's man in New York, who was also the PRC's ambassador to Canada. Kissinger told Nixon, "We don't have to go as far as the Chinese, but I would lean—" before Nixon interrupted and blurted: "I want to go damn near as far. Now, understand: I don't like the Indians." Kissinger responded, "We ought to lean pretty close to the Chinese and make it an international [action]," but he was again interrupted. Nixon repeated his theme: "Let's remember the Pakistanis have been our friends . . . and the damn Indians have not been."[66] Kissinger hoped to coordinate with the Chinese and other powers in order to diplomatically isolate India and its Soviet Bloc supporters.

At Kissinger's suggestion and with Nixon's approval, the State Department sent a démarche to Gandhi on November 27. To the Indians, the note said: "Military engagements along India's border with East Pakistan have increased in number and strength. Tanks, aircraft and regular forces have been involved on both sides."[67] A message to Brezhnev from Nixon was similar and explicit: "The recent border incidents . . . in the Jessore section of East Pakistan have been of particular concern to me, as I am sure they have been to you. . . . [T]here appears to be an imminent danger of full-scale hostilities between India and Pakistan."[68] Despite the Nixon administration's efforts to deescalate the situation, decisions in New Delhi and Islamabad had been made, and the war was a foregone conclusion by late November. India had thrown down the gauntlet, and the fatalistic Pakistani leader decided to pick it up with a bungled attempt to take out Indian forward airbases on December 3.[69]

Nixon and Kissinger decided to fight the battle in the United Nations, in allegiance with China, and to make the Indo-Pakistani war a litmus test in U.S.-Soviet relations. Kissinger and, particularly, Nixon were disinclined to believe the Indian side of the story and instead trusted the Pakistanis. From the vantage point of the Oval Office, Yahya had served as an honest broker in opening to China and had accepted American recommendations for a peaceful resolution of the crisis despite, as they saw them, exaggerated reports of his strong-arm tactics. Nixon and Kissinger, at the same time, believed that Gandhi had moved away from two decades of Indian nonalignment and had allied the world's most populous democracy with the Soviet Union. Furthermore, they believed she had lied to them during her trip to Washington.[70] Long before the war had started, India's quantitative and qualitative military superiority, they surmised, would prevail against Pakistan. Unanswered questions included the status of West Pakistan and whether or not it would be Balkanized, the fate of Kashmir, and whether or not East Pakistan would gain independence, become part of India, or some combination thereof. White House tapes and the escalating vigor with which Nixon and Kissinger pressed the issue of West Pakistan through back channels to the Soviet Union suggest that the two men believed West Pakistan was in peril.

Dobrynin's absence from Washington from before the start of actual hostilities through the short war meant that Soviet chargé d'affaires Yuli Vorontsov became Kissinger's primary back-channel interlocutor. Comparing Vorontsov to Dobrynin, Kissinger lamented in retrospect that Vorontsov "had authority only to receive and transmit messages, not to negotiate."[71] At the time, however, Kissinger saw advantages in Vorontsov vis-à-vis Dobrynin. "It's better with this guy because he's got to report it," Kissinger claimed, whereas "Dobrynin would have argued with you and tried to pitch. . . . [I]t would have been harder . . . to stop Dobrynin."[72]

In a succession of increasingly strident warnings to the Soviets to restrain India and encourage a cessation of hostilities on the Subcontinent, Kissinger met with and talked to Vorontsov repeatedly during the first three weeks of December 1971, sometimes hourly.

Kissinger called Nixon on the morning of December 3 to inform him it appeared that "West Pakistan has attacked because [the] situation in East [was] collapsing." In response, Kissinger suggested canceling the aid programs to India and noted: "State believes and I agree that we should take it to the Security Council once actions are confirmed. If major war [develops] without going to the Security Council it would be a confession of poverty." As for the Pakistani attack on India, Nixon saw it as being akin to "Russia claiming to be attacked by Finland."[73] Immediately responding to the news, Kissinger convened an emergency WSAG meeting, the high-level crisis management team headed by Kissinger with members from the NSC, CIA, the State Department, and the Defense Department.[74] CIA director Richard Helms confirmed that the Pakistanis had attacked the Indians, an act, the group largely agreed, likely provoked by Indian actions over the preceding two weeks—although confirming intelligence was not available. The group also discussed how to cut aid to India and put the decision to cut aid to Pakistan on hold. The rest of the decisions centered around action at the United Nations—the timing of a Security Council meeting, drafting a speech for the U.S. ambassador to the United Nations, George H. W. Bush, and keeping apprised of events on the ground half a world away.[75]

Despite the onset of hostilities, the U.S.-Soviet back-channel dialogue on the war itself, handled via Vorontsov, did not commence in earnest until the afternoon of December 5, 1971. Before Kissinger met with Vorontsov that afternoon, Nixon and Kissinger conferred by telephone about how to handle the response to the Soviets on the morning of December 5. Kissinger told the president that a backgrounder by Joe Sisco had influenced press coverage in the *New York Times* and the *Washington Post* toward the administration line: "That India is largely to blame for the outbreak of hostilities and [the coverage] lists all the things the Indians have rejected." Noting the course of resolutions at the Security Council, Kissinger informed the president that the American efforts for a cease-fire and withdrawal had the support of the Chinese, and only Russia and Poland had opposed the efforts. Kissinger was displeased with the Soviet behavior and told Nixon: "Now, what the Russians this morning have launched is a blistering attack on Pakistan in TASS and in effect, have warned China against getting involved. What we are seeing here is a Soviet-Indian power play to humiliate the Chinese and also somewhat us." If the United States failed to support Pakistan, Kissinger warned, "if we collapse now, the Soviets won't respect us for it; the Chinese will despise us and the other countries will draw their conclusions."[76]

In another conversation later that morning, Kissinger saw the linkage between South Asia and the Middle East. A failure to act decisively over South Asia would have repercussions elsewhere. "This is going to be a dress rehearsal for the Middle East in the spring," Kissinger warned, "and in fact we ought to consider seriously getting Vorontsov in and telling him if the Russians continue this line, these talks on the Middle East and others just aren't going to be possible." After agreeing to bring Vorontsov in to meet with Kissinger, Nixon decided he wanted to send a letter to Brezhnev and have Kissinger deliver an oral note to Vorontsov. Nixon directed: "The President would send this in writing but he wants this oral message to go from him; I don't want to use the hotline; you know, give him a little of that crap . . . first in the Mid-East we made very great progress and . . . Dr. Kissinger will discuss [this] with Dobrynin when he returns. . . . Now, on India-Pakistan we find your attitude very hard to understand and what are you going to do?"[77]

Kissinger then directed NSC staffer Helmut Sonnenfeldt to draft a telegram, and ordered Haig to prepare talking points according to the president's telephone instructions, in preparation for a meeting with Vorontsov at 4:00 p.m. on December 5.

As scheduled, Kissinger met with Vorontsov in the Map Room at the White House. Kissinger told the chargé d'affaires that "a letter for the General Secretary would be delivered the next day, but in view of the urgency of the situation, the president wanted it transmitted to Moscow immediately." At a time of improving relations, Kissinger continued, "the President did not understand how the Soviet Union could believe that it was possible to work on the broad amelioration of our relationships while at the same time encouraging the Indian military aggression against Pakistan." The president believed that Indian "aggression" in instigating armed conflict with Pakistan violated the established order and the UN charter and wondered why "a member country of the United Nations was being dismembered by the military forces of another member country which had close relationships with the Soviet Union." Using the direct Nixon-Brezhnev channel to further linkage, the United States "did not see how the Soviet Union could take the position that it wanted to negotiate with us security guarantees for the Middle East and to speak about Security Council presence in Sharm El-Sheikh, while at the same time underlining the impotence of the Security Council in New York." The statement by the official Soviet press, TASS, "which claimed that Soviet security interests were involved was unacceptable to us and could only lead to an escalation of the crisis." Although President Nixon wanted to "work for the broad improvement of our relationship," Soviet actions and words made the policymakers in the White House develop "severe doubts, both because of the Subcontinent and because of developments in Vietnam."[78]

After briefing the president about his meeting with Vorontsov, Kissinger called the chargé to convey the president's response to the Soviet leadership when he heard that Vorontsov had told Kissinger that the Indo-Pakistani War would be over in a week. Kissinger told Vorontsov that the president "would like you to report to Moscow that in a week or so it may be ended, but it won't be over as far as we are concerned if it continues to take the present trend." Kissinger emphasized that the president wanted to be perfectly clear that the crisis was "a watershed" in superpower relations.[79] The reference to a "watershed" in U.S.-Soviet relations would be repeated several times before the Indians accepted the Pakistani surrender on December 16.

The next day, Kissinger had Nixon's formal letter delivered to Vorontsov at the Soviet embassy, but not via "usual channels."[80] Nixon's carefully drafted letter expressed "profound concern" about the developing situation in South Asia. The president stated "the objective fact now is that Indian military forces are being used in an effort to impose political demands and to dismember the sovereign state of Pakistan. It is also a fact that your Government has aligned itself with this Indian policy." Still hoping to move from confrontation to cooperation, Nixon wrote the general secretary that it was his understanding from his September meeting with Gromyko that the United States and Soviet Union were "entering a new period in our relations which would be marked by mutual restraint and in which neither you nor we would act in crises to seek uni-lateral advantages." Soviet support for India's "open use of force against the independence and integrity of Pakistan, merely serves to aggravate an already grave situation," Nixon warned. The only solution, in the presi-dent's determination, was that, "Urgent action is required and I believe that your great influence in New Delhi should serve these ends."[81]

The Soviet reply took several hours but was equally firm. Vorontsov met with Kissinger at 11:00 p.m. to personally deliver Brezhnev's mes-sage. According to Vorontsov, Brezhnev argued that the root cause of the conflict was the "result of actions of the Pakistani government against the population of East Pakistan" and that the Soviet Union desired "a politi-cal settlement in East Pakistan on the basis of respect for the will of its population as clearly expressed in the December 1970 elections." In the mind of the Soviet leader, the United States did not act "actively enough and precisely enough . . . towards removing the main source of tension in relations between Pakistan and India." Soviet policy meant that "the Soviet representative in the Security Council has been instructed to seek such a solution that would closely combine two questions: a proposal for an immediate cease-fire between Pakistan and India and a demand that the Government of Pakistan immediately recognize the will of the East Pakistani population." Brezhnev vigorously disputed Nixon's argument that the India-Pakistan crisis would be a watershed in U.S.-Soviet rela-tions: "Differences in the appraisal of specific events in the world . . . may arise, and there is nothing unnatural in that. However, if in such cases, instead of business-like search for realistic solutions, to start talk-ing about a 'critical stage' or 'watershed' in Soviet-American relations, it would hardly help finding such solutions, and would make it still harder to envisage that it will facilitate improvement of Soviet-American rela-tions and their stability."[82]

In the face of Soviet pushback, Nixon determined to take an even harder line with the Soviets and to use additional signals, some public and some private, to reiterate the importance of preserving West Pakistan. To increase pressure on India and demonstrate to the Soviet Union that the United States was serious about West Pakistan, Nixon authorized the movement of the USS *Enterprise* task force to the Bay of Bengal, reiterated to Vorontsov—through Haig—that the White House viewed the South Asian crisis as a watershed in U.S.-Soviet relations, and that he expected a written reply to the letter of December 6. Furthermore, Nixon and Kissinger called in the Soviet agriculture minister, Vladimir Matskevich—then visiting Washington—to the Oval Office to convey to the Soviet leadership the seriousness with which American policymakers viewed the Indo-Pakistani war. Nixon discussed the crisis with a number of advisors, including Kissinger, Secretary of State Rogers, Attorney General John Mitchell, and U.S. ambassador to the U.N. George H. W. Bush. The exchanges were noteworthy for the linkage between South Asia and U.S. foreign policy goals of exiting Vietnam and achieving a Middle East peace settlement. Clearly informed by the memory of the Jordanian crisis of September 1970, both Nixon and Kissinger wanted to play it tough with the Soviets on India-Pakistan and save West Pakistan from dismemberment.[83] Both men also determined that forcing a change in Soviet behavior was worth risking the summit, and—like earlier discussions about the May 20 interim SALT agreement—even the back channel itself.

In a brief afternoon discussion on December 6 about cutting off aid to India, Kissinger raised the late-night meeting the previous evening and the receipt of the Soviet oral note from Vorontsov: "I really read the riot act to him . . . about Soviet participation. And we're sending a note that you dictated today over to . . . Brezhnev." Nixon blurted out: "I don't know whether it'll do any good. Goddamn them, they haven't done anything yet!" Alluding to the Jordanian and Cienfuegos crises, Kissinger exclaimed: "My worry is, Mr. President, that . . . we may get into a summer 1970 situation if we don't show some firmness with them, now. Every time we've been tough with them, they've backed off."[84] The theme of playing it tough with the Russians clearly appealed to Nixon.

When Kissinger met again with the president two hours later, the men discussed the "big game" and the high stakes that they perceived to be at risk.

> NIXON: We'll play the big game. . . . There are too many other games we have to play. . . . We have to live to fight another day. The Subcontinent's another thing—
> KISSINGER: . . . Well, the Subcontinent, as such, isn't worth it, Mr. President—
> NIXON: But I know what it is that's involved. It involves our relations with China and Russia. . . . That's our game—

Kissinger saw the whole Nixon foreign policy as being in peril. "The Soviets are . . . again edging up to this 1970 position, where they think they can sort of play us, while at the same time they're really putting it to us," Kissinger responded. "This can then be a dress rehearsal for the Middle East and any other area—Vietnam." Kissinger doubted that the Soviets were counseling restraint to Hanoi and wondered aloud if the Soviets acted "to put it to us and embarrass the Chinese."

Returning to South Asia, Nixon counseled staying the course in the United Nations and working with the Chinese. "Let's not separate from the Chinese at the U.N.," he told Kissinger, "That I will not do." Kissinger reported a positive change in Chinese behavior toward the United States at the United Nations as a means by which to influence Soviet behavior: "Well, Bush called me and he said that the Chinese at the U.N., who had been very aloof and suspicious of him, now at the Security Council, whenever he comes in, smile at him, nod to him, and sort of tell him he's doing the right thing." Kissinger added, "It also will keep the Russians honest."

The remaining questions revolved around courting the Chinese while remaining steadfast and tough with the Soviets. Nixon suggested sending a message to the Chinese, "to try to think of something to consent to." Kissinger offered a two-pronged approach: to tell the Chinese, first, "that the president has sent a very sharp note . . . to the Russians. Secondly, that if their national interest dictates their taking certain actions . . . that we would not stand for the . . . intervention of any other countries." Kissinger again appealed to Nixon's sense of bravado: "It's a daring game, but we've always done well with the daring games." Nixon saw a Chinese feinting maneuver as a good strategy, and, with U.S. backing, the Soviets would not dare to attack China.[85]

Similar themes dominated another Oval Office conversation the following night. Kissinger described the succession of communications with the Soviets and noted that the administration's most recent response was a "pretty tough one." When Nixon queried as to the specific content, Kissinger replied:

Well, we said this threatens the whole climate of confidence we've tried so hard to establish. I told him yesterday that things are exactly the opposite of what they should want. They're driving us into aligning ourselves with countries that we have no particular parallel interest in on the Subcontinent. And I said, "How can you . . . talk to us about Security Council guarantees if you thwart the Security Council?" And I threatened them that we would not carry out the Middle East negotiations. . . . I haven't talked to you about this—and we can't do it—but they have been bugging me to come to Moscow. I don't want to do it. I've just tried to use it because of the Rogers problem. But they've sent me a formal invitation, now. I don't want to do it, but he raised it again yesterday. And I said, "under these conditions there'd be no chance at all talking about it."

Nixon agreed that it was an inopportune time to raise the issue of a summit-planning trip (for which Kissinger had so strenuously lobbied with the Soviets without Nixon's full knowledge) but said it was essential to play it "cool" with the Russians. Earlier in the conversation, Nixon had expressed his hope to downplay Commerce Secretary Maurice "Maury" Stans's recent trip to the Soviet Union by not holding a press conference, so as to send a signal to the Soviets that more was at stake than just the Subcontinent. The Soviets would divine the hidden message: Détente was at risk, as were the economic and trade issues that Stans had worked out when he was in the Soviet Union. At the end of the conversation, Nixon reiterated to Kissinger, "Let's cool it on the Stans thing," thereby linking another aspect of U.S.-Soviet relations to a favorable outcome on the Subcontinent.[86]

To convey the message to the Soviets that Nixon expected a formal response to his letter of December 6, Kissinger had Haig call Vorontsov at 3:50 p.m. on December 8. The conversation was cool and correct. Haig told the Soviet chargé that Kissinger wanted the message to be delivered "as soon as possible." In a direct rebuke to the Soviet oral response, Haig continued, "the president does not feel a response at this time is necessary until he receives a response to his written communication, and he wanted it understood that the 'watershed' term which he used was very, very pertinent, and he considers it a carefully thought-out and valid assessment on his part."[87] Although no record has been published, it is likely that Vorontsov cabled Moscow immediately, because he delivered Brezhnev's formal response the next morning at 8:20 a.m.

While Haig was communicating with Vorontsov, Nixon was meeting with John Mitchell and was soon joined by Kissinger in the president's hideaway office in the Executive Office Building. Kissinger candidly assessed the sequence of events and determined that it was an earlier failure to act tough with Prime Minister Gandhi and the Russians that allowed the war to commence: "The mistake was that we should have understood that she was not looking for pretext; that she was determined to go. And secondly, we should have been much tougher with the Russians." Nixon inquired what the White House could have done earlier. Kissinger explained:

> We should have told them what we finally told them last Sunday [December 5, 1971] that this would mark a watershed in our relationship, that there could be no Middle East negotiations if this thing would grow. . . . And thirdly, we should have, once the cat was among the pigeons, when they moved on November 22, we had cut [aid] off, as you wanted, but we couldn't get the bureaucracy to do. We could have cut off economic aid the first or second day, plus all of arms instead of waiting ten days and diddling around.

A minute later, the discussion turned to the military situation in West Pakistan, and the issue of the recently announced Moscow summit came into question if the Soviet response proved to be confrontational:

> KISSINGER: Well the trouble is we have to convince the Indians now. We've got to scare them off an attack on West Pakistan as much as we possibly can. And therefore we've got to get another tough warning to the Russians. I mean, but you pay a price because you are risking the summit. On the other hand, the summit may not be worth a damn if they lose, if they kick you around. . . . Militarily in Pakistan we have only one hope now: to convince the Indians that the thing is going to escalate, and to convince the Russians that they're going to pay an enormous price.

China also came into play as a potential bluff. Kissinger suggested sending a note to the Chinese, saying, "If you are ever going to move this is the time." "All right, that's what we'll do," Nixon added. Mitchell clarified, "All they have to do is put their forces on the border." Kissinger then warned: "Mr. President, if our bluff is called, we'll be in trouble. . . . But if our bluff isn't [called], if we don't move, we'll certainly lose." The president ordered, "What we have to do, Henry, is to get it out, calmly and cold-bloodedly make the decision." Nixon added, "No more goddamn meetings to decide this."

Returning to the theme of Chinese posturing—and posturing instead of attacking was being suggested—Nixon said: "As I look at this thing, the Chinese have got to move to that damn border. The Indians have got to get a little scared." To add pressure to the Indians, Kissinger suggested moving an aircraft carrier to the Bay of Bengal under the cover of evacuating American civilians from East Pakistan. Nixon agreed that the same "pretext" was used during the Jordan crisis. The three men all dismissed reports from the U.S. ambassador to India, Kenneth Keating, that the Indians had no "annexationist" plans for East Pakistan, because they felt Indian assurances could not be trusted. With a lawyer's grasp of a complicated trial, Mitchell was a voice of reason: "I know there are time factors here that people aren't taking into consideration. That the Pakistanis in East Pakistan are going to keep the Indians busy for quite a while before they can move west." It was not "inconceivable," in Kissinger's opinion, that the "Chinese [would] start a little diversion—not a huge one—but enough to keep the Indians from moving too many troops west." As the discussion concluded, Nixon gave his orders for a WSAG meeting the next day: "Keep as much of it under the hat as you can. What I mean is let's do the carrier thing. Let's get assurances to the Jordanians [to send reinforcements to Pakistan]. Let's send a message to the Chinese. Let's send a message to the Russians. And I would tell the people in the State Department not a goddamn thing they don't need to know."[88]

In a phone conversation with Kissinger later that evening, Nixon again suggested canceling the summit. Kissinger responded: "No, I wouldn't do that yet. . . . That's too drastic." If Kissinger didn't get the president's point, Nixon emphasized, "I want you to know that I'm prepared."[89]

Vorontsov arrived at the White House on the morning of December 9 to deliver the more mollifying letter from General Secretary Brezhnev to President Nixon. Brezhnev offered "considerations in detail" in response to Nixon's December 5 letter. His comrades in the Kremlin considered the "situation" on the Subcontinent important because it lay "in the immediate proximity to the borders of the Soviet Union." Using more apologetic language, Brezhnev noted that the superpowers had been in communication, but through no fault of the United States and Soviet Union, "military confrontation still could not have been averted." The Soviet leader placed the blame on the doorstep of Pakistan, for it was the "reprisal by the Pakistani authorities against those political forces in East Pakistan which were given full confidence by the people in the December 1970 elections," which had caused the exodus of refugees to India and had provided the spark to the proverbial fuse. Brezhnev pledged Soviet support to reach a cease-fire and a political settlement. The letter avoided any questioning or even mentioning of a watershed in U.S.-Soviet relations and instead emphasized "overcoming the crisis." Brezhnev stressed that a cease-fire would serve as a practical first step toward negotiation and asked that the United States "exert due influence upon President Yahya Khan and his Government" to achieve that end. The Soviet leader ended by asking Nixon for a "calm and balanced approach."[90]

If Brezhnev had hoped for a "calm and balanced approach," he was likely upset by Vorontsov's extremely urgent cable describing the delivery of Brezhnev's letter to Kissinger. Echoing the taped discussions Kissinger had had with the president over the preceding two days, Vorontsov reported:

> Kissinger said, as if speaking on his own behalf, that if India turns all its troops against West Pakistan "in the wake of East Pakistan" and tries "to secure a complete victory" over Pakistan, then the United States ("unlike our conduct with regard to events in East Pakistan, where the situation is rather complex and politically complicated") would prevent a crushing defeat of Pakistan in that case, and to that end would even be willing to undertake steps of a military nature: "The Indians must not forget that the U.S. has allied commitments with respect to defending Pakistan from aggression."

Referring to a press briefing he had given on December 7, Kissinger told Vorontsov that the United States had been using its influence to compel Yahya into accepting a number of concessions and that it had also con-

Left to right: Interpreter Viktor Sukhodrev, Soviet ambassador to the United States Anatoly Dobrynin, Soviet foreign minister Andrei Gromyko, President Richard Nixon, Secretary of State William Rogers, and National Security Advisor Henry Kissinger in the Oval Office, September 29, 1971. Following the group meeting, Nixon met privately with Gromyko and moved U.S.-Soviet discussion of the Middle East to the Kissinger-Dobrynin channel. Rogers was not informed that the major component of his portfolio had been effectively moved to Kissinger's purview. (RNPLM)

ducted a number of meetings with Bangladeshi representatives in moving toward a political solution in East Pakistan. Kissinger argued that Indian actions had undercut these efforts.[91]

To up the ante and emphasize Pakistan's deteriorating situation, at Kissinger's suggestion, Nixon took a hard-line position when he received Soviet agriculture minister Matskevich at the White House at 4:00 p.m. on December 9, 1971. A background memo Kissinger prepared that day noted that Matskevich was in Washington for meetings with U.S. secretary of agriculture Earl Butz and that the Soviet was "the first senior Soviet Minister apart from Gromyko to visit this country in your Administration." Kissinger speculated that "the Soviets may always have intended to ask for an appointment" since Alexei Kosygin had received Maury Stans in Moscow, but "their request now is undoubtedly related importantly to the India/Pakistan crisis." Kissinger saw the meeting as a Soviet attempt "to sidestep any implication that the India/Pakistan war need have adverse impact on U.S.-Soviet relations." Although Soviet motives in asking for

U.S. secretary of agriculture Earl Butz, Soviet agriculture minister Vladimir Matske-vich, Nixon, and Kissinger, December 9, 1971. Despite the smiles, Nixon used the meet-ing to convey to the Kremlin that the Soviet backing for India in the Indo-Pakistani War was a "watershed" in U.S.-Soviet relations. (RNPLM)

A 1971 Herblock Cartoon.
(© The Herb Block Foundation)

"HOW AWFUL! IT'S A GOOD THING I TOOK
OFF MY DARK GLASSES IN TIME TO SEE
THIS."

the meeting were debatable, Kissinger clearly expressed the purpose of the meeting for the American side: "To convey to the Soviet leadership your view of the India/Pakistan conflict and its potential implications for U.S.-Soviet relations."[92]

After a friendly introduction in which he recalled an earlier encounter in Moscow in 1959, the president pleaded with Matskevich: "I believe that you as one who is very close to the Chairman, and, of course, you as your top ranking representative . . . I want you to know how strongly I feel personally about this issue, and it may be that as a result of this conversation you could convey to Chairman Brezhnev a sense of urgency that may lead to a settlement."[93] Intending that his guest serve as a one-way channel to pass along the ominous implications of an Indian attack on West Pakistan directly to Brezhnev, Nixon warned Matskevich: "The first requirement is a ceasefire. The second requirement is that India desist from attacks in West Pakistan. If India moves forces against West Pakistan, the United States cannot stand by. The key to the settlement is in the hands of the Soviet Union. If the U.S.S.R. does not restrain the Indians, the U.S. will not be able to deal with Yahya. If the Indians continue their military operations, we must inevitably look toward a confrontation between the Soviet Union and the United States."[94] Reviewing the meeting the following day, Kissinger assured Nixon that the message that the United States would protect West Pakistan would reach the Soviet leadership. The following exchange is particularly telling for Nixon's perception of the Indians and a sense that the Soviets were pulling the Indian marionette strings:

NIXON: But these Indians are cowards. Right?
KISSINGER: Right, but with Russian backing. You see, the Russians have sent notes to Iran, Turkey, to a lot of countries threatening them.[95] The Russians have played a miserable game.
NIXON: So we'll do the same thing, right?
KISSINGER: Exactly.
NIXON: Threatening them with what? If they come in and what?
KISSINGER: They'll do something. They haven't said what they'll do. But they'll settle now. After your conversation with Matskevich yesterday, they're going to settle.[96]

Kissinger met with Vorontsov on the morning of December 10 and delivered a terse letter from Nixon to Brezhnev asserting that Brezhnev's proposals "concerning the political evolution of East Pakistan appear to be met" but that it would need to be followed by "an immediate cease-fire in the West."[97] In the discussion that followed, Kissinger allowed Vorontsov to copy the verbatim text of an aide-mémoire from November 5, 1962, between then Pakistani leader Ayub Khan and U.S. ambassador Walter McConaughy, in which the Kennedy administration reaffirmed previous assurances to assist Pakistan if it was attacked by India.[98] With the Indian advance into East Pakistan, the attention of the White House intensified on the threat of an Indian attack on West Pakistan. As Nixon warned in his letter, if the cease-fire in the West did not take place immediately, the United States "would have to conclude that there is in progress an act of aggression directed at the whole of Pakistan, a friendly country toward which we have obligations." Nixon continued to urge the Soviets "in the strongest terms to restrain India" from looking westward.[99]

On the evening of December 11, Kissinger and a small entourage met again secretly with PRC permanent representative to the United Nations and ambassador to Canada Huang Hua. Kissinger told Huang, "Incidentally, just so everyone knows exactly what we do, we tell you about our conversations with Soviets; we do not tell the Soviets about our conversations with you." He then described the White House response: the United States had canceled $87 million in loans and $14 million in military aid to India, had called Vorontsov and Matskevich to the White House on December 9, and had dispatched the USS *Enterprise* to the Bay of Bengal. Although the United States was legally barred from "giving equipment" or even "permitting friendly countries which have American equipment to give their equipment to Pakistan," Kissinger stated, "arrangements" had been worked out through third-party countries—Jordan, Saudi Arabia, Iran, and Turkey. The United States would "not protest with great intensity" if such countries decided "that their national security requires shipment of American arms to Pakistan."

Kissinger then raised a matter "of some sensitivity." The United States would share information with the Chinese about "Soviet dispositions on your borders" and, vaguely, "if the People's Republic were to consider the situation on the Indian subcontinent a threat to its security, and if it took measures to protect its security, the US would oppose efforts of others to interfere with the People's Republic." "We are not recommending any particular steps," Kissinger continued. "We are simply informing you about the actions of others." With the imminent defeat of the East Pakistani Army, Kissinger added, "We are looking for a way to protect what is left of Pakistan [that is, West Pakistan]."[100] The national security advisor basically asked the Chinese to move troops to apply pressure on India while assuaging Chinese concerns about Soviet forces. Left unsaid was the fact that there were logistic difficulties of moving Chinese troops toward India along the frozen Himalayan passes and that such a move could risk escalation. The suggested military posturing reflected the diplomatic goal of preserving West Pakistan.

In addition to the Nixon-Brezhnev letters in November and December 1971, Nixon also elevated the exchange to the "Hot Line" between Washington and Moscow to show the symbolic and time-sensitive importance of the events on the Subcontinent. After failing to receive an immediate response to Nixon's December 10 letter, Kissinger called Vorontsov the next afternoon to inform the Soviets that the United States would "proceed unilaterally," presumably at the United Nations, if it did not hear back from the Soviet leadership. Vorontsov informed Kissinger that Moscow had dispatched the first deputy Soviet minister of foreign affairs, Vasily Kuznetsov, to India "in direct connection to whatever we have discussed here." Kissinger pessimistically replied: "I cannot stress to you sufficiently seriously how gravely we view the situation. . . . You have to understand that we have not made a move for 72 hours in order to give us a chance of moving jointly." When Vorontsov pressed as to the meaning of unilateral moves, Kissinger replied darkly, "we will of course move unilaterally again in the U.N., but we may also take certain other steps which were not irrevocable."[101]

The Soviets had not responded when Kissinger met with the president in the Oval Office on the morning of December 12. The president and his advisor covered the same ground, such as India's defiance—with Soviet backing—of the UN General Assembly vote which called for an immediate cease-fire, the lack of criticism in the United States of Indian actions, the necessity of putting out the administration line, and a hypothetical Armageddon scenario if the war spiraled out of control. The men worried aloud that an Indian attack on West Pakistan might provoke Chinese action in support of Pakistan against India, which, in turn, could escalate even further if the Soviets moved against China to support India. Nixon acknowledged that part of the problem was a "plague on both . . . houses . . . because Pakistan mishandled the refugee situation in the beginning," but that was "true only of East Pakistan." Nixon believed it would be "crystal clear" "naked aggression" if India continued military action after East Pakistan was "wrapped up." Kissinger explained that Indian foreign minister Swaran Singh had "refused to give an assurance" that India did not "have any territorial . . . ambitions." Singh had vaguely mentioned "minor rectifications," a code word, in Kissinger's opinion, that meant Southern Kashmir. Nixon asked Kissinger how to deal with the Soviets, and Kissinger suggested using the hotline. Nixon replied: "That is my next move. Put it by the hotline to Brezhnev."

A few minutes later the president asked about the "advantage of the hotline" and queried if the message would be made "more urgent." He added: "The public record doesn't bother me a bit. If it makes it more urgent to them, it's good." Kissinger suggested a public statement as to the evolving situation in South Asia. The reasons were threefold: "We have to do a public statement to impress the Russians, to scare the Indians, [and] to take a position with the Chinese." The discussion quickly returned to the drawbacks and merits of using the hotline with the Soviets, and to the possibilities of a Sino-Soviet nuclear exchange. This particular discussion is tinged with a sense of doom. Fortunately, there is also a sense of hope as President Nixon assessed the situation and saw the scenarios involving nuclear war as unlikely contingencies:

NIXON: Are we being over anxious on the hotline? No, we're not. Basically, all we're doing is asking for a reply. We're not letting the Russians diddle us along, point one . . . And, second, all we're doing is to reiterate what I said to the Agriculture Minister and what you said to Vorontsov. Right?

KISSINGER: Right.

NIXON: Does that sound like a good plan to you?

KISSINGER: It's a . . . typical Nixon plan. I mean it's bold. You're putting your chips into the pot again. But my view is that if we do nothing, there's a certainty of a disaster.

NIXON: Yeah.

KISSINGER: This way there's a high possibility of one, but at least we're coming off like men.

Encouraging Chinese troop movements against India entailed risks, but Nixon saw them as more of a means of forcing Indian restraint in Pakistan. With U.S. backing, a Soviet attack on China in support of India was, in the president's estimation, unlikely:

NIXON: The reason that I suggested that the Chinese move is they talked about the Soviet divisions on their border and all that sort of thing. You know that the Soviets at this point aren't about to go ripping into that damn mess, having in mind the fact of their gains from the Indian thing . . .

KISSINGER: The Chinese, well, we asked, but that's not the reason they're doing it.

NIXON: The way you put it, Henry, the way you put it is very different as I understand. You said, "Look, we're doing all these things, why don't you threaten them?" Remember I said, "Threaten, move a couple of people." . . . Look, we have to scare these bastards. . . .

KISSINGER: My feeling is, Mr. President, leaving completely aside what we've said, if the outcome of this is that Pakistan is swallowed by India; China is destroyed, defeated, humiliated by the Soviet Union; it will be a change in the world balance of power of such magnitude . . . that the security of the United States for—maybe forever, certainly for decades—we will have a guaranteed war in the Middle East, then . . .

NIXON: The point is, the fact of the matter is I'd put [it] in more Armageddon terms than reserves when I say that the Chinese move and the Soviets threaten and then we start lobbing nuclear weapons. That isn't what happens. That isn't what happens. What happens is we then do have a hotline to the Soviets and we finally just say now what goes on here?

KISSINGER: We don't have to lob nuclear weapons. We have to go on alert.

Nixon noted that the Armageddon scenarios were, however, hypothetical: "Well, we're talking about a lot of ifs. Russia and China aren't going to go to war." Kissinger disagreed, but Nixon pointed out that the timing was just wrong for a world war. The president counseled prudence: "Well, let me put it this way. I have always felt that India and Pakistan, inevitably, would have a war. And there can always be a war in the Mideast. As far as Russia and China [are] concerned there are other factors too overwhelming at this particular point for them to go at each other."[102]

Less than two hours later, Vorontsov called Kissinger with an "immediate reply" to the president's message: "The first contacts with the Government of India and personally with Prime Minister I. Gandhi . . . testify to the fact that the Government of India has no intention to take any military actions against West Pakistan. The Soviet leaders believe that this makes the situation easier and hope that the Government of Pakistan will draw from this appropriate conclusions."

Vorontsov said he had not "been instructed to say this," but in his "personal capacity" he wanted Kissinger to know that Foreign Minister Gromyko had returned from vacation, and the Soviet ambassador to the United Nations had "been discussing with the authorities in delegation along the lines we discussed with the president," with "all kinds of guarantees."[103] Less than an hour before embarking on December 12 to join President Nixon on a trip to the Azores for a summit with French president Georges Pompidou to discuss the international monetary situation following the collapse of the Bretton Woods system, Kissinger called Vorontsov to tell the Soviets that the United States was going to make a move in the UN Security Council. Vorontsov questioned the urgency of the move but noted that the Kremlin was "talking very actively with the Indians" and believed there would be "results in several hours."

Kissinger reiterated that the United States had already waited to take joint action with the Soviet Union. Vorontsov claimed that the time differences rather than "ill-will" were the root cause of the delay and that the Soviets were "thinking of everything together: the ceasefire, status war, withdrawal of all forces." Vorontsov repeatedly assured Kissinger that the United States and USSR were in agreement, and that there was a chance for cooperation. As Kissinger had prefaced in his phone conversation with Vorontsov, another letter from Nixon to Brezhnev went out via the "hotline" at 11:30 a.m. The message was curt: "[A]fter delaying for 72 hours in anticipation of your [formal] reply . . . I had set in train certain moves in the United Nations Security Council. . . . These cannot now be reversed. I must also note that Indian assurances still lack any concreteness. I am still prepared to proceed along the lines of set forth in my letter of December 10, as well as in conversations with your chargé d'affaires Vorontsov, and my talk with your Agriculture Minister."[104]

The hotline message reflected the belief in the White House that India would attack West Pakistan, regardless of Indian or Soviet pronouncements to the contrary.

Immediately before his departure for the Azores, Kissinger conferred with the president again and called Vorontsov to soften the blow of the hotline message. Kissinger told Vorontsov that the White House would "work it out in a spirit so there are no winners or losers." Nixon would use the United States in the UN Security Council "to come up with a compromise as far as the U.N. is concerned in which everybody gives up a little." Vorontsov replied that the Kuznetsov mission in New Delhi was "very important" and that the Soviets were seeking "a solution acceptable to you, to us, the Indians and to Pakistan." The next day, December 13, the Soviets responded with a brief hotline message of their own, which stated they were conducting a "clarification of all the circumstances in India" based on the back-channel exchanges.[105]

The Conclusion of the Indo-Pakistani War and the Moorer-Radford Affair

The two-day trip to the mid-Atlantic archipelago for meetings with Marcelo Caetano and Georges Pompidou gave Kissinger and Nixon a brief respite from the Indo-Pakistani War, but the intensity of the crisis ratcheted up even before the two had returned to American soil. As soon as Air Force One landed at Andrews Air Force Base, members of the press scurried to report the potentially groundbreaking news that the president might cancel the Moscow summit. The source of the news was none other than some comments Kissinger made on the plane that were supposed to be "unattributed," a journalistic rule of thumb known as the "Lindley Rule."[106] In violation of a gentleman's agreement dating back to the 1950s, the *Washington Post* attributed the comments to Kissinger on the front page the next morning.[107] When the airwaves started carrying news even before the newspapers hit the street, Kissinger shifted to immediate damage control and instructed White House press secretary Ronald Ziegler to issue a denial.

The *Post* story distracted Nixon's and Kissinger's attention from what would become a much larger problem inextricably linked to the India-Pakistan crisis: the Anderson leaks. An investigative journalist in the mold of turn-of-the-century muckrakers, Anderson later topped Nixon's much publicized "enemies list." Unbeknownst at the time to the president and the national security advisor, Anderson's syndicated column of December 14 provoked a White House investigation when Admiral Robert Welander, the head of the JCS-NSC liaison office, noticed a telling mistake in the Anderson column.

Welander recognized that the second paragraph of the Anderson article mentioned that several American ships were steaming to the Bay of Bengal, including the "guided missile destroyer . . . *Tartar Sam*."[108] Welander knew no ship of the name existed, but that the missile destroyers that had been dispatched used the Tartar SAM—a Surface-to-Air Missile. The article also included verbatim quotes from the high-level WSAG meetings, later cluing investigators in as to the significance of the leaks. Welander informed Haig, who then referred the matter to John Ehrlichman and the White House "Plumbers," which had been assembled in the wake of the publication of the Pentagon Papers earlier that year.[109] The dust had not even begun to settle from the Indo-Pakistani War when the Plumbers investigation turned up some alarming news. Under polygraphic interrogations on December 15 and 16, Yeoman Charles Radford revealed that the leadership of the U.S. military had been spying on the White House through the JCS-NSC liaison office, and, more specifically, on Kissinger—the linchpin in the back channels to the Soviets—since November 1970.[110]

Before the Radford affair popped up on the White House's radar, the main U.S.-Soviet back-channel dialogue centered on the failure of the superpowers to work together at the United Nations. By December 15, the Security Council was deadlocked. Representing Pakistan at the UN Security Council session on the 15th, Zulfikar Ali Bhutto eloquently argued that the Security Council's failure to act effectively legalized Indian aggression against Pakistan. Bhutto then stormed out of the session.

The Kissinger-Vorontsov exchanges at a December 15 White House meeting reflected the differences of opinion and the UN deadlock: The United States continued to support a U.K. resolution, while the Soviets pushed a Polish resolution.[111] The real emphasis of the meeting was preventing hostilities in West Pakistan, coupled with a sense that a failure to maintain solidarity in the United Nations could reflect poorly on the status of U.S.-Soviet relations.[112]

The Nixon White House was clearly displeased that the United States and the Soviet Union could not agree to jointly call for a simple cease-fire and withdrawal. Both superpowers had raised the stakes by dispatching naval forces to the Bay of Bengal, and rising tension in the back-channel exchanges reflected increasing antagonism. In a phone call with Kissinger on the morning of December 16, Nixon vented his anger with the Soviets over the course of events. If the Indians failed to accept a cease-fire after the United States had privately applied pressure to the Soviets, Nixon suggested telling the Russians, "You proved to be so untrustworthy we can't deal with you on any issues." Kissinger saw some hope for the Soviets pushing the Indians into accepting a cease-fire but asked, "If they don't get a ceasefire, what do we do then?" Nixon suggested a strong stance intimately tied to his ideas of linkage: "Cut off the Middle East talks, pour arms into Israel, discontinue our talks on SALT and the Economic Security Council can go [to] the public and tell them what the danger is." Nixon continued: "I would go further. We have to stop our talks on trade, don't let Smith have any further things on the [SALT] Middle East[113] and stop seeing Dobrynin under any circumstances." On the point of no longer seeing Dobrynin, Kissinger concurred: "That is right. Break the White House channel."[114]

With much greater speed than the carefully crafted and symbolic actions of the Kissinger-Vorontsov exchanges, the meeting with Matskevich, the hotline messages, and the frequent phone calls between the White House and the Soviet embassy, the war in South Asia ended rather abruptly. On the afternoon of December 16, 1971, India accepted Pakistan's unconditional surrender in the East, and hostilities quickly came to a close the next day after India announced a cease-fire in the West. Negotiations over war reparations, POWs, and the political settlement for East Pakistan—now the new nation of Bangladesh—lasted for several months.

Upon Dobrynin's return to Washington, Kissinger talked with him on January 20, 1972.[115] The tensions had ebbed from the peak on the morning of December 16, 1971. Kissinger reported his conversation with Dobrynin to Nixon:

> KISSINGER: I made some jokes about India-Pakistan. He said, "Let's put it behind us. Let's work positively for the future." And I'm having dinner with him tomorrow night. . . . He was very conciliatory and very—somewhat apologetic.
> NIXON: About what?
> KISSINGER: India–Pakistan.
> NIXON: You think so?
> KISSINGER: Yeah. I said to him, "You know, Anatoly, every time you leave town I know you're doing something mischievous 'cause every time you're out of town things are in crisis. He said, "Oh, I can tell you some interesting things." He said, "Let's put it behind us . . ."
> NIXON: He'll probably say that Kuznetsov tried—
> KISSINGER: Well, that I believe. But that, in fact, there's no doubt. Because we have the telegram from the Soviet Ambassador to India, Pegov, who told the Indians on Friday, which was the 10th, that they should take Kashmir as quickly as possible. And on Sunday Kuznetsov showed up and everything began to turn. So the signals were clearly changed after your conversations with that Agricultural Minister. . . . There's no question. No question.[116]

The lesson Nixon and Kissinger took away from the Indo-Pakistani conflict was that the United States needed to act tough with the Soviets, which reinforced their earlier impressions of dealing with the Soviets during the Jordan crisis. Nixon learned another lesson—one that would lead to his downfall—in the wake of the South Asian crisis when dealing with the Moorer-Radford affair: the art of the cover-up.

Early on the evening of December 21, 1971, Attorney General John Mitchell, Ehrlichman, and Haldeman met with the president to describe the quasi-spy ring and formulate a response. Ehrlichman reported to the president how White House investigator David Young had checked the leaked and published documents against classified manifests and had determined that the documents had been leaked from the NSC-JCS liaison office. Young had concluded that "there [were] only two men in that office: one the Admiral [Welander], and one the yeoman [Charles Radford]," who could have leaked. Ehrlichman continued: "So they [the investigators] began interviewing both of them, and they polygraphed both of them. And the yeoman obviously is the guy. He knew Jack Anderson. He had had dinner with Jack Anderson the previous Sunday. His wife and Jack Anderson's wife were Mormons and friends, and were doing things together, and so on and so forth. He had been stationed in India for two years, so this is probably about the India-Pakistan thing. So there was motive, opportunity, and access—the whole thing."

For roughly thirteen months, the yeoman had "systematically stolen documents out of Henry's briefcase, Haig's briefcase, people's desks—anyplace and everyplace in the NSC apparatus . . . and has duplicated them and turned them over to the Joint Chiefs, through his boss."

Ehrlichman then described the original aim of the interrogations: "We had been working on this with the idea that perhaps they can link him to the Anderson. . . . Then it developed, of course, that this sailor is a veritable storehouse of information of all kinds, as he reads and retains everything that comes through." How could such a breach occur under their noses? Moreover, how could the White House maintain its back channels—such as the Kissinger-Dobrynin channel—and establish a security regimen in the executive offices? Mitchell and Ehrlichman both agreed that the Moorer-Radford affair should be handled quietly and that the liaison office should be reorganized and moved to the Pentagon. When Nixon raised the possibility of prosecuting the Joint Chiefs, Mitchell counseled, "I agree with you, but we have to take it from there as to what this would lead to if you pursued it by way of prosecution of Moorer, or even a public confrontation, you against the Joint Chiefs aligned on that side directly against you." Mitchell continued, "What has been done has been done. I think that the important thing is to paper this thing over."[117] Although Nixon wavered over the course of action over the following days, he eventually agreed to Mitchell's recommendation.

On the heels of press criticism over the handling of India-Pakistan, the Moorer-Radford affair also set off alarm bells about Henry Kissinger and, indirectly, the intricate web of back channels of which Kissinger was the center. Kissinger had good reason to be despondent, as he felt his position in the White House had deteriorated as a result of South Asia and the Moorer-Radford affair. It is a testament to his abilities and resiliency that he remained, in President Nixon's view, "indispensable" to the China and Russia trips.

In a Christmas Eve conversation in the Executive Office Building, Nixon lamented to Ehrlichman that on India-Pakistan: "Henry thinks that the whole world thinks that he's failed, and that we've failed, and so forth. That's bullshit, don't you agree?" Ehrlichman rejoined, "Well, Henry, of course, sees his reputation as sort of a reputation for the ages and as a sort of [Prince Klemens von] Metternich of the '60s and '70s." Honing in on the negative press coverage, Ehrlichman opined as to the source of Kissinger's melancholy:

> EHRLICHMAN: Well, what I mean is he's saying now that the
> Administration is being charged with this mistake and
> that the president should discipline his Secretary of State,
> and that the fellows in the Administration should back
> up the president, and, you know. It's a sort of a detached,
> dissociation kind of a position, which, I think, concerned
> me. He's tired, worked to death with it, didn't you say
> confronted with the charge of having made a mistake?
> NIXON: He reads about himself all the time.
> EHRLICHMAN: Now, that's a mistake.
> NIXON: He reads about himself all the time and, John, for
> Christ's sakes, he can't keep anything in perspective.

Moments after this criticism, Kissinger "walked in, unbidden," to discuss the Moorer-Radford affair among other concerns, including South Asia.[118] Nixon and Ehrlichman tried to convince Kissinger that the Moorer-Radford affair should be handled delicately. The president argued that the spy ring was nothing new. The problems, Nixon hypothesized, "may be just endemic in the government. It's people who just feel that everybody else should find out what the hell's going on." A few minutes later, Nixon told Kissinger: "You see, Henry, if you were to throw Moorer out now . . . the shit's going to hit the fan. That's going to hurt us. Basically it's already over. Nobody else will do it. It happened while you were here and you get blamed for it." Ehrlichman added, "It weakens the institution, and it weakens the military." Nixon interrupted, "You need to protect . . . the only hard line institution in damn government." Seemingly unconvinced and still depressed, Kissinger departed after roughly a half hour of discussion.

Almost as soon as the door shut, Ehrlichman and Nixon returned to their armchair analysis of Kissinger's insecurities on the negative press coverage on India-Pakistan and the Moorer-Radford affair. "He's got his back against the wall on a mistake. And he's being criticized. And he doesn't like it," Ehrlichman said, returning to the theme of press coverage. Nixon defended the record: "None of us are mistaken. . . . The question is about whether State made one, but there's no mistake in policy. Henry knows very well that we did the right thing." Nixon wished aloud that Kissinger would stand up to the critics but admitted: "Henry is holding us together. That poor fellow is an emotional fellow. Now, Henry's got to know it and you know very well that we cannot move on Moorer."

Ehrlichman, who had observed Kissinger for three years, offered a candid assessment. "There's nobody more arrogant when things are going great," Ehrlichman said. Kissinger was normally "cool under fire" and "beautiful, you know, when . . . making decisions and calling shots, but then the aftermath is just total depression," Ehrlichman continued. His interest clearly piqued, Nixon asked, "He goes straight to depression then?" In response, Ehrlichman suggested getting Kissinger "some psychotherapy."

The line of discussion then shifted to the effect of public opinion on Kissinger's psyche. The president dismissed the effect of press coverage of India-Pakistan on U.S. public opinion and questioned how and why it had so affected his national security advisor. Ehrlichman believed it was more than public opinion: "No, but see he's not interested in public opinion. He's interested in . . . what Marquis Childs writes, and what Joe Kraft writes, and what [James] Reston thinks . . . because that's Henry's world. Those are the people because he has no family, no personal life, so that's his cosmos." When Nixon admitted that he had "spent a lot of time on [Kissinger]," Ehrlichman responded that the national security advisor was worth it. "Well, I think you have to," Ehrlichman admitted. "I think that's really the price you pay for what we're doing."[119]

More so than perhaps any other presidential advisor, Dr. Henry A. Kissinger remained indispensable for managing foreign policy and the intricate web of back channels from the White House. In the aftermath of India-Pakistan and the Moorer-Radford affair, Kissinger and the back channels he oversaw remained essential to the fulfillment of the administration's foreign policy objectives.

Ultimately, the situation on the Subcontinent defied the attempts of the superpowers to manage the crisis. The actions of Indira Gandhi, Yahya Khan, Zulfikar Ali Bhutto, and Mujibur Rahman were more important in determining the final outcome than those of Nixon, Kissinger, Vorontsov, and Brezhnev. Nevertheless, the reliance of the Nixon White House on back channels with the Soviet Union—and using back-channel diplomacy to tilt to China at the United Nations during the Indo-Pakistani War—was triangular diplomacy in action. As Jussi Hanhimäki has argued, the tilt toward Pakistan itself was, essentially, a tilt toward China. The actors on all sides were playing roles partially prescribed by Cold War divisions. The procedures they established would prove more useful as Nixon went to China and as the North Vietnamese launched the largest offensive since 1968 against South Vietnam.

Vietnam in U.S.-Soviet Back Channels, November 1971–April 1972

We have to be sure we don't lose [in Vietnam] for reasons that affect China. They affect Russia. They affect the Mideast. They affect Europe. That's what this is all about. Now, having said all that, we don't want to be dumb about it; that's really what it gets down to, because we have a very delicate public opinion situation in this country.

—Richard M. Nixon, February 2, 1972

On March 30, 1972, North Vietnamese Army forces initiated a major offensive against South Vietnam across the Demilitarized Zone (DMZ). North Vietnam was supplied in large measure by the Soviet Union, while the United States supported South Vietnam with nearly seventy thousand troops on the ground and massive aid packages. In the months before the offensive began, the White House used both public and private channels in a futile attempt to deter an attack, reduce Soviet aid to North Vietnam, and enlist Soviet assistance in arranging negotiations with the North Vietnamese. These efforts failed because Hanoi was determined to settle the conflict by force of arms, regardless of the Kremlin's foreign policy calculus. U.S.-Soviet back channels had inherent limitations, even while they were being used to reinforce linkages between Vietnam, the Middle East, Germany-Berlin, SALT, and the summit.

From the beginning of "the Channel" between Kissinger and Dobrynin, Vietnam was the central link in a structure, ordered by Nixon

Kissinger and Dobrynin, March 1972. (RNPLM)

and constructed by Kissinger, of tying improvement in one area of relations—trade, for example—to improvement in other areas. As Raymond
Garthoff has argued, ending the war in Vietnam became a "crucible" for
triangular diplomacy—playing the Chinese and the Soviets off of each
other to achieve progress in Vietnam.[1] After the Easter Offensive had
been thwarted, President Nixon admitted to Kissinger: "Vietnam poisons our relations with the Soviet [Union], and it poisons our relations
with the Chinese. We have suffered long and hard, and God knows how
. . . we get out of it."[2] Recognizing the Soviet desire for trade and technological exchanges, in addition to groundbreaking agreements on the
limitation of offensive weapons and the perennial Cold War flashpoint of
Berlin, Nixon and Kissinger had long hoped to use the Soviets as good-
faith intermediaries to the North Vietnamese to settle the Vietnam War.
The Easter Offensive forced a reassessment and changed the equation for
the policymakers in the White House.

The offensive was not unexpected, although the Americans and South
Vietnamese did not know the exact timing, details, or scale of the attack.
In fact, American intelligence had noticed increased infiltration rates of
troops and supplies along the Ho Chi Minh Trail through Laos and Cambodia over the preceding months. The North Vietnamese Politburo had
approved the plan of attack for a 1972 dry-season offensive in May 1971
and decided not to put forward a counterproposal to American negotiating terms in November 1971.[3] Although he did not have direct knowledge
of the North Vietnamese decisions, Nixon read Hanoi's intentions and
responded in kind.

In NSC meetings, cabinet meetings, phone conversations, and in candid conversations across the executive offices, Nixon and his advisors had
discussed a number of contingencies since the previous autumn. Because
a diplomatic solution seemed elusive, Nixon moved to bolster America's
remaining assets in Southeast Asia. While continuing the phased withdrawal of American ground forces from Vietnam, the United States reinforced American naval and air power in the region.

From a military standpoint, the Nixon administration used the two-
pronged strategy known as "Vietnamization." On the one hand, Nixon
hoped to protect U.S. forces being withdrawn from Vietnam. On the
other, he wanted to bolster Saigon's ability to defend itself against a Communist attack. During the previous three years, the Nixon administration

sought to deter a coordinated attack like the Tet Offensive of 1968, which had discredited President Johnson.[4] The secret bombing of Cambodia and American side actions into Cambodia and Laos during Nixon's thirty months in office failed from a public relations standpoint, regardless of whether or not they stemmed from the strategy of attacking enemy supply lines. Continued and expanded troop withdrawals, however, increasingly made these public relations shocks palatable to the "silent majority" to which Nixon appealed.

By 1971, the White House had used a combination of private and public channels to convey to the Kremlin the deadlocked status of the secret negotiations in Paris between the United States and North Vietnam. On the president's orders, Kissinger had attempted to deliver a number of messages to the North Vietnamese through the Soviets—and through almost anybody who would act as an intermediary—to deter the expected offensive and warn of an escalatory response. The Channel became the primary means to telegraph American intentions, simultaneously applying pressure on the Soviets to restrain the North Vietnamese while warning that there would be serious consequences and drastic action on the part of the United States in the event of a North Vietnamese offensive. The Nixon administration used back channels with the Soviets in concert with public statements, symbolic actions, and other, more traditional, foreign policy mechanisms.

Between November 1971 and April 1972, U.S.-Soviet back channels, particularly the Kissinger-Dobrynin channel, focused on Vietnam and planning for the Moscow summit. In early 1972, Nixon further consolidated the control of the entire U.S.-Soviet relationship, to the point of having the National Security Council prepare sanitized versions of communications with the Soviets for Secretary of State Rogers.[5] The Channel and the Nixon-Brezhnev exchanges allowed both sides to preview, state, and reinforce policy goals. Back channels proved reliable but had realistic limits. Back channels also ensured that Kissinger and Dobrynin became personally vested in the détente policy of their respective governments, to the point of consulting each other to mitigate the adverse impact of decisions and public pronouncements.

Despite attempts to link a Vietnam settlement to U.S.-Soviet détente, Nixon's and Brezhnev's eventual willingness to consider Vietnam outside of U.S.-Soviet relations allowed détente to proceed. In addition to the fre-

Nixon with Irina and Anatoly Dobrynin, 1969. Three years later, Nixon used the auspices of a ladies' tea between his wife, Pat Nixon, and Irina Dobrynin to convey the U.S. interest in proceeding with the summit meeting planned for May 1972. (RNPLM)

quent Kissinger-Dobrynin meetings and the Nixon-Brezhnev exchanges, the White House used secret symbolic gestures and targeted news leaks. For example, Kissinger personally influenced several columns by syndicated journalist Joseph Kraft by feeding information over the phone, and the president personally coordinated a ladies' tea between his wife and Ambassador Dobrynin's wife, Irina, to signal that the United States wanted to work with the Soviets on détente.

Domestic political considerations also factored into the conduct of U.S.-Soviet back-channel diplomacy. It is not coincidental that the timing of the North Vietnamese offensive and the president's trips to Beijing and Moscow occurred before the November 1972 presidential and congressional elections. The back-channel exchanges on Vietnam are flavored with a sense of the elections and the possible political impact of Nixon's decisions to visit Poland following the Moscow summit, postpone a Middle East settlement beyond the summit (and the election), and attempt to curtail the adverse impact of the North Vietnamese offensive on American domestic opinion.

When the North Vietnamese canceled a secret negotiating session scheduled for April 24, Nixon reconsidered whether or not to send Kissinger on a secret trip to Moscow to plan for the summit. While considering the application of expanded force against North Vietnam, Nixon begrudgingly sent Kissinger with instructions to make Vietnam the primary topic of discussion at the Kremlin. Ironically, the Soviets began to push for the delinkage of Vietnam from détente in the back channel— basically accepting the arguments Nixon and Kissinger had been pushing—at the same time Nixon was reconsidering détente.

Negotiations Stall, Infiltration Up

By 1971, the American military wanted to support the Army of the Republic of Vietnam (ARVN) in taking the fight into ostensibly neutral Laos and Cambodia to destroy North Vietnamese supply lines and delay a Communist offensive. In March, Kissinger reported to the president that as a result of the Lam Son 719 operation, it was "probably not possible" for the North Vietnamese to launch an offensive "next year [1972], before April and May."[6] Several days later, Kissinger explained that the attack on North Vietnamese logistics had denied Hanoi stockpiles it would need to mount an offensive.[7] Likewise, at a Senior Review Group meeting in April 1971, in the wake of the Laos operation, Kissinger probed Vietnam experts, like the CIA's George Carver and Paul Walsh, on the logistical supplies and infiltration rates that the North Vietnamese would require to support a major offensive in South Vietnam. The Group concluded that a countrywide offensive would not be possible until the next dry season, roughly from November 1971 through May 1972.[8]

U.S.-Soviet back channels, however, ultimately failed to produce progress in the Vietnamese peace negotiations. The Channel allowed Kissinger to transmit proposals to the North Vietnamese via Moscow, and, the Nixon administration hoped, to use Soviet pressure to influence the North Vietnamese. For example, toward the end of a meeting with Dobrynin at the Soviet embassy in January 1971, Kissinger raised the prospect of a withdrawal of American forces from Vietnam in exchange for a cease-fire and the separation of military from political issues. Kissinger used the guise of discussing Alexi Kosygin's interview with *Asahi Shimbun,* a Japanese newspaper, in which the Soviet premier had "indicated a Soviet willingness to engage itself in the process of a [Vietnam] settlement." The Soviets made good on their offer by transmitting the proposal almost verbatim, from Dobrynin's cable on the meeting with Kissinger, via the Soviet ambassador to Hanoi.[9] Despite some progress in negotiations, facilitated in part by the Soviet Union, the forward momentum had stalled by November 1971 as Hanoi prepared to launch its offensive. The cease-fire-for-withdrawal episode is but one example of the limits of superpowers to influence their client states; the messages may be transmitted in good faith by back channels or through more regular diplomacy, but the intended audience may not listen to the message.

The Nixon administration emphasized in private channels with the Soviets that either North Vietnam could negotiate and the Soviet Union could act as an intermediary, or the United States could act "unilaterally"— a code for stepped-up military action. When Kissinger met with Gromyko in late September 1971, he emphasized that the United States had reached the "last phase of the war." Kissinger reported that he had told the Soviet leader the administration "would either go unilaterally, which we were reluctant to do, or we would go by way of negotiation."[10] Similarly, Kissinger kept Dobrynin apprised of the negotiations he was personally conducting with the North Vietnamese, negotiations that were hidden from the American public.

Whether or not the Soviets genuinely wanted to assist, the U.S. peace negotiations with the North Vietnamese had clearly reached an impasse. After the United States had made proposals and counterproposals to

Hanoi in September and October 1971, the North Vietnamese decided not to respond after postponing several meetings.[11] Adding insult to injury, as Henry Kissinger later summarized the chain of events, "less than forty-eight hours before I was supposed to leave for Paris, Hanoi informed us that Le Duc Tho would not be present because he had 'suddenly become ill.' No alternative date was offered; no expression of readiness to settle accompanied the message; there was still no comment on our major new proposal over a month after we had transmitted it."[12] Nixon and Kissinger discussed Le Duc Tho's apparent illness, which they diagnosed as diplomatic in nature, and determined that the North Vietnamese were delaying in order to build up for an offensive.

The Nixon administration responded to the deadlocked negotiations by marrying force with diplomacy, and it conveyed its intentions via back channels with the Soviets. In the absence of negotiations, the immediate response would be more bombing. Nixon told Kissinger: "I think a one-day shot at this point next week might be very much in order. . . . What the hell harm does it do? . . . I don't want them to think, well, they can pull this goddamn illness gag and keep delaying on this thing." As to the real reason behind the North Vietnamese cancellation, Nixon hypothesized: "They are off balance. These bastards are off balance, and they may be waiting . . . for the Congress to screw us." With the Chinese and Soviet summit meetings very much on his mind, the president wanted to exercise some restraint. He told Kissinger: "Well, Henry, don't give three days. I don't want to give the Chinese any excuses . . . or the Russians, but I think we can give 'em a one-day crack."[13]

The next day, Kissinger told the president: "I just think that a reputation for ferocity usually helps, rather than hurts, even with the Chinese and the Soviets, because you could argue that they might say to the Hanoi chiefs he [Nixon] really meant what he said. . . . With the Le Duc Tho turndown, then they [the Soviets and the Chinese] can say we were provoked."[14] At a dinner meeting not long after the North Vietnamese rejection, Kissinger told Dobrynin that the United States had lost patience and "if there were a North Vietnamese attack, then we would respond without restraint."[15] Playing it tough on Vietnam would send a signal to the Soviets and the Chinese that a North Vietnamese failure to negotiate and an attempt to infiltrate troops and supplies would be met with force.

Several days later, on November 20, Nixon candidly described to Kissinger a middle-of-the-night thought he had had about dealing with the North Vietnamese. The conversation foreshadowed the massive bombing campaign, known as Operation Linebacker, that Nixon used in response to the Easter Offensive months later. Nixon darkly articulated his dual-track, carrot-and-stick approach to a Vietnam settlement and simultaneously linked the war in Vietnam to broader policy initiatives and the domestic political context.

> NIXON: We have more of a card than we think regarding
> settlement. . . . I'm sure it must have occurred to you,
> Henry, that regardless of how the election comes out in
> November, I will still be President until January 20th, and
> I'll be Commander-in-Chief. And, if I should have lost,
> I would certainly—*certainly*—not go out with my tail
> between my legs. Now, if those prisoners are not back by the
> time of the election, if we should lose the election, the day
> after that election—win, lose, or draw—we will bomb the
> bejeezus out of them. Because then, to hell with history!
> . . . You know, *just knock the shit out of 'em* for three months.
> Now—
> KISSINGER: That's the best—I had not thought of that.
> NIXON: You see what I mean?
> KISSINGER: Right.
> NIXON: Now, you have to seize it. Put that into a bargaining
> equation there. . . . They're right: to do anything before
> the election would pose a problem, politically. But, do they
> realize that they have to deal with, here, a man, who if he
> wins the election will kick the shit out of them, and if he
> loses the election will do it even more? Now, there's where
> we are. . . . And, incidentally, I wouldn't worry about a little
> slop over, and knock off a few villages and hamlets, and the
> rest. . . . *This would be war.* . . . I wouldn't worry about a
> Soviet ship, you know, that was in Haiphong Harbor—[16]

Nixon pressed forward with both continued troop withdrawals and targeted attacks against North Vietnamese airfields and staging areas in the heaviest air strikes since 1968. The administration later used back channels to soften the blow to the Soviets and portrayed the air assaults as a reaction to North Vietnamese offensive preparations. Eschewing the complicated rules of engagement that had been used during the Johnson administration, Nixon personally directed the loose interpretation of "protective-reaction" strikes against targets in North Vietnam.[17] In his memoir *Ending the Vietnam War,* Kissinger summarized the administration's response to Hanoi's failure to negotiate:

> On December 23, we bombed supply complexes in North Vietnam south of the 20th parallel for two days, to editorial and congressional outrage. We sent strong notes to both Beijing and Moscow—with which summits had been scheduled—summarizing our exchanges with Hanoi and warning that an offensive would evoke the most serious retaliation. We did not think either capital would prove helpful in the negotiation, but we considered it probable that they had their own objectives to protect at the forthcoming summits and that they would therefore prefer to avoid a crisis.[18]

The volume level in U.S.-Soviet back channels about Vietnam rose through 1971, and by the beginning of 1972 resembled a broken record. The White House used private channels to tell Moscow it should restrain its ally and bring Hanoi to the negotiating table, because if the North Vietnamese launched an attack there would be drastic consequences. Increasingly, another subtext entered into the Channel: The United States would be responding to North Vietnamese intransigence, separate from the policy of détente with the Soviets. The U.S. presidential and congressional elections loomed on the distant horizon, while the China trip in February and the Moscow summit in May served as two bookends for the predicted start of a North Vietnamese dry season offensive in 1972. Nixon and Kissinger suffered from no illusions that the Soviets and the Chinese were enabling a North Vietnamese offensive. They wanted to play the Soviets and Chinese off of each other, support South Vietnam, continue troop withdrawals, and pull off two summit meetings in less than six months. Once again, at least in terms of dealing with the Soviets, back channels telegraphed American intentions.

The Soviets hedged their bets by aiding North Vietnam while moving toward détente, simultaneously seeking an opportunity to disrupt Sino-American rapprochement. Unfortunately, Soviet aid enabled the North Vietnamese and threatened to derail détente, too. In fact, in December 1971—in the wake of the South Asian crisis—the Soviets increased their military aid to North Vietnam.[19] The CIA later estimated that the Soviets had supplied $375 million to the North Vietnamese in military aid alone.[20] In a phone conversation with the president in January, Kissinger reported that the Russians were putting the North Vietnamese up to the offensive in order to overshadow the presidential trip to China in February. Kissinger explained, "We have an intelligence report today . . . in which one of their people in Paris says they're going to do it [launch an offensive] so that they, in February . . . can overshadow your trip to Peking." Kissinger qualified the statement by adding: "I don't think they've got that much power. . . . On the other hand . . . it's a double-edged sword for them, because if they do it at that time you're overshadowing their offensive." The president chuckled in agreement.[21] The warnings in the back channels continued the attempt to deter a North Vietnamese offensive.

At a mid-January 1972 Senior Review Group meeting, Kissinger again inquired as to the predicted offensive. He worried that any simultaneous military action could disrupt Nixon's February trip to Beijing. Kissinger drew two conclusions from a discussion with the CIA's Norman Jones. Kissinger summarized: "The first is that if they keep the present rate of supply, they could not launch an offensive next month. The second is that if they want to increase supply rate—and launch an offensive—they can do so." Jones believed that North Vietnamese preparations would take two more months, putting the start of the offensive in mid- to late March.[22]

Irked by Soviet maneuvering and delays during the South Asian crisis, the White House decided to play it tough about a North Vietnamese offensive through the back channels with the Soviets. Dobrynin had just returned from nearly two months in the Soviet Union for "consultation," so "the Channel" was back in play.[23] Before he met with the recently returned Soviet ambassador, Kissinger confided to Nixon that in order to forestall a North Vietnamese offensive, he would not mince words with Dobrynin. Kissinger both flattered the president and promised to stay on message when he told Nixon he would scold Dobrynin: "Now look. You've watched the president. Time and again he's done things which you would have not predicted, [he's] run enormous risks, and I'll tell you now he's going to do it again if this Vietnam offensive comes off at the scale at which we're now seeing it develop."[24]

In a four-hour dinner meeting at the Soviet embassy on January 21, 1972, Kissinger celebrated Dobrynin's return to Washington and discussed the status of U.S.-Soviet relations with the summit less than five months away. Kissinger reported to the president that despite "an atmosphere of effusive cordiality, buttressed by slugs of vodka and cans of caviar," he had warned the recently returned Soviet ambassador that "if a Communist offensive occurred," the United States "would certainly take the strongest possible action, which in turn would have effects on [the U.S.-Soviet] relationship." Kissinger added, "It was clear that the Soviet Union might think it could embarrass us in Peking." Dobrynin repeated assurances that the Soviet Union "had no interest in an offensive," and "the last thing the Soviet Union wanted was a confrontation with the United States in the months before the Moscow summit."[25] Nixon upped the ante the following week.

January 1972 was a busy month. Less than two weeks after the State of the Union address, Nixon made public the fact that Kissinger had been conducting secret negotiations with the North Vietnamese since 1969. In a major televised speech on January 25, 1972, Nixon offered a withdrawal of American forces within six months of an agreement and described what he deemed to be the successful process of Vietnamization. Nixon explained the course of secret negotiations but noted that the enemy had rejected a settlement. After the abortive Paris session in November, Nixon noted, Hanoi had increased infiltration into South Vietnam and had conducted offensive operations in Laos and Cambodia. The president expressed a willingness to negotiate through any acceptable channel, pledged to continue Vietnamization, but vaguely warned, "If the enemy's answer to our peace offer is to step up their military attacks, I shall fully meet my responsibility as Commander in Chief of our Armed Forces to protect our remaining troops."[26]

Using the Channel to reinforce the message from the January 25 speech, Kissinger called Ambassador Dobrynin from the Lincoln Sitting Room. Without Nixon's presence in the room, which activated the taping system, the back-channel vignette would have been lost to history.[27] During the carefully choreographed phone call, Kissinger clearly used the back channel to send a message to the North Vietnamese to warn against offensive action but also signaled a willingness to negotiate through the Soviets:

> If there is any way get to your allies and make clear to them that, now, they can, of course, start . . . raging . . . and use their usual adjectives . . . and that would be a very unhelpful approach. . . . On the other hand, we are willing, if there's any chance at all of a constructive outcome, to meet with them again and to bring this war to a reasonable conclusion. But they cannot tempt us into a military . . . outcome or there'll be very serious consequences. . . . The president has again asked me to say that if your government thought a meeting in Moscow would speed things up I remain ready to do that. . . . We don't want to be in a position where they launch an offensive and we then react to their offensive without having made it clear . . . because, we will certainly, in case of an offensive, have to take drastic measures. . . . They have given us no choice. It's simply not proper . . . not to respond to a serious proposal transmitted through another government and then separately at their own request. . . . And we are perfectly willing to have another confidential channel, or to do to it in other channels, but that's entirely up to them. . . . We have kept every secret when there was any prospect of a constructive outcome.[28]

In a letter Kissinger delivered to Dobrynin three days later, Nixon explained to the Soviet leadership that the purpose of his January 25 address had been to reaffirm his administration's "desire to reach a negotiated settlement of the Indochina war." The president categorically reiterated: "The North Vietnamese nevertheless seem intent to keep on trying to embarrass the United States by a major military offensive," to which the United States "would have no choice but to react strongly." Holding out an olive branch, Nixon asked for the Kremlin's assistance in ending the war and promoting peace, "without in any way compromising its principles."[29] Again, the White House used back channels and private letters to reinforce a public statement but also to temper the statement by signaling a willingness to compromise.

The analysis from the Soviet embassy following the January 25 speech accurately assessed Nixon's motivation and message. Dobrynin recognized "a strong domestic political slant in connection with the election campaign that is getting under way." The Soviet ambassador took Nixon's threats seriously and viewed the speech as "a way of preparing Americans for such actions and be a kind of preventive measure in order to derail possible DRV offensive operations in advance."[30] At the meeting on January 28, following a discussion of the Middle East, Dobrynin reported that Kissinger raised the topic of Vietnam "at length" and that his thoughts were "essentially a repetition" of what the White House had said earlier.[31] The back channels achieved a tactical function of buttressing the point with the Soviets that the United States would respond to a North Vietnamese offensive with considerable force.

Bureaucratic Centralization and the Channel

It was against the backdrop of the anticipated Easter Offensive and the summit meeting in Beijing that Nixon and Kissinger consciously moved, via the Channel, to make Ambassador Dobrynin a coconspirator in the bureaucratic turf wars within the Nixon administration. Although he occasionally voiced doubts about Kissinger, and Kissinger periodically offered his resignation for perceived and real transgressions in the "bureaucracy," the president remained firmly committed to a centralized foreign policy run by Kissinger.[32] On one occasion in late 1971, Nixon worried to Haldeman that Kissinger might resign: "Fundamentally, we've got to decide: does Henry want to go to Peking and Moscow? If so, he must not have any more talk at all, or any more thought . . . that he can do trips and then he'd quit. Aw, for Christ sakes he's out of his goddamned mind! That's when we need him."[33]

Nixon moved decisively in early 1972 to bolster his national security advisor by fully centralizing control over foreign policy in the White House. This essentially continued the trends he had initiated earlier, such as the expansion of the Channel to include U.S.-Soviet deliberations on a Middle East settlement at his private meeting with Gromyko in September 1971. Back-channel diplomacy had independently allowed rapprochement with the Chinese and progress with the Soviets on the way to the summit. It made sense for Nixon. Conveying a presidential directive and a vigorous exertion of executive control, Kissinger informed Secretary of State Rogers on January 14: "The President has directed that henceforth meetings with representatives of the Soviet Embassy in Washington on any topic and with representatives of foreign governments on the Middle East situation be cleared with him. In conjunction with these clearances, the president wishes to have a memorandum outlining the objective of the meeting and the manner in which it will be conducted. Following the meeting, the president wishes to have a written memorandum for the record covering the contents of the decision."[34]

After some debate between Nixon, Kissinger, Rogers, Haldeman, and Attorney General John Mitchell, Nixon followed up on the matter and "established a 'basic operating procedure' with regard to issues relating to the Soviet Union, as well as China, the Middle East, Cuba, and Chile." Nixon further "directed that he be informed of and approve any proposed actions taken on these matters beforehand and that all meetings with representatives from these areas be cleared with him in advance."[35] Nixon wanted White House control of foreign policy, especially on détente and Sino-American rapprochement, which meant backing Kissinger.

In a candid conversation among Nixon, Haldeman, and Kissinger on February 2, the three discussed how to largely exclude Rogers and the State Department from the decision-making process by using Dobrynin. Haldeman reported that Rogers had "sent over a really crappy memo" which stated that the secretary intended to meet with the Soviet ambassador. There were a number of complications arising from a meeting between the secretary of state and the Soviet ambassador, including the fact that Rogers had received sanitized versions of communications with the Soviets that omitted any mention of back-channel exchanges. Rogers was in the dark on a number of issues. Nixon counseled: "Well, the better thing to do is to tell Dobrynin. . . . I think that's the best thing, because Dobrynin well knows, Henry, where the power is now, don't you think?"

Nixon basically advocated informing the Soviet ambassador that Rogers was ignorant of nascent summit plans, on the Middle East, and even about the existence of the back channel. The problem was, as Kissinger responded to the president's suggestion, "You can't tell Rogers not to meet with Dobrynin." The Channel certainly had its own set of complications, as became evident during the course of the conversation:

KISSINGER: It's murderously dangerous if [Rogers] goes through the Middle East with [Dobrynin]. And, if Dobrynin has

two positions on every issue, it's—Dobrynin has already
asked me whether we couldn't shut off Sisco, and I told him,
"No, we couldn't do that, because—"

HALDEMAN: Well, he has a problem enough on the letter, too.

KISSINGER: Well, yeah. Well, I've sent him a copy of the letter,
an edited copy of the letter . . . taking out those parts which
refer to my conversations, of the Brezhnev letter. But I want
it . . . to live up to the spirit of what we had agreed to do,
and also this letter—

NIXON: You're doing it exactly right.

Kissinger stressed the importance of the Middle East discussions in
the Channel as a means to influence the Soviets: "It's the one thing we've
got which gives them a stake in your reelection. And it's the one thing
we've got which gives them a stake in having you in Moscow unimpaired.
. . . Because only you can deliver the Israelis."

The linkages were apparent, and the back channels could be used as
an amplifier with the Soviets. Once again, the domestic political considerations of White House image crafting for the summit meetings in the
Communist capitals became even more important:

KISSINGER: Another thing, Mr. President, the results of the
Moscow Summit are the ones that are going to be very
tangible.

NIXON: Yeah, I know.

KISSINGER: And they have to be yours. I mean, there can't be
stories how the Peking was White House, and the Moscow
was . . . [that] State made you do it.

In a bureaucratic fight, Nixon agreed with Kissinger that the State
Department was trying to be relevant on the Moscow summit and the
impending visit to Beijing just three weeks away:

NIXON: It's that they want to have this meeting so that the little
assholes at State came in and told me—

HALDEMAN: Told you how to conduct yourself.

NIXON:—the Chinese wear a different kind of dress than we do, and that they're very—you know, their history is this and that. Well, they don't know a goddamned thing, and I'm not going to have 'em tell me that. I'm just, you know, I'm going to cut 'em off. . . . I'm not going to have it.[36]

Between February and May 1972, the Kissinger-Dobrynin channel reached its apogee and became an essential safety valve as well as a vehicle to move toward détente and a successful summit meeting. In one of the most significant back-channel exchanges in the published record, the Soviet ambassador candidly reported to the Kremlin how far the Channel had gone at a meeting on February 3, 1972. At the meeting Kissinger showed Dobrynin the sanitized texts that had been passed to Rogers and described the secretary's ignorance of matters like SALT and the summit. Dobrynin noted that Kissinger had brought him into his confidence and wanted to exclude the State Department from the summit planning.

According to Dobrynin's memcon—Kissinger did not produce a record of the meeting—the national security advisor wanted "to avoid having this [summit] agenda formally recorded in any way through State Department channels." Proclaiming the domination of the Channel, Dobrynin wrote: "In fact, it is a unique situation when the Special Assistant to the president secretly informs a foreign ambassador about what the Secretary of State knows and does not know concerning relations between two states at the level of the president of the U.S. and leaders of the other state—the Soviet Union." Dobrynin added, "All of this once more goes to show that discussion of and decision-making on the main, most sensitive issues are now being carried out primarily by two individuals: Nixon and Kissinger."[37] As Nixon had postulated, Dobrynin knew very well where the power was.

Moving Toward the Summit

Recognizing the limits of back-channel messages to the Soviet leadership on Vietnam, Nixon realistically saw the North Vietnamese pursuit of their own interests and, in anticipation of the offensive, ordered the movement of several aircraft carrier task forces to the South China Sea. Nixon also loosened the interpretation of "protective reaction" strikes against North Vietnamese airfields and SAM sites. Following a briefing by CIA director Richard Helms and chairman of the Joint Chiefs of Staff Admiral Thomas Moorer, Nixon described for his cabinet the obstacles a North Vietnamese offensive would present for his overall foreign policy and the link to domestic opinion. For better or worse, the major foreign policy initiatives were linked, and Vietnam was the linchpin. Nixon philosophized: "We have to be sure we don't lose for reasons that affect China. They affect Russia. They affect the Mideast. They affect Europe." "That's really what it gets down to," the president continued, "because we have a very delicate public opinion situation in this country." After discussing the North Vietnamese buildup along the DMZ, Nixon added: "The only thing to do if the other guy gives you a, you know, a slap on the wrist [is] you kick him in the groin. That's one theory. That's what we've got to do here."[38]

When Kissinger met again with Dobrynin on February 7, Dobrynin delivered Brezhnev's reply to Nixon's letter of January 25, and the discussion focused largely on taking the U.S.-Soviet relationship to a new level. Brezhnev's letter was short and more moderate than the White House had expected considering the president's disclosure of Kissinger's secret negotiations with Hanoi—a revelation that raised red flags for Soviets, themselves engaged in confidential diplomacy with the United States through Kissinger. "The reaction of the [North] Vietnamese to the U.S. proposals is quite understandable to us," Brezhnev wrote Nixon. He continued, "It is not difficult to understand . . . [due] to the very fact of the disclosure by the U.S. . . . of the confidential negotiations." Without belaboring the point, the general secretary added that Moscow told Hanoi that the United States wanted to restore confidential contacts, and he pledged a readiness to overcome obstacles.[39]

The back-channel meeting on February 7 focused on shifting gears toward the nuts and bolts of the approaching summit meeting and included substantive discussion on a Brezhnev visit to the United States, planning for the Moscow summit, the German treaties, trade, and the Middle East. Kissinger asserted that Dobrynin "wished to point out" that the Brezhnev letter "was deliberately phrased in a very conciliatory fashion." Furthermore, "none of the arguments made against the president's peace plan were embraced by the Soviet Union; they were all ascribed to the [North] Vietnamese." As he had done during the phone call on January 25, Kissinger reiterated his offer to go to Moscow to secretly negotiate with the North Vietnamese. The meeting ended with an exchange about the function of the back-channel correspondence between Nixon and Brezhnev, which would be reserved "for the most crucial issues" as the summit approached.[40]

China: Driving a Wedge between the Soviets and the North Vietnamese

Tactically, Kissinger decided to use the idea of a peace meeting with the North Vietnamese in Moscow—an idea he thought extremely unlikely, if not impossible—to push the peace negotiations past the China trip and the trip to the Soviet Union. Communicating the idea with the Soviets through the Channel would bolster American credibility about pursuing meaningful negotiations, while the inevitable North Vietnamese rejection could drive a wedge between Hanoi and Moscow. After all, hadn't Kissinger been arguing via the Channel that American military actions were a reaction to North Vietnamese intransigence and stonewalling? Kissinger explained his thinking to the president on February 14, 1972, the third anniversary of the Kissinger-Dobrynin channel:

> KISSINGER: I believe the more we can get the Russians to press for a meeting in Moscow, which they want for their reasons, the more eager Hanoi will be to have the meeting in Paris because Hanoi will under no circumstances, in my view, settle in either of the other Communist capitals.
>
> NIXON: I see.
>
> KISSINGER: So the reason . . . I'm going to see Dobrynin tomorrow and I'm going to put it to him again that I'm eager to meet them in Moscow. And I'll bet it's a poker game. . . . I already know they proposed a meeting in Paris.
>
> NIXON: Yeah.
>
> KISSINGER: There isn't a chance of a snowball in hell that they will accept a meeting in Moscow. They've already objected in October so they—
>
> NIXON: Did it work?
>
> KISSINGER: But if Moscow proposes a meeting, it's to them a sign that Moscow is eager to settle. I'm certain that Moscow

is playing such a big game that they are not going to let Hanoi screw it up in May. So they're up against a whole series of deadlines. Then they see you—if you look at the press, say look at *Time* and *Newsweek* this week, it's a little play of the State of the World report, which is on the whole positive. But above all it's China. So they know for the next 3 weeks.[41]

The domestic political calendar again weighed into the Sino-Soviet-Vietnamese triangle as the president's trip to Beijing approached. The next day, February 15, less than a week before his departure to China, and demonstrating the complete ascendancy of Kissinger, Nixon toyed with the idea of excluding Secretary of State Rogers from both the Peking and Moscow summit meetings. The president couched it in terms of precedence and political expediency:

NIXON: You know, Henry, my recollection is that when Eisenhower took his trips he didn't take [Secretary of State John Foster] Dulles. . . . But my point is, I don't believe we should have a situation where the Secretary of State travels every time we go. It's just a total pain in the ass. You can't have two VIPs on any trip. It's a rule we always have in politics, you know. . . . We really shouldn't have Bill going on this. He should go separately on his own trips. What do you think? Or do you disagree?

KISSINGER: Well, it's going to be a pain in the neck. There's no question.

NIXON: But, I mean on anything; not just this, but all. I don't think the Secretary of State needs to go along on the goddamned trips.[42]

Later that afternoon, Kissinger met with Dobrynin at the Soviet embassy. According to Kissinger, Dobrynin seemed "friendly but still somewhat more reserved than at previous meetings." Vietnam only came up in passing in a discussion primarily orbiting around Lend-Lease debts that dated back to World War II, Most Favored Nation (MFN) status for the Soviet Union and other trade concerns, grain sales to the Soviet Union,

the Middle East, and SALT.[43] Both men skillfully avoided the eight-hun-
dred-pound gorilla in the room: Nixon's impending trip to China.

The meeting was noteworthy only because Kissinger delivered another
letter from Nixon to Brezhnev that Tuesday afternoon. The president wrote
that he had overseen exchanges in the confidential channel and in regular
negotiations. Then he got to the point: "I believe that it might be helpful
to outline for you my views on the topics which should be reserved for discussion within the existing confidential channel and those which would
be better left to negotiations." The Kissinger-Dobrynin channel would
be "best suited" for discussion of the Middle East, Vietnam, and SALT.
Additionally, the back channel could "perhaps" be used for "some preliminary exchanges on Mutual Force Reduction [MBFR]," which dealt with
force reductions in Europe. Kissinger and Dobrynin could also discuss
the "overall objectives" for the May summit, and "especially discussions
as to the final outcome of the meeting, to include consideration of a final
statement or joint communiqué." Nixon visualized "that normal channels
should be used to advance our respective positions on a full range of bilateral issues, including trade, cultural exchanges, environment, health and
space cooperation." The president was "confident" that the summit would
be "an important milestone in the improvement of relations between our
two countries."[44] In a word: détente. To be achieved via the back channel.

"Nixon Sees [Z]hou in Two Sessions of Policy Talks" was emblazoned
in large, capitalized, italic font down the right column of the front page
of Nixon's hated *New York Times* on February 23. Katharine Graham's
Washington Post, another newspaper Nixon detested, went a step further,
showing the picture of a beaming president at the Peking Ballet, flanked
by Madame Mao and a young female interpreter, dominating the left column, with an even larger headline, "Chinese Press, TV Play up Nixon
Visit," and more pictures on the right side. Both the *Times* and the *Post*
described how he had been received as "a public sensation" in the People's
Republic.[45] In contrast to the warm reception Nixon received in China,
Brezhnev's response to his letter, delivered that same morning in Washington, D.C., was considerably cooler. Brezhnev noted that the confidential exchanges had increased "precisely in this way that we agreed with
the president to conduct preparation for the summit meeting." Brezhnev
then noted the disparity between confidential exchanges and public statements and took particular exception to the president's own message to

Congress on foreign policy (which had been written by Kissinger): "In the United States more and more frequently statements are made and documents published, which contain totally groundless reproaches addressed to the Soviet. . . . And this is being done not by private persons or small functionaries. What is meant here is the statements of the president himself and such a document as his foreign policy report to the U.S. Congress outlining the fundamental approach to the questions of relations with foreign states, including the Soviet Union."

Brezhnev said he hoped that the public and private exchanges could be conducted in a "business-like" manner and agreed that détente was a worthy goal "in the interests of our peoples, and other peoples of the world."[46]

From February 17 through February 28, the president was on his historic trip to China or in transit, but the return to Washington meant an immediate return to business as usual.[47] The president's triumphant return also signaled that gears had shifted in U.S.-Soviet back channels, and both sides used them to alleviate some of the tensions added by Sino-American rapprochement.

On February 28 the president and Mrs. Nixon got off *The Spirit of '76* aircraft at 9:15 p.m. at Andrews Air Force Base, gave some brief remarks, and arrived at the White House aboard the presidential *Marine One* helicopter less than forty-five minutes later. An hour after his arrival, Nixon called Kissinger, who reported with glee that California governor Ronald Reagan said he had "never doubted" the president on America's defense commitments to Taiwan and the Peking summit.[48] The result of the Peking summit, the jointly issued Shanghai Communiqué, left enough wiggle room for Nixon to open a relationship with China without abandoning Taiwan, which pleased Reagan, the Right's standard-bearer. Kissinger also predicted that Arizona senator and 1964 GOP presidential nominee Barry Goldwater, a.k.a. "Mr. Conservative," and *National Review* editor William F. Buckley Jr. would be harder to convince.[49]

Toward the end of the call, Kissinger brought up the content of the February 23 Brezhnev letter. Evidently, Goldwater and Buckley weren't the only people with ruffled feathers over the Sino-American rapprochement. With the China trip behind him, Nixon advocated assuaging Brezhnev via the back channel with Dobrynin:

NIXON: Well, I think on this meeting with Dobrynin [scheduled for March 1] it's probably worth it if you would bring him in for a minute just to say, "Hello," to me. . . . I just think it's just a good little touch, you see.

KISSINGER: Well, my frank opinion is to do it after, not right this minute.

NIXON: Why?

KISSINGER: Because I'm worried that these sons-of-bitches—

NIXON: The Chinese?

KISSINGER:—may just get it back to the Chinese, that you saw Dobrynin right after [seeing them]—

NIXON: Fine, fine, fine. But, you can see him?

KISSINGER: Oh, I'll see him Wednesday. I am having lunch with him.

NIXON: Um-hmm. And then you tell him, though, because he may say, well, the president would like to see him. . . . Say, "Yes, the president does want to see you, because prior to the trip [to Moscow], Mr. Ambassador, the president wants to have a good off-the-record talk with you to get your advice." How about that? Something like that?

KISSINGER: Oh, that's good.[50]

Like a television set with a broken tuner, the Channel seemed stuck on discussion of China in the immediate aftermath of the Peking summit. The tension of the first meeting after the summit, on March 1, is palpable in Kissinger's descriptive memorandum of the conversation. Making good on a pre–Peking summit promise of briefing the Soviet ambassador on the trip, Kissinger found Dobrynin "extremely jovial, but clearly under instructions not to ask any questions or show any excessive interest." Kissinger pointedly noted that "[Dobrynin] violated these instructions consistently."[51] Dobrynin's account of the same meeting is much less colorful, but significantly more detailed.[52] The two barely mentioned Vietnam in either account, and both sides seemed more conciliatory when talking about the geostrategic situation and the means by which to move ahead with détente.

The two sides conducted additional back-channel meetings during March 1972 in a constructive spirit by ironing out the details of the division of labor between the White House and other agencies on matters like Lend-Lease and trade. Kissinger and Dobrynin arranged to send the U.S. secretary of agriculture, Earl Butz, to the Soviet Union to work out a deal for a massive grain sale. The Departments of State, Commerce, Agriculture, and even the National Aeronautics and Space Administration (NASA) coordinated through the White House on the agreements to be signed at the Moscow summit. Vietnam remained in the background as the U.S. intelligence saw increasing buildup for an offensive. The meetings mainly focused on the March 17, 1972, joint announcement that the Moscow summit would start on May 22, 1972. Kissinger and Dobrynin had more detailed discussions on SALT and the Middle East, and even the president made an appearance to allay any Soviet fears about the U.S. commitment to détente. Dobrynin remembered asking Nixon about his personal thoughts about the summit. According to Dobrynin's memoirs, Nixon replied: "Here is Henry, whom I trust completely. Whatever he says comes directly from me. There is no man in the administration who can speak on my behalf with greater authority. It is true, Bill Rogers is an old friend of mine and has all necessary authority as secretary of state. But he is locked together with a great bureaucratic machine. His staff cannot be controlled, nor can it keep things in strict confidence. That is why I do this kind of thing through Kissinger."[53]

In any form of communication, there is often a dichotomy between intended and received signals. In the case of the importance of the back channel, the Soviets, and particularly Ambassador Dobrynin, understood exactly what President Nixon had meant. Aside from an exchange at a meeting on March 10, reported by Dobrynin, the discussion on Vietnam remained status quo.[54]

Linkage via the Channel: The "Polish Bloc," the Middle East, and Germany-Berlin

On the morning of March 28, Kissinger met with Nixon in the Oval Office to discuss summit-planning details—namely, the duration of the trip, a postsummit stopover in Poland after a brief stay in Iran, and how to handle the matters via the Channel. The two first briefly discussed Vietnam, noting that American bombing raids had resulted in "massive casualties" on "concentrated" enemy positions. They then discussed the Soviet proposal that Nixon stay for eight days at the Kremlin. A trip to Poland could cause a potential snafu because it could offend the political sensitivities in Kremlin, which considered Poland a satellite nation and wanted to minimize independence of action in the Warsaw Pact. As a result of the Sino-Soviet split and harsh talk and party congresses over the preceding decade, Moscow already had tense relations with Romania and Albania, which backed Beijing. Nixon also did not make any other foreign visits on his way to or from China a month earlier, and the Soviets might not want to share the spotlight. Nixon, however, saw an opportunity for domestic political gain. The president told Kissinger to work out "the Polish thing" with Dobrynin: "They want it for some purposes, but they may be underestimating what it can do in serving our own purposes. In terms of foreign countries we can visit, a Polish visit is by far the most important."

Polish Americans, in the president's estimation, made up a "most politically powerful ethnic" voting bloc. "The Poles vote as a bloc; the Italians do not," Nixon the politician continued. "The Italians split up a great deal because they've been more assimilated into the community. The Poles . . . live in their little ghettos, still, in Philadelphia, New York, Chicago, Cleveland, Detroit . . . in terms of voters, it's an enormous wallop." Nixon the foreign policy president then conceded: "Now, having said that, naturally, we can't do anything, visit any place like that, which is going to hurt us in a foreign policy way. Now, the Russians, you've just got to feel it out with Dobrynin and see what it is."

Nixon and Kissinger also had to figure out how to reassure NATO that the trip to the Soviet Union did not weaken the alliance, but without offending the Soviets. Kissinger raised the idea of using the secretary of state. Rogers apparently had *some* purpose. Nixon decided that Rogers should skip the presidential trip to Tehran and "go directly to NATO. Absolutely." Kissinger counseled, "Well, the way to handle NATO is if Rogers would peel off when you go to Baku and Teheran, it gives him two-and-a-half days at NATO." When Kissinger raised the possibility that Rogers could rejoin the president in Warsaw, Nixon raised his voice: "No, he doesn't need to rejoin me in Poland. He should go to NATO. Goddamnit, that's what he's supposed to do there!"

Returning to the possible Polish stopover, Kissinger repeated his handling instructions for Dobrynin: "And I think the way to handle Poland, given the situation you describe, is to tell the honest truth to Dobrynin, to say exactly what we're up against. Why we want it, but give them the choice of vetoing it." Kissinger reassured the president: "They won't veto it. . . . And if they try to veto it, we can get so many points with them." Talk of the Polish stopover came full circle as Nixon and Kissinger returned to the topic of a presidential stay in the Kremlin, a rare honor being bestowed upon the president, "a guarantee of the success," in Kissinger's mind. After all, he continued, Eisenhower stayed in the Kremlin only one night, while French president Charles de Gaulle—a leader Nixon respected for his strength—had stayed only two nights. Nixon had been invited to stay all eight nights.

As the summit became more and more of a reality, Kissinger told Nixon about his evolving Middle East strategy to be handled via the back channel and at the summit. Kissinger advocated fighting secrecy with secrecy:

KISSINGER: My fear is that the Israelis have enough wind of what we're planning, that you will come back and you will be asked, "Are there any secret deals?"

NIXON: Yeah, I know.

KISSINGER: Therefore, what we should do in my judgment is to make a secret deal to make a secret deal. You see what I mean?

NIXON: Huh.

KISSINGER: In other words, agree with the Russians . . . you've offered them that I'd go over there after the summit, for example—

NIXON: Yeah. Yeah.

KISSINGER: We must make the deal. And we must—

NIXON: That's the problem.

KISSINGER: And we must, we must brutalize the Israelis.

NIXON: Yeah.

KISSINGER: I think we should do it right *after* the election, though, and not before the election. There'll be the goddamndest brawl.

NIXON: There could be.

KISSINGER: Because I also don't know how you would trigger it before the election without being at the verge of a Middle East war.

In a quiet, almost inaudible tone of voice, Nixon explained that his pro-Israel stance would not help him in the election. Domestic politics and foreign policy were inescapably linked: "We've checked the situation with regard to what we call 'the Jewish vote,' and we get about 12%." With resignation, he continued: "We're not gonna get any more than that. And if we get any less than that it isn't gonna make a hell of a lot of difference, because 12% of what is basically 6% and so forth, and most of the places are not too important." The president persisted: "Now, the other side of the coin is that if they want to make a brawl about this . . . they're gonna find that there are gonna be more people on the side of not getting the United States involved in a Middle East conflict than there are gonna be on the other side." Kissinger suggested "brutalizing the Israelis" but granted that "the way to brutalize them is get a war scare started in the Middle East. . . . And then you side against them. I think you're better off without a war scare there in an election year." More importantly, Kissinger said: "I think we get more out of the Russians by dangling it in front of them than by delivering it. I would like to have something going on. I look at the Israeli thing as a cold-blooded enterprise." The linkages between the Middle East, the Channel, and the summit arose again:

KISSINGER: Mr. President, you can make the deal at the summit. What I would like to get done at the summit is the interim agreement. That we can publicize.
NIXON: Can you do that?
KISSINGER: Yes.
NIXON: That's all we need. . . . How can you make an interim agreement? The Israelis won't even agree to what's necessary to get that.
KISSINGER: They'll do it for us.
HALDEMAN: You think they will?
KISSINGER: Yeah. The interim they'll do. My worry—
NIXON: The interim is fine. Then let them make the final one later.

The Middle East had now been removed from the State Department's hands for good (during the Nixon administration, at least) and brought under direct presidential purview through the Channel. Seeing the Third

World through a Cold War lens, Nixon said: "My view of the Middle East has nothing to do with Israel or the Arabs; it has a hell of a lot to do with Russia and the United States. . . . And State does not understand it that way." The major obstacle to creating a settlement was not the Soviet adversary, however, but the Israeli ally:

KISSINGER: But the Israelis have to be handled with exceptional trickiness, because their intelligence is so good.

NIXON: I know. And also they know they've got us by the balls.

KISSINGER: Well, to some extent they have us by the balls, but I think it's in our interest to move on them as early in the new term as you can.

NIXON: Yeah.

KISSINGER: So it's done by the time. We have to get the Russians out of the Middle East. . . .

NIXON: That's right, too. . . . And we've got to get into the Middle East. We've got to be in other than in Israel. That's the point.

KISSINGER: Well, once they are out, we are in a better position to go in.[55]

At Kissinger's March 28 luncheon meeting at the Soviet embassy, Dobrynin delivered a letter from Brezhnev to Nixon. Brezhnev and his colleagues promised to "closely follow the course of preparation for the May meeting in Moscow as well as all the events attendant to that preparation." Brezhnev first stated common ground with the United States over the Quadripartite Agreement on West Berlin, adding that the adoption of the agreement "will indeed make a major step on the way to strengthening the détente and ensuring security in Europe." The general secretary then moved on to strategic arms limitations and agreed that both sides should cease any new construction of land-based ICBM silos, thus beginning a freeze in July 1972. The SALT and ABM agreements would be, in Brezhnev's eyes, "such an important step in the relations between our countries, that its significance can hardly be overestimated." Brezhnev also hoped for "more detailed considerations on the Middle East settlement," as had been done with the September 1971 visit of Gromyko to Washington and through the back channel. Almost as an afterthought, Brezhnev brought up the vague concept of "making conditions most suitable for our meeting." He warned "that continued bombings of the DRV . . . push the developments in Vietnam in a direction opposite to peaceful settlement—can only complicate the situation."[56]

The Offensive Begins

The actual start of the offensive proved anticlimactic because of an element of uncertainty. During a morning meeting on March 30, an anonymous staffer briefly interrupted the discussion between Nixon, Kissinger, and Haldeman to hand the NSC advisor a note. Kissinger read the note and quickly explained that the long-anticipated offensive had begun as North Vietnam attacked eight fire-support bases across the DMZ.[57] Or, as Haldeman recorded in his diary, almost as an afterthought: "The North Vietnamese have attacked South Vietnam. The attack that we've been concerned about and waiting for."[58] Stumbling for words, Nixon unleashed a staccato barrage of questions: "What's the situation? . . . This is an attack on a broad front? . . . How?"

The White House spent most of the next few days wondering whether it was "a real attack or just a blip," as Kissinger phrased it when he explained the situation half a world away to the president. The linkage between Vietnam and an improvement in U.S.-Soviet relations proved too powerful for the president to resist, as he immediately connected the offensive to Kissinger's upcoming afternoon meeting with Dobrynin:

> NIXON: I think you should tell Dobrynin that we're rather
> surprised by this attack . . . and you can say, "Look, you
> don't know . . . the president has said he wants to make the
> best possible arrangement with Brezhnev. . . . We're on the
> same track, but an attack on North Vietnam may make it
> impossible. It may spoil it." . . . I'd play it very hard.
> KISSINGER: In fact, at the end of [Brezhnev's] letter, he had
> a rather mild expression of hope that we wouldn't bomb
> North Vietnam. And I can just take off from that and say . . .
> we have showed great restraint.[59]

The central issue remained whether or not the Soviets knew about the offensive and how much they had done to make it possible by supplying

North Vietnam. Moscow provided war materiel like sophisticated Surface-to-Air Missiles (SAMs), mobile artillery, heavy tanks, and the more basic supplies like petroleum, oil, and lubricants (POL). Against the backdrop of the Sino-Soviet conflict, both Moscow and Beijing aided Hanoi to show that each was committed to socialism and the support of socialist revolution.[60]

Predictably, the administration responded to the enemy's offensive military action with increased bombing and gave the Soviets a preview of the reaction via the Channel. Nixon instructed Kissinger to tell Dobrynin that the United States had exercised "great restraint *since this*." Nixon unabashedly warned: "Now, instead we're going to have to do it. And *it's only because they're attacking*. And you've just got to keep, have them *knock off this attack or we're going to bomb them*." The president added: "But I'd tell him, 'Now look, Mr. Ambassador, I cannot vouch for what [Nixon] won't do. I mean don't think that it's going to be limited to what we have done before.'" The president emphasized that Kissinger should tell Dobrynin not to assume that the U.S. response against North Vietnam would "be limited to the kind of a bombing we've done before."[61] Nixon later floated the idea of using nuclear weapons against Hanoi but actually only mentioned the atomic option in passing. Listening to the conversation, one gets the sense that the Nixon White House sincerely believed that the Soviets would get the message.[62] Nixon and Kissinger had stayed on message inside and outside the special back-channel relationship with the Soviet leadership. Even still, the long-anticipated offensive had begun, and matters would only be complicated as the military situation in Southeast Asia developed.

Events in Vietnam imperiled the summit in both Washington and Moscow. The United States used back channels in coordination with more regular diplomacy to send subtle and not-so-subtle signals that the linkages could be used as levers to apply pressure. The Nixon White House wished to express a willingness to deal with the Soviets on the summit but had to appear not too willing, lest it be seen as overeager and weak. Contradictory impulses abounded. Nixon wanted to appear tough but not too tough, to seem like a madman but also appear rational.

Once Kissinger received confirmation that the North Vietnamese drive across the DMZ was an actual offensive, he invited Dobrynin to the White House for an urgent meeting early in the afternoon on April 3. The start of the offensive was "just as well," Kissinger told the president that morning, adding: "We can now precipitate. I'm going to get Dobrynin in and I'm going to tell him, I'm just going to threaten him with the non-ratification of the Berlin treaty." Agreeing, Nixon responded: "Keep in mind the fact that you—that we—still want to drive a hard bargain on the summit. Oh, they want that summit. . . . They can't trade Vietnam for this."[63]

Dobrynin met with Kissinger late that afternoon to discuss the developing offensive and its potential effects on U.S.-Soviet relations. Although he did not produce a memorandum of the conversation, Kissinger described his encounter in two phone calls to the president. In the first phone call, right after Dobrynin had left, Kissinger told the course of the discussion and his playing it tough with the Soviets through the back channel:

> KISSINGER: I told him what you said and he said, "Isn't it
> amazing what a little country can do to wreck well-laid
> plans?" I said, "The President wants you to know we will
> under no circumstances accept a defeat there and we will
> do what is necessary not to." He said, "What do you want
> us to do?" I said, "First, to show restraint and secondly you
> have to ask yourselves whether this isn't the time to bring an
> end to the war. There is, after all, when I look around the
> world I see no areas where we should be in conflict." He said
> he did not either—not even in Vietnam. Then I brought
> up the Berlin thing. I said, "Look, here we are. We get the
> ratification thing coming up in Germany, the president
> has been asked to write to Brandt, but he can't under these
> circumstances and he wants you to know if we should lose
> in Vietnam that is the last concession we will make this
> year." He said, "You aren't going to lose. In our assessment
> you can't lose."[64]

Dobrynin matter-of-factly reported the meeting back to Moscow, adding interesting detail to what Kissinger had told the president. Dobrynin relayed Kissinger's assessment that the United States was "talking about a large-scale armed invasion of South Vietnam." Kissinger, the ambassador told Moscow, said that the United States had secretly arranged to

meet with the North Vietnamese in Paris on April 24, but Hanoi duplici-
tously launched the offensive. Dobrynin told Moscow how the White
House saw the situation in personal terms and that, according to Kissinger, Hanoi wanted to "personally humiliate" Saigon and Washington
as the U.S. election season approached. Kissinger added, "Nor is it out of
the question . . . that these North Vietnamese actions are also directed
against the president's trip to Moscow."[65]

Then came the remarkable point, as Dobrynin recorded, laying the
foundation for the actual course of action. The United States would delink
Vietnam from détente if the Soviets overlooked the response Nixon would
be "forced to undertake" against North Vietnam. The White House recognized that Moscow and Hanoi were allies, but, "at the same time, the
president is also well aware that Moscow did not perform any planning or
encourage Hanoi at this particular time to carry out the current offensive
by North Vietnamese troops against South Vietnam; rather it is an independent action by the DRV Government itself."[66] The North Vietnamese
pursued their own national interests, separate from and even at crosscur-
rents with Soviet interests. The subtext was that the United States and
the Soviet Union should do whatever was necessary in their own national
interests apart from their respective allies.

According to Dobrynin, Kissinger explained that the White House
hoped that U.S. action would "not be viewed in Moscow as being deliberately directed against the interests of the Soviet Union and that all this
will not negatively impact Soviet-U.S. relations in other fields and in other
parts of the world, such as Europe." Kissinger described that, keeping
Brezhnev's letter of March 27 in mind, Nixon had "ordered that during
the initial stage U.S. retaliatory actions should be fairly limited in scope."
There could be "no guarantees" over the longer term, however, because
everything would depend on military developments in Vietnam. Kissinger pleaded for perspective, as Dobrynin reported that he said, "We
would very much like to hope that this crisis will not seriously affect the
incipient process of visible improvement in Soviet-U.S. relations and will
not get in the way of a constructive outcome to the meeting in Moscow." Contrary to what Kissinger had told the president about Dobrynin's
response, Dobrynin wrote, vaguely, that he had simply repeated Moscow's
"fundamental view."[67] In retrospect, it appears that Kissinger was not the
only one who had to appear tough to his superiors.

If the Soviet Union could not overlook the American reaction, Kissinger warned, it would immediately sacrifice the Berlin treaty, SALT, trade, and the other components of the framework of peace. In another phone call on April 3, for example, Kissinger told Nixon: "I think the Russians are going to do something [for us on Vietnam]. They're not going to risk everything." Nixon inquired, "You think that got across to Dobrynin?" "Oh, he'll get it back," Kissinger promised. Nixon agreed: "He will pass the word: They are risking the summit, they're risking Berlin—I mean the German treaties . . . and our whole relationship." Kissinger replied, "I told him, 'We just can't consider sending a message to Brandt [to help with the Bundestag ratification] under these conditions.'"[68] Although the groundwork for the actual summit meeting was largely in place, the developing situation in Southeast Asia would add twists and turns to the story.

A Kissinger-Dobrynin meeting on April 6 essentially reinforced their exchange of three days earlier. According to Dobrynin, "Kissinger devoted a considerable amount of time to the situation in Vietnam" and again argued that the offensive was in part designed to upset the summit meeting. Kissinger also believed Hanoi wanted to influence American public opinion and discredit President Nixon. Dobrynin summarized Kissinger's comments with regard to the Soviet Union as "mainly centered on two themes, albeit in a rather veiled way." First, Kissinger's remarks indicated Nixon's desire for the Soviet Union "to still exert some restraining influence on Hanoi." Second, Kissinger conveyed "a de facto appeal by the White House" for the Soviets to "not allow the events in Vietnam to have a serious impact on the meeting in Moscow." Dobrynin saw the implied context of "heavy bombing of the DRV that is being planned by Washington," although Kissinger "did not directly frame the issue that way."[69]

Kissinger's report to Nixon of the conversation stressed less of the conciliatory response to the Soviets and added fuel to the crisis mentality provoked by the offensive. Kissinger wrote that Dobrynin tried to downplay the offensive, arguing that the White House "took the situation too gravely." When Dobrynin inquired as to whether or not the White House seriously believed the Soviet Union had anything to do with planning the offensive, Kissinger boasted later to Nixon, he told Dobrynin that there were "only two possibilities, either they planned it or their negligence made it possible. In either event, it was an unpleasant eventuality."[70]

Dobrynin unmistakably got the message. In an extremely urgent and top-secret cable back to Moscow, the Soviet ambassador wrote that the situation in Vietnam was "aggravating the overall international situation and our relations with the U.S., and [would] further aggravate them in advance of the Moscow meeting." Public opinion inside and outside the United States was "tensely following" the developments. Using Soviet phraseology, Dobrynin noted that "the Soviet Union's arms shipments have been quite important in the patriotic forces' successes," but Moscow's "political stature and prestige" could also be used to prevent the "events in Vietnam from escalating into a major international crisis." Dobrynin advocated a Soviet initiative with public statements promoting peace and private entreaties to both Hanoi and Washington. Dobrynin also recommended the use of confidential channels to Nixon "in a rather flexible way to leave the door open to further constructive dialogue" and warned that "the Chinese, too, could serve as a confidential intermediary between Hanoi and Washington."[71] Kissinger's efforts to exacerbate the Soviet fear of Sino-American cooperation to settle Vietnam had an effect, demonstrating both the essence and the partial effectiveness of triangular diplomacy. Dobrynin encouraged rhetorical support of North Vietnam while trying to work out an arrangement behind the scenes. Back channels were ideally suited to both Kissinger's and Dobrynin's purposes.

In addition to the back-channel approaches, Kissinger relied on his carefully cultivated contacts in the media to send messages to the Soviets indirectly. For example, Kissinger used his long-standing relationship with syndicated columnist Joe Kraft to hint at the White House deliberations and send a message to the Soviets, who carefully monitored what the American Fourth Estate said. Kraft called Kissinger on the morning of April 9 to talk about the offensive in Vietnam and its potential effects on U.S.-Soviet relations. The journalist told Kissinger that "people around town" had told him that the North Vietnamese offensive was "not a calculated plan" by the Soviet leadership but stemmed more from the "Soviet inability to say 'no' to the North Vietnamese." Kissinger agreed. "It would not be harmful if you speculate along these lines," Kissinger told the columnist; "It would be helpful, in fact."

Kraft then inquired as to the significance of the March 1972 mission by the head of Soviet air defense, Marshal Pavel Batitsky, to Hanoi. Kissinger responded that there were two possible theories as to Moscow's motives for supporting North Vietnam. First, Kissinger stated, was "a very farsighted plan" whereby the Soviets could challenge "the U.S. first in the Subcontinent and in Southeast Asia, and when we come to Moscow we are coming in total weakness." "The other theory," Kissinger continued, "is [that] they see the opportunity to outmaneuver Peking in Hanoi. Hanoi keeps bleeding equipment out of them and . . . also they don't know a big offensive is planned and they get sucked in." Kissinger expressed his opinion that it was "blundering rather than a master plan."

The larger stakes for the Soviets were a major factor. Kraft asked if the Soviets understood the "impact on Germany." Kissinger replied: "If this turns into a Soviet-U.S. crisis, it complicates the passage of these treaties in an enormous way. There is no question we could stop passage of these treaties if we wanted to." The White House might also retaliate if it discovered proof of Soviet involvement in the offensive. Without acknowledging the existence of the Channel, Kissinger told Kraft, "If we were convinced this was carefully planned, we would have to get Dobrynin out of here." Kissinger noted that the Soviets could conspire, "but for big stakes and not putting all into the hands of a client," it remained unlikely.[72]

A half hour later, Kissinger reported the conversation with Kraft to Nixon. "I told him it was not a conspiracy," Kissinger explained, "but incompetency." Blowing off some steam, the president responded: "We all know what this is. It is a damn conspiracy. The Indian thing, the UAR and this is a massive attempt on the Soviet part to put it to us." The conversation continued with the theme of the imperiled summit, the need for forceful action in Vietnam, and the interlinked aspects between Hanoi, Moscow, Beijing, and American politics:

> [KISSINGER]: They haven't understood all the implications. I don't believe they would put the test to us into an area where their intelligence is so bad. They don't know how this can be going. I think they saw a chance of picking up a cheap trick against Peking and blundered into a confrontation with us again. That is more worrisome than the other. If it is a conspiracy, we could turn it off . . .
>
> [NIXON]: We are coming to the point—with Safire working on the draft—of knocking off of the Soviet Summit becomes more and more a possibility.

[KISSINGER]: I am afraid so. I do not have another view. I do not
think we can survive a Soviet Summit as a country if we are
humiliated in Vietnam. Unless they accept rules of conduct,
we may have to confront them. It is easy for me to say. But if
one looks at an election on that platform . . .

[NIXON]: The country would be done then.

[KISSINGER]: I think our bargaining position in Moscow,
if it came out of a position of total weakness, would be
hopeless.[73]

Kraft published his column titled "The Russian Role" two days later.
Discounting murmurs from Pennsylvania Avenue that the North Vietnamese offensive was a "prelude to a new set of peace offers" to surface
at the Moscow summit, the journalist countered, "The White House, on
the eve of summit talks full of implications for the presidential election,
is about as good a judge of Communist intentions as a baby is of candy."
Kraft clearly took a hard line, but the question was whether or not the
Soviets would get the message. Kraft wrote that the "Soviet Ambassador
. . . almost certainly reassured the White House that Moscow wanted
the summit meeting to go ahead, and with it the various moves toward
détente with the West." By repeating the assessments of "the hard-line
Kremlinologists," Kraft endorsed their position. Through aid and equipment deliveries, the Soviets had to know that Hanoi was preparing a
major offensive. Echoing the private conversation with Kissinger, Kraft
wrote, "The initial Soviet reaction was to steer the North Vietnamese
toward a more peaceful settlement," but "the North Vietnamese refused."
In the face of North Vietnamese independence, however, the Soviets saw
an opportunity to weaken Nixon's bargaining position at the upcoming
summit. Kraft noted, "On the basis of visits by Marshal Batitsky and others, the Russians decided that instead of trying to head off the offensive,
they should play it down as a mere bagatelle that need not get in the way
of détente with the West."

Again repeating the Kremlinologists' line, Kraft warned, "Nixon
would find himself in an awful fix." Kraft saw two alternatives. Under the
first scenario and with his position undercut, Nixon could "yield to a very
tough Soviet approach, accepting arms control terms highly favorable to
Russia, and at best disguised surrender in Vietnam." Alternately, Nixon

could "dig in very hard, bombing North Vietnam flat, breaking off the various negotiations for détente, and forcing a return to Cold War across the board." Kraft qualified the two alternatives and advocated a third course: "Maybe these forebodings are exaggerated. Maybe the Russian leaders did not know of the offensive and its scope. Maybe the fighting in Vietnam will have eased off before the summit. Maybe the Russians truly do want détente with the West." Kraft's "fall-back position" amounted to postponing the Moscow summit "to a more favorable time."[74]

Kraft's columns would be used in conjunction with other news stories fed by the White House to foreshadow the actual cancellation crisis. First, however, other signals would be used, including giving Ambassador Dobrynin a personal stake in the summit.

Back Channels by Other Means

On April 9, Nixon also told Kissinger to tell Dobrynin, "the Summit is on the line now." The president amplified the warning: "I think he has to know with this going as it is that we are under enormous pressure. The whole Summit is being jeopardized. Our hold card is to play more with the Chinese." Kissinger responded, "I have talked to him sternly twice last week." Kissinger had continued the explicit linkage with Berlin: "I sent a message to [Egon] Bahr. They [Bonn and Moscow] requested a letter from you recommending ratification of the treaties. I was against it and sent a message saying under the circumstances—since this is the second time Soviet arms are engaged in an offensive—we are reassessing the whole policy." Kissinger assured the president that the message would get through to the Soviets, albeit in a circuitous fashion, claiming that Bahr would "run to the Soviet Ambassador—we have some intelligence on him. He gave back exactly what we gave him here." Nixon inquired whether he should write another message to Brezhnev, but Kissinger advised against it: "The danger is if they don't see a way out they may have to confront you. They got the message and I would save this. Let me work out a scenario for you."[75] Kissinger put one of his top men, Helmut Sonnenfeldt, on options to send more signals to the Soviets.[76]

Ambassador Dobrynin attended a private screening of a newsreel of Kissinger's two trips to China in the top-secret White House Situation Room on April 9. The meeting was both social and political, as Mrs.

Dobrynin joined her husband and Kissinger's parents attended. Talking one-on-one out of earshot of their family members, Kissinger and Dobrynin conducted an ad hoc back-channel meeting. The national security advisor told the ambassador: "Anatol, we have been warning you for months that if there were an offensive we would take drastic measures to end the war once and for all. That situation has now arisen."[77]

Dobrynin summarized Kissinger's comments at the private screening in greater detail: Hanoi had gambled with the offensive; the White House had been showing restraint; restraint occurred "not for lack of resources" with the steady buildup of air power and naval assets; Washington's restraint showed "primarily a desire to not overly complicate U.S.-Soviet relations"; the United States sought negotiations with the North Vietnamese but remained cagey as to whether Kissinger would actually meet Le Duc Tho in Paris on April 24; U.S. "counter-operations" were not aimed at the Soviet Union but would be necessary if Hanoi continued "its offensive operations." Once again, Kissinger argued against the conspiracy theory: "By all indications, Hanoi was acting on its own in this case." Also, the United States would appreciate Soviet assistance in resolving the matter and communicating with the North Vietnamese, but it "boiled down to the premise that he has repeated more than once: further developments depend entirely on Hanoi."[78]

The president publicly picked up on the theme the following day at the signing of the Biological and Toxin Weapons Convention. Nixon reflected that it served as "a subtle occasion to apply pressure on the Soviets." With Dobrynin in attendance, Nixon aimed his remarks at the Soviet Union with a general statement about the responsibility of the great powers not to "directly or indirectly encourage any other nation to use force or armed aggression."[79] Recently published evidence from the Soviet Archives shows that the signals, back-channel and otherwise, increasingly fell on receptive ears, at least in the Soviet embassy. Dobrynin cabled Moscow and suggested that the Soviets attempt to facilitate a meeting between North Vietnamese prime minister Pham Van Dong and President Nixon in Moscow. Instead of viewing Vietnam as a liability in U.S.-Soviet relations, Dobrynin wrote, "Hanoi must realize that given Nixon's trip to Moscow we have additional opportunities to influence him in terms of support for the struggling Vietnamese people."[80]

Back-channel diplomacy became a family affair, with the president and Kissinger personally directing the star performance of Mrs. Thelma Catherine Nixon (affectionately known as Pat) from the Oval Office following the signing of the Biological and Toxin Weapons Convention.[81] After the ceremony, Dobrynin wrote, "Nixon passed on to me a request from his wife to meet with my wife to discuss certain 'women's aspects' of the trip to the Soviet Union."[82] Nixon, however, wrote in his memoirs that Dobrynin "called Kissinger and suggested that the ladies' meeting be arranged for the next day," a fact the Soviet ambassador left out of the official record.[83] During an early-afternoon discussion, Nixon and Kissinger briefly reviewed the idea before the president asked a White House operator to find his wife.[84] In the short phone conversation that ensued, Nixon asked Mrs. Nixon to see Mrs. Dobrynin "for foreign policy reasons," whereupon Mrs. Nixon agreed.[85] Following some additional conversation in the presence of the president, Kissinger called Dobrynin to confirm the details. After Kissinger thanked Dobrynin for the idea, Dobrynin interjected: "No, no, no. The pleasure is ours, our duty really." Kissinger explained that Mrs. Dobrynin should enter "through the diplomatic entrance . . . the same place you do." The ambassador noted, "The car will be the same," and Kissinger explained that somebody would meet the ambassador's wife.[86]

Nixon took a particular interest in using his wife as a back-channel agent to the Soviets. At the president's request, Kissinger briefed Mrs. Nixon on the "foreign policy reasons" related to the upcoming tea.[87] According to Nixon's daughter Julie Nixon Eisenhower, at dinner that same evening the president had explained to Mrs. Nixon: "The Russians are acting badly. . . . We've got to shake them up." The president advised his wife "to tell Madame Dobrynin how much she was looking forward to seeing Russia again, and then to add it was a pity that what was happening in Vietnam might force a cancellation of the visit."[88] Adding to sense of secrecy, the meeting "never appeared on the First Lady's official schedule." The president's daughter provides the most detailed description of the meeting, from personal interviews with her mother and access to her father's personal daily diary:

> After a perfunctory discussion about some of the places Mrs. Nixon had visited on her last trip to Russia and about Moscow in the spring, Mother mentioned that she did hope nothing would

happen to prevent the next visit from taking place. Madame Dobrynin squeezed Mother's hand and nodded vigorously, saying, "Oh, yes, yes." As Mother remembers, "She went right home and told her husband about our meeting, and he immediately called Kissinger and assured him that the Soviets were in favor of the visit."[89]

In Nixon's retrospective estimation, the meeting "was very successful. Pat showed great skill and subtlety."[90] Nixon spoke on the phone with Kissinger not long after the tea. The president proudly told his NSC advisor:

NIXON: Then Mrs. Nixon raised this point: "I just hope it won't hurt the visit." Mrs. Dobrynin squeezed her hand and said, with almost tears in her eyes, "I hope not. I hope not." [laughs] So, we got *that* message across.

KISSINGER: Did she mention Vietnam?

NIXON: Oh, hell yes! That's what she talked about.

KISSINGER: Oh, good.

NIXON: My wife did, yes. Oh, it was right on—You know how she'd do it? Right on the nose. . . . So, that message goes back. Right.[91]

The use of a back channel, kept off the White House appointment logs and quietly arranged by the president and the national security advisor, achieved several objectives. First, it gave Ambassador Dobrynin a personal stake in the summit. The fact that Dobrynin characterized the idea as the Americans' and made scant reference to it in his memcons or cables shows that the White House achieved the first objective. Second, Nixon carefully scripted and choreographed the meeting, clearly conveying the intended diplomatic signal that the United States remained interested in the summit but events in Vietnam might force its cancellation. Lastly, the meeting subtly reinforced the belief that the dominant faction in the Kremlin, led by Leonid Brezhnev, wanted the summit because of the known personal ties between the Dobrynin and Brezhnev families.

During a conversation on April 12, Kissinger reported the results of an earlier meeting with Dobrynin. Kissinger noted that the Soviet ambassador had reaffirmed that "Mrs. Dobrynin was moved to tears by Mrs. Nixon and has written a personal letter to Mrs. Brezhnev." Nixon then asked, "I think the Russians want the summit, don't you?" Kissinger replied: "I think the Russians must. The whole position of Brezhnev depends on the goddamn summit." Earlier in the conversation, Nixon told Kissinger: "If they can guarantee secrecy to Russia, I think you should go to Russia. . . . Also there's some advantage in your sort of finding out what Brezhnev is like for us."[92]

Kissinger's Secret Trip to Moscow

From April 12 through April 17 Kissinger met with and talked to Dobrynin or Vorontsov repeatedly about Vietnam. The issues were serious, and Kissinger characterized some of the back-channel exchanges as having been "acrimonious."[93] Through regular meetings, Kissinger and Dobrynin also discussed the status of peace negotiations with the North Vietnamese and the possibility, which Kissinger deemed remote, that the Soviets would arrange a U.S.-DRV contact negotiation in Moscow. Most importantly, on April 12, Nixon tentatively agreed to send Kissinger to Moscow on a secret trip to plan the details for the summit, now only weeks away. Nixon had responded to a Soviet request that Kissinger had promoted for months. With the president taking a pessimistic view of the Soviet role in enabling North Vietnam by supplying the offensive, Kissinger said he took a tough, uncompromising stance in his meetings with the Soviets. The Channel was used to assuage the president's concerns.

In the memcon of the April 12 meeting with Dobrynin that Kissinger prepared for the president, he wrote that he had told the Soviet ambassador, "You are responsible for this conflict, either because you planned it or because you tried to score off the Chinese and as a result have put yourself into the position where a miserable little country can jeopardize everything that has been striven for for years." Kissinger wrote, "I was also bound to tell Dobrynin that I was not authorized to discuss any of the other subjects with him." He reported that Dobrynin acquiesced and used the memo to reinforce the idea of a secret trip, giving credit to the Soviet ambassador: "Dobrynin replied that it seemed to him that a visit by me to Moscow was more urgent than ever. . . . He felt that I should go and discuss Vietnam with their leaders and at the same time accelerate preparations for the Summit." Kissinger, of course, promised to "put this proposition to the president," and get back to Dobrynin.[94]

Dobrynin called Kissinger "from a gas station" at 3:15 p.m. Kissinger told Dobrynin, "I called you [earlier] because I just talked to the president and I am leaving town for a couple of hours and I wanted to get word to you." Kissinger explained that Nixon was "inclined to approve the secret trip of mine to Moscow if we can do it in conjunction with the Paris thing, a week from Saturday and Sunday." There were some caveats, Kissinger explained: "It's not yet 100 percent sure; the president is going to Camp David—he wants to think about it overnight." Dobrynin replied: "I understand. I think it is very helpful. I will pass this information to Moscow."[95]

The Soviet ambassador conflated his meeting and phone conversations with Kissinger in his own memcon for the Kremlin and in his journal. Dobrynin couched Nixon's reconsideration of Kissinger's trip in diplomatic terms and accentuated the positive in his own report to the Kremlin. "Upon further reflection, and particularly taking into account the worsening situation," Dobrynin cabled the Politburo, "President Nixon believes that a brief trip by Kissinger to Moscow is, nevertheless, advisable." Nixon now expected that Kissinger would meet with Brezhnev and Gromyko, to "exchange of views in Moscow." Kissinger could then fly from Moscow directly to Paris, "where his secret meeting with DRV representatives is scheduled to take place."[96]

As had become standard practice, soon after the meeting Kissinger called Nixon, reporting that Dobrynin had called the president's decision to send Kissinger to Moscow "the most cheerful news he's had all day." Kissinger immediately qualified the statement: "I didn't even say you . . . had agreed. I just said that you were considering it seriously and you'd let me know finally tomorrow." Kissinger jovially described Dobrynin's reaction, "Oh, Mr. President, he was *slobbering*." When Kissinger used the term "slobbering" about himself, he typically meant that he had applied insincere flattery. When Kissinger used the term about others, it often meant that the slobberer was eating out of his hand like a hungry dog. All signs indicated that the Soviets remained onboard with the summit and the secret trip: "Then Brezhnev saw the Hanoi ambassador today and made a statement of support, and I showed this to my Soviet expert [Sonnenfeldt] who doesn't know a damn thing about Vietnam. And, I said, "What do you think?" He said, 'If we made a statement like that about an ally I would conclude that we're getting ready to screw them.'"

Nixon urged Kissinger to maintain a tough line with Soviets and inquired as to the weather in Vietnam. Kissinger replied, "By tomorrow . . . we can make a massive strike."[97]

And strike is what the U.S. forces did, with increasing frequency and violence. The American military response to the Easter Offensive relied on an abundance of heavy B-52 bombers, F-4 fighter-bombers, an array of naval gunfire, and an arsenal of sophisticated laser-guided bombs. U.S. Air Force historian Wayne Thompson has written that Nixon "gathered a more formidable (if less numerous) air armada than the North Vietnamese had yet encountered." A raid of 12 B-52s on Vinh, North Vietnam's gateway to the south near Ho Chi Minh's birthplace, paved the way for more aggressive attacks over the coming month. Although the raid "was not very effective" on April 10, it signaled the beginning of the American counteroffensive directly against North Vietnam. From the start of the offensive, Nixon expanded bombing authorities and allowed strikes deeper into North Vietnam, first beyond the 19th and then the 20th parallels.[98]

At the president's personal insistence, the surge of airpower that began the previous fall continued through April and May 1972 with the deployments of additional aircraft and carrier forces to Southeast Asia.[99] The president ordered JCS chairman Admiral Moorer to use additional B-52s and focus on Thanh Hoa's Bai Thuong Airfield and logistic supplies during the April 13 raid. Moorer also told Kissinger that U.S. submarines had surfaced right next to Soviet cargo ships, an effective form of harassment sure to signal the Soviets then supplying North Vietnamese offensive actions.[100] Back-channel exchanges, however, remained largely divorced from the military operations, other than to signal that the United States had reacted to Moscow's direct supply to Hanoi's offensive.

Back in Washington, Kissinger and Dobrynin met again on April 13, this time to discuss the "principal areas" of Kissinger's upcoming April 24 meeting with the North Vietnamese. Kissinger told Dobrynin the United States wanted "serious negotiations" as long as the North Vietnamese agreed to meet. Furthermore, the United States was "prepared to withdraw its troops completely from South Vietnam . . . without leaving any U.S. bases or U.S. 'residual' forces there," but only if Hanoi released all American POWs. The United States would not depose the Thieu government, but it would support elections and an interim coalition government. Of greater significance, the United States would halt military aid to Saigon once the POWs arrived home safely and provided that Hanoi would "not seek continuation of similar assistance from its allies." In the case of a so-called "clean situation," Kissinger added, "Washington would be willing to accept any outcome of the conflict, since it would become a purely internal Vietnamese issue."

According to the Soviet ambassador, Kissinger explained that the White House would not "for domestic political reasons, on account of the elections," accept "such an uncertain situation" in which the survival of South Vietnam might be at stake. Of course, however, a flip side of the coin existed, a "subtext," as Dobrynin described it: "What is needed is a turn either towards peace or towards major military actions." Aside from the obligatory statement at the end of the memo that Dobrynin had "firmly rejected Kissinger's attempts to use the above considerations," Dobrynin wrote that he had expressed the Soviet willingness "to prepare to assist in overcoming the difficulties that arise along this road."[101]

From April 13 through the 15, the second string of the back channel went into play to finalize the arrangement for the secret trip during Nixon's state visit to Canada. On April 14, Vorontsov delivered a handwritten note to Haig noting that a Soviet navigator and radio operator would fly inconspicuously aboard a commercial Aeroflot flight to New York. To avoid having to file visa requests for the fliers with the U.S. embassy in Moscow, the note stated "the White House should arrange for their delivery from New York (straight from our plane) to Washington D.C." The Soviets also requested vital info on the flight and promised to accommodate the crew. Appealing to Kissinger's repeated requests that the trip be confidential, the note read, "All measures are going to be taken by the Soviet side to ensure the full secrecy."[102]

President Nixon used a trip to Canada to continue the theme he had included in his comments on April 10 to the Canadian Parliament that summit meetings could create an "unrealistic euphoria." The president again warned, "Whether the great powers fulfill that responsibility depends not on the atmospherics of their diplomacy, but on the realities of their behavior."[103] The address included the line, "The great powers cannot avoid responsibility for the aggressive actions of those to whom they give the means for embarking on such actions." Kissinger had originally argued against the line, believing it too provocative against the Soviets on Vietnam, and had initially convinced the president to delete the phrase. With the offensive developing, however, Nixon reconsidered and included the tougher line.[104]

Nixon's hard-line stance for military action against Hanoi seemed to be vindicated the next day, April 15, when the White House learned that the North Vietnamese had canceled the Paris meeting scheduled for April 24. In response, Nixon considered canceling or postponing Kissinger's trip to Moscow—and possibly the summit itself. Nixon recalled that this was the "meeting that the Soviets had hinted might be the decisive one for reaching a settlement."[105] Soviet assurances conveyed via the back channel, however, had amounted to little of substance on the Vietnam negotiations. Nixon's forebodings soon erupted into a full-fledged crisis in the White House over whether or not to cancel the Moscow summit and what military actions to take against North Vietnam. First, however, Nixon weighed his options with his chief of staff and his national security advisor.

As Haldeman recorded in his diary, on the return flight from Canada, the three discussed whether or not Kissinger could go to Moscow in light of the North Vietnamese cancellation.[106] Years later, Nixon recalled that he "laid down the law hard" and that Kissinger could not go to Moscow "under these circumstances." "I told him that what the Russians wanted to do was to get him to Moscow to discuss the summit," Nixon explained, but "what we wanted to do was to get him to Moscow to discuss Vietnam." Nixon recognized that this "shook" Kissinger because he "desperately" wanted "to get to Moscow one way or the other." Kissinger "took it in good grace," and Nixon began more seriously considering stronger options—a blockade, for example—against North Vietnam.[107]

Not long after arriving back in Washington, Nixon and Kissinger met in Nixon's hideaway office in the Old Executive Office Building. The two explored the options, and Nixon reluctantly agreed that Kissinger could go to Moscow, "with the condition that the primary subject for discussion [would be] Vietnam." Nixon stressed, "Unless there's something positive, tangible to offer that [then] the president is going to take action." As he had over the preceding two weeks, Nixon linked Vietnam to the ratification of the German treaties. Nixon told Kissinger: "We may still go. In other words, let me put it this way: As I look at going to the summit, Henry, we cannot go . . . if the South Vietnamese are on the rocks." Kissinger replied, "Impossible." Nixon continued: "We could go—and I'll make this concession—if the situation is still in flux, with the understanding that we will discuss it at the summit and something is going to come out of it at the summit." Making the linkage clear, the president pontificated: "They want the summit. They want it badly. And you're going to of course hold over their heads. . . . I don't know if the blockade is going to worry them, but the German thing is. And . . . I'll sink that without any question." Nixon later added: "If the Russians don't come up with anything here, we have no choice but to blockade. I really have no doubt about it."

Once again, Kissinger dismissed the idea that the Soviets wanted to cause trouble when genuine détente was nearly at hand. Instead, he returned to his realpolitik roots and argued that both Moscow and Hanoi were pursuing their own national interests. Kissinger explained: "I'll say this for the Russians. They are bloody-minded sons-of-bitches. But Hanoi hasn't fought for 35 years in order to be pushed around by the Russians either." Again, the question was which lever to apply. "So we have the problem that we must let Soviet pressure on Hanoi begin to operate," Kissinger argued, "and we must bring home to the Soviet Union that you are really deadly serious about this." Nixon was willing to reveal Kissinger's secret trip if the Soviets did not help bring the war in Vietnam to a swift conclusion. "I'd just reveal it," he told Kissinger. Nixon thought aloud: "Now, Dr. Kissinger went to Moscow at their suggestion and it didn't do a damn thing. Under the circumstances, I'm calling off the Russian summit and I'm blockading. I wouldn't let them call off the summit." Echoing his boss, Kissinger offered: "I agree completely. I would list all the sins." Nixon replied: "Right. They're furnishing arms. They're doing this. They didn't help."[108] Of more immediate concern was how to send a message to the Soviets. The State Department was not involved, and the back channel was suited to the task.

Later that afternoon, Kissinger called Vorontsov to the White House to deliver an oral note to the Soviets. Kissinger read aloud as Vorontsov quickly took it down:

The President questions what progress can be made in Moscow if the Soviet Union cannot assure even a meeting on an agreed date. The President remains prepared to send Dr. Kissinger to Moscow to see whether a basis can be found to bring the war in Vietnam to a rapid and just conclusion and to seek to prevent consequences which could jeopardize what both sides have worked so hard to accomplish and brought so near to fruition. Needless to say, Dr. Kissinger will be instructed to deal with the Summit agenda in a constructive, comprehensive, forthcoming and generous manner.[109]

Dobrynin transmitted the oral note Vorontsov had retrieved to Moscow. Dobrynin's cable noted the American willingness to meet with the North Vietnamese "in order to continue the search for a rapid peace settlement in Vietnam." While Hanoi blocked peace, Washington would continue to bomb Hanoi and Haiphong. The bombing of Hanoi-Haiphong would "be immediately stopped as soon as agreement is reached on holding the private meeting on April 24." Kissinger again claimed that Hanoi's offensive was an attack on the presidency and on the summit. The American reaction, an "unavoidable step," Kissinger stated, "should not come as a surprise to the Soviet leadership . . . since the president and he, Kissinger, had repeatedly informed Moscow during the past year through the Soviet Ambassador that the United States would need to resort to decisive measures."[110]

When Kissinger met with Dobrynin on the evening of April 15, Dobrynin recalled that the national security advisor "did not try to conceal his anger" as the ambassador tried to flesh out details of the American desire for peace in Vietnam.[111] Why would Kissinger not meet with the North Vietnamese on May 6? Kissinger retorted that it was too late. Dobrynin asked if the secret trip to Moscow would still occur. Kissinger reported to Nixon afterward:

I said we wanted to make sure that there was some major progress toward a Vietnam settlement; this was the principal reason for my going. He said of course in Moscow they were rather looking at it the other way: The principal reason for my going was to prepare the Summit, and also to talk about Vietnam. I said there had to be some progress. He said they could not promise progress. I said, but Vietnam had to be the first item of the agenda, which would affect all others. Dobrynin said, well, we can agree on that; Vietnam will be the first item on the agenda.

According to Kissinger, the tables had turned. Through an "extremely friendly" Soviet ambassador, the Soviets now believed "the great powers must be able to put differences aside to settle fundamental issues."[112] Naturally, Kissinger again took a hard line. Dobrynin's more detailed memo essentially confirmed that Kissinger had acted tough but seemed amenable to go to Moscow. Dobrynin warned his bosses: "On the whole, the current mood in the White House is quite clear: unless they get some kind of understanding with the Vietnamese . . . in the next few days, they will significantly expand the bombing of the DRV, even if this could jeopardize the May meeting in Moscow. Virtually the same view is now being expressed in all of the channels through which we maintain contact with the various political circles, including the current administration's opposition in the U.S. Congress."[113]

Kissinger called the president soon after the meeting with Dobrynin and reported: "We got some pretty quick action out of our Soviet friends—Dobrynin was in slobbering over me—first of all he had a message from the North Vietnamese for us which was a lot more conciliatory than the one that they gave us in Paris." After recounting some of the details of the meeting with Dobrynin, Kissinger emphasized that the Soviets seemed "very anxious" for the secret trip and that Vietnam would "be the first agenda item" and that the Soviets recognized "the urgency." The Soviets had clearly moderated their stance, since "in the past they had even refused to pass messages, much less take sides." Kissinger emphasized, "Vietnam is agenda item one."[114] An hour later, Nixon explained the possible consequences if the secret trip was canceled or failed to produce some movement on compelling the North Vietnamese to the negotiating table: "You see, when you meet with them it's either got to be on the way to settlement or we blockade."[115] The Soviets were letting up, and Nixon did not intend to let his guard down.

As Kissinger had informed Vorontsov and Dobrynin earlier that day, U.S. air and naval forces had struck Hanoi and Haiphong from April 15 to 16. As an unintended consequence, several Soviet ships were hit in the large-scale attacks. Vorontsov delivered a fairly muted diplomatic protest on April 16. The note simply stated: "As a result of the American air raids against Haiphong a damage was also caused to some of the Soviet ships in that port. Moreover, there are casualties on the Soviet ships—several persons were killed from among the Vietnamese workers." The note warned that "all appropriate steps" would be taken "to protect Soviet ships wherever they would be."[116] The White House believed the low-key protest signaled Moscow's willingness to see Kissinger's secret trip through. Kissinger's Soviet expert, Helmut Sonnenfeldt, wrote that the note raised two possibilities: (1) "It lays the basis for disrupting the Summit and the HAK mission if this later becomes their choice," and (2) "It threatens military responses by Soviet vessels (an unsurprising threat in these circumstances)." In the final analysis, Sonnenfeldt postulated: "While the note seemingly rejects our manner of dealing with DRV maneuvers over the secret talks, it ends up by assuring us that Moscow has nevertheless transmitted our last proposal. The Soviets are thus in a position where the DRV has now explicitly made cessation of bombing a precondition to secret talks while the Soviets have not (except in the elliptical manner indicated above) made it a precondition either to the Wednesday mission or to acting as an intermediary with Hanoi."[117]

The back-channel delivery of the note and the continued signals from Dobrynin and Vorontsov convinced the White House that the Soviets wanted to separate Vietnam from détente. As Kissinger told Nixon on the afternoon of April 16: "Mr. President, leaving aside the fact now of this last two days, the mere fact that they want me to go there while we are at least substantially bombing the North [is significant]. I mean, we weren't exactly playing tiddley winks last week."[118]

The secret trip was still on. Kissinger secretly left for Moscow on April 20, with Ambassador Dobrynin in tow. It was, after all, the quickest way to get the Soviet ambassador back to Moscow.[119] Several questions remained. Would Nixon be willing to delink Vietnam in the end? With regard to the counteroffensive against North Vietnam, how far would be too far for the Soviets to swallow? Should Nixon preemptively cancel the summit? The questions would be answered in the coming weeks.

The Easter Offensive demonstrated the limits of linkage and the limits of back channels. Nixon hoped to enlist the Soviet Union to reduce aid to North Vietnam and restrain the DRV from precipitous offensive action. Furthermore, Nixon expected that the Soviets could facilitate productive U.S.-DRV peace negotiations while the United States removed

A 1972 Herblock Cartoon.
(© The Herb Block
Foundation)

"DR. KISSINGER, I PRESUME?"

itself from Southeast Asia. Even as the back channels demonstrated the limited utility for handling the larger problems of the Vietnam War, U.S.-Soviet back-channel diplomacy proved its worth as a tactical instrument for conveying Nixon's limited ambitions in Vietnam relative to détente. Back channels served as an important mechanism for facilitating the summit, allowing continued discussion on the Middle East sheltered from the State Department and encouraging the Soviets to separate détente from Vietnam. In the wake of the South Asian crisis, with a historic trip to China and with a North Vietnamese offensive at the forefront of his worries, Nixon moved in early 1972 to fully consolidate and bureaucratically centralize U.S.-Soviet relations in the back channels.

From a tactical standpoint, the White House used back channels to telegraph American intentions. During the deadlock in the secret negotiations with the North Vietnamese, Kissinger used the Channel to inform the Soviets that Hanoi refused to negotiate, that time was running out for meaningful negotiations, and the United States would be forced to react "unilaterally." Nixon and Kissinger also used the Channel to warn the Soviets that the U.S. response to the anticipated DRV offensive would be severe. Playing on Soviet fears related to Sino-American rapprochement, the White House encouraged the Soviets to separate their own interests from those of their North Vietnamese ally.

The Soviet-American relationship was by no means limited to confidential diplomacy. Back channels reinforced public statements but also tempered them. For example, Kissinger's call to Dobrynin following Nixon's January 25 speech, followed by a letter from Nixon to Brezhnev, softened the blow of Nixon's disclosure of the secret negotiations between Kissinger and the North Vietnamese. The communications gave the impression that the United States was being forced to react to North Vietnamese intransigence by disclosing the negotiations and preparing military countermeasures to a North Vietnamese buildup. The U.S.-Soviet back-channel relationship was based on more than just the Channel, as Nixon personally dropped in on Kissinger-Dobrynin meetings, communicated the major issues via the Nixon-Brezhnev exchanges, and directed the April 11 ladies' tea between Pat Nixon and Irina Dobrynin. Nixon used these meetings to signal that although he wanted détente, the North Vietnamese offensive could endanger the summit. Kissinger did his part, reinforcing the messages he discussed with Dobrynin and Vorontsov with targeted leaks to influential columnists like Joseph Kraft.

In the months preceding the offensive, Nixon and Kissinger enlisted Dobrynin to further exclude the State Department on the Middle East negotiations with the Soviets and to further centralize and reinforce power in the White House. Détente was the bailiwick of the back channel, and personal stakes reinforced its desirability for both sides. Domestic political considerations also flavored back-channel exchanges—for example, the episode that disclosed that the president needed a stopover in Poland for domestic political reasons. Back channels also reinforced linkages between Vietnam and other, unrelated areas like Germany-Berlin, the Middle East, and SALT.

Ironically, just as the Soviets signaled a willingness to treat Vietnam separately from détente via the back channels, Nixon started to blur the lines between Hanoi and Moscow. Moscow signaled the willingness to delink Vietnam from détente by accepting Kissinger's last-minute, secret trip to Moscow and put forward only muted protest for U.S. attacks on Soviets ships in Haiphong Harbor on April 16. Nixon had maintained that détente and Vietnam were tied together, and he increasingly saw the Kremlin's military aid to Vietnam as the very factor that had enabled the offensive in the first place. Nixon feared a South Vietnamese collapse and was determined to use massive force to prevent or postpone that possibility. Nixon worried that his massive reaction would be interpreted by the Soviets as an escalation and would force them to cancel or postpone the summit in solidarity with their Communist ally. By mid-April 1972, Nixon begrudgingly agreed to send Kissinger to Moscow but insisted that the primary agenda be centered on a Vietnam settlement rather than planning for the summit. Nixon's attitude foreshadowed a full-blown "cancellation crisis" over the summit as he considering mining Haiphong Harbor and dramatically expanding bombing strikes directly against North Vietnam.

7

Cancellation Crises

Good God, I mean, we can't go [to Moscow] with Russian tanks and Russian guns killing South Vietnamese and Americans. Hell, no, we're not going to go. We won't go. It isn't just a reasonable summit. . . . That's what he [Brezhnev] has to understand.
—Richard Nixon, April 15, 1972

Keep very close sessions with Dobrynin so that if you sense that even one word, and if he ever raises the subject of cancellation, you go out and say that the president has canceled the summit. [Do] not let those sons-of-bitches say they did!
—Richard Nixon, May 1, 1972

On May 8, 1972, two weeks before his departure to Moscow for a historic summit meeting with the Soviet leaders, President Richard Nixon gave a short but major address on Vietnam to a national prime-time television audience. In a somber tone, the president read from a carefully crafted script in the Oval Office.[1] In response to a massive North Vietnamese offensive launched on Easter weekend, the president explained, he had ordered American naval and air assets to mine "all entrances to North Vietnamese ports." U.S. forces would "take appropriate measures . . . to interdict the delivery of any supplies. Rail and all other communications will be cut off to the maximum extent possible." Nixon argued that the North Vietnamese had "flatly and arrogantly refused to negotiate an end to the war and bring peace. Their answer to every peace offer . . . has been to escalate the war."

Furthermore, American actions were directed against North Vietnam, and "not . . . against any other nation," with that "other nation" being thinly disguised diplospeak for the Soviet Union. Extending an olive branch to the Soviets, Nixon suggested to Brezhnev and the Soviet leadership: "We are near major agreements on nuclear arms limitation, on trade, on a host of other issues. . . . We do not ask you to sacrifice your principles, or your friends, but neither should you permit Hanoi's intransigence to blot out the prospects we together have so patiently prepared."

In one short speech, Nixon sent different messages to three different audiences. To Hanoi, the president served notice that he had taken off the proverbial gloves. To the domestic audience, Nixon tried to undercut mounting congressional and public opposition to the war by explaining that he had designed his actions to protect the lives of the sixty thousand Americans who remained in South Vietnam and to prevent "turning 17 million South Vietnamese over to Communist tyranny and terror." Lastly, Nixon appealed to the leadership in the Kremlin. During Kissinger's April 20–24 secret trip to Moscow, Nixon explained, the Soviets had "indicated they would use their constructive influence" with their North Vietnamese ally to encourage peace talks in Paris. On May 2, Kissinger had traveled to Paris for a meeting facilitated by the Soviet Union. It was Hanoi—not Moscow—that responded with "bombastic rhetoric" and "flatly refused" meaningful negotiations.[2]

Media coverage the next day highlighted the conundrum in which decision makers in Washington and Moscow found themselves. Robert Semple reported in the *New York Times* that Nixon's announcement "seemed to stun much of official Washington, but reaction from the public was not clear." Semple added, "Some observers here wondered whether Mr. Nixon's plans to cap an election-year whirlwind of dramatic diplomacy with the Communist world could or would survive [the] speech."[3] Another article in the *Times* noted "it was clear that the Nixon Administration, in seeking to prevent a confrontation with the Russians, was trying to keep the Nixon visit to Moscow alive."[4]

U.S.-Soviet back channels, and specifically the Kissinger-Dobrynin channel, were instrumental to Nixon's decision-making process and the resolution of a cancellation crisis in the weeks before the Moscow summit. Nixon considered canceling the summit even as Kissinger finalized plans to go on a secret trip to the Soviet Union in April to discuss Vietnam and the summit planning. As the president became determined to take strong action in response to the continuing North Vietnamese offensive and the deteriorating military situation in South Vietnam, he worried that the

Soviets would cancel the summit in solidarity with their ally in Hanoi. The Nixon administration had maintained since 1969 that the improvement of U.S.-Soviet relations would be linked to progress in the U.S. peace negotiations with the DRV, and expected the Soviets to restrain their ally and facilitate substantive diplomacy.

In the lead-up to the Easter Offensive, however, the Nixon White House laid the groundwork to encourage the Soviets to consider détente separately from Vietnam, conveying a tacit modus vivendi via the confidential channel with Dobrynin. While Nixon pondered the possibility of canceling the summit, the administration also used back channels to read Soviet intentions. Ultimately, Treasury Secretary John Connally emerged as the pivotal figure in Nixon's decision to place the onus of any cancellation or postponement of the summit on the Soviets. Domestic opinion polls buttressed the president's decision since the American public did not see the Moscow summit as interrelated to the situation in Vietnam.

Once Nixon decided to move forward with détente with the Soviet Union while both bombing and mining North Vietnam, the White House continued to assess the Soviet reaction via back channels but also focused on effectively removing the Indochina impediment as an issue in the improvement of U.S.-Soviet relations. Following the president's May 8 speech, Kissinger used his relationship with Dobrynin to mitigate the blow to the Kremlin, going so far as to clear drafts of the presidential speech and communications with Dobrynin to remove or soften offending language.

Memoir accounts by Soviet policymakers, in addition to declassified American intelligence reports, show that the Kremlin itself was divided over the course of action and had its own cancellation crisis. After a showdown with hard-liners, such as Ukrainian first secretary and CPSU Politburo member Petro Shelest, the Soviet leadership lined up behind Brezhnev, Gromyko, and Kosygin in favor of the summit while rhetorically condemning the American bombing-mining campaign against North Vietnam. The summit thus became the successful product of U.S.-Soviet back-channel diplomacy.

The Secret Trip

On April 19, Nixon and Kissinger discussed the latter's upcoming secret trip to the Soviet Union, the situation in Vietnam, and a back-channel meeting the national security advisor had just concluded with the Soviet ambassador. Kissinger painted a picture of the reception he expected in Moscow, and his tough line with Dobrynin emphasizing Vietnam:

> KISSINGER: I said, "Anatol, I want you to know this. We will
> continue to bomb while I am in Moscow. I don't want Mr.
> Brezhnev to feel that while he's seeing me and his ally's
> being bombed that you didn't know that. . . . Don't consider
> that a surprise." He said, "I understand." He said, "But you
> promised me no escalation." I said, "No, I promised you no
> attacks on Hanoi-Haiphong."
> NIXON: Right.
> KISSINGER: He said, "That's no escalation."

Although Kissinger said U.S. forces would not bomb Hanoi or Haiphong during the secret trip, he advocated bombing the port of Thanh Hoa, sixty miles to the south. Lest the Soviets forget that Vietnam remained the Nixon administration's primary concern, Kissinger surmised that the continued bombing would send "a good signal to the Russians."[5] Nixon agreed with Kissinger's reasoning and remained determined to continue the use of force: "Crack 'em now when we've got a chance. . . . When it means something militarily, take it. Take it out." The two men continued:

> KISSINGER: They are not talking from strength. . . . They're
> scared of the blockade. . . .
> NIXON: That's right. And the president isn't bluffing. . . . You
> told him that?
> KISSINGER: [Laughs] Oh-oh.
> NIXON: You ought to remember, if you ever talk about my
> [playing] poker, I didn't win by bluffing. . . . I very seldom
> lost a pot when I was called, because I knew pretty well
> when I was going to be called, [and] I always had the cards.
> . . . You've got to have a little bluff in your game, but the key
> to my success in poker was playing a very different kind of
> a game. I would bluff at times, but then when I knew that I
> didn't have the cards I got the hell out. But whenever I was

called in the game, I usually won. That's why I won $10,000 when I was in the service. Not bad?

KISSINGER: That's extraordinary.[6]

As the discussion progressed, Kissinger called the meeting a dress rehearsal for the summit, complete with a backup presidential plane that would be used for secure communications, bypassing the U.S. embassy in Moscow and the State Department. Nixon inquired, "You don't have to use [U.S. ambassador to the Soviet Union Jacob] Beam?" "No," Kissinger replied. Nixon opined that this was "good," although both the president and the NSC advisor failed to foresee the logistical hurdles of ferrying messages to and from the presidential plane parked an hour away from Kissinger's accommodations at a military airfield.[7] "There was an additional delay," Kissinger remembered, "caused by interference with the communications."[8] Although initially ascribed to atmospheric conditions, Kissinger remembered a similar problem during his 1973 "shuttle diplomacy," giving credence to the conjecture that the communications problems were caused by Soviet eavesdropping or jamming. Soviet espionage efforts and American counterespionage efforts were almost comical, with the Soviets offering the use of a safe to store classified information and the American use of a "babbler," a recording of gibberish voices, to confound KGB eavesdroppers.[9]

While Nixon and Kissinger spoke in the Oval Office, Dobrynin sent an urgent telegram to Gromyko, recommending negotiating tactics and an agenda for Kissinger's arrival. Dobrynin described the view from Washington at length and noted with regard to the linkage between Vietnam and U.S.-Soviet détente, "The White House realizes that it is essentially unrealistic to try to get us to halt the DRV's current offensive." In exchange for a successful summit meeting, Kissinger might ask on the president's behalf for "some guarantee" that during the preelection period, through November 1972, "no new major DRV offensive . . . will become possible as a result of major new shipments of Soviet offensive weapons." Nixon would be tough, Dobrynin wrote, and the president did "not intend to retreat when confronted with force." "From a tactical standpoint," Dobrynin recommended emphasizing "discussion of various issues related to the May meeting, devoting only the requisite amount of time to Vietnam." In preelection maneuvering, "the White House will probably nonetheless make [the] . . . trip public, possibly emphasizing for the domestic American audience that he went there chiefly to discuss Vietnam." The longtime Washington-watcher saw potential progress in discussions with Kissinger on SALT, European matters like Berlin, and the Middle East because Kissinger was "authorized to make decisions on the spot" and had "a very great deal of influence over Nixon." Dobrynin predicted Kissinger would also focus on the draft statement of principles to be signed at the summit.[10]

No sooner had Kissinger and Dobrynin left U.S. airspace en route to Moscow than Nixon sent revised instructions for the upcoming talks. Alexander Haig served as the intermediary between the president and Kissinger in increasingly testy exchanges over the course of the trip. Reflecting on the briefing book Kissinger had prepared in advance of the trip, Nixon got right to the point in the "eyes only" telegram to Kissinger: "Brezhnev is simple, direct, blunt and brutal." The president added: "You will find that his interest during your talks with him will be to filibuster in order to spend relatively little time on Vietnam. Our goal in talking to him is solely to get action on Vietnam." After all, the president surmised, summit planning could have been arranged via the back channel with Dobrynin in Washington. The president then suggested, "It might be worthwhile to indicate quite bluntly that from now until the summit, the Soviets should desist from strong rhetoric in support of Vietnam." Nixon rationalized that the United States should use force to counter the North Vietnamese offensive. The Soviets needed to understand that "as long as the invading North Vietnamese are killing South Vietnamese and Americans in the South the president will have to resort to bombing military installations in the North that are supporting that invasion." Nixon added that the joint announcement of the secret trip "*must*, at the very least, include some wording to indicate, directly or indirectly, that Vietnam was discussed and progress made on it."[11] Kissinger immediately replied that the message had been received and would "be carried out meticulously."[12]

Kissinger arrived in Moscow on the evening of April 20 and was greeted by the head of security for the summit, KGB general Sergei Antonov, and First Deputy Foreign Minister Vasily Kuznetsov. Kissinger and his crew were whisked away by a "terrifying" high-speed motorcade to a guesthouse on Vorobyevskii Road in the Lenin Hills above the Moscow River.[13] Kissinger later described the encounter with Antonov to Nixon and Rosemary Woods, the president's longtime secretary: "The head of their State Security, General Antonov, greeted me at the airport and said he had a whole bunch of girls, all 25-years and younger. . . . The crudeness of these guys is not to be believed." Hinting at the classic Soviet intelligence honeypot to compromise foreign officials, Kissinger continued: "When I said I want[ed] to take a swim—and that's also under the State Security—so, again . . . they asked, 'Do I want masseuses to come in?'" Nixon responded: "Masseuses? They use those for that purpose? . . . It takes all the fun out of it." Kissinger described Antonov's persistence: "And they brought it up on every occasion. . . . We went past the Moscow film studio and I said I know a lot of actresses in Hollywood. He said, 'Try my girls. They've got a lot more experience.'"[14]

Kissinger met with Gromyko and Dobrynin at 11:00 p.m. Kissinger's secretary, Julie Pineau, sat in on the meeting and made the stenographic record, which revealed a hopeful, playful, and short meeting that laid out the general course of discussions over the coming days. Gromyko used the meeting to reinforce the importance of the back channel and the goal of a successful summit. "As regards the forthcoming meetings," Gromyko told Kissinger, "you will certainly be aware from the communications made to the president through channels you are familiar with that we attach very great importance to the meetings and talks with the president." As the meeting ended, Gromyko again praised the American back-channel agent: "You are not unfamiliar to us. . . . [Dobrynin] is familiar to you. . . . And we are your friends, your partners." Kissinger replied, "I am here with the attitude that we will make major progress."[15] The Soviet foreign minister gave the back channel a seal of approval. In his memoir, Kissinger recollected, "Gromyko's eagerness, within four days after a massive B-52 attack in the Haiphong area, dramatized to me that the summit could be used as a restraint on Soviet conduct while we pursued our strategy for ending the war."[16]

That evening, Kissinger reported back to the president that he would not fall into a "summit trap." Kissinger called the atmosphere "effusive" and said Brezhnev would personally conduct the meetings over the coming days. He reported with satisfaction that the Soviets were ready to have some "concrete considerations" on the situation in Vietnam, but he added a caveat to the president's instructions: discussion on Vietnam should not be deferred until the summit itself.[17]

The next day, Kissinger, Sonnenfeldt, and Lord met with Brezhnev, Gromyko, Dobrynin, Brezhnev's political advisor Arkady Aleksandrov-Agentov, and veteran Soviet translator Viktor Sukhodrev. After opening pleasantries and philosophical pronouncements about the spirit of warmth and frankness, Brezhnev and Kissinger steered the discussion to the summit and Vietnam. Brezhnev's "priority was clearly the summit and U.S.-Soviet relations, not Vietnam," Kissinger wrote in his memoirs.[18] After some jokes about burning down the State Department and the Foreign Office, Kissinger assured Brezhnev, "You can be absolutely certain, Mr. Secretary, that these discussions will never leave the White House and will be seen only by the president and no one else."[19] Earlier comedy aside, the State Department would not be privy to the back-channel records—at least not for two decades.

As he had with Dobrynin in the previous months, Kissinger laid the proposed summit agenda on the table for Brezhnev. Arms control—namely, SALT—was the first priority. The agenda also stated that the United States wanted to make "important progress" on European security and "other European questions" like the German treaties, and the Middle East. The United States "would consider" other issues, such as Most Favored Nation status for the Soviet Union, long-term credits, Lend-Lease, and science and technology transfers, but progress in these areas would remain linked to the "obstacle," the "problem of Southeast Asia."[20]

Kissinger then presented the Vietnam issue as Nixon had repeatedly directed. He explained to the general secretary that the Nixon administration had two main objectives in Southeast Asia. First, the United States sought "an honorable withdrawal of all our forces" and, second, "to put a time interval between our withdrawal and the political process which would then start." "We are prepared to let the real balance of forces in Vietnam determine the future of Vietnam," Kissinger told Brezhnev. "We are not committed to a permanent political involvement there, and we always keep our word."[21] The discussion then turned to some of the broader details of the proposed settlement and a timetable:

KISSINGER: [W]e cannot withdraw our forces without getting our prisoners back and without some perspective of what follows afterward. This North Vietnam refused to do. But if we can get this, we are prepared to withdraw all our forces without any residual forces, and to close all bases within a period of months, which remains to be negotiated, but is not an obstacle to a solution.

AMB. DOBRYNIN: Within this year?

MR. KISSINGER: Yes, by the end of this year. By the end of the year. The number of months will not be a question of principle. We have said six months [from the agreement] in our last proposal.[22]

After several exchanges, Brezhnev conveyed the Soviet view on Vietnam in longer soliloquies. According to Brezhnev, the United States "started the war, the U.S. . . . intensified it when Kosygin visited Vietnam [in February 1965]."[23] As the leading socialist country, the Soviet Union had the duty to aid North Vietnam. Countering Kissinger's point, Brezhnev opined, "I certainly don't think that the bombing at this time will help President Nixon get elected." He added, "We are going to the summit meeting at this particular time—surely on our part this is the best assistance to the president." Brezhnev argued that the United States should delink the war from détente. "As regards Soviet assistance in Vietnam," he said emphatically, "I wish to say very clearly and openly that in the recent period there have been no additional agreements with regard to Soviet supplies." After all, the Soviet Union had little real influence in Hanoi. "I am sure you are aware," he continued, "that throughout the history of the Vietnam war we have nothing to do with the planning of the war. . . . They never ask us to take part in the planning or ask for our acceptance."[24]

Brezhnev also attempted to twist American efforts at triangular diplomacy by blaming the Chinese for enabling and profiting from the North Vietnamese offensive. "Take a look at the Chinese press concerning Vietnam," Brezhnev argued. "It is now saying that the Soviet Union is now rendering immense assistance to Vietnam." Brezhnev urged Kissinger and Nixon to "bear in mind that powerful forces in the world are out to block the summit meeting." There was more than met the eye. "It certainly would be quite a big gift to the Chinese if the meeting did not come off," the general secretary added. "It would only help China." Alluding to the Sino-Soviet split and describing the negative ramifications of the Cultural Revolution, Brezhnev suggested that Chinese policies lacked consistency and principle.[25] Kissinger, however, did not take the bait.

The meeting ended on a positive note as Brezhnev came back to the summit meeting and what he saw as the main point of the secret trip: the improvement of bilateral U.S.-Soviet relations. Brezhnev explained, "The main issue between our two countries is the relations between the United States and the Soviet Union, our two countries." Brezhnev told Kissinger he hoped these principles would be embodied in the statement to be released at the end of the summit, a U.S.-Soviet analogue to the Sino-American Shanghai Communiqué. During this first meeting with the general secretary, Kissinger mostly stuck to the script the president had prepared, roughly outlined the expected course of negotiations with the North Vietnamese, and "did not immediately put forward a formula for breaking the procedural deadlock with Hanoi." Brezhnev was not interested in specifics at this first meeting. Kissinger recalled, "I thought I had reached the limit of what the traffic would bear in that meeting." He saw positive signs as a result of the first meeting with the top Soviet leaders and believed, in retrospect, that "Brezhnev's response was mild in the extreme." Kissinger wrote, "It was a measure of Brezhnev's commitment to the summit that he listened to these provocative remarks without demur."[26] The record, as described above, shows that the remarks were less provocative than Kissinger remembered. Nevertheless, the emphasis remained on improving relations.

At Camp David later that evening, Nixon listened intently when General Haig read Kissinger's report over the phone from the White House. Kissinger cabled that he had "not yet discussed one substantive issue other than Vietnam" and that "Brezhnev indicated considerable readiness to help bring about a meeting [between the United States and the DRV]." Brezhnev had gone so far, in fact, that he had read aloud from a telegram from Hanoi that rejected a meeting in Moscow in "particularly insolent terms." Nixon, however, was unconvinced of the Soviets' sincerity, and the U.S. administration knew Hanoi would reject the meeting. The president gave Haig the thankless task to "get Henry stiffened up." Nixon then criticized Kissinger: "Henry better understand that Brezhnev is playing the typical sickening game. . . . Henry is so easily taken in by flattery. . . . Shake him up hard!"[27]

In self-imposed isolation at Camp David, the president increasingly believed that the United States should have continued to strike Hanoi and Haiphong during Kissinger's visit. Hanoi had not halted its offensive, so why should Washington let up on the bombing strikes? Camp David provided a good cover for Kissinger's back-channel trip, but it also made for its own set of difficulties. As Nixon stewed that Kissinger had not been tough enough with the Soviets, the communications problems combined with the eight-hour difference in time zones meant that Nixon was constantly behind events in Moscow. His friend, the Cuban American financier Bebe Rebozo, who was staying with the president at Camp David, bolstered his instinct to play it tough with Moscow.[28] The president also received "hawkish injections" from Treasury Secretary John Connally.[29]

Haig sent a message to Kissinger on the evening of April 21. The communications had become such a problem that Haig recommended using alternate arrangements, perhaps through Gen. Brent Scowcroft or even "with the cognizance of Ambassador Beam." The situation required clear communication. The state of affairs in South Vietnam was deteriorating, especially around An Loc, a provincial capital seen as the gateway to Saigon. Haig relayed the president's order that Kissinger should return on April 23, unless significant progress on a Vietnam settlement were made: "He states that from his perspective the settlement of Vietnam is in order of magnitude ten times more important than the Soviet summit and he is fully prepared to sacrifice summit if need be."

Haig ended the telegram with a note about a recent poll by Albert Sindlinger, which basically signaled to Kissinger that the president favored a hard line with the Soviets and the North Vietnamese. The poll showed a sharp rise in the president's popularity, a rally-around-the-president effect, due to the escalation of fighting in Vietnam. More ominously, Haig reported, George Wallace's popularity had also risen.[30] After running as an independent in 1968, Wallace had returned to the Democratic fold as a candidate for the presidential nomination and, Nixon feared, threatened his own reelection with a potential to divide the Right.

Kissinger and his full entourage met again with the Soviet contingent on April 22, and the discussion touched upon a number of issues far beyond Vietnam—in contravention of the president's stream of orders. The discussion started on the statement to be issued at the end of the summit, the Basic Principles, and continued with banter about the respective bureaucracies. Brezhnev was gregarious throughout the meeting and frequently interrupted the talks to eat snacks, smoke his ubiquitous cigarettes, or to go off on tangents and tell jokes. When Kissinger brought up Vietnam, he divided his presentation into procedural and substantive parts. On procedure, Kissinger proposed a public plenary meeting with the North Vietnamese on April 27. The substance would be a private meeting with Le Duc Tho on May 2, because, as Kissinger explained, "the plenaries are a waste of time." Brezhnev offered to communicate the proposal and Kissinger fleshed out the details: "We shall ask that the North Vietnamese withdraw the divisions that entered South Vietnam after March 29. . . . We will then withdraw the air and naval forces which we have introduced since March 29. . . . We shall then stop the bombing of North Vietnam completely."

Kissinger continued that all POWs held by both sides for more than four years be immediately released. Brezhnev responded by restating it was for "the U.S. side to find the method to extricate itself" but that he found such American proposals "constructive." Kissinger again stressed the president's seriousness. "We had no intention two weeks ago to add any new element to the North Vietnamese problem," Kissinger stated, but the offensive had forced the situation as "an attack on the institution of the Presidency."

The high point of the drama broke when Brezhnev offered Kissinger a cake in the middle of his spiel about Vietnam. In response to the solicitation, Kissinger humorously replied, "I can never refuse the General-Secretary." When the conversation returned to Vietnam, the national security advisor essentially repeated himself, and Brezhnev replied that bombing was not the answer and then asked to discuss SALT. Kissinger agreed and added, "I cannot understate [overstate?] the seriousness and determination of the president not to be pushed by military action."[31] After a short recess, the participants returned to chat about SALT.

Sessions in Moscow: SALT and ABM

The two sides made some progress on a freeze on Submarine-Launched Ballistic Missiles (SLBMs) and the number of launchers and sites for respective ABM systems during the second day of the secret trip. Echoing Raymond Garthoff, the historian David Reynolds has recently written that Kissinger made "a serious mistake" in the back channel on arms control, specifically over failing to include SLBMs in the interim SALT agreement. In discussions with Dobrynin, Kissinger had focused on "offensive strategic weapons," a synonym for Inter-Continental Ballistic Missiles (ICBMs), and had "not explicitly included submarine-launched ballistic missiles, apparently failing to realize that American building programs were in limbo." Kissinger tried to rectify the "real problem" in the spring of 1972 after the Pentagon refused to accept a SALT agreement that did not include SLBMs.[32] "Thinking out loud" at a back-channel meeting in March 1972, Kissinger suggested to Dobrynin that the SALT agreement set a Soviet ceiling of 950 SLBMs.[33] Brezhnev readily accepted such a high ceiling and essentially repeated Kissinger's own offer back to him at the meeting on April 22. The high ceiling would allow the Soviets to continue to build missile submarines for some time. Nevertheless, Kissinger accepted the SLBM formula and a proposal on ABM systems, allowing SALT I to draw to its conclusion at the summit meeting.

Whether the SLBM limitation was a mistake or not, the participants at the time actually considered it to be one of the back channel's achievements. Brezhnev told Kissinger, "So now you have something to take back, a proposal from your confidential channel."[34] Unfortunately for historians and arms control experts, the details and finer points have blurred the big picture. Perhaps the controversy boils down to a fundamental question: At what point do the numbers of strategic warheads and launchers become irrelevant? Whether the Soviet Union could be permitted to build 950 submarine-based launchers or 650 launchers seemed beside the point at the time and in retrospect. Could the Soviet Union for all intents and purposes have destroyed the United States in a first *or* a retaliatory strike with 650 versus 950 SLBMs? The answer is yes. The general secretary made a good point when he noted: "It doesn't make any difference what kind of rocket you die from."[35] Although Kissinger may have lost track of some of the details in complicated negotiations carried out in the back channel, the significance of the settlement proved more important than quibbling about a negotiating point. As Gromyko concluded: "True, [SALT I] concerned only ground-based intercontinental and submarine-based ballistic missiles. . . . SALT-1 nevertheless was enormously important in limiting the nuclear arms race."[36] Thus, the back channel proved effective at breaking deadlocks and managing the overall tone of the U.S.-Soviet relationship but, in retrospect, seems to have been less successful at handling detailed, technical negotiations.

At the end of the marathon session, Kissinger asked when the secret trip should be publicly announced and said, "I believe that after my return we should make a brief public announcement that I have been here." "Otherwise," he warned, "it could leak out." Kissinger then recommended that the text be worked out the next day in sessions with Gromyko. Brezhnev consented to the request "in advance" but cautioned that he had not discussed it with his colleagues and that the Politburo understood that the trip was purely confidential. Kissinger reassured the general secretary: "It will remain confidential while I am here."[37]

Signs that a cancellation crisis was looming over the summit appeared in a series of terse telegrams between Kissinger and Haig on April 22. Kissinger could not believe that Nixon wanted him to discuss only Vietnam with the Soviets, stating: "I am astonished both by the tone and the substance of your communications. . . . We were unaware of communications failure. . . . We need support, not constant strictures." He considered Brezhnev's behavior consistent with American goals: "Brezhnev wants a summit at almost any cost. He has told me in effect that he would not cancel it under any circumstances." Whether or not the Soviets knew about the offensive, Kissinger saw "three opportunities":

(A) We may get help in deescalating or ending the war.
(B) If not, we can almost surely get his acquiescence in pushing NVN to the limit.
(C) We can use the summit to control the uproar in the U.S.

Kissinger said that eventually he needed to talk about the summit arrangements, part of the rationale behind the trip in the first place, and that he should stay until Monday, April 24. "In sum I am not sure they are able to deliver on Vietnam," Kissinger stated, "but they will stand aside and they will have the summit. We can use this as cover for other actions. Why not play out the string?" As for a course of action, he suggested stepped-up bombing raids up to the 20th parallel against North Vietnam, calling for a private meeting with the North Vietnamese on May 2, and going "all-out" if the meeting failed.[38]

Haig apologized but said that the president considered the offensive to be a concerted conspiracy between Hanoi and Moscow. According to Haig's first message, the president feared, "if we get no assist[ance] from the Soviets and then proceed with stringent action against the North, at the last minute, the Soviets might cancel the summit on their own thereby further complicating the domestic situation."[39] Haldeman, who was one of the few privy to the flurry of exchanges, wrote in his diary that Nixon felt the United States could not "show any overt weakness." The chief of staff noted that the president feared "the effect on our people, the hawks, who are now enthusiastic, but could be turned off pretty rapidly if, as a result of Henry's trip, we backed off."[40]

Four hours later, Haig cabled Kissinger that Nixon was concerned about the public reception of the secret trip. "He hopes that announcement you work out with Gromyko will explicitly mention that Vietnam was discussed if at all possible," Haig wrote. "If not, it is then essential that the implication that Vietnam was discussed is clear."[41] In a message two hours later, Haig wrote that Kissinger's strategy had finally taken root with the president: "He is, in fact, becoming increasingly optimistic that the delicate balancing act which you have established is getting us the best of all worlds by (1) inflicting maximum psychological and military pressure on Hanoi, (2) enabling him to reassure hawks here that punishment of Hanoi will continue while (3) totally disarming doves who will be completely puzzled by implications of Moscow visit and commencement of plenaries."[42]

At the end of the day, Kissinger reported the results of his meetings and private discussions with Brezhnev and Dobrynin after the formal sessions with the larger groups had ended. Brezhnev repeated the line that China—not the Soviet Union—was behind the offensive: "The enemies of the summit in Hanoi and Peking were trying to wreck the summit and we had to thwart them." Brezhnev, Kissinger reported, "said he would do anything to deescalate the fighting but he could not ask North Vietnam to withdraw its troops." Kissinger wrote that the summit remained secure. Brezhnev "made it clear that we would have to cancel the summit; he would not."

The Channel went into play between sessions. Kissinger cabled: "[Brezhnev] next sent Dobrynin to ask what they should do. Dobrynin stressed that if we confined bombing to present limits there was no chance of canceling summit and they were extremely anxious to have it. Dobrynin told me that the Politburo would meet tomorrow and we would hear something on Monday." Kissinger again stressed the necessity of staying the extra day. "We have nothing to lose by staying and much to lose by leaving," Kissinger admonished. "They are keeping us from nothing and have been most conciliatory on all issues in their control and have promised to transmit our proposals to Hanoi. They are not using the summit to keep us quiet; we are using the summit to impose restraints on them." Furthermore, "Brezhnev has spent more time with me than with any other foreign visitor. To kick them in the teeth now would be an absurdity."[43]

As he had foreshadowed for the president, Kissinger shifted gears to discuss topics other than Vietnam in greater detail his last two days in Moscow, April 23 and 24. The Middle East dominated the discussion between Kissinger and Gromyko on April 23, but the national security advisor and the Soviet foreign minister also discussed the wording of the joint announcement acknowledging the secret trip.[44] Kissinger wrote to Haig: "Please keep everybody calm. . . . Must we blow it in our eagerness to bomb targets which will not move and when the delay is only one week?"[45] In a message several hours later, Kissinger again recommended bombing up to the 20th.[46]

On the evening of April 23, Moscow time, Haig wrote Kissinger that the president understood the need to stay until April 24 and left it to Kissinger's "best judgement [sic] as to precise departure time provid[ed] you are convinced that constructive discussions on Vietnam are taking place." Haig also communicated Nixon's suspicions about Soviet maneuvering and attempts to play Kissinger against the bureaucracy on the ABM settlement and SLBM ceiling, since the White House had received conflicting reports from the SALT delegation in Helsinki. Haig attempted to summarize the president's thinking about the perceived linkage between the secret trip to Moscow and a collapse in Vietnam. Linkage seemed now to be a double-edged sword. According to Haig, Nixon believed that "our agreement to resume plenaries despite the announcement of your visit to Moscow will convey impression of US collapse." Haig suggested that he had a calmer head than the president and agreed with Kissinger's own thinking that the resumption of plenaries, "when accompanied by intense bombing up to the twentieth parallel," would show "Moscow has blinked and provide a firm base for further escalation [against North Vietnam] if required."[47]

Clearly agitated, Kissinger replied, "All I can say is that if this is [the] President's attitude he had no business approving the Moscow trip." As for Vietnam, Kissinger disagreed with the president's conspiracy theory about collusion between Moscow and Hanoi on the course and scale of the offensive. On the contrary, Kissinger believed that the Soviets had done what they could to transmit American proposals but that they enjoyed only limited influence in Hanoi. As for the most recent breakthrough on SLBM numbers and on ABMs, Kissinger stressed that it was an achievement of the back channel. It was "exactly the scheme we advanced in the special channel." Rather than the Soviets playing the SALT delegation against him, Kissinger contended that the Soviet deputy foreign minister in charge of the Soviet SALT delegation in Helsinki, Vladimir Semenov, was "under instructions to make no further move" until the president gave the go-ahead. Kissinger sarcastically added, "If the president likes to run down his own accomplishments that is his business."[48]

The president himself dictated a message directly to Kissinger both attempting to assuage the national security advisor and to more clearly elaborate his thinking on Vietnam. First, Nixon expressed his confidence in Kissinger and wrote, "I have read each one of your messages carefully and have been enormously impressed with how you have had exactly the right combination of sweet and sour in dealing with them." Nixon wanted Kissinger to return on the evening of Monday, April 24, because the cover story that Nixon was at Camp David with Kissinger was becoming implausible. Also, Nixon wanted time to review the results and to confer with Kissinger on both the announcement of the secret trip and a major speech he had prepared announcing the withdrawal of additional American troops from Vietnam. He worried that the Soviets had achieved their goal of discussing the summit, while there was only "intangible" progress on Vietnam, namely the symbolism that the Soviet leadership had met with Kissinger three days after the United States had struck Hanoi-Haiphong and had damaged Soviet ships. Nixon warned, "We cannot be oblivious to the fact that while they have agreed to send messages, secretly, they will be continuing to send arms, publicly." The summit in Moscow would serve American "long term interests," but the offensive, backed by Soviet weapons, meant that the summit would "be judged as a success or failure depending upon whether we get some progress on Vietnam." As for the SLBM agreement with the Soviets, Nixon recognized a "shade of difference" with the proposal Semenov had made to Smith in Helsinki. It would now be a question of credit: Would Smith and the SALT delegation get the credit, or would Kissinger and, by extension, President Nixon?

Nixon's primary worries at this point were public relations and politics, closely intertwined in the election year: "What I am trying to emphasize is that we must face the hard fact that we have now convinced the country that Soviet arms and Soviet tanks have fueled this massive invasion of South Vietnam by the North. Having done so, it is only logical that our critics on both right and left will hammer us hard if we sit down and meet with the Soviets, drink toasts, sign communiqués, etc., without getting progress on Vietnam."

Nixon ended his memo trying to buck up the national security advisor: "Just remember we all know we couldn't have a better man in Moscow at this time than Kissinger."[49]

Kissinger's final meetings on the secret trip, on April 24, primarily wrapped up discussions over the preceding days, although Kissinger became irritated by a minor dispute with the Soviets regarding the announcement of the secret trip.

In a morning session with the full Soviet contingent of Brezhnev, Gromyko, Dobrynin, Aleksandrov-Agentov, and Sukhodrev, Kissinger stressed that there would be no "useful purpose" in repeating himself, but that Vietnam remained "the only obstacle on our side in the way" of a constructive summit meeting. Kissinger insisted that the United States had to meet privately with the North Vietnamese no later than May 2 and expressed appreciation for Soviet assistance in passing messages along to the North Vietnamese. The Channel remained sacrosanct, bypassing the State Department, as Kissinger chatted with Brezhnev:

> KISSINGER: As for our proposals, if you were prepared to communicate them to Hanoi, it would be considered a great courtesy. I showed the note we received from the North Vietnamese to your Ambassador, who sees more of these than our Foreign Ministry.
>
> BREZHNEV: Maybe Rogers' post should be abolished.
>
> DR. KISSINGER: Or maybe Dobrynin should be given an official function.
>
> BREZHNEV: He has a second post—the channel.
>
> DR. KISSINGER: Our policy is, anything that comes to the White House is never let out of the White House. All of your communications go only to [the] President.

Brezhnev also broached the idea of a nuclear nonaggression pact with the United States, a "peaceful bomb," perhaps in a "special document, an understanding that our two countries will not use nuclear weapons against one another." Brezhnev praised and personalized the accomplishments of the secret trip: "You and I have done a big job, a necessary and useful piece of work." Kissinger promised to discuss the idea in the confidential channel with Dobrynin. Trouble was brewing in West Germany over the ratification of the Eastern treaties in the Bundestag, so Kissinger told Brezhnev, "We will use our influence where we can." The roundabout on the Middle East continued in general, vague terms. Kissinger was not sure of a settlement and said, "The President must be able to come back from the Summit and be able to say truthfully that no secret agreements were made." Consultation was needed, but Kissinger was ready to "begin immediately a discussion of principles in the special channels." If a framework could be determined, the summit could be a venue to show some progress, "a public arrangement" on "an interim solution." Brezhnev attempted to back away from the idea of the public announcement of the secret trip, but Kissinger insisted. Brezhnev then departed for a Politburo meeting.[50]

Announcement Imbroglio

Kissinger reconvened with Gromyko in the last session of the secret trip. Kissinger had an outburst when Gromyko tried to change the agreed-upon language of the announcement unveiling the secret trip. The Soviet draft omitted the parts about "useful" and "frank" discussion, and the fact that the Soviets had invited him to Moscow.[51] Gromyko nonchalantly told Kissinger: "I am not empowered to make any changes. It is his [Brezhnev's] decision." Kissinger coldly responded, "It will make a bad impression on the president that you refuse to call useful a series of talks in which we settled SALT and the basic principles of our relations, and had useful talks on the Middle East." Ambassador Dobrynin entered the room, and Kissinger explained the situation to his back-channel counterpart: "Anatol, I have been telling the Foreign Minister what the situation is. What conclusion is the president to draw? He will conclude that you maneuvered him into getting me over here, which you wanted for whatever reasons of your own, while reserving the right to suggest publicly that it wasn't very significant." That would be unacceptable for Kissinger: it would undermine the back channels and exacerbate Nixon's fears, possibly derailing the summit. Kissinger explained: "But you are paying a hell of a price for nothing. . . . You know, you have the habit that when someone drops a nickel you will do anything to get the nickel, even if you lose a million dollars of goodwill in the process. There are many in Washington who oppose this. As a friend, I can tell you I have been telling Washington that you have made significant concessions. Now you are telling me that you have tricked me. You are weakening my arguments."

When Gromyko opined that it was "a most impossible interpretation" that the Soviets had maneuvered Kissinger to Moscow to discuss the summit and ignore Vietnam, Kissinger took the unorthodox step of reading from the president's most recent memo. Gromyko excused himself and returned ten minutes later with the general secretary's permission to accept the "new" draft.[52] Kissinger later called the imbroglio over the announcement "petty," and a "crude maneuver" at a "stormy session." Afterward, Kissinger wrote, "all was again serene and jovial, as is the way of Soviet negotiators when they have at last discovered what the negotiating limits are. . . . The Soviets now needed some time to make their influence felt [in Hanoi]."[53] Following the last session, Kissinger commenced the "painful duty" of informing Ambassador Beam about the trip and then returned home. Kissinger regretted keeping Beam in the dark about the trip and characterized Beam as "a true professional. . . . He conducted himself with gentle, unassuming skill during his tour of duty in Moscow." Moreover, Kissinger, added, Beam "deserved better than this apparent vote of no confidence that our strange [back-channel] system imposed on him."[54]

Kissinger Returns

Kissinger arrived at Camp David on the evening of April 24 and had a mini-debriefing with Nixon, Haldeman, and Haig in the Birch Lodge of the presidential retreat. The president, normally known for his formality—a man photographed walking along the beach in a suit—forgot to zip his fly, "so during the entire conversation it was noticeably open." Haldeman wrote in his diary, "The meeting went pretty well, although it was pretty tense at the beginning." According to the chief of staff, the conflict-averse president "was all primed to really whack Henry, but backed off when he actually got there." The cable traffic during the secret trip no doubt contributed to the atmosphere. Haldeman wrote that Haig had called earlier and relayed that Kissinger "felt we had not backed him, and he was very distressed that he had been sabotaged and undercut." Despite frosty greetings, the participants exited the fifty-five-minute meeting "in good spirits," went straight to the helipad, and departed for the White House.[55]

The next morning, April 25, Nixon went to Kissinger's office, and the two carried the discussion over to the president's EOB hideaway office.[56] With a number of brief interruptions from other staff members, Nixon and Kissinger met alone for an hour and had a wide-ranging discussion that brought everything together—a more personal rehash of Kissinger's secret trip, the military situation in Southeast Asia, the status of the Vietnam peace negotiations, the summit, and the great stakes on the line. Everything was linked, and Kissinger saw both opportunities and perils on the horizon. Nixon continued his Vietnam-centric view and described public support for his bombing measures in response to the offensive:

> NIXON: I'm surprised, incidentally, [I've been thinking] of this whole business of Gallup's poll, and I don't give a shit about polls, but they show that we've got—that even though it's a slight majority, but the majority favor bombing. Shit, that means that after I talk, it'll be 60%, I assure you.
> KISSINGER: [That's the best], Mr. President, and I believe, if you pull this off—and I now think the chances are 60–40— your popularity is going to skyrocket even more.

For the president, Kissinger's report on the secret trip confirmed his belief that the leading faction in the Kremlin had a personal stake in the summit but also real policy concerns like the Berlin agreement. Nixon noted: "Brezhnev desperately needs this one. He sees about this vote in the Bundestag . . . and Brandt might go down." Kissinger answered, "Yeah . . . Even if Brandt doesn't go down . . . his treaty does then." The president then compared the summit with Vietnam:

> NIXON: I have a feeling, Henry, that I've been thinking a lot about it. I know that we're going to be sorely tempted to

save the summit at almost any cost. . . . Let me put it in the political context: I am convinced now that we could lose in Vietnam, that I could camouflage it in a way by going to the Russian summit, that it would appear "well, he did the best he could," and we'd win the election. . . . On the other hand, I am convinced that the American people, if we lose in Vietnam after all of this, this is the great struggle between the left and the right, the great struggle between the peaceniks and the patriots, and we cannot lose it.

Nixon's solution of strikes against North Vietnam had become standard operating procedure, but the president had escalation on his mind:

NIXON: We've got to be thinking in terms of an all-out bombing attack. . . . Now, by an all-out bombing attack I am thinking of things that go far beyond: I am thinking of the dikes; I'm thinking of, naturally, the railroads. . . . I've talked to Al about what we had in mind. He said, "It's really simple. We'll gradually move up." And I said, "Al, enough of this goddamn gradualism—"

KISSINGER: I agree with that—I mean, I agree with you.

NIXON: Yeah . . . And, incidentally, I think I will sink the Russian summit. But, I think on the other hand, if it saves Vietnam there might be a Russian summit at some time in the future.

Kissinger explained his personal view to Nixon: "You cannot go and meet Brezhnev if you have either pulled off your confrontation or if you've been defeated." He reassured the president: "That guy will never understand. So, I'm with you 100 percent. And, second, we have, however, a big problem of striking always from a good position." "We've done it in a masterful way of," Kissinger haltingly continued with a chuckle, "sweet and sour, and never being just butchers."

Ambassador Dobrynin factored in the equation as Kissinger flattered the president for his skill. Kissinger reported: "Well, Dobrynin told me at lunch just before we left, he said never has he seen a weak hand played with such masterful skill as you've played Vietnam. . . . I mean, domestically he said." After some discussion about what would constitute a major breakthrough in the Vietnam peace negotiations, Kissinger described Gromyko's hope that tougher American military actions could be delayed past the summit, a kind of tacit agreement:

> KISSINGER: Now, one thing Gromyko told me yesterday . . . [He said], "Look, why don't you have the summit, and after the summit do what you want. Then we will understand." I'm not saying you should do it. It's just delaying us and we can't afford the delay.
> NIXON: Just like we did with the Chinese.
> KISSINGER: Well, no. It's important we did it. Before the Chinese summit we didn't hit North Vietnam at all.[57]

Kissinger's back-channel relationship with Dobrynin took on a new function during the secret trip as the Soviet ambassador served as a personal intermediary so that Brezhnev could maintain plausible deniability with his Kremlin colleagues. Kissinger pointed out: "At the end of every day, Dobrynin came over and talked to me. What Brezhnev obviously did was to use his underling to tell me things so that he wouldn't be around, so that he could tell his top people he hadn't said it." Nixon interrupted, "I would do the same thing." Kissinger described a particularly significant episode during the secret trip that signaled Brezhnev's acquiescence to the American military moves against North Vietnam, so long as the United States avoided hitting the Hanoi-Haiphong complex. In response, Nixon suggested wording for a back-channel message to the Soviets:

> NIXON: You should tell Vorontsov you just had a very discouraging . . . meeting with the president. I want you to put this down. This is very important. "First of all, in one sense, it was one of the best meetings and one of the most hopeful meetings we've ever had. He was enormously impressed with Brezhnev's frankness, with the messages, with the personal communication that has now been established between him and Brezhnev. And, he thinks the summit can be the great event of the century." Put that in. I should write that to Brezhnev. "On the other hand, the president," put it,

"has been shocked by the fact that despite the meetings in Moscow, [North Vietnam has] launched this new offensive, and under the circumstances he's said he has made the following decision: that while this offensive occurs we are going to have to kick 'em."

Kissinger interjected that there were built-in political constraints for Brezhnev. "Our problem with the Russians is this, Mr. President," Kissinger added. "[Brezhnev] does seem to me to have trouble in the Politburo. . . . People tell me that. We don't want him to be accused that we bombed Haiphong three days before I got there." After discussing a creative plan "to sink two or three ships in the mouth of the Harbor of Haiphong," Kissinger returned to the political dilemma for the Soviet leadership and Dobrynin's merits:

> KISSINGER: Incidentally, Mr. President, I've seen these guys in action, there're two guys who've got their asses in a sling: One is Dobrynin; the other is Brezhnev. I really believe, and, uh—
> NIXON: And Dobrynin has some influence because he's so smart.
> KISSINGER: And because he's a member of the Central Committee—
> NIXON: That's right. And they respect him. And they know he talks to you. . . . We know he brokers every damn little conversation.

Kissinger reported that Dobrynin proved extremely useful in rectifying the imbroglio over the joint announcement disclosing the secret trip.

> KISSINGER: And Brezhnev, for example, when he said to me, "I don't want an announcement." He said, "I don't want any announcement." He said, "It's too embarrassing for us. . . . Must you have it?"
> NIXON: [laughs] Ha.
> KISSINGER: Dobrynin was winking at me.
> NIXON: Is that right?

KISSINGER: You know, he was coaching me. And I said, "Yes, we must have it—"

NIXON: Dobrynin knows we've gotta have it.

KISSINGER: But my point is that . . . Dobrynin was helping me out. . . . When I really laid into Gromyko yesterday, Dobrynin took a walk with me, and he said, "You may not believe this, but you did me the biggest favor that has ever been done. These guys think that they can maneuver the president, and I've told them, 'If you think Kissinger is tough, wait 'til you meet the president.'"

NIXON: He said that?

KISSINGER: And he said, "This was a tremendous lesson that you can't push these guys beyond a certain point."

As the conversation drew to a conclusion and the tape abruptly cut off, Kissinger intimated that the Soviets had limits when it came to influencing Hanoi, just like the United States could not always corral Saigon: "Now, how much they can do with these goddamned North Vietnamese—Hell, we can't make the South Vietnamese do everything we want them to—"[58]

The White House shifted to public relations mode later that afternoon, April 25, over the announcement of Kissinger's trip and Nixon's speech on Vietnam the next day. Nixon told Haldeman they must "program" conservative hawks, like Arizona senator Barry Goldwater, and explain that the president was focusing on Vietnam—not on the summit meeting. The bombing of North Vietnam would continue "relentlessly." After rehearsing his speech on Vietnam with Haldeman, Nixon returned to the topic of Kissinger's trip and guidance for White House press secretary Ronald Ziegler. Nixon stated, "I don't think that makes a goddamned bit of difference to the American people, do you think, the fact that we covered up the fact that Henry Kissinger was in Moscow?" Haldeman seemed unsure. Nixon explained: "No, but I mean what you've got to say [is]: Where secret negotiations will help the cause of peace they will be secret, gentlemen. We'll do what is necessary. That's the way to handle it. And we didn't lie to 'em." "We set it up as a cover," Nixon continued, "and it worked, Bob."

Kissinger and Zeigler entered the Oval Office right after Zeigler had read the announcement of Kissinger's secret trip at the morning press briefing on April 25. Kissinger again recounted parts of his secret trip for the president before the discussion turned to the military situation in Vietnam. With Zeigler present, Kissinger described the situation in the Kremlin.

> KISSINGER: I think they got there by stupidity. . . . I don't think that he [Brezhnev] thought they would start such a huge offensive.
>
> NIXON: Before the summit?
>
> KISSINGER: Before the summit. He thought they would start a sort of typical offensive. That if they won it would be embarrassing for us; if they lost, it would make Hanoi more dependent on them. . . . He said, "I didn't think—realize until ten days ago how deadly serious this was." I think—I mean he has really fantastic problems at home, because Brandt is falling on his face, now the summit is falling on its face, or at least it's in danger, and—
>
> NIXON: We always think here that losing the summit is the worst thing that could happen to us; it isn't. Losing the summit might be the worst thing that could happen to him. . . . You see my point?
>
> KISSINGER: His whole policy has been based on the fear [that] we are using the summit against him to blackmail him.

Lest Brezhnev be in too much of a bind, Nixon suggested an ameliorative approach to the general secretary in a private letter transmitted via Vorontsov. Nixon recommended another letter expressing gratitude for the reception Kissinger and his retinue had received in Moscow but also restating that Vietnam remained the "only" issue.[59] The actual letter, which Kissinger delivered later that day, did not refer to Vietnam.[60]

In a late-night television and radio broadcast to the nation the next evening, April 26, Nixon described three decisions he had made on Vietnam. Nixon described a 95 percent reduction in U.S. casualties since he took office, and noted that U.S. forces in Vietnam had been reduced from 549,000 on January 20, 1969, to 69,000 by May 1, 1972. He expected to withdraw 20,000 more troops by July 1, 1972. Nixon then gave the nation the details of the most recent proposal to the North Vietnamese, which included an immediate cease-fire, the exchange of all prisoners of war, the withdrawal of U.S. forces within six months of an agreement, and internationally supervised elections in South Vietnam. "One month before such elections," Nixon explained, "President Thieu and Vice President Huong would resign." When the United States had made the identical offer in October 1971, "intelligence reports began to indicate that the enemy was building up for a major attack. . . . Finally, 3 weeks ago, on Easter weekend, they mounted their massive invasion of South Vietnam."

The contrast between offers of peace and war at a time of peace—Easter weekend—could not be starker. Although upward of 120,000 North Vietnamese were fighting in South Vietnam, Nixon pointed out: "There are no South Vietnamese troops anywhere in North Vietnam. . . . There are no United States ground troops involved." After painting a rosy picture from the report of the U.S. commander in Southeast Asia, Gen. Creighton Abrams, Nixon announced his belief that Vietnamization was working, that the Paris talks would resume, and that bombing raids would continue against North Vietnam. Nixon added: "I have flatly rejected the proposal that we stop the bombing . . . as a condition for returning to the negotiating table. They sold that package to the United States once before, in 1968, and we are not going to buy it again in 1972."

The rhetoric was classic Nixon, who again contrasted his actions in the name of peace with those of the North Vietnamese that reflected their intransigence. Nixon justified the use of American power against North Vietnam to protect withdrawing U.S. forces, to continue the withdrawal program, and "to prevent the imposition of a Communist regime on the people of South Vietnam against their will." The president turned again toward talk of peace, reminding his audience of his "historic journey for peace" to China, which would be followed up by a historic summit in Moscow. The issue was also credibility—presidential credibility: "If the United States betrays the millions of people who have relied on us in Vietnam, the president of the United States, whoever he is, will not deserve nor receive the respect which is essential if the United States is to continue to play the great role we are destined to play of helping to build a new structure of peace in the world."[61]

Kissinger met with Dobrynin in the Map Room on April 28. According to Dobrynin, the "entire conversation . . . essentially centered around one topic: the results of his trip to Moscow."[62] Kissinger jumped into discussion of Vietnam, specifically Brezhnev's dispatch of Konstantin Katushev to Hanoi to pass along the American proposals and attempt to restrain Hanoi. Katushev was publicly seen as one of Brezhnev's protégés,[63] so his departure within hours of Kissinger's own from Moscow meant one of two things for Kissinger. Either Brezhnev was seriously transmitting the American proposals and applying pressure on Hanoi to attend the private meeting on May 2, or, according to "Asian communist" sources, it was to reassure Hanoi that it still enjoyed Soviet support. Dobrynin chose not to qualify either "version" of the Katushev mission.[64]

The White House Cancellation Crisis

On May 1, 1972, a news report fueled fears of a South Vietnamese collapse, and Soviet support for North Vietnam factored into discussions within the Nixon administration to consider canceling the summit. Peter Osnos of the *Washington Post* reported from Saigon "that the military situation in northern South Vietnam" was "rapidly reducing the prospects that government forces will be able to stop the enemy."[65] Haig reported to the president that Quang Tri, the capital city of the northernmost South Vietnamese province, was going to pieces, and Nixon acknowledged the United States could do little to prevent it.[66] Quang Tri fell that evening, and, in response to the failure, South Vietnamese president Nguyen Van Thieu shuffled military leaders.[67]

When he met with Kissinger on May 1, Dobrynin delivered a letter from the general secretary to President Nixon. Brezhnev conveyed his view that events in Vietnam were largely beyond either Soviet or American control. Brezhnev wrote: "We cannot have 100-percent assurance that everything will go just the way it is desired. . . . This question is, of course, not a simple one. As I already told Dr. Kissinger, on the turn that the developments in Vietnam will take, very much will depend, even irrespective of our wishes."[68] The Soviet leader hoped "to prevent a new aggravation of the situation around Vietnam" and thereby avoid the dangers action against North Vietnam would entail "for advancing the relations between our countries and for improving the entire international situation."[69]

Late that afternoon Nixon instructed Rogers and Kissinger to "play it in the terms that the plans for the summit are going on on-schedule [and] that nothing we have done so far has affected it detrimentally." Nixon noted the Soviets might cancel in response to "strong attacks" by U.S. forces to counter the North Vietnamese offensive but predicted "that the summit will move forward."[70]

Earlier that day Kissinger had received a memo from Winston Lord suggesting "a watershed decision" over military action would be made on May 3. The memo ostensibly backed the option of increased military action against North Vietnam because, Lord argued, "Moscow, getting the dangerous message, will choose to pressure Hanoi rather than scuttle the summit." Lord ascertained, from Kissinger's April 20–24 planning trip in Moscow, "that the Soviets (or at least Brezhnev) [were] panting for the summit."[71]

At a meeting later that evening the centrality of Vietnam in the discussion over possible Soviet summit cancellation loomed large as Nixon conferred with Kissinger over whether or not to bomb Hanoi and mine North Vietnamese harbors to curb the offensive and boost South Vietnamese morale. Kissinger warned it was "very conceivable" that the Soviets would cancel the summit after the next series of strikes against Hanoi and Haiphong.[72] Kissinger said the situation demanded decisive force and expressed his support for "really wrapping it up."

The discussion shifted to damage control and preemptive cancellation in the event of any perceived Soviet move to abandon the summit. Nixon inquired: "How will they cancel? I mean, is there any way we can find out?" The back channel provided the means by which to evaluate the Kremlin's line. The president ordered Kissinger: "Keep very close sessions with Dobrynin so that if you sense that even one word, and if he ever raises the subject of cancellation, you go out and say that the president has canceled the summit. [Do] not let those sons-of-bitches say they did!"[73] Kissinger digested Nixon's instructions and soon departed for Paris to conduct the secret session with Le Duc Tho, the meeting to which the North Vietnamese had acquiesced at Soviet behest with the Katushev visit.[74] Outwardly, Nixon seemed confident that the Channel could be used to gauge the Soviet pulse on Vietnam.

On the morning of May 2, the president and Haig met in the Oval Office. Haig reported a cable he had just received from Kissinger that described the Paris negotiations with North Vietnam's Le Duc Tho as the

278   NIXON'S BACK CHANNEL TO MOSCOW

"least productive on record."[75] Hanoi refused to negotiate, despite Soviet assurances. Haig dejectedly added that the North Vietnamese did not even serve warm tea. The Soviets had delivered the North Vietnamese to the conference table, but to no effect. The news of North Vietnamese obstinacy hardened Nixon's opinions about taking strong action against the DRV and toward canceling the summit.

Nixon confessed to Haig his unhappiness with Kissinger's approach toward negotiations with both the North Vietnamese and the Soviets, noting: "I do not believe they ever react to anything unless there're very, very powerful incentives." In Nixon's opinion, Kissinger's meeting with Le Duc Tho failed because "Henry was wrong in not wanting to strike [Hanoi-Haiphong] before he went [to Paris]. . . . I think for Henry's meeting to be any success at all, we [had] to hit the sons-of-bitches before we went. . . . He'd say, 'Well then that would risk the meeting.' The point is he went there empty handed."[76] Nixon apparently forgot about strikes on Thanh Hoa, but the point is that Kissinger did not want Hanoi to have a pretext to cancel the meeting after the Soviets had strong-armed them into the meeting in the first place.

In the Oval Office, Nixon and Haig broached Kissinger's return from Paris and Nixon's belief that Kissinger's approach to the Soviets had been problematic for failing to adequately address the topic of Vietnam. When the subject of canceling the summit came up, Nixon told Haig, "I think we've got to take a hard look at canceling the summit right now." Haig responded with a hard-line position: "Well, I think we have to rack 'em and rack 'em good, and see what the reaction is after the two-day strike. . . . I don't think they'll cancel it based on that."[77] The president then compared the options of mining or blockading North Vietnamese ports and solicited Haig's military expertise.

Nixon continued to absorb news of Kissinger's failed negotiations with Le Duc Tho during a discussion with Haldeman. He pondered preemptive cancellation and also commissioned his chief of staff to conduct an opinion poll to gauge the public feelings on the summit and actions in Vietnam. Nixon acknowledged the great deal of personal investment that had been put into the summit planning:

> NIXON: I think we better cancel the Russian summit. Now this
> is the one that just breaks Henry's heart, because—

HALDEMAN: What about postponing it?

NIXON: No, then they'd cancel.

HALDEMAN: Yeah. You could make it look like you were. If
you postpone indefinitely, just announce you will not go
to the summit under these conditions. . . . Don't say, "I'm
canceling." Don't say, "I'll never go," but say . . . ."Under
the present conditions I will not go, and therefore I have
cancelled my plans for the May 22 departure. . . . What
becomes of the summit depends on what happens in other
places." Then they can come back and say we cancelled the
summit. You've still taken the initiative.

NIXON: No, I haven't. You see all this is very painful to me. I
know all of our people around here, it's especially painful
to Henry because he sees basically our goal for everything
in great jeopardy; I mean all of our schemes and this and
that. But on the other hand, we've got to look at what else
you can do, and what else do you do . . . is to, you know,
continue to just whack 'em out there [and] have the Russians
cancel the summit. That's the worst of both worlds.

HALDEMAN: Um-hmm. If you cancel the summit you gain
something from it. If they cancel it, it hurts you.

NIXON: If they cancel it, it looks like . . . peace has suffered a
great blow because of our failure in Vietnam, the president's
stubbornness and all that sort of thing.[78]

As the conversation progressed, the president put the issues of the Easter Offensive into context and predicted that the United States would "be
in a position then when the offensive will have, frankly, run its course and
they will not have succeeded."[79] If that scenario played out, Nixon could
continue with the summit—provided American actions did not compel
the Soviets to cancel.

Haig returned to the Oval Office as Haldeman departed. The two men
discussed arrangements and an agenda for a meeting on the presidential
yacht *Sequoia* upon Kissinger's return from Paris later that evening. Nixon
told Haig to send Kissinger a message indicating that "The critical question that we must discuss tonight is my growing conviction—to use those
terms—that we should move to cancel the summit." As in earlier conver-

sations, Nixon again criticized Kissinger's negotiations with the North Vietnamese, but this time he tempered his criticism with praise. "Henry's judgment has been really fantastically good on so many things," the president told Haig, "but I think we have to realize that his judgment with regard to negotiations with the North Vietnamese has been faulty." Nixon added, "Throughout he's always been hopeful, and he's always read more into it than was there." Haig hypothetically put himself in the Kremlin and cautioned the president: "If I were in Moscow and were driven by the convictions I think they're driven by, I'd screw us. . . . I think that we've seen nothing to cause us to think otherwise."

Nixon contemplated the potentially disastrous consequences of an American abandonment of South Vietnamese president Nguyen Van Thieu, an ever-recurring North Vietnamese demand. With encouragement from Nixon, Haig opined that the whole region of South East Asia would "career about the dominoes." The men rattled off a list of countries that would hypothetically fall to communism in the event of a South Vietnamese collapse.

The dialogue concluded with talk about the war and the possibilities of canceling the summit. "Let me say that if I thought that continuing it could save the war, we would continue it," Nixon mused. "To hell with the summit."[80] Haig recollected that Nixon "talked almost exclusively about hard options: blockade, the bombardment of strategic targets in the Hanoi-Haiphong agglomeration, destroying the railroads, mining the harbors, interdicting shipping from whatever source to stop the materials of war from getting through to the enemy."[81] The meeting adjourned, and Nixon went to his EOB office for the remainder of the afternoon.

Kissinger met up with Haig and joined the president that evening for dinner aboard the *Sequoia*. The dinner was anything but a pleasure cruise, and the men discussed the agenda Nixon had set beforehand. Kissinger came back from Paris emboldened to confront the North Vietnamese militarily, but he saw three choices that he outlined in a memo to the president: (1) go through with the summit; (2) bomb Hanoi and Haiphong while leaving summit cancellation up to the Soviets; or (3) postpone the summit until after the climate had changed. Above all, Kissinger leaned toward the second option because "it would give the Russians the onus of the decision whether or not to cancel the summit" and would "gain us the best of both worlds concerning the summit and Vietnam."[82] Reflecting later, Kissinger judged the summit to be Nixon's primary concern and posited that his boss was worried about a repeat of the U-2 crisis when the Soviets shot down CIA pilot Francis Gary Powers and ceremoniously canceled a four-power meeting with President Eisenhower, French president Charles de Gaulle and British prime minister Harold Macmillan. Kissinger believed Nixon "was determined that any cancellation or postponement should come at his initiative."

Kissinger presented himself as more practical and the possibility was worth running "whatever risk was necessary."[83] Continuing the wedge strategy, the advisor suggested using "Moscow's eagerness for the summit" to separate Moscow and Hanoi.[84] Moscow had facilitated the meeting with the North Vietnamese but could not deliver concrete results. The North Vietnamese had their own interests in mind, and the "brutal" private meeting on May 2 reflected the situation on the ground. Kissinger explained: "Quang Tri had fallen the day before. Pleiku was in peril. An Loc was now surrounded. . . . For all Le Duc Tho knew, a complete South Vietnamese collapse was imminent." "What the May 2 meeting revealed," Kissinger added, "was Hanoi's conviction that it was so close to victory that it no longer needed even the pretense of negotiation."[85]

Nixon worried about the problems a summit cancellation by the United States would cause at home and abroad, but the potential drawbacks always remained peripheral to the issue of Vietnam. On this, he remained consistent: he could not go to the summit if Saigon could collapse at any moment, and he would resort to overwhelming force before allowing it to collapse. Although Kissinger has not denied this, he has insisted that the president was dead set on canceling the summit. Nixon stressed that Kissinger "felt that there was now almost no chance that the Soviet Summit could take place, and he agreed with my initial inclination that we should cancel it immediately in order to prevent the Soviets from doing so first. . . . The problem, as Kissinger saw it, was that we could not bomb and have the summit too."[86]

Kissinger claimed that Haig and Connally tipped Nixon's decision in favor of Kissinger's own preferred course of action, that of bombing and not preemptively canceling the summit. Kissinger biographer Walter Isaacson has argued convincingly that "the prospect of losing the summit horrified Kissinger. Although his fury at the North Vietnamese had heightened his conviction that a hard military blow was necessary, he had no stomach for a breakdown in negotiations and further domestic turmoil." Kissinger's staff believed the Soviets would cancel the summit, or worse, in response to strong American action in Vietnam.[87] Consequently, Kissinger acknowledged the need for some display of force against the intractable North Vietnamese. The balancing act came into play, and the differences in options became largely academic. Should the United States expand bombing of North Vietnam to include Hanoi, Haiphong, and other targets farther north? Should the United States bomb *and* mine?

Nixon's "presidential style" may offer some explanation as to why his and Kissinger's accounts of the decision vary. First-person accounts have shown that Nixon generally used different advisors as sounding boards to weigh the pros and cons of each issue. The president discussed the ramifications of action against North Vietnam and summit cancellation throughout early May 1972, and what Nixon told Kissinger differed from what he was telling Haig and Haldeman. First and foremost a politician, Nixon was all too aware of the effects of public opinion, which was why he ordered Haldeman to set up a poll. The president probably went through the scenarios in his head and did so aloud while he was trying to get a handle on what course of action was politically palatable.

Early in the morning on May 3, 1972, Nixon told Haldeman about the meeting the previous night on the *Sequoia*. Nixon reported that "Kissinger has reached the conclusion [that] what we ought to do is to, rather than bomb this weekend, is to announce we're not going to the summit. . . . [I] tend to agree with his assertion last night." "However," Nixon added, "I want to see this poll. . . . If not going to the summit is going to be a plus then it's worth doing."[88] Conversely, if public opinion could (and did) swing in favor of the summit, it would be worth going. On that same morning, the *Washington Post* reported that a telephone poll by Opinion Research Corporation (conducted April 27–29) showed "that 7 out of 10 Americans support[ed] President Nixon on his decision to bomb North Vietnam."[89] If he could not gauge public opinion on the summit, at least Nixon had some confidence from the poll that he could safely escalate against Hanoi.

Nixon's talk with Haldeman also confirmed his later recollection that canceling the summit did not make sense. The president rhetorically queried, "What do we get from canceling?" He then answered his own question: "Canceling the summit we certainly lose with the doves. It hardens the opposition on the war in Congress. Frankly, it's a hawk. It prepares the way for bombing, but the key is what happens then?"[90]

Kissinger briefly met with Dobrynin at the White House on the morning of May 3, to deliver a letter from Nixon to Brezhnev about the "deeply disappointing" results of the Paris peace session the previous day. The military situation in South Vietnam was deteriorating and "since Dr. Kissinger's visit to Moscow and our agreement to resume talks, the DRV has started offensive actions. . . . Hanoi obviously hopes that the pressure of its offensive will force us to accept terms tantamount to surrender." The president warned, "The fact remains that Soviet military supplies provide the means for the DRV's actions and promised Soviet influence if it has been exercised at all has proved unavailing." Nixon wrote he "would welcome having on an urgent basis [Brezhnev's] own assessment of the situation."[91]

In another conversation with Haldeman later that morning, Nixon focused on the negative consequences of canceling the summit. Haldeman wrote that cancellation of the summit could lead to "a collapse of the Nixon foreign policy." He again raised the prospect of postponing the summit, to which the president replied, "If we cancel the summit or postpone the summit, which any way you call it it's a dodge, and it's bound to lead to . . . massive propaganda." The summit would also distract from Vietnam and would provoke the Democrats to say at their party convention, "Here we are, a President who was going to go to Moscow and bring us a generation of peace [who] has now bogged us down in an unwinnable, desperate war in Vietnam."[92]

After Haldeman left the Oval Office, Nixon met with Kissinger to discuss the broader political implications in the event of a summit cancellation. The president favored a two-day air strike against North Vietnamese targets because, in addition to being domestically favorable, "it would give some encouragement to the South Vietnamese, give some pause to the Russians, and some pause to Hanoi." The heart of the matter was "whether we honestly feel that canceling the summit could have—could be a decisive factor or even a substantial factor in resolving the situation in Vietnam." The president answered, "On that point, I have grave doubts." In this instance, Nixon moved away from preemptively canceling the summit and toward placing the decision in the Soviet court.

With a rather gloomy outlook, Kissinger estimated that a "slightly better than 50–50 chance" existed that the Soviets would cancel in response to increased American bombing strikes against North Vietnam. Still, he argued for action—albeit the more restrained action of bombing and not a full naval blockade, which would surely be more likely to provoke the Soviets to cancel. Kissinger praised his boss for his "toughness" and stressed that the success of the summit hinged on a number of factors. "Now you could say you could go to the summit, go through with it, don't sign these principles, don't give them credit, and don't make a deal on the Middle East. Well, then, you'll have a pretty empty summit." The former Harvard professor lectured: "Now to get out of the summit what you want, you have to come back and be able to talk about peace. . . . In other words, you give the Soviets a certificate of good conduct."[93] Kissinger hoped Vietnam would be a nonissue for the summit, and he again argued in favor of a two-day bombing strike on Hanoi and Haiphong.

Public opinion also helped to clarify the decision. The poll Haldeman had conducted the day before at the president's behest "showed that most Americans, 60 percent or more, believed that he should go to Moscow, no matter what was happening [in Vietnam]."[94] In terms of public approval, going through with the summit was a nondecision. Before he had the results of the poll, however, the president had Haldeman and Kissinger get John Connally's read on the situation.

Reaching a Decision: May 4, 1972

For all intents and purposes, the president finalized the decision to go through with the summit while both bombing and mining North Vietnam on the morning of May 4, 1972. That morning, Haldeman reported the results of his meeting with Kissinger and Connally. Haldeman told the president, "I didn't have to give my pitch." Nixon exclaimed, "I'll be damned," and then inquired, "You didn't have to talk about polls?" Haldeman replied that he had talked about polls at the end of the meeting with Connally, but the treasury secretary "said his position is, first of all, [that] you've got to face one fact: you cannot lose the war in Vietnam." Haldeman continued: "He put that to Henry. . . . You've got to go in and bomb Hanoi and Haiphong. You've got to do anything else that's gonna make a difference." Echoing Nixon's own talk about the use of force against North Vietnam, Connally told Haldeman and Kissinger:

"Bomb for seriousness, not just for a signal, to knock out whatever their capabilities are, whatever the targets are there. . . . If the railroad complex is important, demolish it. If the port's important, demolish it. Power plugs, communications bases, whatever there is, and don't worry about killing civilians."

Nixon asked whether that included the blockade option in addition to bombing. Haldeman continued: "Including the blockade. [. . .] Number two, you're absolutely wrong in your—Henry is—in your position that you should be the one to cancel the Soviet summit." Haldeman reported that Connally had hammered the point: "If the Soviet summit is to be cancelled, make the Soviets cancel it. Don't you do it, because if the hope for peace is gonna be shattered by anybody in this world have it shattered by the other guy. Don't shatter it yourself." After a moment's pause, the president stated: "I hadn't thought of that. He's absolutely right. . . . Absolutely right."[95]

In a conversation on May 5, Nixon and Kissinger recounted Connally's assessment of a course of action:

NIXON: Connally, with his, you know, with his animal-like
    decisiveness, and which I also have, but I'm much more—
KISSINGER: You're much more subtle.
NIXON: Through the years I've put much more layers of subtlety
    on it. But anyhow, Connally marched quickly to the point.
    He says, "Look, the summit is great. I hope you don't knock
    it off. I think you can do both, and I hope you can do
    both. I think you will do both." But, he says, "Even if you
    don't, you're going to do the first things first. You've got to
    remember [that] you can do without the summit, but you
    cannot live with a defeat in Vietnam."[96]

Nixon realized that the publicly supported escalation in bombing would likely decrease the odds that South Vietnam would collapse by boosting South Vietnamese morale and disrupting North Vietnamese supply lines. The question in the interim was how to phrase the action without seeming wishy-washy or provoking the Russians to cancel. Against Kissinger's fears of Soviet cancellation, Nixon would conclude that the benefits would outweigh the costs for Moscow.[97]

Even with the decision more or less made to proceed with both bombing and mining, though, Nixon continued to go through the various possibilities over and over to make sure he had not overlooked any contingency. China also entered into the discussions as a factor of U.S.-Soviet relations, as a point of contrast and as an opportunity. In another conversation with Kissinger on May 4, Nixon sought to use action against Vietnam to keep the momentum moving forward on Sino-American rapprochement by playing the Chinese off the Soviets (and vice versa). Nixon instructed Kissinger: "Let's make it a point to write a direct letter, a message from me to Zhou Enlai, saying why we're doing this; that the Russians have . . . proved to be not trustworthy. . . . And what we do now in Vietnam is not directed against them but against the Russians." Kissinger concurred, "Oh, yes. Mr. President, we have come back from every crisis stronger, and I think we're going to become stronger because of this one."[98]

In a conversation on May 5, Nixon advised Kissinger "to be incredibly cool and particularly outgoing," with Dobrynin. Nixon worried that the Soviets had got wind of his ruminations of canceling the summit meeting, so he wanted to reassure the Soviets and even suggested flattery. The president continued: "Act as if everything was going ahead on schedule, but act very, very nice. Say how [grateful] you are, how pleased Mrs. Nixon is with the graciousness of Mrs. Dobrynin, and all that. Because now that the die is cast, we are going to play this in the most vicious way we can with those bastards."[99]

Ironically, Dobrynin cabled Moscow on May 5 that Nixon appeared ready to finally delink Vietnam from the substantive achievements of a summit meeting.[100] The Soviet ambassador could not have predicted the proceedings in the executive offices that week, but he uncharacteristically misread signals from Kissinger at a lunch meeting at the Soviet embassy. Dobrynin wrote of the encounter, "By all indications, until the Moscow summit the White House will try to refrain from making particularly major decisions on far-reaching military measures against the DRV, so as not to come into conflict with us and not to jeopardize the Moscow meeting, as long as the situation in South Vietnam does not turn into a disaster during this interval."[101]

As if to reiterate the Russian inability to pressure Hanoi's hand at the negotiating table, Brezhnev wrote to Nixon on May 6 that only the

Vietnamese and the United States could settle the conflict. The Soviets expressed their willingness to encourage renewed DRV-U.S. peace negotiations.[102] Although the Soviet Union could put forward rhetorical arguments or act as an intermediary between the United States and the DRV, the Soviet leaders projected the image that Southeast Asia was only a peripheral concern for them. Members of the Nixon White House continued to stress Brezhnev's personal stake in détente and that "business as usual"—planning for the summit and negotiations—continued as before.

Nixon wavered at times in his determination to proceed with the bombing-mining counteroffensive and to let the onus of summit cancellation rest with the Soviets. In a meeting with Haldeman on May 5, for example, Nixon pointed out that Kissinger was too friendly with Dobrynin and that the relationship had some drawbacks:

> NIXON: He's never going to get anything from the Russians. Henry's always saying he's going to get something out of the Russians . . . through some senior man down there. Christ, there was a delegation that's been down there. . . . He goes through this litany, time and time again and again. In fact, he really shouldn't be lunching with Dobrynin today. . . . Probably he should have canceled it, but he thought that was too much of a signal. I don't know why in the hell he would be doing it today. Do you?
>
> HALDEMAN: Except that he had it set.
>
> NIXON: Well, of course. I'd just postpone it. By God, after that meeting, I'd postpone it. But I did give him some good advice, because Henry tends to overreact one way or the other, and I didn't want him to go over there and be cold, and menacing, and the rest. But I said: "Slobber over the son-of-a-bitch. Dobrynin treats us that way. Slobber over him. Make it appear that we're not going to do anything." We've got to do something, you know. It's like the bluff with poker. You don't shout it out and the rest when you've got the cards. You just sit there and that's the whole key to it.[103]

On the morning of May 8 Nixon met with his NSC on the topic of action against North Vietnam. The NSC confirmed the president's choice to escalate the bombing and commence mining against North Vietnam. The advisors agreed that the United States would need to take a conciliatory attitude toward the Soviets and thereby evade the cancellation issue. Nixon officially gave the order to execute Operation Linebacker, the name for the massive bombing and mining of the DRV, and Hanoi-Haiphong in particular, following the meeting. Nixon announced the decision on television that evening.[104]

Kissinger met with Dobrynin to give some forewarning before Nixon's televised address. The ambassador recollected that he "sharply criticized the military actions as a crude violation of international law, including freedom of the seas."[105] Dobrynin conveyed the deep Soviet apprehension about interference with Soviet ships, which could potentially be construed as "an act of war."[106] Kissinger tried to assuage Soviet fears with a conciliatory tone and had previously warned Dobrynin in earlier conversations about "drastic" U.S. military actions. He assured him "that Soviet vessels would not be attacked." Retrospectively, Dobrynin felt that, "on the whole, the conversation was rather tense, especially when I insisted and managed to have one offensive passage deleted from the draft of Nixon's announcement. Frankly, I began worrying about the summit."[107] Kissinger's account backs up Dobrynin's sense of foreboding and notes that, at Dobrynin's suggestion, Nixon had removed a latent criticism of the Soviets for the failure of the Paris peace talks on May 2 that had been backed up by "Soviet assurances."[108] Dobrynin's recommendation probably signaled the Soviet leadership that the Americans remained willing to compromise. Such personal intervention certainly reflected the ambassador's preference for a successful summit.

As a concession for the Soviet acceptance of the military escalation and to encourage the summit, Kissinger also delivered a letter from Nixon to Brezhnev. Nixon justified the American military action as a means to "effectively preclude further supplies of aggression from reaching North Vietnam." The president challenged Brezhnev to rise to the occasion and subtly suggested that the Vietnam issue be put aside: "This is a moment for statesmanship. It is a moment when, by joint efforts, we can end the malignant effects on our relations and on the peace of the world which the conflict in Vietnam has so long produced."[109] The United States also signaled its readiness for "peace," a code word to the Soviets that the Nixon administration wanted to proceed with the summit.

Brezhnev waited several days to reply, and in the interim the Soviets sent mixed signals about the summit, mostly due to three factors. First, several Soviets died in North Vietnam due to the increased American bombing raids, and it is likely that the Kremlin held off on a definitive answer on the summit until it was satisfied by the American response to their protests. Second, the ratification of the long-sought West German "Eastern treaties" with the Soviet Union and Poland entered into the equation, at least until May 9, when Kissinger "was able to inform Ambassador Dobrynin that the Bundestag *would* ratify the . . . treaties."[110] Third, the mixed signals may have been a result of a behind-the-scenes Kremlin power struggle that finally ended at a May 19 Central Committee plenum. "In Moscow," according to Dobrynin, "the summit literally hung in the balance."[111]

Damage to Soviet shipping proved to be the primary inhibitor on Soviet policy following Nixon's televised announcement of May 8. Dobrynin lodged a formal protest with Kissinger about damage to Soviet shipping in Cam Pha within two days of American military escalation. Dobrynin protested the "criminal activity of the U.S. Air Force that had killed some crewmen on Soviet vessels in North Vietnamese waters" and "demanded that the United States guarantee the safety of Soviet vessels and Soviet sailors' lives."[112] Kissinger excused himself and returned a few minutes later. The national security advisor said the president had requested that Dobrynin "deliver to Brezhnev his deep personal regret, especially for the casualties, an offer to pay damages, and his assurance that he was ordering the military command to prevent any recurrence."[113] When Kissinger queried if the Soviets' use of the private channel could be interpreted as "a desire to keep matters at low key," Dobrynin replied that "he was not sure yet . . . however, he thought it was a somewhat encouraging sign as far as future relations were concerned."[114] As further encouragement and as a sign of continuing arrangements for the summit, however, Dobrynin said Moscow wanted Soviet minister of foreign trade Nikolai Patolichev to meet with President Nixon. Kissinger arranged the meeting between Nixon and Patolichev for the next morning and later estimated that the conversation with Dobrynin, "if not yet the turning point, deflated the pressure."[115]

When Brezhnev's reply to Nixon's May 8 letter arrived in the afternoon on May 11, the general secretary again stressed that the American

May 11, 1972. Nixon met with Soviet trade minister Nikolai Patolichev (*speaking with Nixon*) and Ambassador Dobrynin (*second from left*). Just three days earlier, Nixon had announced a major escalation of mining and bombing operations against North Vietnam, in response to the largest Communist offensive since 1968. Less than a week earlier, Nixon had considered preemptively canceling the Moscow summit meeting because Soviet weapons and materiel had made the North Vietnamese "Easter Offensive" possible. The back channel allowed a tacit agreement that (aside from strong rhetoric) Nixon would overlook the Soviet aid to North Vietnam and that the Kremlin leadership, headed by Leonid Brezhnev, would overlook the American escalation. (RNPLM)

bombing campaign was a dangerous affront to maritime freedom of navigation and a contravention of international law. Through Brezhnev's letter, the collective Soviet leadership expressed dismay at the American bombing campaign and the perils it entailed for the freedom of navigation. The "complete destruction" of one Soviet ship and "a loss of human lives among Soviet seamen" subjected "Soviet-American relations to a severe test."[116] Tellingly, Brezhnev did not mention the summit, the absence of which set off alarm bells in the White House that Soviets might cancel the meeting.

Dobrynin tried to allay Kissinger's concerns of a Soviet cancellation. According to Dobrynin, Kissinger "repeatedly" inquired about the summit, and asked if the Soviets "had any objections to the White House publishing the statement that it had received a reply from the Soviet leadership confirming that the summit meeting was still on." Dobrynin answered, "there were no grounds for such a statement, as the summit had not been directly discussed in the exchange of letters." When Kissinger queried whether or not the Soviet government could "confirm its readiness to hold the summit as scheduled," Dobrynin again said that that thorny issue had not been dealt with directly.[117]

Immediately after the two-hour meeting with Dobrynin, Kissinger went to the Oval Office to discuss the Soviet ambassador's response with the president. Kissinger reported that he had given Dobrynin three assurances: "One, we will do nothing in addition to what we're already doing. . . . Two, there'll be no attacks on Soviet ships; Three, there'll be no interference with Soviet ships on the high seas." Kissinger argued that if the Soviets had decided against the summit, they would have done so after the president's May 8 speech. The ratification of the German treaties in the Bundestag also remained a moderating factor in the Soviet calculus. Kissinger told the president: "Well, we've got them where the hair is short. They're dying about that German Treaty." The national security advisor added, "I think we've pulled this damn thing off." Nixon asked if Dobrynin seriously "expected we would interfere with their ships." Kissinger replied, "I think it's like the Cuban Missile Crisis, Mr. President, where they constructed a victory by saying they got a promise from us not to invade, which we had no intention to do anyway." Kissinger dismissed press criticism of Operation Linebacker. "They were charging in here, saying this was the day World War Three starts, the mines are activated," he told the president. "And instead," Kissinger chuckled, "you see the Russian minister of foreign trade." Dobrynin pointed out to Kissinger that the Patolichev meeting with the president after the president's announcement was a "Politburo decision." In the same conciliatory spirit, Kissinger recommended a "personal assurance" to the Soviets that the U.S. military strikes against North Vietnam would be turned down right before and during the summit. Nixon and Kissinger agreed this was a good course of action. While Nixon opined that Dobrynin was "obviously on edge a bit," he noted that the Soviets wanted a positive summit. The president praised Kissinger's moderate approach:

NIXON: Henry, the way you handled it was just right. You said we're not going to do any more, but we're not going to do any less. . . . We aren't going to hurt any Russian ships.

KISSINGER: Right. And then, Monday, I figure I should tell him
that starting Thursday, there'll be no more attacks in the
Hanoi-Haiphong area. . . . That helps us with Hanoi, too,
when they see we made a deal with Russia. By that time,
Mr. President, they'll have worked it over for ten days. . . .
[The Soviets] won't do a damned thing until the German
treaties are ratified.
NIXON: You don't think so?
KISSINGER: No. And they want to save it from you. . . .
NIXON: But if we give them that, it has to be a straight quid pro
quo, don't you think?
KISSINGER: They won't cancel it now. There's nothing in it for
them to cancel it a day before you go there.[118]

Although Dobrynin could not completely address Kissinger's anxiety
about a summit cancellation on May 11, the news looked better on May
12 with the Soviet reply to Nixon's apologies and assurances regarding
damage to Soviet shipping. The Soviets maintained their strict position
about the dangerous American impediments to the freedom of navigation
and vaguely warned of "dangerous consequences" in the event of repetition, but they seemed to accept Nixon's mollifying response.

The Soviets' mixed signals diminished, and the tacit understanding about Vietnam returned in a modified form. Nixon's response to the
Soviet protests had been sufficiently apologetic, and both sides seemed to
acquiesce to less forceful position statements. The two sides quietly agreed
to disagree on contentious issues and to keep up appearances. A Soviet
position paper delivered by Oleg Sokolov to General Haig on May 14,
for example, requested that if the DRV and United States had decided to
reconvene peace negotiations, "it would in many ways be favorable to the
Soviet-American meeting" if President Nixon made "a public announcement about such [an] agreement in advance, before Mr. Nixon's visit to
Moscow."[119]

The Dobrynin-Kissinger private channel also turned to the lighter
side of preparations for the "forthcoming summit" when Dobrynin
specified that the car-loving Brezhnev would prefer, as a gift from the
Americans, "some sort of Cadillac" and that the general secretary preferred the color to be black.[120] Perhaps the bombing of North Vietnam

would not stand in the way of the general secretary's desire to sample Detroit's finest.

The Kremlin's Cancellation Crisis

Brezhnev had committed the Soviet Union to détente with the United States and a summit meeting, although Nixon's decision for a massive escalation in Vietnam created a dilemma. Brezhnev's foreign policy advisor Andrei Aleksandrov-Agentov recollected years later: "The Soviet leadership had to raise the subject so that they could justify themselves in front of their colleagues, in front of the Central Committee, and in front of the public."[121] Dissenting hard-line elements in the CPSU led by Petro Shelest took issue with Brezhnev's détente initiative and sought to either cancel outright or indefinitely postpone any summit meeting. Brezhnev used the opportunity to replace Shelest as the first secretary of the Ukrainian Communist Party with one of his allies and protégés, Vladimir Scherbitsky. A CIA memorandum written just two months after the dispute in the Kremlin summarized:

> There were rumors in Moscow that following President Nixon's speech on 8 May announcing U.S. plans to step up military pressure on Hanoi, Shelest was one of those who argued against going ahead with the summit meeting. The timing of the announcement of Shelest's demotion . . . just one day before President Nixon's arrival, strongly suggests that this was indeed the case. . . . Shelest's demotion is certainly being read by the party rank and file as signaling a victory for Brezhnev and the forces favoring détente.[122]

Several Soviet policymakers have described the episode in their memoirs, including Dobrynin, Aleksandrov-Agentov, Arkady Shevchenko, Oleg Kalugin, and Petro Shelest himself.[123] Dobrynin provided an overview of the Soviet cancellation crisis in his memoirs, but the account must be taken with caution, because the Soviet ambassador was at his post in the United States when the showdown in the Politburo occurred on May 19, 1972. As the Soviet ambassador to the United States and as Kissinger's primary back-channel interlocutor, Dobrynin also had a personal and professional stake in improved U.S.-Soviet relations. Despite this necessary disclaimer, however, Dobrynin's analysis and recollections remain a very valuable source on Soviet decision making. Dobrynin claimed that "the military leadership headed by Marshal [Andrei] Grechko opposed the meeting, and so did President [Nikolai] Podgorny." Others, such as "[Mikhail] Suslov, the chief ideologist, and many prominent party figures were undecided, while Kosygin and Gromyko favored a summit." The man in the center, Brezhnev, "was well aware that if he refused to receive Nixon our relations would be adversely and profoundly affected." In the final analysis, Dobrynin saw Brezhnev's decision as a cost-benefit analysis comparing U.S.-Soviet relations with Soviet-North Vietnamese relations: "The leadership in Hanoi, while our ideological allies, doggedly avoided informing us about their long-term plans in Southeast Asia . . . notwithstanding our considerable military and economic aid. . . . The final verdict of the Politburo was to go ahead with the summit, because its members recognized that the alternative would amount to handing Hanoi a veto over our relations with America."[124]

Shelest considered the summit the culmination of Brezhnev's efforts to consolidate his power and less of a cancellation crisis per se. In an interview three decades later, Shelest noted that he had been expendable, "vulnerable to the will of the Party elite." Shelest essentially confirmed that Nixon's bombing and mining campaign angered Podgorny, but the Soviet president had accepted Shelest's removal, Scherbitsky's promotion, and the summit meeting as a fait accompli. Shelest wrote that Brezhnev clearly enjoyed his "success in international politics, but that his supporters were politically blind bootlickers."[125]

The Kissinger-Dobrynin channel was an essential element in the resolution of the Soviet and White House cancellation crises provoked by the North Vietnamese Easter Offensive. Although the White House had paved the way for the Soviets to delink Vietnam from the improvement in U.S.-Soviet relations in the months before the offensive, by mid-April Nixon had begun to believe that Moscow had colluded with Hanoi and enabled the offensive in the first place. The president reluctantly sent Kissinger on a secret trip to Moscow with instructions to focus on Vietnam. While the national security advisor was in Moscow, Nixon upped the ante and ordered Kissinger to discuss *only* Vietnam. With a time lag and communications failures, Kissinger instead took the initiative and achieved results on an SLBM ceiling and on the number of ABM sites, but only after the Soviets had essentially arranged to facilitate communication with Hanoi. Although the Soviets did not make any promises, the North Vietnamese agreed to meet with the Kissinger for a private session in Paris on May 2. The secret trip proved to be the height of the back channel, with a direct vote of confidence from both the leadership in the Kremlin and the White House.

The failure to achieve results at the May 2 meeting with the North Vietnamese hardened Nixon's determination to take more drastic measures against North Vietnam. Nixon and Kissinger feared that the escalation would force the Soviets to cancel the summit in solidarity with Hanoi. Yet, on the advice of Treasury Secretary John Connally, and atop the foundation Kissinger laid in the back channel, Nixon decided on May 4, 1972, to go through with mining and bombing operations against Hanoi-Haiphong. The president announced the decision on May 8, but not before he directed Kissinger to use his back-channel relationship with Ambassador Dobrynin to both soften the blow and probe the Soviet reaction to the escalation. Public opinion polls bolstered Nixon's decision making and factored into several back-channel exchanges with Dobrynin. The summit became the culmination of the back-channel relationship, and the personal diplomacy ameliorated relations across the Iron Curtain.

Conclusion

At the Summit, Achieving Détente

NIXON: Well, you know it's been a long war, and we'll do our best
with no doubt. It's just we have to realize that . . . there is [not]
anything much left to do, unless you're going nuclear . . . and
we won't do that. I mean, what else is there to do, Henry? . . .
There isn't another thing. They'll say, "Talk to the Russians."
We have. "Talk to the Chinese." We have. "Talk to the North
Vietnamese." We have. "Bomb them." We have. "Mine them."
We have. "Stop their offensive." We have. "Vietnamize." We
have. What in the name of God—?

KISSINGER: We've got to get out now.

—December 14, 1972

Nixon arrived at Moscow's Vnukovo Airport for the summit on May 22,
1972, on a rainy, overcast day. "Because of the war in Vietnam the Politburo had decided to accord Nixon a reserved public welcome," Arkady
Shevchenko remembered, "and only a small number of people saluted
him at Vnukovo and on Moscow's streets."[1] In contrast to the muted
arrival, most of the plenary sessions at the summit were conducted with
pomp and circumstance, and each day of the summit concluded with a
formal ceremony for a plethora of agreements being signed.

There were many agreements. In addition to the Interim Agreement
on the Limitation of Strategic Offensive Arms and the Anti-Ballistic Missile Treaty, both of which had a back-channel element, seven other agreements or treaties were signed concerning cooperative efforts in science and
technology, medicine, public health, environmental protection, collabora-
tion in space exploration, and avoiding naval incidents at sea. The mood

Kissinger escorts Anatoly and Irina Dobrynin with their grandchild along the White House grounds, 1973. In the course of contacts over many years, Kissinger and Dobrynin formed a friendship based on mutual respect for each other's talents and the realization that they represented governments that did not always see eye to eye. (RNPLM)

was extremely positive. The head of the SALT delegation in Helsinki and Vienna, Ambassador Gerard Smith, remembered "the image of a Kremlin topped by a floodlighted Star-Spangled banner."[2] The American flag declared to the world—and to the throngs of media in attendance—that the Soviet leaders were hosting the American president in a historic summit. Back channels made the summit possible, and they would continue operating outside the spotlight of the formal delegations.

Nixon, Dobrynin, and Kissinger at Camp David in 1973. (RNPLM)

The events in Vietnam colored the summit behind the scenes on May 24, 1972, at a private session at the secluded Novo Ogaryevo dacha outside Moscow. Soviet president Nikolai Podgorny proclaimed to Nixon, Kissinger, and some NSC aides: "You are murderers. You have the blood of old people, women, and children on your hands." The Soviet leader, a member of the ruling "troika" along with Brezhnev and Kosygin, emphatically asked the president of the United States, "When are you finally going to end this terrible war?"[3] The tone of the meeting contrasted sharply with the jovial method of getting to the dacha, when General Secretary Brezhnev "abducted" President Nixon, "physically propelling him into his . . . big ZIL limousine" and then taking him for a high-speed hydrofoil ride on the Moscow River.[4]

In a sense, the meeting, convened at Brezhnev's suggestion to discuss "outstanding issues," was a continuation of the back-channel diplomacy that had brought leaders together in the first place.[5] Secretary of State Rogers was not there because Soviet foreign minister Andrei Gromyko was not present; it was a matter of protocol. As Brezhnev's primary aide, Alexei Aleksandrov-Agentov, remembered, "The question [of Vietnam] was raised not in the gilded St. Catherine's Hall in the Kremlin, not in the presence of both extensive delegations, but in a narrow circle almost in secret." In contrast to the large plenary sessions, the number of participants on both sides at the secluded dacha was small: Only Brezhnev, Kosygin, Podgorny, Aleksandrov-Agentov, and the translator Viktor Sukhodrev made up the Soviet delegation. Nixon, Kissinger, John Negroponte, and Winston Lord comprised the American side. There were no State Department or Foreign Ministry note-takers. Aleksandrov-Agentov noted that during the verbal lashing about Vietnam, Nixon's and Kissinger's faces were "increasingly flushed blood red," and he expected "an explosion in place of negotiations." Nevertheless, Nixon "restrained himself."[6] According to Kissinger, Nixon "endured it in dignified silence." Kissinger then recalled: "Suddenly the thought struck me that for all the bombast and rudeness, we were participants in a charade. . . . The Soviet leaders were not pressing us except with words. They were speaking for the record, and when they had said enough to have a transcript to send to Hanoi, they would stop."[7]

The private dinner at Novo Ogaryevo reaffirmed the tacit agreement that had been reached in back channels. Nixon would overlook the fact that Soviet arms had enabled the North Vietnamese Easter Offensive, and Brezhnev would overlook Nixon's escalation of the war through the bombing and mining of Hanoi-Haiphong, including the damage to Soviet shipping. In other words, the Soviets and the Americans agreed to disagree. As Aleksandrov-Agentov noted: "Our party told him that we could not dictate anything to the Vietnamese, but we could pass the Americans' reasoning to them. Podgorny could go for that purpose to Hanoi, if, of course, the Americans ceased their bombing for that time. This is where we ended. There were no promises made on our side about decreasing (or, even less so, stopping) deliveries of weapons to Vietnam."[8]

The public focus remained on the inauguration of a new era of détente. Georgi Arbatov, the head of the U.S.A. Institute and a participant at the summit, recollected, "Though Brezhnev raised the issue of Vietnam, the meeting resulted in a real breakthrough in Soviet-American relations, marking the beginning of the period of détente."[9]

The United States and the Soviet Union had moved from potentially

A 1972 Herblock Cartoon.
(© The Herb Block Foundation)

". . . IT WAS ANNOUNCED TODAY
THAT THE PRESIDENT HAD A
SECRET MEETING WITH
DR. KISSINGER TO DISCUSS FUTURE
SECRET MEETINGS ABOUT SECRET
MEETINGS WITH . . ."

apocalyptic confrontation toward détente. And, yet, the period of détente was short-lived. The honeymoon period was over by the time Egypt and Syria attacked Israel in October 1973, and the superpowers went on nuclear alert. Granted, there were some lasting achievements, such as the ABM Treaty, the SALT I agreement, and even lesser-known details such as the universal space dock that allowed an American Apollo spaceship to dock with a Soviet Soyuz craft in orbit in 1975. With updates, the basic design exists to this day in the International Space Station. Despite the achievements and the goodwill generated, however, both sides continued to pursue national interests at the expense of maintaining détente. The back-channel means by which impasses were broken and agreements were reached could not indefinitely shelter negotiations from politics or personalities. Roles changed, as did the players. Crippled by Watergate, Nixon could no longer deliver concessions to the Soviets after the middle of 1973. Although Kissinger remained national security advisor when he became secretary of state in September 1973, the back channel moved out of the White House to Foggy Bottom. The decline and collapse of détente, however, is a story for another study.

This study has traced the evolution of U.S.-Soviet back-channel diplomacy toward the goal of achieving détente during Nixon's first term. Back channels were established because both the White House and the Kremlin believed such confidential diplomacy could be useful. When Nixon entered office in January 1969, he brought certain ideas about the conduct of diplomacy, and an inclination to use confidential diplomacy outside the State Department. Even before he had assumed the presidency, Nixon set up two back channels to the Soviets: one, through his longtime associate Robert Ellsworth, went directly to the Soviet embassy; the other was between Henry Kissinger and KGB agent Boris Sedov.

Kissinger, too, had a history with secretive back-channel diplomacy, having taken part in the 1967 attempt to develop a bombing-halt-for-negotiations approach (the San Antonio formula) to the North Vietnamese during the Johnson administration. Nearly everyone has assumed that Kissinger's secret negotiating style was sui generis when it was implemented during the Nixon administration. Kissinger's December 1967 trip to Moscow under the auspices of the Soviet-American Disarmament Study Group (SADS) in an attempt to revive the Pennsylvania negotiations, however, demonstrated that he had begun to develop his ideas for linkage between Moscow and Hanoi more than a full year before he became Nixon's national security advisor.

Dobrynin enjoyed high-level access during the Kennedy and Johnson administrations. However, the Channel with Kissinger overshadowed earlier back channels both in breadth and depth. The Soviet leadership actively endorsed two-track discussions when Kissinger suggested the idea in February 1969.

Just because both sides favored back-channel diplomacy did not mean that it was necessarily effective—at least not for the first twenty months of the Nixon administration. In fact, the back channel expanded significantly in the wake of the 1970 Cienfuegos crisis, when Kissinger used the contact with Dobrynin to bypass Secretary Rogers and the State Department in a bureaucratic power grab, ostensibly to keep the mini-crisis contained. The gambit worked, and both sides steadily expanded their reliance on back-channel diplomacy in response to a series of crises.

The White House and the Kremlin made known to each other their dissatisfaction with the state of U.S.-Soviet relations at the end of 1970 and moved decisively in 1971 to build the Channel. The back channel came to be used as both a brake and an accelerator to moderate the pace of negotiations and to link unrelated areas. For example, at the start of 1971, Kissinger and Dobrynin accelerated discussions to break an impasse on SALT and the Berlin negotiations, both of which were being negotiated through formal channels. When the Soviets made a politically profitable summit meeting contingent on a Berlin access agreement in the spring of 1971, Nixon and Kissinger applied a back-channel brake to slow progress at the Four-Power Talks in Berlin in response. In the Strategic Arms Limitation Talks (SALT), the Nixon administration used the back channel to insist on limitations for both offensive and defensive weapons. In the case of SALT, the back channel was used to bypass the formal negotiations, whereas it supplemented the Berlin negotiations.

U.S.-Soviet back channels, but specifically the Kissinger-Dobrynin channel, served as a button for each side to play on the other's anxieties or desires. The issue of China became the primary back-channel button for the Nixon administration's efforts at triangular diplomacy—playing the Soviets and the Chinese off of one another. Until the advent of Ping-Pong diplomacy and the breakthrough via the Pakistani channel in April 1971, however, the Nixon administration's efforts existed more in thought than in deed. The Channel was also the forum where Kissinger and Dobrynin, respectively, telegraphed anxieties, goals, and underlying motivations of U.S. and Soviet policies.

After the March 1969 Sino-Soviet border clashes, the Soviets inadvertently displayed their concern about a possible Sino-American rapprochement. The show of fear, and the continued interest displayed in back-channel meetings, demonstrated to the White House that triangular diplomacy could offer tangible gains. The Soviet move to raise the price of a superpower summit meeting served as an inadvertent push factor in the White House effort to achieve better relations with Beijing. The penalty for the Soviets was the fact that Nixon went to the Beijing summit in February 1972 before the Moscow summit in May.

During the Indo-Pakistani War of 1971, White House–directed back channels bypassed the State Department and acted as a kind of safety valve. Contrary to earlier critiques, the record indicated that Nixon and

Kissinger did not realistically risk World War III. Earlier histories have, however, correctly assessed the personal experiences and prejudices that motivated White House policy. Through back channels, Nixon and Kissinger insisted that the Soviet response constituted a "watershed" in U.S.-Soviet relations because the Soviet Union supported India while the United States—or rather, the White House—supported Pakistan. Pakistani president Yahya Khan had facilitated the Sino-American rapprochement, and, as has been described elsewhere, U.S. support for Pakistan was essentially a tilt toward China. During the war, the White House used a steady escalation of warnings to the Soviets, including frequent back-channel communications to Soviet chargé d'affaires Yuli Vorontsov; inviting the visiting Soviet agriculture minister, Vladimir Matskevich, to the White House; activating the Moscow-Washington hotline; dispatching the USS *Enterprise* carrier task force; and encouraging the Chinese to move troops to the Sino-Indian border to press India to desist from moving toward West Pakistan. Some of these moves doubtless entailed some risk of escalating the conflict. The Soviets certainly understood the meaning of the repeated back-channel messages and signals, especially after Kissinger hinted that the Nixon administration might cancel the Moscow summit if the Soviets did not take a more helpful role.

Whether or not West Pakistan was imperiled is another debate that cannot be resolved without research in Indian and Soviet records, but the White House was resigned to the fact that Yahya could not protect East Pakistan against an Indian attack. What Nixon and Kissinger did fear, however, was that the Indians would move on West Pakistan, perhaps to settle the long-standing dispute over Kashmir or even to dismember West Pakistan. The White House therefore coordinated its actions at the United Nations with the Chinese and used back-channel messages to the Soviets to imply that there was a U.S. commitment made during the Kennedy administration that obligated the United States to assist Pakistan in the event of an attack.

In the aftermath of the crisis, Nixon questioned Kissinger's emotional stability due to his response to the South Asian imbroglio, and particularly his response to the Moorer-Radford affair. The episode itself was a by-product of the surreptitious use of back channels by the White House and involved the military spying on the civilian government. In the end, however, Nixon quietly swept the Moorer-Radford affair under the rug and resolved to retain Kissinger until his usefulness had been exhausted.

The U.S. war in Vietnam was both a constant focus of Nixon's foreign policy and a central topic in U.S.-Soviet back channels. During the first two years of the administration, Nixon and his foreign policy team developed the strategy of Vietnamization, whereby American troops would be withdrawn and gradually replaced by trained, South Vietnamese regulars. The administration also pursued both public and private negotiations with the North Vietnamese and sought to compel the Soviet Union and China to exercise a restraining influence over their ally, reduce tensions, and serve as a broker between Washington and Hanoi. The results were mixed. Moscow did on occasion serve as a good-faith intermediary between the United States and North Vietnam. Moscow did not, however, reduce its material aid to North Vietnam and was not in a position to dictate terms to Hanoi, even if it had wanted to. The Easter Offensive in the spring of 1972 demonstrated that the North Vietnamese were still determined to settle the conflict by force. Nevertheless, the back channels with the Soviets served as a means by which Nixon and Kissinger relayed to the Kremlin that the United States would respond to any North Vietnamese attack with overwhelming force. The offensive ultimately provoked cancellation crises both in Washington and Moscow, but for different reasons. Back-channel diplomacy provided a safety valve whereby Nixon could overlook Soviet aid to North Vietnam, and Moscow could overlook the American response to the Easter Offensive, allowing both sides to proceed with the summit.

With such a rich record available to scholars, it seems fair to draw several conclusions about the strengths and weaknesses of back-channel diplomacy. Back channels had a range of politically useful functions, such as avoiding embarrassing leaks, preventing potential opposition from coalescing, and maximizing the amount of political credit that accrued to the administration. Back channels were also useful in overcoming bureaucratic inertia and resistance, and sheltering politically controversial topics, such as arms reductions or limitations on ABM systems, from a capricious Congress and/or public. Private channels could be used to reinforce public messages and vice versa.

Back channels also enabled both sides to maintain confidence in the other's good faith, despite the vicissitudes of U.S.-Soviet relations. Starting in 1971, the Channel was instrumental in overcoming impasses in the negotiations over SALT and the Quadripartite Agreement over Berlin, and served as an accelerator and brake in negotiations. Back channels gave policymakers on both sides a personal stake in the improvement in relations and served as a reliable, direct connection from the Kremlin leadership—specifically Brezhnev and Gromyko—to the White House. The relationship also functioned as a powerful tool in bureaucratic warfare, allowing Kissinger to outmaneuver rivals for the direction of U.S. foreign policy, such as Secretary Rogers, just as it elevated Dobrynin's and Gromyko's prominence within the Soviet policymaking elite.

My work on back channels has introduced several ideas related to the conduct of U.S.-Soviet diplomacy during the early years of détente, such as its potential to reinforce linkage; the accelerator-and-brake means by which both sides either sped up or slowed down progress in formal channels; the concept of a "back-channel button" to potentially play off of each side's anxieties; and the safety-valve concept, where the Channel served as the avenue to release tensions on areas peripheral to U.S.-Soviet relations like Cienfuegos, South Asia, and Vietnam.

The use of back-channel diplomacy also entailed a number of drawbacks for different policy actors. Bypassing the State Department, ACDA, the SALT delegation, and other parts of the bureaucracy created friction and undermined the legitimacy of the administration's achievements in the eyes of others. As Secretary of State Rogers told H. R. Haldeman regarding SALT, "There's no need for me to be involved, but I do have to be informed."[10] It could be argued that the overreliance on Kissinger caused resentment and robbed the system of spontaneity. Although Kissinger and Dobrynin were certainly two beneficiaries of back-channel diplomacy—Dobrynin became a full member of the Central Committee; Kissinger became a celebrity, which, ironically, undermined his effectiveness as a back-channel intermediary—others, namely Rogers and Ambassador Gerard Smith, were two of the victims. The example of Ambassador Kenneth Rush, who was aware of the back channel and actually informed discussions between Kissinger and Dobrynin, indicates that coordination of back channels with official channels may have struck a better balance between maintaining secrecy and effectiveness, as opposed to the wholesale exclusion of the traditional foreign policy apparatus.

Back channels also resulted in duplication of effort and negotiators working at cross-purposes, as demonstrated on a number of occasions during the SALT negotiations. Control over the Channel—or lack thereof—also resulted in the "Semenov slipups," and sometimes allowed other opportunistic parties outside the Channel to take advantage of the situation. As Smith, Garthoff, Dobrynin, and others have noted, it was simply impossible for Kissinger to master all of the esoteric minutiae of detailed technical negotiations, even if the back channel was successful in achieving the initial May 1971 agreement and the April 1972 settlement of the SLBM question. In fact, the SLBM issue arose only because it was not adequately addressed with Dobrynin in the first place.

Back channels blossomed to deal with specific issues when they served a limited function, and they were the means by which the United States and the Soviet Union achieved détente more broadly. Ultimately, the story of achieving détente involved more than back channels; it was about the ambitions of the concerned parties and the policies they pursued. Back channels were not a panacea. Long-term success ultimately depended on some fundamental basis for agreement, and the areas for agreement had begun to dwindle before 1974. In a broad sense, as Kissinger himself recognized, back-channel structures could not be carried on indefinitely. The Channel was not meant to replace traditional diplomacy, only to augment it.

Ironically, the same mentality and modus operandi—a reliance on secrecy, distrust of public discourse, desire for political gain—that led to the use of back channels destroyed Nixon's presidency when it was applied to domestic politics. What was acceptable in the international arena was simply inapplicable at home, with lamentable consequences for both détente and U.S.-Soviet relations. Perhaps identifying the reason for his own downfall, in his farewell speech at the White House on August 9, 1974, Nixon warned, "Always remember, others may hate you, but those who hate you don't win unless you hate them, and then you destroy yourself."[11]

Acknowledgments

Thank you to the University Press of Kentucky's editorial board and acquisitions editor Allison Webster for accepting my manuscript for publication. A special thank you to Susan Murray, my copyeditor, who exercised considerable skill to improve the manuscript and corral my consistent inconsistency. Thanks also to Grant Hackett, who prepared the index, and to Ila McEntire, who performed the final edits and transformed the manuscript into a book.

I would like to express my gratitude to CDR Youssef Aboul-Enein, USN, for his encouragement and for helping me navigate the publication waters. Youssef secured public release clearances with the Defense Department, circulated the manuscript, and used his own experiences as an author and book reviewer to identify the University Press of Kentucky as the best venue. Youssef also connected me to Dr. Christina Lafferty for helpful feedback and encouragement and arranged for Ms. Dorothy Corley to help edit and refine the manuscript while she was on a humanitarian mission to Zambia. We need more such young American women and men who do not shy away from global problems.

I am grateful for the advice, encouragement, and true friendship from Dr. Anand Toprani. Anand possesses one of the finest minds I have encountered, and he has helped me in innumerable ways to refine my thinking, improve my writing, and challenge my assumptions.

This book relies heavily on the Nixon Tapes, which is both a blessing and a curse: a blessing because of the fly-on-the-wall perspective, but a curse because accurate transcription is time-consuming and the audio quality ranges from decent to unintelligible. I therefore encourage readers to listen to the audio and come to their own interpretations. To facilitate this end, I worked with Luke Nichter and the National Security Archive to make the entire collection of digital audio available at nixontapes.org.

This book would not have been possible without the rich resources at the former Nixon Presidential Materials Project at the National Archives in College Park, Maryland (later the Richard Nixon Library and Museum in Yorba Linda, California); the Library of Congress; the Cold War International History Project; George Washington University's Gelman Library; and the nonprofit National Security Archive, which is led by the dynamic Thomas Blanton. I thank the archivists and librarians at these fine institutions, who often toil in anonymity, for the work they do every day to preserve our past, inform our present, and teach lessons for our future. At the above institutions, I thank Fred Graboske, William Cowell, Steve Greene, Maarja Krusten, John Powers, Jon Fletcher, Melissa Heddon, Aleksandr Gorokov, Barbra Tschida, Oksana Prokhracheva, Robert Lintott, and Svetlana Savranskaya.

I thank the reviewers in the Department of Defense's Office of Prepublication and Security Review for reviewing and clearing the manuscript for publication. The prerequisite disclaimer is included in the front matter of this book.

Thank you to my colleagues and students at the U.S. Naval War College for providing an intellectually rigorous and enjoyable work environment.

I thank Jeffrey Kimball, David Wolff, James Rosen, Len Colodny, Max Holland, Vlad Zubok, and W. Taylor Fain for providing documents or transcripts over the years. James Rosen provided outstanding and extensive comments and suggestions on draft chapters. This book would not have been possible without Jim Hershberg, Hope Harrison, Gregg Brazinsky, Bill Burr, and Chris Tudda. I appreciate the assistance, feedback, and encouragement I had during the early stages of this work from Tyler Anbinder, Muriel Atkin, MT, Douglas Kraft, John Carland, Jim Siekmeier, Kent Sieg, Seth Center, Mark Hove, Tom Pearcy, John Wilson, Artemy Kalinovsky, Thomas Schwartz, Lubna Zakia Qureshi, Stephen Randolph, Vlad Zubok, Hugh Wilford, Salim Yaqub, Dennis Kux, Ken Hughes, Jeff Burson, Avi Moscowitz, Terrance Rucker, James Person, Tanvi Madan, Thomas Faith, Jason Roberts, Jaideep Prabhu, Sarah Mergel, James and Lillian Charapich, and Yvonne and Keith Fredlake.

Thank you to Dr. Henry Kissinger and his office of talented professionals for responding to my many inquiries over many years. Thank you to Raymond Price for answering questions and allowing me to interview him.

Thank you also to the Herblock Foundation for permission to reprint political cartoons from the incomparable Herbert Block.

Thank you to my parents, Richard and Toni Moss, without whom I wouldn't have been here to write this book. Thank you also to my in-laws, Steven and Jane Schonfeld, without whom my wife, Amy, wouldn't be here to help.

I thank my Amy, who always provides love and support as we weather the storms that life throws at us. I also thank my son, Samuel, for his unstinting love and sweetness, and for putting up with his dad working on this book instead of playing more chess, Minecraft, or Wii, or discussing mathematics. My second son, Daniel, was fortunate to be too young to remember my work on this book.

Unlike the *mudéjar* craftsmen in Moorish Spain who intentionally included flaws in their mosaic, wood, or stone masterpieces because only God is perfect, I'm certain I made unintentional errors and apologize in advance.

Notes

Foreword

1. The quote that the Nixon Tapes are "the gift that keeps on giving" is widely attributed to investigative reporter Bob Woodward, of Watergate fame, who also apparently listens to the tapes as he drives (Bob Woodward, "Landon Lecture," March 29, 2000, www.mediarelations.k-state.edu/newsreleases/landonlect/woodwardtext300.html).

2. Jay Solomon, "Secret Dealings with Iran Led to Nuclear Talks," *Wall Street Journal*, June 28, 2015, www.wsj.com/articles/iran-wish-list-led-to-u-s-talks-1435537004.

3. Peter Kornbluh and William M. Leogrande, "Cuba Confidential: Inside the Crazy Back-Channel Negotiations That Revolutionized Our Relationship with Cuba," *Mother Jones,* August 12, 2015, www.motherjones.com/politics/2015/07/secret-negotiations-gross-hernandez-kerry-pope-obama-castro-cuba.

4. Scott Horton, "Beltway Secrecy: In Five Easy Lessons," *Harper's,* August 28, 2015, http://harpers.org/blog/2015/08/beltway-secrecy/.

5. Office of the Historian, U.S. Department of State, "Biographies of the Secretaries of State: William Pierce Rogers," https://history.state.gov/departmenthistory/people/rogers-william-pierce.

6. Slavophilism was a nineteenth-century, romantic, nationalistic, intellectual movement centered in Moscow that idealized Russia's past, held the organic peasant commune (*obshchina*) in high regard, and steadfastly supported the Eastern Orthodox Church and tsarist autocracy. The Slavophiles saw a distinct Russian destiny in contraposition to Europe and the world (Andrzej Walicki, *The Slavophile Controversy: History of a Conservative Utopia in Nineteenth-Century Russian Thought,* trans. Hilda Andrews-Rusiecka [Oxford: Clarendon, 1975]).

7. "Kissinger-Dobrynin Memcon (U.S.)," February 18, 1970, U.S. Dept. of State, *Soviet-American Relations: The Détente Years, 1969–1972,* with forewords by Henry A. Kissinger and Anatoly Dobrynin (Washington, DC: U.S. GPO, 2007).

Preface

1. Nixon Tapes (hereafter NT), Executive Office Building (hereafter EOB) 308–13, December 22, 1971, in U.S. Dept. of State, *Foreign Relations of the United States* (hereafter *FRUS*), *1969–1976,* vol. 2, *Organization and Management of Foreign Policy, 1969–1972* (Washington, DC: U.S. GPO, 2003), 68.

2. NT, EOB 308–13; "Eisenhower Executive Office Building," www.whitehouse.gov/1600/eeob.

314 Notes to Pages xiv–3

3. NT, Oval Office (hereafter OVAL) 639–30, December 21, 1971, in James Rosen, "The Men Who Spied on Nixon: New Details Reveal Extent of 'Moorer-Radford Affair,'" *Fox News,* December 15, 2008, www.foxnews.com/politics/2008/12/15/men-spied-nixon-new-details-reveal-extent-moorer-radford-affair/. Rosen has been at the forefront of documenting the Moorer-Radford affair with the Nixon Tapes. See also James Rosen, "Nixon and the Chiefs," *Atlantic Monthly,* April 2002; and James Rosen, *The Strong Man: John Mitchell and the Secrets of Watergate* (New York: Doubleday, 2008).

4. NT, OVAL 640–5, December 21, 1971, partial transcript in Brinkley and Nichter, *The Nixon Tapes* (New York: Houghton Mifflin Harcourt, 2014), 335–39. Feldman, *Poisoning the Press: Richard Nixon, Jack Anderson, and the Rise of Washington's Scandal Culture* (New York: Farrar, Straus and Giroux, 2010), 157–97.

5. Rosen, "The Men Who Spied on Nixon."

6. NT, EOB 308–13.

7. NT, OVAL 639–30.

8. NT, EOB 308–13.

Introduction

Epigraphs: U.S. Dept. of State, *Soviet-American Relations: The Détente Years, 1969–1972* (Washington, DC: U.S. GPO, 2007), xi, xxi, hereafter cited as *Détente Years.*

1. Arbatov claimed he introduced Kissinger to Dobrynin (Georgi Arbatov, *The System: An Insider's Life in Soviet Politics* [New York: Times Books, 1992], 178). Kissinger's account differed slightly (Kissinger, *White House Years* [New York: Little, Brown, 1979], 112–14, hereafter cited as *WHY*).

2. "Conversation with Ambassador Dobrynin," *Détente Years,* 4.

3. Kissinger, *WHY,* 113.

4. "Kissinger-Dobrynin Memcon (U.S.S.R.)," February 14, 1969, *Détente Years,* 4–6, italics in original.

5. Kissinger-Dobrynin Telcon, February 15, 1969, 3:15 p.m., Henry A. Kissinger Telephone Conversation Transcripts (Telcons) [hereafter cited as HAK Telcons], Richard Nixon Presidential Library and Museum (hereafter RNPLM), Yorba Linda, CA. The HAK Telcons are arranged in four series: Chronological File, Anatoli Dobrynin File, Home File, and Jordan File. The Telcons are keyword and participant searchable at the Digital National Security Archive through ProQuest's subscription service. See www.proquest.com/products-services/databases/dnsa.html.

6. Memorandum of Conversation, February 17, 1969, in U.S. Dept. of State, *FRUS, 1969–1976,* vol. 12, *Soviet Union, January 1969–October 1970* (Washington DC: U.S. GPO, 2006), 37–42; H. R. Haldeman, "Entry for February 15, 1969," *The Haldeman Diaries: Inside the Nixon White House. The Complete Multimedia Edition,* CD-ROM (Santa Monica, CA: Sony Electronic Publishing, 1994); "Nixon-Dobrynin Memcon (U.S.S.R.)," *Détente Years,* 14–18.

7. Kissinger-Harriman Telcon, February 19, 1969, 1:05 p.m., HAK Telcons.

8. Richard M. Nixon, *RN: The Memoirs of Richard Nixon* (New York: Touchstone, 1978), 369, hereafter cited as *RN*.

9. Anatoly Dobrynin, *In Confidence: Moscow's Ambassador to America's Six Cold War Presidents* (Seattle: University of Washington Press, 1995), 199.

10. Kissinger, *WHY*, 139.

11. Henry A. Kissinger, foreword to *Détente Years*, ix, xv. On the relationship between President Wilson and his confidant, Col. Edward House, and a comparison between the "special envoy" diplomacy of House and Hopkins, see Anand Toprani, "Extraordinary Diplomacy: Edward M. House and Harry L. Hopkins as Presidential Foreign Policy Advisors & Special Envoys to Europe during the Period of American Neutrality in the First & Second World Wars, 1914–1916 & 1940–1941" (M.Phil. diss., University of Oxford, 2006).

12. Timothy Naftali and Alexandr Fursenko, *"One Hell of a Gamble": Khrushchev, Castro, and Kennedy, 1958–1964* (New York: Norton, 1997). For discussion of President Kennedy's concession to remove Thor and Jupiter missiles from Europe and the behind-the-scenes negotiations within NATO to follow through on Kennedy's pledge to the Soviets, see Philip Nash, *The Other Missiles of October: Eisenhower, Kennedy, and the Jupiters 1957–1963* (Chapel Hill: University of North Carolina Press, 1997).

13. "Telegram 8604 from Kissinger at American Embassy in Paris to Secretary of State Rusk, 'Conversations in Moscow,'" January 4, 1968, 10:09 a.m. (Paris time), National Security File, Vietnam Country File, Box 140, Lyndon B. Johnson Library; "Kissinger-Read Telephone Conversation," January 17, 1968, 7:30 a.m., ibid; "Memorandum from Walt W. Rostow to Lyndon B. Johnson," January 17, 1968, 10:10 a.m., ibid. Kissinger's renewed Pennsylvania efforts coincided with the signals the Johnson administration was then receiving from another peace effort through Romania, known as Packers. In both channels, the DRV signaled a willingness to begin peace negotiations with the United States in exchange for an American bombing halt.

14. Arbatov, *The System*, 178.

15. Lyndon B. Johnson, "Speech before the National Legislative Conference in San Antonio, Texas," September 29, 1967, *Public Papers of the Presidents of the United States: Lyndon B. Johnson, 1967*, bk. 2, 876–81. *Public Papers of the Presidents of the United States* is hereafter cited as *PPP*.

16. Isaacson, *Kissinger: A Biography* (New York: Simon and Schuster, 1992), 121.

17. David Kraslow and Stuart Loory, "The Secret Search for Peace: Unheralded Emissaries Opened Way to Hanoi," *Los Angeles Times*, April 4, 1968, 1, 20.

18. Arbatov, *The System*, 178.

19. The *New Yorker* published a series of five articles by Newhouse from May 5, 1973, to June 2, 1973. John Newhouse, *Cold Dawn: The Story of SALT* (New York: Holt, Rinehart and Winston, 1973), 203–72. Kissinger confirmed Newhouse's was the first account of the Channel (e-mail from Jessee LePorin, Office of Henry Kissinger, to Richard Moss, April 13, 2009).

20. Kissinger, foreword to *Détente Years,* x.

21. Kissinger, *WHY,* 801, 801–6. The documentary record supports Kissinger's assertion. Excluding front matter and the introductions, there are approximately 250 pages of documents for February 1969 through January 1, 1971, or half of the chronological coverage of the *Détente Years* volume. Approximately 750 pages are devoted to the period covering January 1971 through May 29, 1972.

22. Kissinger, *WHY,* 28–32.

23. Jussi Hanhimäki, *The Flawed Architect: Henry Kissinger and American Foreign Policy* (New York: Oxford University Press, 2004), 32–40; Seymour M. Hersh, *The Price of Power: Kissinger in the Nixon White House* (New York: Summit, 1983), 39–41; Gerard C. Smith, *Doubletalk: The Story of the First Strategic Arms Limitation Talks* (New York: Doubleday, 1980), esp. 222–46, 465–73; Gerard C. Smith, *Disarming Diplomat: The Memoirs of Ambassador Gerard C. Smith, Arms Control Negotiator* (Lanham, MD: Madison, 1996), esp. 158–60.

24. Raymond Garthoff, *Détente and Confrontation: U.S.-Soviet Relations from Nixon to Reagan,* rev. ed. (Washington, DC: Brookings Institution, 1994), 179.

25. "U.S.-Soviet Relations in the Era of Détente, 1969–1976" conference, George C. Marshall Conference Center, Washington, DC: October 22, 2007; Jeremi Suri, *Henry Kissinger and the American Century* (Cambridge: Harvard University Press, 2007).

26. The defining work in the study of détente is Raymond Garthoff's *Détente and Confrontation.* Over the last two decades, the trend has been to look at the transnational origins of détente in West German and French efforts to ease tensions with the Eastern Bloc. For a recent multinational view of détente as a conservative response to global revolution, see Jeremi Suri, *Power and Protest: Global Revolution and the Rise of Détente* (Cambridge: Harvard University Press, 2003). For another recent study, see Wilifried Loth, *The Making of Détente: Eastern Europe and Western Europe in the Cold War, 1965–75* (London: Routledge, 2007). In *Britain, Détente and Changing East-West Relations* (New York: Routledge, 1992), Brian White describes the rationale behind British policies in East-West relations from the 1950s onward, and the United Kingdom's reluctance and even opposition to Johnson's or Nixon's Vietnam policies. Mary E. Sarotte traces the negotiations between East and West Germany in the late 1960s and early 1970s and how these policies affected the policies of their respective superpower supporters in *Dealing with the Devil: East Germany, Détente, and Ostpolitik, 1969–1973* (Chapel Hill: University of North Carolina Press, 2001). These aforementioned sources are but a very broad sampling of a large body of literature that has largely focused on the origins and the decline of détente.

27. Records on different topics, such as the 1962 Cuban Missile Crisis and the 1979 Soviet invasion of Afghanistan, are available. Unfortunately, there are limited Soviet documents available for the period 1969–1972. There are a few back doors through former East German records, Romanian archives, etc. (Jonathan Haslam, "Collecting and Assembling Pieces of the Jigsaw: Coping with Cold War Archives," *Cold War History* 4, no. 3 [April 2004]: 140–52).

28. I would like to thank Svetlana Savranskaya of the National Security Archive for access to the Papers of Dmitrii Volkogonov, copied from the files at the Library of Congress, which include a broad sampling of documents from thirteen Soviet archives. Separately, the Cold War International History Project (CWIHP) virtual archive is an amazing resource with translated documents from a number of archives. Soviet leaders' memoirs include Leonid Ilyich Brezhnev, *Memoirs,* trans. Penny Dole (Oxford, UK: Pergamon, 1982); Andrei Gromyko, *Memoirs,* trans. Harold Shukman (New York: Doubleday, 1989); and Dobrynin, *In Confidence.* Dobrynin's Russian-language memoirs, published later, differ slightly from the English-language edition. See *Sugubo Doveritel'no: Posol v Vashingtone pri shesti prezidentach CShA, 1962–1986* (Moscow: Avtor, 1997); Arkady N. Shevchenko, *Breaking with Moscow* (New York: Knopf, 1985); Petro Shelest, *"Spravjniy Sud Istorii she Poperdu": Spogadi, shodenniki, dokumenti, materiali,* ["The true judgment of history still awaits us": Memoirs, diaries, documents, and materials], ed. Juri Shapoval, in Ukrainian and Russian (Kiev: Geneza, 2003); and Oleg Kalugin, *First Directorate: My 32 Years in Intelligence and Espionage Against the West* (New York: St. Martin's, 1994).

29. "Nixon White House Tapes—Online," RNPLM, www.nixonlibrary.gov/virtuallibrary/tapeexcerpts/.

30. Tape logs are not perfect, but they provide a generally solid foundation for identifying participants, times and places of conversations, and subject content. I have cited the tapes by conversation number, which is the easiest way to locate recordings based on the tape logs. Conversations may be several hours in duration so identifying a tape by the time listed in tape logs is not always accurate.

31. Although the Nixon Tapes are a rich historical source, using them—ideally transcribing them with the proper context—requires a number of caveats. It is a time-consuming process, audio quality ranges from decent to unintelligible, and accurate transcription requires multiple reviews, preferably by multiple people who have background knowledge in the subjects being discussed. Transcription is physically taxing and requires frequent breaks to avoid tone deafness and permanent hearing loss. Additionally, the surreptitious recordings captured "natural speech," with stuttering, repetition, verbal tics, false starts, and other problems that make rendering difficult. I have edited out repetition and stuttering, and I have denoted omissions with ellipsis points.

32. Craig A. Daigle, "The Limits of Détente: The United States, the Soviet Union, and the Arab-Israeli Conflict, 1969–1973" (Ph.D. diss., George Washington University, 2008).

33. "Honecker-Brezhnev Memcon," June 18, 1974, obtained and translated by David Wolff.

34. Henry A. Kissinger, "The White Revolutionary: Reflections on Bismarck," *Daedalus* 97, no. 3 (Summer 1968): 890.

1. Precedents and Back-Channel Games, 1968–1970

Epigraph: "Nixon-Dobrynin Memcon (U.S.S.R.)," February 17, 1969, *Détente Years,* 14–15.

1. William Bundy, *A Tangled Web: The Making of Foreign Policy in the Nixon Presidency* (New York: Hill and Wang, 1998), 58. Bundy worked at the Central Intelligence Agency (CIA), the State Department, and the National Security Council (NSC) for Presidents Kennedy and Johnson.

2. Stephen Ambrose, *Nixon: The Education of a Politician, 1913–1962,* vol. 1 (New York: Simon and Schuster, 1987); Stephen Ambrose, *The Triumph of a Politician, 1962–1972,* vol. 2 (New York: Simon and Schuster, 1989); Stephen Ambrose, *Ruin and Recovery, 1973–1990,* vol. 3 (New York: Simon and Schuster, 1991); Robert Dallek, *Nixon and Kissinger: Partners in Power* (New York: HarperCollins, 2007); Irwin Gellman, *The Contender: Richard Nixon—The Congress Years, 1946–1952* (New York: Free Press, 1999); Joan Hoff, *Nixon Reconsidered* (New York: Basic, 1994); Roger Morris, *Nixon: The Rise of an American Politician* (New York: Henry Holt, 1991). Richard Reeves, *President Nixon: Alone in the White House* (New York: Simon and Schuster, 2002); Fredrik Logevall and Andrew Preston, eds., *Nixon in the World: American Foreign Relations, 1969–1977* (Chapel Hill: University of North Carolina Press, 2007).

3. Suri, *Henry Kissinger and the American Century;* Dallek, *Nixon and Kissinger;* Hanhimäki, *Flawed Architect;* Isaacson, *Kissinger;* Schulzinger *Doctor of Diplomacy* (New York: Columbia University Press, 1991); Hersh, *Price of Power;* Marvin Kalb and Bernard Kalb, *Kissinger* (Boston: Little Brown, 1974); Stephen R. Graubard, *Kissinger: Portrait of a Mind* (New York: Norton, 1973).

4. See esp. Hoff, *Nixon Reconsidered,* 156.

5. Stephen E. Ambrose, introduction to *The Haldeman Diaries: Multimedia Edition.* Haldeman described his own approach in *The Ends of Power* (New York: Times Books, 1978), 45–76.

6. U.S. Dept. of State, *FRUS, 1969–1976,* vol. 40, *Germany and Berlin, 1969–1972* (Washington, DC: U.S. GPO, 2008), 509.

7. David J. Rothkopf, *Running the World: The Inside Story of the National Security Council and the Architects of American Power* (New York: Public Affairs, 2005), 108–56.

8. U.S. Dept. of State, *FRUS, 1969–1972,* vol. 2, *Organization and Management of Foreign Policy, 1969–1972.*

9. "Memo from Kissinger to Nixon," April 29, 1969, U.S. Dept. of State, *FRUS, 1969–1976,* vol. 2, *Organization and Management of Foreign Policy, 1969–1972,* 84–88; Kissinger, *WHY,* 321. On the crisis management function of the WSAG, see Asaf Siniver, "The Nixon Administration and the Cienfuegos Crisis of 1970: Crisis-Management of a Non-Crisis?," *Review of International Studies* 34 (2008): 69–88.

10. Kissinger, *WHY,* 29.

11. Nixon-Kissinger Telcon, May 17, 1972, 9:52 a.m., HAK Telcons. Nixon's taping system captured Nixon's side of the conversation. I used the tape to fill in minor gaps, albeit limited to Nixon's speech (NT, Camp David Hard Wire 189–8, May 17, 1972).

12. Milton Viorst, "William Rogers Thinks Like Richard Nixon," *New York Times,* February 27, 1972, 12–13, 30–38.

13. Ibid.

14. Kissinger, *WHY,* 31.

15. Haldeman described the first dispute between Kissinger and Rogers over meeting with the Soviets in his daily diary ("Entry for February 15, 1969," *Haldeman Diaries: Multimedia Edition*); Kissinger, *WHY,* 26–31, 141; "Nixon-Dobrynin Memcon (U.S.S.R.)," February 17, 1969, *Détente Years,* 14–15.

16. Nixon, *RN,* 339.

17. NT, OVAL 650–12 between Nixon, Ehrlichman, and Shultz, January 18, 1972.

18. Jonathan Aitken, *Charles W. Colson: A Life Redeemed* (Colorado Springs: WaterBrook, 2005), 22.

19. Rosen, *The Strong Man,* 146–49. For more on the "Henry problem," a.k.a. the Kissinger-Rogers dispute, see Dallek, *Nixon and Kissinger,* 248–52.

20. NT, OVAL 648–4, January 17, 1972; entries for January 17–18, 1972, *Haldeman Diaries: Multimedia Edition;* see also NT OVAL 650–12; and NT, OVAL 650–13, January 18, 1972.

21. For the letter to Rogers, see "Editorial Note," U.S. Dept. of State, *FRUS, 1969–1976,* vol. 14, *Soviet Union, October 1971–May 1972* (Washington, DC: U.S. GPO, 2006), 116–17.

22. Hoff, *Nixon Reconsidered,* 150.

23. David Greenberg, *Nixon's Shadow: The History of an Image* (New York: Norton, 2004) thoroughly traces Nixon's relationship with the press.

24. NT, OVAL 823–1 between Nixon and Kissinger, December 14, 1972. This is the same conversation in which Nixon decided to go through with the "Christmas Bombing" against North Vietnam.

25. Anthony Summers, *Arrogance of Power,* with Robbyn Swan (New York: Viking, 1997), 88–99. Summers repeatedly cited Nixon's psychotherapist, Dr. Arnold Hutschnecker. Dallek, *Nixon and Kissinger,* 30. Dallek relied on a confidential, secondhand source—an "analyst" who studied under Dr. Arnold Hutschnecker—to claim: "'[Nixon] didn't have a serious psychiatric diagnosis,' although he had 'a good portion of neurotic symptoms'" (ibid.).

26. "Entry for February 6, 1969," *Haldeman Diaries: Multimedia Edition.*

27. Seymour Hersh, "Kissinger and Nixon in the White House," *Atlantic Monthly,* May 1982, 25–58. Portions of the article were reprinted in Hersh's critical biography of Kissinger, *The Price of Power.* See also Jonathan Schell, *The Time of Illusion* (New York: Knopf, 1975), 32–34.

28. "The Pentagon Papers: Secrets, Lies, and Audiotapes," National Security Archive Electronic Briefing Book (hereafter NSAEBB) No. 48 (April 2001), www.gwu.edu/~nsarchiv/NSAEBB/NSAEBB48/nixon.html.

29. Rosen, *Strong Man,* 156–57.

30. William Beecher, "U.S. Urges Soviet to Join in a Missiles Moratorium," *New York Times,* July 23, 1971, 1, 4.

31. Smith, *Doubletalk,* 253.

32. NT, OVAL 545–1 between Nixon, Kissinger, and Haldeman, July 24, 1971.

33. Director of Security Howard J. Osborn to CIA Deputy Director for Man-

agement & Services, "Press Allegations re: Use of [Central Intelligence] Agency Polygraph," May 9, 1973, MORI DocID 1451843, DNSA, "Family Jewels" Collection, through Proquest online.

34. Raymond Price, interview by Luke Nichter and Richard Moss, March 6, 2008, New York City.

35. Suri, *Power and Protest.* esp. 4–6, 261.

36. Dobrynin, *In Confidence*, 186.

37. Ibid.

38. Kalugin, *The First Directorate*, 110–11.

39. Kissinger, *WHY*, 50.

40. U.S. Dept. of State, *FRUS, 1969–1976*, vol. 12, *Soviet Union, January 1969–October 1970* (Washington, DC: U.S. GPO, 2006), 1n2.

41. U.S. Dept. of State, *FRUS, 1964–1968*, vol. 14, *Soviet Union* (Washington, DC: U.S. GPO, 2001), Documents 217–38, www.state.gov/r/pa/ho/frus/johnsonlb/xiv/.

42. Nixon, *RN*, 345.

43. "Kissinger to Nixon," December 18, 1968, U.S. Dept. of State, *FRUS, 1964–1968*, vol. 14, *Soviet Union*, www.state.gov/r/pa/ho/frus/johnsonlb/xiv/1416.htm.

44. Kissinger, *WHY*, 50.

45. "Kissinger to Nixon," December 18, 1968, U.S. Dept. of State, *FRUS, 1964–1968*, vol. 14, *Soviet Union*.

46. Rusk transmitted Kissinger's note and his assessment to President Johnson at his Texas ranch ("Rusk to Johnson," December 31, 1968, U.S. Dept. of State, *FRUS, 1964–1968*, vol. 20, *Arab-Israeli Dispute, 1967–1968* [Washington, DC: U.S. GPO, 2001], www.state.gov/r/pa/ho/frus/johnsonlb/xx/2676.htm).

47. "Kissinger-Sedov Memcon," January 2, 1969, U.S. Dept. of State, *FRUS, 1969–1972*, vol. 12, *Soviet Union*, 2, italics in original.

48. Henry A. Kissinger, "The Viet Nam Negotiations," *Foreign Affairs* 2, no. 2 (January 1969): 211–34.

49. "Kissinger-Sedov Memcon," January 2, 1969, U.S. Dept. of State, *FRUS, 1969–1976*, vol. 12, *Soviet Union, January 1969–October 1970*, 1–4.

50. Ibid., 3n7.

51. Kissinger, *WHY*, 50. See also Garthoff, *Détente and Confrontation*, 30–31.

52. Richard Nixon, "Inaugural Address," January 20, 1969, *PPP, 1969*, 1–4.

53. "Nixon to Rogers," January 20, 1972, *Détente Years*, 3–4.

54. "Nixon to Laird," February 4, 1969, U.S. Dept. of State, *FRUS, 1969–1976*, vol. 1, *Foundations of Foreign Policy 1969–1972*, Document 10, www.state.gov/r/pa/ho/frus/nixon/i/20701.htm. The letters are nearly identical.

55. Kissinger, *WHY*, 130.

56. Kalugin, *First Directorate*, 112. Dobrynin did not mention Sedov in his memoir, *In Confidence*.

57. "Note from Soviet Leaders to President Nixon," U.S. Dept. of State, *FRUS, 1969–1976*, vol. 12, *Soviet Union, January 1969–October 1970*, 42n1.

58. Kalugin, *First Directorate*, 112–13.

59. U.S. Dept. of State, *FRUS, 1969–1976*, vol. 12, *Soviet Union, January 1969–October 1970*, 1n2. Unfortunately, the volume does not identify the Lebanese American citizen with ties to the KGB.

60. Kissinger-Sedov Telcon, April 17, 1970, 5:50 p.m., HAK Telcons.

61. Dobrynin, *In Confidence*, 200.

62. Kissinger, *WHY*, 140.

63. Dobrynin, *In Confidence*, 8, 200.

64. "Kissinger to Nixon Memo," February 18, 1969, *Détente Years*, 19.

65. "Kissinger-Dobrynin Memcon (U.S.S.R.)," February 21, 1969, *Détente Years*, 20–25.

66. Vorontsov replaced Cherniakov as counselor-minister during the summer of 1969.

67. "Kissinger-Dobrynin Memcon, March 3, 1969 (U.S.)," March 6, 1969, *Détente Years*, 27.

68. "Kissinger-Dobrynin-Nixon Memcon (U.S.S.R.)," May 14, 1969, *Détente Years*, 59.

69. "Kissinger-Dobrynin Memcon (U.S.)," December 29, 1969, *Détente Years*, 110.

70. Dobrynin, *In Confidence*, 200.

71. "Kissinger-Dobrynin Memcon (U.S.S.R.)," March 11, 1969, *Détente Years*, 39.

72. "Dobrynin to Foreign Ministry," March 13, 1969, *Détente Years*, 39–44.

73. "Kissinger-Dobrynin Memcon (U.S.S.R.)," June [11], 1969, *Détente Years*, 70. The memorandum was misdated as June 12. Dobrynin's memorandum was first published in CWIHP *Bulletin* 3 (Fall 1993): 63–67.

74. See *Détente Years*, 82, for how Kissinger recounted his session with the North Vietnamese in Paris in August 1969 to Dobrynin.

75. "Dobrynin to Foreign Ministry," March 13, 1969, *Détente Years*, 39–45.

76. Kissinger, *Ending the Vietnam War*, 57.

77. "U.S. Aides Oppose Raids in Cambodia," *New York Times*, March 26, 1969, 5; William Beecher, "Raids in Cambodia by U.S. Unprotested," *New York Times*, May 9, 1969; "Foe Shells Major U.S. Base," *Washington Post*, May 18, 1969, 14; Kissinger, *Ending the Vietnam War*, 68.

78. "Dobrynin to Foreign Ministry," April 15, 1969, *Détente Years*, 53–56. The proposal was known as the "Vance Mission" after Cyrus Vance, the man envisioned as an emissary to Moscow to broker a package deal on arms control and Vietnam. It is uncertain whether or not the Soviets passed along the proposal, which was otherwise considered a failure (Isaacson, *Kissinger*, 167).

79. "Kissinger-Dobrynin Memcon (U.S.)," April 15, 1969, *Détente Years*, 51–53.

80. "Kissinger-Dobrynin Memcon (U.S.S.R.)," April 24, 1969, *Détente Years*, 56–58.

81. Kissinger, *Ending the Vietnam War*, 61–62.

82. "Kissinger-Dobrynin-Nixon Memcon (U.S.S.R.)," May 14, 1969, *Détente Years,* 59–62.

83. Kimball, *Vietnam War File,* 121–98, esp.197–98; Kimball, "Nixon and Kissinger Obfuscations about Vietnam: What the Documents Show," *History News Network,* February 2, 2004, http://hnn.us/articles/3073.html.

84. Kissinger suggested that Nixon call after thirty minutes to summon Dobrynin. Memorandum from Kissinger to Nixon, "Your Meeting with Ambassador Dobrynin," May 14, 1969, NSC Institutional Files (hereafter cited as H-Files), President's Trip Files, Box 489, RNPLM. See also *Détente Years,* 58–59.

85. "Kissinger-Dobrynin-Nixon Memcon (U.S.S.R.)," May 14, 1969, *Détente Years,* 59–62.

86. Richard Nixon, "Address to the Nation on Vietnam," May 14, 1969, *PPP, 1969,* 369–75.

87. "Kissinger-Dobrynin Memcon (U.S.)," June 11, 1969, *Détente Years,* 62–64.

88. "Kissinger-Dobrynin Memcon (U.S.S.R.)," June [11], 1969, *Détente Years,* 64–70, italics in original.

89. "Kissinger-Dobrynin Memcon (U.S.)," September 27, 1969, *Détente Years,* 77–78.

90. Nixon-Kissinger Telcon, September 27, 1969, 4:40 p.m., HAK Telcons.

91. Kissinger, *Ending the Vietnam War,* 90. For the record of the meeting, see "Memo from Kissinger to Nixon with August 4, 1969 transcript attached," August 6, 1969, U.S. Dept. of State, *FRUS, 1969–1976,* vol. 6, *Vietnam, January 1969–July 1970* (Washington, DC: U.S. GPO, 2006), 330–43.

92. "Kissinger-Dobrynin Memcon (U.S.)," September 27, 1969, *Détente Years,* 77–78.

93. "Kissinger-Dobrynin Memcon (U.S.S.R.)," October 9, 1969, *Détente Years,* 79–81.

94. "Dobrynin to Foreign Ministry," October 10, 1969, *Détente Years,* 81–83.

95. Kissinger-Dobrynin Telcon, October 17, 1969, 4:40 p.m., HAK Telcons.

96. "Note from the Soviet Leadership to President Nixon," undated, *Détente Years,* 88–89.

97. "Nixon, Kissinger, Dobrynin Memcon (U.S.)," October 20, 1969, *Détente Years,* 86–87.

98. "Nixon, Kissinger, Dobrynin Memcon (U.S.S.R.)," October 20, 1969, *Détente Years,* 90–97.

99. "Dobrynin to Foreign Ministry," October 23, 1969, *Détente Years,* 99.

100. William Burr and Jeffrey P. Kimball, *The Secret Alert of 1969, Madman Diplomacy, and the Vietnam War* (Lawrence: University Press of Kansas, 2015); William Burr and Jeffrey Kimball, "Nixon's Nuclear Ploy," *Bulletin of the Atomic Scientists,* 59, no. 1 (January/February 2003): 28–40; Scott D. Sagan and Jeremi Suri, "The Madman Nuclear Alert: Secrecy, Signaling, and Safety in October 1969," *International Security* 27, no. 4 (Spring 2003): 150–83.

101. Burr and Kimball, "Nixon's Nuclear Ploy." Rick Perlstein attributes the can-

cellation of Duck Hook to the Mobilization to End the War protests and death of Ho Chi Minh (Perlstein, *Nixonland: The Rise of a President and the Fracturing of America* [New York: Scribner, 2008], 418–29).

102. For Nixon's July 15, 1969, letter to Ho Chi Minh and Ho Chi Minh's reply of August 25, see *PPP, 1969*, 910–11.

103. Kissinger to Nixon, "Your Meeting with Ambassador Dobrynin, Monday, October 20, 1969," October 18, 1969, *Détente Years*, 83–85.

104. H. R. Haldeman, [handwritten] entry for October 20, 1969, H. R. Haldeman Journal, Vol. 3, RNPLM. In *WHY*, Kissinger wrote in error that Dobrynin did not take notes. This is contradicted by Haldeman's Journal, Kissinger memcon of the October 20, 1969, meeting, and Dobrynin's memcon. *Détente Years*, 90–98.

105. "Nixon, Kissinger, Dobrynin Memcon (U.S.S.R.)," October 20, 1969, *Détente Years*, 90–97.

106. Dobrynin, *In Confidence*, 206–7.

2. At a Crossroads

Epigraph: NT, OVAL 501–18 between Nixon, Kissinger, and Laird, May 19, 1971.

1. Richard M. Nixon, "Remarks Announcing an Agreement on Strategic Arms Limitation Talks," May 20, 1971, *PPP, 1971*.

2. NT, Cabinet Room (hereafter CAB) 58–4, between Nixon and his cabinet, May 20, 1971.

3. Kissinger, *WHY*, 1216–17.

4. Dobrynin, *In Confidence*, 209.

5. Kissinger, *WHY*, 833.

6. Ibid., 144; Dobrynin, *In Confidence*, 208. In the one thousand pages of the official record of the back channel, *U.S.-Soviet Relations: The Détente Years*, only 25 percent deals with the period February 4, 1969, through December 24, 1970. In contrast, approximately 75 percent of the volume covers from January 1971 through May 29, 1972. The results are similar when examining the primary repository of the American collection of back-channel exchanges in the President's Trip Files of the National Security Council Files at RNPLM. Less than two standard Hollinger boxes in the President's Trip Files cover 1969–1970, whereas it takes more than six Hollinger boxes to cover 1971–1972 (NSC Files, President's Trip Files, Boxes 489–495). The same comparison cannot be made with Russian records, which do not have a publicly accessible inventory/finding aid.

7. Dobrynin, *In Confidence*, 206–7. The assertion, of course, depends on what defines a "*major* crisis."

8. Kissinger, *WHY*, 144.

9. On the Soviet deployment of men and missiles to Egypt, see Kissinger, *WHY*, 558–93; Nixon, *RN*, 479–83; Garthoff, *Détente and Confrontation*; Isabella Ginor, "'Under the Yellow Arab Helmet Gleamed Blue Russian Eyes': Operation *Kavkaz* and the War of Attrition, 1969–70," *Cold War History* 3, no. 1 (October 2002): 127–56; and Dima Adamsky, "'Zero-Hour for the Bears': Inquiring into the Soviet Deci-

sion to Intervene in the Egyptian-Israeli War of Attrition, 1969–1970," *Cold War History* 6, no. 1 (February 2006): 113–36. On the Cambodian incursion, see Kissinger, *WHY*, 433–521; Kimball, *Nixon's Vietnam War*, 129–33; Kimball, *Vietnam War File*; and William Shawcross, *Sideshow: Kissinger, Nixon, and the Destruction of Cambodia* (New York: Simon and Schuster, 1979). On the Jordan crisis, see Kissinger, *WHY*, 594–631; U.S. Dept. of State, *FRUS*, 1969–1976, vol. 24, *Jordan, September 1970* (Washington, DC: U.S. GPO, 2008). On Cienfuegos, see Kissinger, *WHY*, 632–52; Siniver, "The Nixon Administration and the Cienfuegos Crisis of 1970; and U.S. Dept. of State, *FRUS, 1969–1976*, vol. 12, *Soviet Union, January 1969–October 1970*. On the election of Salvador Allende in Chile, see Kissinger, *WHY*, 653–83; Hersh, *Price of Power*, 252–54; Daniel Michael, "Nixon, Chile and Shadows of the Cold War: United States–Chilean Relations during the Government of Salvador Allende, 1970–1973" (Ph.D. diss., George Washington University, 2004); and Lubna Zakia Qureshi, *Nixon, Kissinger, and Allende: U.S. Involvement in the 1973 Coup in Chile* (New York: Rowman and Littlefield, 2008).

10. Dallek, *Nixon and Kissinger*, 248–51. Dallek's unique citation format makes it extremely difficult to identify Nixon Tape conversations, and Dallek excluded Nixon's general philosophy about religion and policy debates in one repeatedly referenced conversation, NT, OVAL 464–25 between Nixon, Haldeman, Shultz, and Ehrlichman, March 9, 1971. In the same conversation, Haldeman and Ehrlichman agreed that they were not the right people to take on health-care policy decisions due to their background as Christian Scientists, just as Kissinger's Jewish background would make it hard for him to remain objective on Israel.

11. Kissinger, *WHY*, 559. For a discussion of Kissinger's Jewish background, see Suri, *Henry Kissinger and the American Century*, 252–53.

12. Kissinger, *WHY*, 560–62.

13. U.S. Dept. of State, *FRUS, 1969–1976*, vol. 12, *Soviet Union, January 1969–October 1970*, 364.

14. Kissinger, *WHY*, 562.

15. Ginor, "Under the Yellow Arab Helmet," 141–43.

16. "Kissinger-Dobrynin Memcon (U.S.)," March 10, 1970, *Détente Years*, 132–34.

17. "Memorandum of Conversation," March 10, 1970, U.S. Dept. of State, *FRUS, 1969–1976*, vol. 12, *Soviet Union, January 1969–October 1970*, 433–37.

18. "Kissinger-Dobrynin Memcon (U.S.S.R.)," March 10, 1970, *Détente Years*, 134–38.

19. Nixon, *RN*, 477.

20. "Kissinger-Dobrynin Memcon (U.S.)," March 20, 1970, *Détente Years*, 138–39.

21. "Kissinger-Dobrynin Memcon (U.S.S.R.)," March 20, 1970, *Détente Years*, 139–41.

22. "Kissinger-Dobrynin Memcon (U.S.)," February 10, 1970, *Détente Years*, 121–22; "Kissinger-Dobrynin Memcon (U.S.S.R.)," March 10, 1970, ibid., 123–25.

23. Nixon, *RN,* 482.

24. Kissinger, *WHY,* 605.

25. Ibid., 632.

26. Although soccer is not a national pastime like baseball, Cubans have long played the game. Garthoff, *Détente and Confrontation,* 89n40.

27. Haldeman, *The Ends of Power,* 85–86, italics in original.

28. The CIA detected the construction activities and warned that the Soviets might use Cuba as a base to service ships, submarines, and/or aircraft. The detection of a Soviet flotilla en route to Cuba set off red flags, and daily U-2 spy-plane flights began on September 14. A flight on September 16 photographed the installation and provided the evidence that construction was taking place rapidly (Kissinger, *WHY,* 636–37).

29. Memorandum from Kissinger to Nixon, September 18, 1970, U.S. Dept. of State, *FRUS, 1969–1976,* vol. 12, *Soviet Union, January 1969–October 1970,* 622–24.

30. H. R. Haldeman, entry for September 20, 1970, H. R. Haldeman Journals, vol. 6.

31. Kissinger, *WHY,* 641.

32. "Paper Prepared by the Chairman of the Joint Chiefs of Staff (Moorer)," undated, U.S. Dept. of State, *FRUS, 1969–1976,* vol. 12, *Soviet Union, January 1969–October 1970,* 632–35; Memorandum from Kissinger to Nixon, "Soviet Naval Facility in Cuba," September 22, 1970, ibid., 636–44.

33. Kissinger, *WHY,* 633, 641.

34. Ibid., 642.

35. The "strategic advantage" was not simply the prospect of extended submarine capabilities in the Caribbean with the construction of the base in Cienfuegos but also the Soviet ICBM buildup, which surpassed that of the United States in 1970. The United States maintained a clear superiority in terms of warheads due to the use of MIRVs.

36. Italics denote material that was redacted in the published *Haldeman Diaries: Multimedia Edition.*

37. "Entry for September 20, 1970," H. R. Haldeman Journals, vol. 6. Vorontsov raised the understanding on August 4, 1970, and Kissinger replied after studying the historical record (Documents 74–76, *Détente Years,* 185–88; Kissinger, *WHY,* 632–35).

38. Kissinger-Dobrynin Telcon, September 24, 1970, 3:04 p.m., HAK Telcons.

39. Kissinger-Nixon Telcon, September 24, 1970, 6:40 p.m., HAK Telcons.

40. Kissinger-Dobrynin Telcon, September 24, 1970, 7:00 p.m., HAK Telcons.

41. "Kissinger-Dobrynin Memcon (U.S.)," September 25, 1970, 10:00 a.m., *Détente Years,* 191–92.

42. "Kissinger-Dobrynin Memcon (U.S.)," September 25, 1970, 5:30 p.m., *Détente Years,* 193–94.

43. "Kissinger-Dobrynin Memcon (U.S.S.R.)," September 25, 1970, *Détente Years,* 194–97.

44. Dale Van Atta, *With Honor: Melvin Laird in War, Peace, and Politics* (Madison: University of Wisconsin Press, 2008), 276–77. Van Atta wrote that Kissinger had leaked the story to Cyrus L. Sulzberger, and cited Sulzberger's memoir. While Van Atta's claim that Kissinger leaked for his own advantage and to prompt the president to action is logical, Sulzberger's memoir does not back up the claim (Sulzberger, *An Age of Mediocrity* [New York: Macmillan, 1973], 654–57, 660).

45. Kissinger, *WHY*, 645.

46. "Kissinger-Dobrynin Memcon (U.S.S.R.)," October 6, 1970, *Détente Years*, 199–202.

47. "Kissinger-Dobrynin Memcon (U.S.)," October 9, 1970, *Détente Years*, 202–4. "Kissinger-Dobrynin Memcon (U.S.S.R.)," October 9, 1970, ibid., 204–8. Garthoff wrote that the original settlement over the Cuban Missile Crisis was "spongy" and that important details had never been settled, such as the stipulation that the removal of Soviet missiles from the island be verified by inspection (Garthoff, *Détente and Confrontation*, 87–95).

48. Kissinger, *WHY*, 650.

49. Ibid., 651.

50. Ibid., 652.

51. "Entry for September 26, 1970," *Haldeman Diaries: Multimedia Edition*, italics in original.

52. "Entry for October 14, 1970," *Haldeman Diaries: Multimedia Edition*, italics in original.

53. "Entry for December 28, 1970," *Haldeman Diaries: Multimedia Edition*.

54. Richard M. Nixon, "Inaugural Address," *PPP, 1969*, www.nixonlibraryfoundation.org/clientuploads/directory/archive/1969_pdf_files/1969_0001.pdf.

55. "Minutes of National Security Council Meeting," Washington, January 29, 1969; Memorandum from Kissinger to Nixon, "Actions Resulting from the National Security Council Meeting of January 29, 1969," January 31, 1969; National Security Decision Memorandum (hereafter NSDM) 6, February 5, 1969, all in U.S. Dept. of State, *FRUS, 1969–1976*, vol. E-2, *Documents on Arms Control and Non-Proliferation, 1969–1972* (2007), http://history.state.gov/historicaldocuments/frus1969–76ve02/ch1.

56. "Kissinger-Dobrynin Memcon (U.S.S.R.)," June 12, 1969, *Détente Years*, 66; "Rogers, Gromyko, et al., Memcon (U.S.)," September 22, 1969, ibid., 73–74. See also CWIHP *Bulletin*, no. 3 (Fall 1993): 63–67.

57. John W. Finney, "Senate Approves Treaty to Block Nuclear Spread," *New York Times*, March 14, 1969, 1; "Telegram 200453 from the Department of State to All Diplomatic Posts," December 2, 1969, 2013Z, U.S. Dept. of State, *FRUS, 1969–1976*, vol. E-2, *Documents on Arms Control and Non-Proliferation, 1969–1972*, www.state.gov/r/pa/ho/frus/nixon/e2/83452.htm.

58. Dobrynin, *In Confidence*, 243. The Soviets also suffered a number of accidents related to their biowarfare program, such as the unintentional release of weapons-grade anthrax spores in Sverdlovsk in 1979 (Robert A. Wampler and Thomas S. Blan-

ton, "Anthrax at Sverdlovsk," Briefing Book No. 61 [November 15, 2001], www.gwu
.edu/~nsarchiv/NSAEBB/NSAEBB61/). For a chilling account of the Soviet Union's
bioweapons program, see Judith Miller, Stephen Engelberg, and William Broad, *Germs: Biological Weapons and America's Secret War* (New York: Simon and Schuster, 2002).

59. Acting Secretary of State Elliott Richardson to President Nixon, "MIRV testing," May 22, 1969, NSC Files, ABM–MIRV, MIRV Test Program, Vol. I, Box 845, RNPLM.

60. NT, OVAL 493–10 between Nixon, Haldeman, and Haig, May 6, 1971.

61. NT, OVAL 681–2 between Nixon, Haldeman, and Kissinger, March 9, 1971, in U.S. Dept. of State, *FRUS, 1969–1976*, vol. 32, *SALT 1, 1969–1972* (Washington, DC: U.S. GPO, 2010), 674.

62. Richard Nixon, "Statement on Deployment of the Antiballistic Missile System," March 14, 1969, *PPP, 1969*; Newhouse, *Cold Dawn*, 11–12, 64–65.

63. Newhouse, *Cold Dawn*, 11–12.

64. Kissinger, *WHY*, 195–225.

65. NT, OVAL 482–22 between Nixon, John McClellan, Clark MacGregor, and Kenneth E. BeLieu, April 19, 1971.

66. "Kissinger-Dobrynin Memcon (U.S.S.R.)," February 21, 1969, *Détente Years*, 20–25. The modified Sentinel program accepted by the Nixon administration became known as "Safeguard" because Nixon used the word "safeguard" so many times when announcing the ABM program (Van Atta, *With Honor*, 188–89).

67. Kissinger, *WHY*, 145.

68. "Telegram from Dobrynin to Foreign Ministry," March 13, 1969, *Détente Years*, 43; see also ibid., 55–56.

69. Kissinger, *WHY*, 145.

70. Van Atta, *With Honor*, 188–93.

71. "Dobrynin to Soviet Foreign Ministry," March 12, 1969, *Détente Years*, 39–45. Before departing to Moscow for consultations, Dobrynin wrote that Kissinger's influence on foreign policy was "predominant," although divisions still existed within the administration ("Kissinger-Dobrynin Memcon [U.S.S.R.]," June [12], 1969, ibid., 64–70).

72. "Memcon of Meeting between Rogers and Gromyko (U.S.)," September 22, 1969, *Détente Years*, 71. For "Grim Grom," see Shevchenko, *Breaking with Moscow*, 154; for Shevchenko's excellent portrait of Gromyko, see ibid., 144–62.

73. "Kissinger-Nixon-Dobrynin Memcon (U.S.)," October 20, 1969, *Détente Years*, 86–87.

74. Kissinger, *WHY*, 149.

75. Newhouse, *Cold Dawn*, 43–44.

76. Gerard Smith, "Memcon, February 9, 1970," U.S. Dept. of State, *FRUS, 1969–1976*, vol. 32, *SALT 1, 1969–1972*, 178–80.

77. Richard Nixon, *U.S. Foreign Policy for the 1970's: A New Strategy for Peace, A Report to the Congress by Richard Nixon* (Washington DC: U.S. GPO, 1971). For a description, see Dallek, *Nixon and Kissinger*, 179–83.

78. "Area defense" would provide blanket ABM coverage for a geographical area and would involve a larger number of radars and interceptor missiles. "Point defense" would be designed to protect a specific location, such as an ICBM field. Similarly, a "thin" defense could ring the continental United States and use long-range interceptor missiles to take out incoming missiles, whereas a "thick" defense would use a large number of interceptors to protect an ICBM field or a city.

79. "Kissinger-Dobrynin Memcon (U.S.)," February 18, 1970, *Détente Years,* 125–27.

80. "Laird Says Russia Takes ICBM Lead," *Washington Post,* January 12, 1970, A2.

81. "Kissinger-Dobrynin Memcon (U.S.)," February 18, 1970, *Détente Years,* 125–27.

82. It is uncertain whether Kissinger and Dobrynin could have tackled the MIRV dilemma in the Channel since deployment began in 1970—before the Channel was fully operational. By the time Nixon took office, the United States had already flight-tested the 3-MIRV Minuteman III ICBM.

83. "Kissinger-Dobrynin Memcon (U.S.S.R.)," February 18, 1970, *Détente Years,* 127–32.

84. Newhouse, *Cold Dawn,* 50.

85. "Kissinger-Dobrynin Memcon (U.S.)," March 10, 1970, *Détente Years,* 132–34.

86. "Kissinger-Dobrynin Memcon (U.S.S.R.)," March 10, 1970, *Détente Years,* 134–38.

87. "Kissinger-Dobrynin Memcon (U.S.)," April 7, 1970, *Détente Years,* 141–43.

88. "Kissinger-Dobrynin Memcon (U.S.)," April 9, 1970, *Détente Years,* 144–45. Dobrynin's account is essentially identical on the details related to SALT (ibid., 145–48).

89. "Kissinger-Dobrynin Memcon (U.S.S.R.)," April [9], 1970, *Détente Years,* 145–48.

90. "Kissinger-Dobrynin Memcon (U.S.S.R.)," June 10, 1970, *Détente Years,* 159–65.

91. Richard M Nixon, "NSDM 51," April 10, 1970, NSC Files, Subject Files, National Security Decision Memoranda, Nos. 51–96, Box 363, RNPLM.

92. "Kissinger-Dobrynin Memcon (U.S.)," June 23, 1970, *Détente Years,* 165–66. Dobrynin's contemporaneous account corroborated Kissinger's assertions but added some color, for example, that Kissinger was "agitated" ("Kissinger-Dobrynin Memcon [U.S.S.R.]," June 23, 1970, ibid., 166–68).

93. "NSDM 69," July 9, 1970 [signed Richard Nixon, July 4, 1970], H-Files Files, Box H-208, RNPLM.

94. "Memorandum of Conversation between Nixon, Rogers, Kissinger, and William D. Krimer and Gromyko, Dobrynin, and Viktor Sukhodrev (U.S.)," October 22, 1970, *Détente Years,* 217–25, 224.

95. "Kissinger-Dobrynin Memcon (U.S.)," December 22, 1970, *Détente Years,* 241–46.

96. "Kissinger-Dobrynin Memcon (U.S.S.R.)," December 22, 1970, *Détente Years,* 247–48.

97. Kissinger, *WHY,* 817, 1155.

98. For example, a typewritten note attached to the cable in which Dobrynin described Kissinger and the back channel read: "Distribute to members of the Politburo of the CC CPSU and candidate members of the CC CPSU. July 12, 1969. A. Gromyko." Gromyko likely distributed the telegram after he gave an important foreign policy speech at a session of the Soviet Union's Supreme Soviet. The memcon itself is: "Kissinger-Dobrynin Memcon (U.S.S.R.)," June [11], 1969, *Détente Years,* 70. As noted earlier, the memorandum was misdated as June 12, and Dobrynin's memorandum was first published in CWIHP *Bulletin* 3 (Fall 1993): 63–67.

99. Shevchenko, *Breaking with Moscow,* 151–52.

100. Newhouse, *Cold Dawn,* 192–93.

101. Hope Harrison, "The Berlin Wall, Ostpolitik, and Détente," *GHI Supplement* 1 (2003): 9.

102. Marc Trachtenberg, *A Constructed Peace: The Making of the European Settlement* (Princeton: Princeton University Press, 1999); William Glenn Gray, *Germany's Cold War* (Chapel Hill: University of North Carolina Press, 2003); Hope M. Harrison, "Ulbricht and the Concrete 'Rose': New Archival Evidence on the Dynamics of Soviet East German Relations and the Berlin Crisis, 1958–61," CWIHP Working Paper 5, 1993; Hope Harrison, *Driving the Soviets up the Wall: Soviet-East German Relations, 1953–1961* (Princeton: Princeton University Press, 2003).

103. Sarotte, *Dealing with the Devil*; Werner D. Lippert, "Richard Nixon's Détente and Willy Brandt's *Ostpolitik:* The Politics and Economic Diplomacy of Engaging the East" (Ph.d. diss., Vanderbilt University, 2005); Piers Ludlow, ed., *European Integration and the Cold War: Ostpolitik-Westpolitik, 1965–1973* (London: Routledge, 2007); Carole Fink and Bernd Schaefer, eds., *Ostpolitik, 1969–1974: European and Global Responses* (Cambridge: Cambridge University Press, 2008); Julia von Dannenberg, *The Foundations of Ostpolitik: The Making of the Moscow Treaty between West Germany and the USSR* (New York: Oxford University Press, 2008).

104. In September 1970, just one month after Brandt signed the Moscow Treaty, CIA director Richard Helms told *New York Times* correspondent C. L. Sulzberger that the Soviets had thirty-five divisions—more than three hundred thousand troops—on the border with China (Sulzberger, *An Age of Mediocrity,* 660).

105. Anatoly Kovalev, unpublished memoir prepared by Andrei Kovalev, courtesy of Aleksandr Gorokhov, CWIHP. Thank you to Mr. Gorokhov for his assistance with identifying and translating excerpts from the unpublished Kovalev memoir.

106. Hillenbrand, *Fragments of Our Time,* 284.

107. Dallek, *Nixon and Kissinger,* 215–16.

108. "Letter from Brandt to Nixon," December 15, 1970, U.S. Dept. of State, *FRUS, 1969–1976,* vol. 40, *Germany and Berlin, 1969–1972,* 426–27.

109. "WSAG Meeting Minutes," December 18, 1970, U.S. Dept. of State, *FRUS, 1969–1976,* vol. 40, *Germany and Berlin, 1969–1972,* 435–38. In addition to other

signals, Brandt dispatched a minister in his office, Horst Ehmke, to Washington ("Kissinger, Hillenbrand, FRG Ambassador Rudolph Pauls, and Ehmke Memcon," December 22, 1970, U.S. Dept. of State, *FRUS, 1969–1976*, vol. 40, *Germany and Berlin, 1969–1972*, 449–55). See also Willy Brandt, *People and Politics*, 289.

110. "Telegram from Gromyko to Dobrynin," January 4, 1971, *Détente Years*, 255–56.

111. On December 22, 1970, Kissinger and Dobrynin agreed to meet on Thursday, January 7, 1971, but the meeting was originally postponed until January 11 because Kissinger was in San Clemente with the president.

112. Kissinger-Dobrynin Telcon, January 6, 1971, 8:45 a.m., [San Clemente], HAK Telcons.

113. Kissinger-Dobrynin Telcon, January 6, 1971, 12:35 p.m., [San Clemente], HAK Telcons.

114. Kissinger-Dobrynin Telcon, January 7, 1971, 12:05 p.m., [San Clemente], HAK Telcons.

115. Kissinger-Dobrynin Telcon, January 7, 1971, 1:35 p.m., [San Clemente], HAK Telcons.

116. "Memo from Hyland to Kissinger," January 6, 1971, NSC Files, Country Files, Europe, Germany (Berlin), Box 691, RNPLM.

117. William G. Hyland, *Mortal Rivals: Superpower Relations from Nixon to Reagan* (New York: Random House, 1987), 34–35.

118. Kissinger, *WHY*, 802.

119. "Kissinger-Dobrynin Memcon (U.S.)," January 9, 1971, *Détente Years*, 257–58. Dobrynin's account substantively confirmed what Kissinger wrote, although the ambassador made no mention of SLBMs as a separate issue ("Kissinger-Dobrynin Memcon [U.S.S.R.]," January 9, 1971, ibid., 259–63).

120. Nixon, *RN*, 523.

121. "Kissinger-Dobrynin Memcon (U.S.)," January 23, 1971, *Détente Years*, 265–68. See also Dobrynin, *In Confidence*, 211; and Kissinger, *WHY*, 804.

122. Isaacson, *Kissinger*, 324. See also David C. Geyer, "The Missing Link: Henry Kissinger and the Back-Channel Negotiations on Berlin," *GHI Bulletin Supplement* 1 (2003): 82.

123. "Kissinger-Dobrynin Memcon (U.S.)," January 23, 1971, *Détente Years*, 273–75.

124. Isaacson, *Kissinger*, 323–24.

125. Kissinger, "Memorandum for the President's File," January 31, 1971, U.S. Dept. of State, *FRUS, 1969–1976*, vol. 40, *Germany and Berlin, 1969–1972*, 512–14.

126. Kissinger, *WHY*, 814.

127. "Kissinger-Dobrynin Memcon (U.S.)," February 4, 1971, *Détente Years*, 284–85; "Kissinger-Dobrynin Memcon (U.S.S.R.)," February 4, 1971, ibid., 285–86. "Kissinger-Dobrynin Memcon (U.S.)," February 10, 1971, ibid., 286–89; "Kissinger-Dobrynin Memcon (U.S.S.R.)," February 10, 1971, ibid., 289–93.

128. Kissinger, *WHY*, 810–13.

129. Garthoff, *Détente and Confrontation*, 179–90; Smith, *Doubletalk*, 218–29, 244–46. See chapter 5 for discussion on the resolution of the SLBM issue in April 1972.

130. "Kissinger-Dobrynin Memcon (U.S.)," February 10, 1971, *Détente Years*, 286–89, italics added.

131. "Kissinger-Dobrynin Memcon (U.S.S.R.)," February 10, 1971, *Détente Years*, 289–93.

132. "Telegram from Dobrynin to Foreign Ministry," February 14, 1971, *Détente Years*, 293–96.

133. "Kissinger-Dobrynin Memcon (U.S.)," February 16, 1971, *Détente Years*, 296–97; "Kissinger-Dobrynin Memcon (U.S.S.R.)," February 16, 1971, ibid., 297–98.

134. Kissinger-Dobrynin Telcon, February 22, 1971, 9:23 p.m., HAK Telcons.

135. NT, OVAL 456–5 between Nixon, Kissinger, and Haldeman, February 23, 1971.

136. NT, OVAL 450–1 between Nixon and Butterfield, February 16, 1971.

137. Joseph Kraft, "Arms Control at Bay," *Washington Post*, February 18, 1971, A21.

138. NT, OVAL 451–4 between Nixon and Kissinger, February 18, 1971.

139. NT, OVAL 460–25 between Nixon and Rogers, February 26, 1971, italics added.

140. NT, OVAL 466–12 between Nixon and Kissinger, March 11, 1971.

141. Nixon, *RN*, 523.

142. "Soviet Draft Letter handed to HAK by D," March 12, 1971, 8:00 a.m., NSC Files, President's Trip Files, Exchange of Notes between Dobrynin & Kissinger, Vol. 1 [Part 2] [July 1970–April 1971], Box 497, RNPLM, italics added.

143. "Kissinger-Dobrynin Memcon (U.S.)," March 12, 1971, *Détente Years*, 306.

144. Kissinger, *WHY*, 815.

145. NT, OVAL 467–11 between Nixon and Kissinger, March 12, 1971.

146. Kissinger, *WHY*, 814.

147. Ibid., 815.

148. "Note from Dobrynin on SALT," March 15, 1971, NSC Files, President's Trip Files, Exchange of Notes between Dobrynin & Kissinger, Vol. 1, Part 2, July 1970–April 1971, Box 497, RNPLM.

149. Ibid.; "Memo from Kissinger to Nixon [attached to note of March 15, 1971]," March 22, 1971 [date was handwritten on the typed memo], NSC Files, President's Trip Files, Exchange of Notes between Dobrynin & Kissinger, Vol. 1, Part 2, July 1970–April 1971, Box 497, RNPLM.

150. "Kissinger-Dobrynin Memcon (U.S.S.R.)," March 16, 1971, *Détente Years*, 310–13.

151. NT, OVAL 468–5 between Nixon and Kissinger, March 16, 1971.

152. "Soviet Proposal of Four Power Agreement on West Berlin with attachments," March 18, 1971, NSC Files, President's Trip Files, Exchange of Notes

between Dobrynin & Kissinger, Vol. 1 [Part 2] [July 1970–April 1971], Box 497, RNPLM. Abrasimov was the Soviet ambassador to East Germany until 1971.

153. NT, OVAL 469–13 between Nixon, Kissinger, and Haldeman, March 18, 1971.

154. "Entry for March 18, 1971," *Haldeman Diaries: Multimedia Edition.*

155. "Soviet Note rec'd 4:10 p.m. March 26, 1971," NSC Files, President's Trip Files, Exchange of Notes between Dobrynin & Kissinger, Vol. 1 [Part 2] [July 1970–April 1971], Box 497, RNPLM. See also Kissinger, *WHY,* 816; "Memorandum of Telephone Conversation (U.S.S.R.)," March 26, 1971, *Détente Years,* 323," italics added.

156. Kissinger, *WHY,* 815.

157. Nixon, *RN,* 508.

158. Kissinger, *WHY,* 816.

159. "Kissinger-Dobrynin Telcon (U.S.)," San Clemente, March 26, 1971, 8:20 p.m., *Détente Years,* 323–25.

160. "Backchannel from Smith to Kissinger," March 30, 1971, U.S. Dept. of State, *FRUS, 1969–1976,* vol. 32, *SALT 1, 1969–1972,* 430–31.

161. Shevchenko, *Breaking with Moscow,* 265.

162. "Kissinger-Dobrynin (Moscow) Telcon," April 13, 1971, 7:15 p.m., HAK Telcons.

163. Nixon, *RN,* 523.

164. Kissinger, *WHY,* 816.

165. NT, OVAL 476–8 between Nixon and Shultz, April 9, 1971.

166. Nixon, *RN,* 524. Nixon's memoir account captured the gist of the conversation of NT, CAB 55–1, April 20, 1971.

167. NT, OVAL 481–7 between Nixon and Kissinger, April 17, 1971.

168. NT, OVAL 487–21 between Nixon, Haldeman, and Kissinger, April 3, 1971.

169. Kissinger, *WHY,* 817.

170. "Entry for April 23, 1971," *Haldeman Diary: Multimedia Edition.*

171. Kissinger, *WHY,* 817.

172. Secretary Rogers acknowledged the drawback of the NCA-only option in an earlier discussion with Kissinger (Kissinger-Rogers Telcon," March 15, 1971, 10:55 a.m., HAK Telcons).

173. Kissinger, *WHY,* 817.

174. Ibid., 817–18.

175. "Memorandum of Telephone Conversation (U.S.S.R.)," May 11, 1971, *Détente Years,* 349–51.

176. Dobrynin, *In Confidence,* 215.

177. Nixon, *RN,* 524.

178. Kissinger, *WHY,* 819.

179. NT, OVAL 501–4 between Nixon and Rogers, May 19, 1971.

180. "Entry for March 19, 1971," *Haldeman Diaries: Multimedia Edition.*

181. NT, OVAL 493–10 between Nixon, Haldeman, and Haig, May 6, 1971.

182. NT, White House Telephone (hereafter WHT) 17–142 between Nixon and Kissinger, January 2, 1972.

183. Shevchenko, *Breaking with Moscow*, 169.

184. Dobrynin, *In Confidence*, 218, 217.

185. "Kissinger-Dobrynin Memcon (U.S.)," April 27, 1971, 3:30 p.m., *Détente Years*, 336–37.

186. NT, OVAL 505–18 between Nixon and Kissinger, May 28, 1971, U.S. Dept. of State, *FRUS, 1969–1976*, vol. 40, *Germany and Berlin, 1969–1972*, 715.

187. Geyer, "The Missing Link," 89–90.

188. "Kissinger-Dobrynin Memcon (U.S.)," April 23, 1971, *Détente Years*, 326–28; Geyer, "Missing Link," 85–86.

189. Kissinger, *WHY*, 825.

190. Nixon, *RN*, 524.

191. Lawrence Fellows, "Arms Talks: 'You Give Something, You Take Something,'" *Washington Post*, E2.

3. "Playing a Game," Finding a "Lever"

Epigraph: NT, EOB 317–6 between Nixon and Ehrlichman, January 24, 1972.

1. United States Department of State, *FRUS*, vol. 1, *Foundations of Foreign Policy, 1969–1972*, www.state.gov/r/pa/ho/frus/nixon/i/20700.htm (originally in *Foreign Affairs* 46, no. 1 [October 1967]: 113–25); X [George F. Kennan], "The Sources of Soviet Conduct," *Foreign Affairs* 25, no. 4 [July 1947]: 566–82).

2. Nixon wrote that he had begun to reconsider the approach to the PRC during a worldwide trip in 1967 that became the basis of his *Foreign Affairs* article (Nixon, *RN*, 279–85).

3. Graubard, *Kissinger: Portrait of a Mind*, 252.

4. U.S. Dept. of State, *FRUS, 1969–1976*, vol. 17, *China, 1969–1972* (Washington, DC: U.S. GPO, 2006); U.S. Dept. of State, *FRUS, 1969–1976*, vol. E-13, *Documents on China, 1969–1972* (2006); Chen Jian, *Mao's China and the Cold War* (Chapel Hill: University of North Carolina Press, 2001); Margaret Macmillan, *Nixon and Mao: The Week That Changed the World* (New York: Random House, 2007); "Declassified: Nixon in China," produced by ABC News Productions for the Discovery Times Channel, December 21, 2004; Burr, *Kissinger Transcripts;* William Burr, ed., "The Beijing-Washington Back-Channel and Henry Kissinger's Secret Trip to China," NSAEBB No. 66 (February 27, 2002), www.gwu.edu/~nsarchiv/NSAEBB/NSAEBB66/; William Burr, ed., "New Documentary Reveals Secret U.S., Chinese Diplomacy behind Nixon's Trip," NSAEBB No. 145 (December 21, 2004), www.gwu.edu/~nsarchiv/NSAEBB/NSAEBB145/index.htm; Yukinori Komine, *Secrecy in US Foreign Policy: Nixon, Kissinger and the Rapprochement with China* (Surrey, UK: Ashgate, 2008); Yafeng Xia, *Negotiating with the Enemy: U.S.-China Talks during the Cold War* (Bloomington: Indiana University Press, 2006); Evelyn Goh, *Constructing the U.S. Rapprochement with China, 1961–1974: From "Red Menace to Tacit Ally"* (Cambridge: Cambridge University Press, 2005); Robert

S. Ross and Jiang Changbin, eds., *Re-examining the Cold War: U.S.-China Diplomacy, 1954–1973* (Boston: Harvard University Asia Center, 2001).

5. Richard Nixon, "Inaugural Address," January 20, 1969, *PPP, 1969,* 1–4; Kissinger, *WHY,* 50. See also Burr, ed., "Document 1," NSAEBB No. 145.

6. F. S. Aijazuddin, *From a Head, through a Head, to a Head: The Secret Channel between the US and China through Pakistan* (Oxford: Oxford University Press, 2000), documents the successful Pakistani channel using the personal files of Pakistani leader Yahya Khan. Mircea Munteanu, "Romania and the Sino-American Rapprochement, 1969–1971: New Evidence from the Bucharest Archives," CWIHP *Bulletin,* no. 16 (Fall 2007/Winter 2008), gives insights into the efforts through Bucharest and suggests the strengths and weaknesses of the Romanian channel. See also Macmillan, *Nixon and Mao,* 160–87.

7. Chen Jian, "The Path toward Sino-American Rapprochement, 1969–1972," *GHI Supplement* 1 (2003): 16–52; Burr, ed., NSAEBB No. 145; Yafeng Xia, "China's Elite Politics and Sino-American Rapprochement, January 1969–February 1972," *Journal of Cold War Studies* 8, no. 4 (2006): 3–28.

8. Harold P. Ford, "Calling the Sino-Soviet Split: The CIA and Double Demonology," *Studies in Intelligence* (Winter 1998/1999): 57–71.

9. The Chinese, the North Vietnamese, and the Soviets worked out an agreement in 1967 whereby the North Vietnamese would assume control of Soviet shipments at the Sino-Soviet border according to the CIA ("Intelligence Information Cable: Miscellaneous Observations in Hanoi," June 9, 1967, www.foia.cia.gov; see also Ilya Gaiduk, *The Soviet Union and the Vietnam War* [Chicago: I. R. Dee, 1996]; and Qiang Zhai, *China and the Vietnam Wars, 1950–1975* [Chapel Hill: University of North Carolina Press, 2000]).

10. William Burr, "Sino-American Relations, 1969: The Sino-Soviet Border War and Steps toward Rapprochement," *Cold War History* 1, no. 3 (April 2001): 73–112; Chen Jian and David Wilson, "'All under the Heavens Is Great Chaos': Beijing, the Sino-Soviet Border Clashes, and the Turn toward Sino-American Rapprochement," CWIHP *Bulletin,* no. 11 (Winter 1998): 155–75; Yang Kuisong, "The Sino-Soviet Border Clash of 1969: From Zhenbao Island to Sino-American *Rapprochement,*" *Cold War History* 1, no. 1 (August 2000): 21–52; Viktor M. Gobarev, "Soviet Policy toward China: Developing Nuclear Weapons 1949–1969," *Journal of Slavic Military Studies* 12, no. 4 (1999): 43–47; "Editorial Note," U.S. Dept. of State, *FRUS, 1969–1976,* vol. 12, *Soviet Union, January 1969–October 1970,* 86–87; Ouimet, *The Rise and Fall of the Brezhnev Doctrine;* William Burr, ed., "The Sino-Soviet Border Conflict, 1969: U.S. Reactions and Diplomatic Maneuvers," NSAEBB No. 49 (June 12, 2001), www.gwu.edu/~nsarchiv/NSAEBB/NSAEBB49/.

11. EOB Conversation 317–6.

12. NT, WHT 20–126 between Nixon and Kissinger, February 29, 1972. There is also a telcon, Kissinger-Nixon Telcon, February 29, 1972, 9:00 p.m., HAK Telcons.

13. Dobrynin, *In Confidence,* 202.

14. Aleksandrov-Agentov, *Ot Kollontai,* 212.

15. Garthoff, *Détente and Confrontation,* 108.

16. According to Wikipedia, Zhenbao/Damansky is a small island measuring 0.74 square kilometers (0.29 sq mi). It is located on the Ussuri River on the border between Primorsky Krai of Russia and Heilongjiang Province, People's Republic of China (https://en.wikipedia.org/wiki/Zhenbao_Island).

17. George C. Denney Jr., "USSR/China: Soviet and Chinese Forces Clash on the Ussuri River," March 4, 1969, NSAEBB No. 49.

18. Directorate of Intelligence, "Weekly Review," March 23, 1969, Directorate of Intelligence, "Weekly Review," March 28, 1969, www.foia.cia.gov.

19. Kissinger, *WHY,* 172.

20. Yang Kuisong, "The Sino-Soviet Border Clash of 1969"; Burr, ed., NSAEBB No. 49.

21. "Kissinger-Dobrynin Memcon (U.S.)," March 11, 1969, *Détente Years,* 35–36. Contrary to the times listed in Kissinger's memcon of the meeting, an earlier telcon stated: "Dobrynin said he would like to drop in for 5 minutes since he had some things to tell HAK, and HAK said he had one thing to tell Dobrynin. It was decided that the meeting should take place at the Soviet Embassy this evening between 8:00 and 8:30 p.m." The meeting clearly lasted longer than five minutes (Kissinger-Dobrynin Telcon, March 11, 1969, 5:00 p.m., HAK Telcons).

22. "Kissinger-Dobrynin Memcon (U.S.S.R.)," March 11, 1969, *Détente Years,* 36–39. Kissinger accurately reflected the CIA's view, which reported: "As long as Mao is the dominant figure, major changes in China's international posture do not appear likely. Mao will remain an insurmountable obstacle to any accommodation with the USSR" ("Special National Intelligence Estimate Number 13–69: Communist China and Asia," March 6, 1969, p. 1, www.foia.cia.gov).

23. Kissinger, *WHY,* 172.

24. "Nixon-Kissinger Telcon," *Détente Years,* 36n6.

25. "Telegram from Dobrynin to Foreign Ministry," March 13, 1969, *Détente Years,* 39–45.

26. "Kissinger-Dobrynin Memcon (U.S.)," April 3, 1969, *Détente Years,* 45–46.

27. Peter Grose, "Washington Hopes Peking Meeting Leads to Talks with U.S.," *New York Times,* April 2, 1969, 16.

28. Theodore Sorenson, "Another Opinion: For a New China Policy," *New York Times,* March 30, 1969, E13.

29. Peter Grose, "U.S. and China Stirrings—and Frustrations—over Policy Change," *New York Times,* March 30, 1969, E4.

30. "Kissinger-Dobrynin Memcon (U.S.S.R.)," April [3], 1969, *Détente Years,* 46–49.

31. "Kissinger-Dobrynin Memcon (U.S.)," June 11, 1969, *Détente Years,* 62–64.

32. "Kissinger-Dobrynin Memcon (U.S.S.R.)," June [11], 1969, *Détente Years,* 64–70.

33. Lacking diplomatic relations after 1949, the United States and the PRC

maintained contacts during the mid-1950s, first in Geneva and later in Warsaw. The talks had been sporadic over the course of fourteen years and three previous presidential administrations before Nixon took office (see Yafeng Xia, *Negotiating with the Enemy*, 76–134).

34. "Kissinger-Dobrynin Memcon (U.S.S.R.)," February 21, 1969, *Détente Years*, 20–25. As Kissinger told Dobrynin, the public reasons was the defection of Chinese chargé d'affaires Liao Ho-shu in the Netherlands on January 24. After the Chinese canceled the session scheduled for February 20, 1969, with less than forty-eight-hours' notice, the CIA reported that the Chinese leadership was not ready to engage in serious negotiations (U.S. Dept. of State, *FRUS, 1969–1976*, vol. 17, *China, 1969–1972*, 15n6).

35. Gaiduk, *Soviet Union and the Vietnam War*, 227; *History Declassified: Nixon in China*, documentary produced by ABC News Productions for the Discovery Times Channel, December 21, 2004.

36. Kissinger described another incident involving a "middle-level State Department specialist in Soviet affairs, William Stearman," who "was having lunch with a Soviet Embassy official [Boris Davydov] when, out of the blue, the Russian asked what the US reaction would be to a Soviet attack on Chinese nuclear facilities" (Kissinger, *WHY*, 183). William Burr includes the memcon of the contact Stearman and Davydov, a KGB officer with diplomatic cover ("Document 10," EBB49, National Security Archive; see also Yang Kuisong, "Sino-Soviet Border Clash," 34).

37. William Burr and Jeffrey T. Richelson, "Whether to Strangle the Baby in the Cradle: The United States and the Chinese Nuclear Program, 1960–64," *International Security* 25, no. 3 (Winter 2000/2001): 54–99.

38. Arbatov, *The System*, 176.

39. Aleksandrov-Agentov, *Ot Kollontai*, 215–16. Gaiduk cites portions of Aleksandrov-Agentov in *The Soviet Union and the Vietnam War*, 225–26.

40. Burr, ed., EBB49.

41. Hanhimäki, *Flawed Architect*, 59–60.

42. "Kissinger-Dobrynin Memcon (U.S.S.R.)," October 9, 1969, *Détente Years*, 79–81.

43. "Kissinger-Dobrynin Memcon (U.S.S.R.)," October 20, 1969, *Détente Years*, 89–90.

44. On July 3, 1969, Kissinger commissioned NSSM 63 to explore U.S. policy toward Sino-Soviet differences ("Kissinger to SecState, SecDef, DCI," July 3, 1969, H-Files, Box H-207, RNPLM). On the basis of recommendations developed out of NSSM 63, Nixon directed Stoessel to renew the Warsaw talks ("Nixon, Kissinger, Stoessel Memcon," September 3, 1969, U.S. Dept. of State, *FRUS, 1969–1976*, vol. 17, *China, 1969–1972*, 80–81; see also NIE 11/13–69, August 12, 1969, CIA FOIA).

45. "Sonnenfeldt to Kissinger," December 11, 1969, U.S. Dept. of State, *FRUS, 1969–1976*, vol. 17, *China, 1969–1972*, 145–46.

46. Nixon-Kissinger Telcon, December 13, 1969, 12:59 p.m., HAK Telcons.

47. "Kissinger-Dobrynin Memcon (U.S.)," January 20, 1970, *Détente Years*, 117.

48. "Kissinger-Dobrynin Memcon (U.S.S.R.)," January 20, 1970, *Détente Years*, 120.

49. "Editorial Note," U.S. Dept. of State, *FRUS, 1969–1976*, vol. 17, *China, 1969–1972*, 210–12.

50. "Kissinger-Dobrynin Memcon (U.S.)," June 10, 1970, *Détente Years*, 154–59, quote 159.

51. "Kissinger-Dobrynin Memcon (U.S.S.R.)," June 10, 1970, *Détente Years*, 159–65. The only reference to China in Dobrynin's account is that Kissinger stated that nuclear-armed U.S. carrier-based aircraft were aimed at deterring China, not the Soviet Union (ibid., 160).

52. "Kissinger-Dobrynin Memcon (U.S.S.R.)," July 9, 1970, *Détente Years*, 173–78, quote 177, italics added. Kissinger recorded this meeting but, interestingly, did not mention China ("Kissinger-Dobrynin Memcon [U.S.]," July 9, 1970, ibid., 170–73).

53. "Kissinger to Nixon: Soviet Ambassador Dobrynin's Call on You," February 15, 1969, *Détente Years*, 7; "Memcon (U.S.)," February 17, 1969, ibid., 8–9.

54. "Kissinger-Dobrynin Memcon (U.S.S.R.)," February 21, 1969, *Détente Years*, 25.

55. "Dobrynin to Foreign Ministry," March 13, 1969, *Détente Years*, 44.

56. Dobrynin, *In Confidence*, 207–8.

57. Garthoff, *Détente and Confrontation*, 198–203.

58. "Summit" no date, NSC Files, Box 73, Folder 1, originally from the Nixon Presidential Materials Project at the National Archives and Records Administration, College Park, MD. The records have since moved to RNPLM. Included as part of the Document Reader on "NATO, the Warsaw Pact and the Rise of Détente, 1965–1972," CD-ROM, Machiavelli Center for Cold War Studies, September 2002.

59. Aijazuddin, *From a Head, through a Head, to a Head*, 40–44.

60. "Kissinger-Dobrynin Memcon (U.S.)," March 16, 1971, *Détente Years*, 310.

61. "Kissinger-Dobrynin Memcon (U.S.)," April 26, 1971, *Détente Years*, 331–32; "Kissinger-Dobrynin Memcon (U.S.S.R.)," April 26, 1971, ibid., 333–36.

62. NT, OVAL 489–17 between Nixon and Kissinger, April 26, 1971.

63. "Message from Chou Enlai to President Nixon," [dated April 21, 1971], U.S. Dept. of State, *FRUS, 1969–1976*, vol. 17, *China, 1969–1972*, 300–301.

64. "Kissinger-Dobrynin Memcon (U.S.)," April 27, 1971, *Détente Years*, 336–37.

65. "Kissinger-Dobrynin Memcon (U.S.S.R.)," April [27], 1971, *Détente Years*, 337–38.

66. NT, WHT 2–52 between Nixon and Kissinger, April 27, 1971. The Kissinger Telcon for the conversation has portions that are toned out of the audio on the Nixon tape ("Nixon-Kissinger Telcon," April 27, 1971, 8:18 p.m. HAK Telcons; also published in U.S. Dept. of State, *FRUS, 1969–1976*, vol. 17, *China, 1969–1972*, 303–8).

67. Dallek, *Nixon and Kissinger*, 69.

68. Mao personally approved the invitation (NSAEBB No. 145).

69. Richard M. Nixon, "Press Conference," April 29, 1971, *PPP,* 1971, 592–602, qtd. in *Détente Years,* 341n4.

70. Nancy Bernkopf Tucker, "Taiwan Expendable? Nixon and Kissinger Go to China," *Journal of American History* 92, no. 1 (June 2005): 109–35.

71. NT, OVAL 504–2 between Nixon, Kissinger, and Haldeman, May 27, 1971.

72. NT, OVAL 504–13 between Nixon, Kissinger, and Haldeman, May 27, 1971.

73. "Kissinger-Dobrynin Memcon (U.S.)," June 8, 1971, *Détente Years,* 368–69.

74. "Kissinger-Dobrynin Memcon (U.S.S.R.)," June [8], 1971, *Détente Years,* 371–75.

75. "Summit" no date, NSC Files, Folder 1, Box 73, originally from the Nixon Presidential Materials Project at the National Archives and Records Administration, College Park, MD. The records have since moved to RNPLM. Included as part of the Document Reader on "NATO, the Warsaw Pact and the Rise of Détente, 1965–1972," CD-ROM, Machiavelli Center for Cold War Studies, September 2002.

76. "Dobrynin to Soviet Foreign Ministry," June 10, 1971, *Détente Years,* 375–76.

77. Kissinger, *WHY,* 734.

78. Ibid., 737.

79. For discussions that took place in Beijing, see U.S. Dept. of State, *FRUS, 1969–1976,* vol. 17, *China, 1969–1972,* 359–452; U.S. Dept. of State, *Foreign Relations of the United States, 1969–1976,* vol. E-10, *Documents of American Republics, 1969–1972* (2009), Documents 7–10.

80. "Kissinger-Dobrynin Telcon (U.S.)," July 15, 1971, 9:45 p.m., *Détente Years,* 399–400. Dobrynin's account is nearly verbatim (ibid., 400–401). The oral note can be found in NSC Files, President's Trip Files, Dobrynin/Kissinger 1971 Part 2, Box 492, RNPLM.

81. "Dobrynin to Foreign Ministry," July 17, 1971, *Détente Years,* 401–4.

82. NT, EOB 262–9 between Nixon and Kissinger, July 19, 1971.

83. "Kissinger-Dobrynin Memcon (U.S.S.R.)," July 19, 1969, *Détente Years,* 406–11.

84. Kissinger, *WHY,* 766–67.

85. "Kissinger-Dobrynin Memcon (U.S.)," June 11, 1969, *Détente Years,* 62; "Kissinger-Dobrynin Memcon (U.S.S.R.)," June [11], 1969, *Détente Years,* 64–70.

86. "Kissinger-Dobrynin Memcon (U.S.)," November 18, 1971, *Détente Years,* 520.

87. "Kissinger-Dobrynin Memcon (U.S.S.R.)," November 18, 1971, *Détente Years,* 527.

88. See "Kissinger-Dobrynin Memcon (U.S.)," March 10, 1972, *Détente Years,* 612; "Kissinger-Dobrynin Memcon (U.S.S.R.)," March 10, 1972, ibid., 614. See also Document 114, "Memcon of Kissinger's meeting with Huang Hua," March 14, 1972, U.S. Dept. of State, *FRUS,* vol. E-13, *Documents on China, 1969–1972.*

89. "Memo from Kissinger to Nixon," March 8, 1972, NSC Files, President's Trip Files, Dobrynin/Kissinger 1972, Vol. 9, Box 493, RNPLM.

4. Divergent Channels

NT, OVAL 699–1 between Nixon and Kissinger, March 31, 1972.

1. Kissinger, *WHY*, 848.

2. Nixon, *RN*, 530.

3. Kissinger, *WHY*, 853, 854, 864, 861, 867, 913, 918.

4. Jack Anderson, *The Anderson Papers*, with George Clifford (New York: Random House, 1973), 205–69; Christopher Van Hollen, "The Tilt Policy Revisited: Nixon-Kissinger Geopolitics and South Asia," *Asian Survey* 20, no. 4 (April 1980): 339–61; T. N. Kaul, *The Kissinger Years: Indo-American Relations* (New Delhi: Arnold Heinemann, 1980); Hersh, *Price of Power*, 444–79; Garthoff, *Détente and Confrontation*, 296–322; Bundy, *Tangled Web*, 269–92; Isaacson, *Kissinger*, 371–76; Christopher Hitchens, *The Trial of Henry Kissinger* (London: Verso, 2001), 44–55; Hanhimäki, *Flawed Architect*, 154–84, 187–91; Dallek, *Nixon and Kissinger*, 325–68.

5. Anderson, *Anderson Papers*, 205.

6. F. S. Aijazuddin, *The White House and Pakistan: Secret Declassified Documents, 1969–1974* (Karachi: Oxford University Press, 2004); Roedad Khan, ed., *The American Papers: Secret and Confidential India-Pakistan-Bangladesh Documents 1965–1973* (Karachi: Oxford University Press, 1999); U.S. Dept. of State, *FRUS, 1969–1976*, vol. 1, *Foundations of Foreign Policy 1969–1972*; *FRUS, 1969–1976*, vol. 11, *South Asia Crisis, 1971* (Washington, DC: U.S. GPO, 2005); *FRUS, 1969–1976*, vol. E-7, *Documents on South Asia, 1969–1972* (2009), www.state.gov/r/pa/ho/frus/nixon/e7/index.htm.

7. Gary J. Bass, *The Blood Telegram: Nixon, Kissinger, and a Forgotten Genocide* (New York: Knopf Doubleday, 2013).

8. NT, EOB 309–1 between Nixon, Ehrlichman, and Haldeman, December 24, 1971.

9. NT, WHT 17–13 between Nixon and Rockefeller, December 24, 1971.

10. Yahya Khan's Legal Framework Order (LFO) of March 31, 1970, established the groundwork for the upcoming elections based on population from the 1961 Pakistani census instead of administrative units between East and West Pakistan based on parity.

11. Kissinger, *WHY*, 850.

12. Hersh, *Price of Power*, 446. For a thoughtful treatment of the Bangladesh War and Indo-Pakistani conflict, see Sumit Ganguly, *Conflict Unending: India-Pakistan Tensions since 1947* (Washington, DC: Woodrow Wilson Center Press, 2001).

13. Kissinger, *WHY*, 862.

14. U.S. Dept. of State, *FRUS, 1969–1976*, vol. 11, *South Asia Crisis, 1971*, 3.

15. G. W. Choudhury noted that Yahya heard a tape-recorded account of Mujib's talks with close associates in which Mujib had claimed: "My aim is to establish Ban-

gladesh; I will tear L.F.O. [Legal Framework Order] into pieces as soon as the elections are over. Who could challenge me once the elections are over?" (Choudhury, *The Last Days of United Pakistan* [Bloomington: Indiana University Press, 1974], 98). Siddiq Salik recounted the same story in *Witness to Surrender* (Karachi: Oxford University Press, 1977), 1. In a more recent document collection, F. S. Aijazuddin claims: "[The] process towards representative government was aborted by the self-serving intransigence of Zulfikar Ali Bhutto who, unable to match in the West Wing of Pakistan the clear majority won by Sheikh Mujibur Rahman in the East, refused to accept at a national level the consolation prize of a role in the opposition" (Aijazuddin, *The White House and Pakistan*, xiii–xiv). American policymakers at the time alternated in their views over who was failing to accommodate whom (see U.S. Dept. of State, *FRUS, 1969–1976*, vol. 11, *South Asia Crisis, 1971*, 2–21).

16. Ganguly, *Conflict Unending*, 59.

17. U.S. Dept. of State, *FRUS, 1969–1976*, vol. 11, *South Asia Crisis, 1971*, 45.

18. Ibid., 47; Kissinger, *WHY*, 853. Hersh repeated and amplified the genocide charge in *Price of Power*, 446.

19. Bass, *The Blood Telegram*.

20. U.S. Dept. of State, *FRUS, 1969–1976*, vol. 11, *South Asia Crisis, 1971*, 35. See also HAK Telcons, Chronological File, Box 9.

21. Kissinger's memoranda of conversation in this time period are certainly less detailed than those of his Soviet counterpart, especially on the crisis in the Subcontinent. The absence in Kissinger's records of the meetings of playing on the Soviet fear of China and any kind of linkage between the Indo-Pakistani conflict and China is notable.

22. "Kissinger-Dobrynin Memcon (U.S.S.R.)," March 15, 1971, *Détente Years*, 309.

23. "Kissinger-Dobrynin Memcon (U.S.S.R.)," March 22, 1971, *Détente Years*, 315–17.

24. The Indian ambassador to the United States, L. K. Jha, met with Kissinger on May 21, 1971, and described the situation as "explosive" (U.S. Dept. of State, *FRUS, 1969–1976*, vol. 11, *South Asia Crisis, 1971*, 129).

25. An unclassified postmortem chronology of key events during the Indo-Pakistani crisis prepared by the State Department's Bureau of Intelligence and Research (INR) noted the progression of refugee numbers: 1.48 million on May 6, 1971; 6,733,019 as of July 8, 1971; 8,542,000 as of September 15, 1971; 9,587,000 as of October 29, 1971 (Peter S. Maher, "Indo-Pakistani Crisis—Chronology of Key Events," February 2, 1972, Records Group [RG] 59, 1971 Indian Ocean, Box 296; originally at the National Archives and Records Administration in College Park, MD; a copy is now on microfilm at RNPLM).

26. Ganguly, *Conflict Unending*, 62. For the CIA, Lieutenant General Cushman reported to the WSAG on April 19, "There is no doubt that the Indians are involved in clandestine support activities; they're supplying them with arms, ammunition, food and medical supplies, and have sent in advisors and sabotage teams" (U.S. Dept. of State, *FRUS, 1969–1976*, vol. 11, *South Asia Crisis, 1971*, 77–78).

27. Ganguly, *Conflict Unending*, 52.

28. Geoffrey Warner, "Nixon, Kissinger and the Breakup of Pakistan, 1971," *International Affairs* 81, no. 5 (2005): 1098. Warner cited a telling quote from Nixon in the middle of the South Asian Crisis: "I would tell the people in the State Department not a goddamn thing they don't need to know," Nixon told Kissinger on Dec. 8, 1971 (U.S. Dept. of State, *FRUS, 1969–1976*, vol. E-7, *Documents on South Asia, 1969–1972*, Doc. 165).

29. "Samuel Hoskinson and Richard Kennedy to Kissinger," May 25, 1971, U.S. Dept. of State, *FRUS, 1969–1976*, vol. 11, *South Asia Crisis, 1971*, 146.

30. "Kissinger-Dobrynin Telcon," June 9, 1971, 11:31 a.m., HAK Telcons; "Kissinger-Dobrynin Memcon (U.S.S.R.)," June 10, 1971, *Détente Years*, 374.

31. "Kissinger-Dobrynin Memcon (U.S.S.R.)," June 10, 1971, *Détente Years*, 72.

32. "Kissinger-Dobrynin Memcon (U.S.S.R.)," June 30, 1971, *Détente Years*, 391. In his memoirs, Dobrynin wrote that Kissinger's July trip to Asia ostensibly "was supposed to acquaint him with the rising tensions between India and Pakistan" (Dobrynin, *In Confidence*, 224–25).

33. "Kissinger-Dobrynin Memcon (U.S.)," July 19, 1971, *Détente Years*, 405. Kissinger orally briefed the president right after his July 19, 1971, meeting with Dobrynin. Echoing the memo of the conversation, Kissinger noted that Dobrynin treated him "with a respect [he] hadn't encountered before" (EOB 262–9, July 19, 1971, 5:10–5:35 p.m.).

34. Thank you to Tanvi Madan of the University of Texas, Austin, for this "insurance policy" phrase, which is pertinent and insightful.

35. Soviet foreign minister Gromyko and Indian foreign minister Swaran Singh officially signed the treaty in New Delhi on August 9. For an English translation of the text, see R. K. Jain, ed., *Soviet-South Asian Relations, 1947–1978*, vol. 1 (Atlantic Heights, NJ: Humanities Press, 1979), 113–16.

36. Nixon added about Foreign Minister Singh: "that little son-of-a-bitch is insufferable."

37. Kissinger used the phrase "unshirted hell" frequently, a term that I had not previously encountered. In a 1990 *New York Times* article, former Nixon speechwriter William Safire described the origins of the term, which at that time was being applied to Mexican president Carlos Salinas's treatment of U.S. vice president Dan Quayle (himself another famous user of anachronistic speech and spelling). Safire wrote: "The picture comes to mind of a person tearing his shirt off to castigate another; a second possibility is to berate someone whose shirt has been taken off, as if to receive a whipping. The first picture is more likely the source; the unshirted one is angry and ready to give hell to the clothed recipient" (Safire, "On Language: Keep Your Shirt On," *New York Times*, May 13, 1990). Thank you to Dr. John Carland, formerly of the State Department's Office of the Historian, for sending me the Safire article.

38. NT, OVAL 557–1, August 9, 1971.

39. Kissinger jealously guarded the back channels and quashed a July 1971 sug-

gestion by the U.S. ambassador to the Soviet Union, Jacob Beam, that high-level discussions be initiated. Kissinger's rationale was, obviously, that the high-level channels already existed, but he was not going to reveal their existence to anybody in the State Department. After a conversation with Soviet foreign minister Gromyko, Beam had cabled Washington on July 28 and had called Secretary of State Rogers's attention to the prospect of higher-level contacts to discuss policy. Beam wrote: "I found it particularly interesting that in his survey of US-Soviet relations Gromyko this morning went out of his way to involve President Nixon personally (not always unfavorably) as well as General Secretary Brezhnev. Rather than give comprehensive answer on the spot to [the] question put by Brezhnev to Gromyko about US intentions, I replied indirectly by reference to seriousness of our intent to proceed with negotiations with [Soviet] government. It seems significant Brezhnev asked President be informed and Soviets may be seeking opening for contact at highest political level" ("Telegram 5368 from Beam [Moscow] to State Department [Washington]," RG 59, Central Files 1970–73, US–USSR, RNPLM). When he found out about the telegram from Ambassador Beam, Kissinger called Dobrynin on July 30 and told his counterpart: "Our Ambassador deduced from his conversation with your Foreign Minister that your Foreign Minister was eager for a channel between the president and your Chairman Brezhnev. At any rate we don't want to use a channel through Beam, but through the established channel. He got the impression that Gromyko was hinting that Brezhnev wanted some indication from the president on policy views, but wanted to insure that the channels remain secret." Dobrynin replied: "In this context of what you read, I interpret the words of my Minister—that he raised the question of a different channel, no. I am inclined to interpret it that he simply wants [a] more personal basis between the two bosses. I know our point of view and personally that of Brezhnev and Gromyko. I have no doubts. There is no question on a new channel. We don't want to go through Beam. I am positive this is not the meaning" (Kissinger-Dobrynin Telcon, July 30, 1971, 6:35 p.m., HAK Telcons).

40. "Kissinger to Nixon: Your Meeting with Foreign Minister Gromyko," no date, NSC Files, Kissinger Office Files, Box 71, Country Files, Europe, USSR, Gromyko, 1971–1972, RNPLM.

41. "Kissinger to Nixon: Your *Private Session* with Gromyko, September 29, 1971," September 28, 1971, Henry A. Kissinger (HAK) Office Files, Box 71, Country Files, Europe, USSR, Gromyko, 1971–1972, RNPLM.

42. See chapter 2.

43. NT, OVAL 580–13 between Nixon and Kissinger, September 29, 1971.

44. "Memorandum of Conversation," White House Special Files, President's Office Files, Box 86, RNPLM. See also NT, OVAL 580–18 between Nixon, Gromyko, Kissinger, Rogers, et al., September 29, 1971.

45. NT, OVAL 580–20 between Nixon and Gromyko, September 29, 1971.

46. Richard Sisson and Leo E. Rose, *War and Secession: Pakistan, India, and the Creation of Bangladesh* (Berkeley: University of California Press, 1991), 242, 243. In

addition to Mrs. Gandhi's September trip to Moscow, Sisson and Rose also describe the missions of Soviet deputy foreign minister Nikolai Firyubin under the treaty obligations, and Soviet air marshal P. S. Koutakhov to arrange for immediate military transfers to India.

47. See, for example, Haig-Dobrynin Telcon, October 19, 1971, 10:55 a.m., HAK Telcons.

48. "Dobrynin-Kissinger Memcon," October 9, 1971, 10:40–11:20 a.m., NSC Files, President's Trip Files, Box 492, RNPLM.

49. Haig-Dobrynin Telcon, October 19, 1971, 10:55 a.m., HAK Telcons.

50. Haig-Dobrynin Telcon, October 23, 1971, 12:18 p.m., HAK Telcons.

51. U.S. Dept. of State, *FRUS, 1969–1976*, vol. 11, *South Asia Crisis, 1971*, 505.

52. Dallek, *Nixon and Kissinger*, 339, 340. For the memo, see U.S. Dept. of State, *FRUS, 1969–1976*, vol. E-7, *Documents on South Asia, 1969–1972*, www.state.gov/r/pa/ho/frus/nixon/e7/48213.htm. NT, OVAL 613–15, November 4, 1971. Approximately twenty-six minutes of the conversation are publicly available, which largely encompass setting the agenda for and generalizations about Nixon's forthcoming China trip and the importance of India. The toned-out withdrawal of one hour, forty minutes covers the rest of the meeting. The memorandum for the president's file of the Nixon-Gandhi meeting is published in U.S. Dept. of State, *FRUS, 1969–1976*, vol. 11, *South Asia Crisis, 1971*, 493–99. NT, OVAL 615–23, November 5, 1971.

53. "Kissinger-Dobrynin Telcon (U.S.)," November 15, 1971, *Détente Years*, 519.

54. "Kissinger-Dobrynin Telcon (U.S.S.R)," November 15, 1971, *Détente Years*, 520.

55. On November 16, Kissinger called the ambassador with birthday wishes. During the course of the short phone call, Dobrynin informed Kissinger that he would be leaving Washington to attend a plenum of the Central Committee the following Monday, November 22 ("Kissinger-Dobrynin Telcon," November 16, 1971, 11:45 a.m., HAK Telcons.)

56. *Détente Years*, 527.

57. For example, Raymond Garthoff writes: "On December 3 the Pakistani air force attacked eight Indian airfields in the region around West Pakistan, and Pakistani armored forces thrust into the part of Kashmir administered by India. This action opened the Indo-Pakistani War of 1971" (Garthoff, *Détente and Confrontation*, 298). Garthoff notes: "The reasons for the move by Pakistan are less clear. It may have acted in the hope that, to forestall a wider war, the United Nations and the major powers would press India to accept a cease-fire on both fronts, permitting Pakistan to hold its ground in the East" (ibid., 298n12). See also Dallek, *Nixon and Kissinger*, 341; and Isaacson, *Kissinger*, 374.

58. For example, at a WSAG meeting on November 12, 1971, Joseph Sisco said: "Indian strategy has been to continue the pressure on Yahya and to suck Pakistan in militarily so that the principal onus for starting a war would fall on Pakistan" (U.S. Dept. of State, *FRUS, 1969–1976*, vol. 11, *South Asia Crisis, 1971*, 506).

59. Isaacson, *Kissinger*, 374. Yahya's cable is published in full in Aijazuddin, *The White House and Pakistan*, 364–66. See also U.S. Dept. of State, *FRUS, 1969–1976*, vol. 11, *South Asia Crisis, 1971*, 539n4.

60. To be fair, the tapes were not released until 2000, half a decade after Isaacson's *Kissinger* was published.

61. Sisson and Rose, *War and Secession*, 214.

62. "Minutes of WSAG Meeting," November 22, 1971, U.S. Dept. of State, *FRUS, 1969–1976*, vol. 11, *South Asia Crisis, 1971*, 532.

63. "Nixon-Kissinger Telcon," November 22, 1971, 12:45 p.m., HAK Telcons, also qtd. in U.S. Dept. of State, *FRUS, 1969–1976*, vol. 11, *South Asia Crisis, 1971*, 536–37.

64. U.S. Dept. of State, *FRUS, 1969–1976*, vol. 11, *South Asia Crisis, 1971*, 537.

65. Kissinger, *WHY*, 889. A transcript of the meeting, prepared by Winston Lord, is included in William Burr, ed., "The Lead-Up to Nixon's Trip to China: U.S. and Chinese Documents and Tapes," NSAEBB No. 70, with Sharon Chamberlain, Gao Bei, and Zhao Hun, May 22, 2002, www.gwu.edu/~nsarchiv/NSAEBB/NSAEBB70/doc22.pdf.

66. NT, OVAL 622–1, November 22, 1971.

67. "Telegram from State Department (Washington) to Embassy in Pakistan (Islamabad)," November 28, 1971, 0101Z, U.S. Dept. of State, *FRUS, 1969–1976*, vol. 11, *South Asia Crisis, 1971*, 565–66. Nixon discussed the handling of the notes through the State Department with Kissinger (see NT OVAL 622–1, November 22, 1971).

68. "Telegram from the Department of State (Washington) to the Embassy in the Soviet Union (Moscow)," November 27, 1971, 0103Z, U.S. Dept. of State, *FRUS, 1969–1976*, vol. 11, *South Asia Crisis, 1971*, 569.

69. Indian prime minister Gandhi spoke to her nation on December 3, 1971, noting that the Pakistani Air Force had struck six Indian airfields and was shelling positions along the Indian–West Pakistani border. Pakistan countered that it was responding to "aggressive" Indian reconnaissance over West Pakistan (U.S. Dept. of State, *FRUS, 1969–1976*, vol. 11, *South Asia Crisis, 1971*, 592). The CIA correctly predicted the Pakistani course of action in a September Intelligence Memorandum (see "India Pakistan: Comparative Capabilities in a New Military Confrontation," September 1971, http://foia.cia.gov).

70. Raymond Price, a core member of Nixon's campaign cadre and a presidential speechwriter, accompanied Nixon on a prepresidential trip to India in 1967. Price noted that the difference between Indira Gandhi's public statements and her private statements to Nixon during the trip was "one of the sharpest contrasts." Price explained in his memoirs: "[Gandhi] was then giving the United States vituperative public tongue-lashings for its role in Vietnam. Privately, she stressed that it was vital for the United States to hang tough. Her public posture was partly for domestic political consumption, and partly because she was walking a diplomatic tightrope in her relations with the Soviet Union. Privately, she was deeply worried about China's

ambitions, and she saw US perseverance in Vietnam as essential to checking those ambitions and thereby protecting India itself" (Price, *With Nixon*, 24).

71. Kissinger, *WHY*, 900.

72. OVAL 634–19, December 9, 1971, U.S. Dept. of State, *FRUS, 1969–1976*, vol. E-7, *Documents on South Asia, 1969–1972*.

73. "Kissinger-Nixon Telcon," December 3, 1971, 10:45 a.m., in U.S. Dept. of State, *FRUS, 1969–1976*, vol. 11, *South Asia Crisis, 1971*, 593–94.

74. The minutes of the first meeting were among the leaked documents published by Jack Anderson, in which Kissinger famously said—and has been often quoted in news stories and histories ever since: "I've been catching unshirted hell every half-hour from the president who says we're not tough enough. He believes State is pressing us to be tough and I'm resisting. . . . He wants to tilt toward Pakistan" ("WSAG Minutes," December 3, 1971, 11:19–11:55 a.m., U.S. Dept. of State, *FRUS, 1969–1976*, vol. 11, *South Asia Crisis, 1971*, 597).

75. U.S. Dept. of State, *FRUS, 1969–1976*, vol. 11, *South Asia Crisis, 1971*, 596–604. Kissinger also convened the WSAG on December 4, 1971. Significantly, at the beginning of the meeting, Helms noted how the Soviet Union had shifted its position from opposing an Indo-Pakistani war "to the conclusion that Moscow would not do much to try to halt hostilities." Helms also reported that he had sent Dr. Kissinger a study entitled *Moscow and the Indo-Pakistani Crisis* (not located by State Department historians working on *FRUS*), which discussed "the switch in Soviet attitude in some detail" (U.S. Dept. of State, *FRUS, 1969–1976*, vol. 11, *South Asia Crisis, 1971*, 621n3). The WSAG discussed handling the crisis in the Security Council and aid cutoff—especially to India (ibid., 620–27).

76. Kissinger-Nixon Telcon, December 5, 1971, no time, HAK Telcons. See also U.S. Dept. of State, *FRUS, 1969–1976*, vol. 11, *South Asia Crisis, 1971*, 635–40. Nixon was in Key Biscayne, Florida, so the White House taping system did not capture the conversations, although Kissinger recorded the conversations and had an aide (or aides) type the telcon transcripts of the conversations.

77. "Kissinger-Nixon Telcon," December 5, 1971, no time, in U.S. Dept. of State, *FRUS, 1969–1976*, vol. 11, *South Asia Crisis, 1971*, 642.

78. "Kissinger-Vorontsov Memcon," December 5, 1971, President's Trip Files, Box 492, RNPLM.

79. "Kissinger-Vorontsov Telcon," December 5, 1971, U.S. Dept. of State, *FRUS, 1969–1976*, vol. 11, *South Asia Crisis, 1971*, 649.

80. Kissinger-Vorontsov Telcon, December 6, 1971, 3:32 p.m., HAK Telcons.

81. "Nixon to Brezhnev," December 6, 1971, *Détente Years*, 532.

82. "Brezhnev to Nixon," December 6, 1971, NSC Files, President's Trip Files, Box 492, RNPLM. In a memo from Kissinger to Nixon, prepared by Kissinger's veteran aides Peter Rodman and Winston Lord, the Soviet oral reply was summarized more succinctly and with the edge taken off: "The Soviets linked a cease-fire to a demand that Yahya immediately recognize East Pakistani autonomy, and they objected to our treating the India/Pakistan crisis as a watershed or critical

stage in US-Soviet relations" (Memorandum for the president from Henry Kissinger, December 8, NSC Files, President's Trip Files, Dobrynin/Kissinger 1971, vol. 8, Box 492, RNPLM). A cover memo indicates that Rodman and Lord drafted the memo and said, "you may wish to forward this to the president." A handwritten annotation states, "not sent."

83. For Nixon's views on the Jordan crisis, see Nixon, *RN*, 483.

84. NT, OVAL 630–2, December 6, 1971. Thank you to W. Taylor Fain for providing draft portions of the transcript. This abbreviated conversation is also significant for the discussion of the U.S. diverting military aid to Pakistan via Iran.

85. NT, OVAL 630–10, December 6, 1971.

86. NT, OVAL 630–20, December 6, 1971.

87. "Haig-Vorontsov Telcon," December 8, 1971, 3:50 p.m., *Détente Years*, 533n3.

88. NT, EOB 307–27 between Nixon, Kissinger, and Mitchell, December 8, 1971, U.S. Dept. of State, *FRUS, 1969–1976*, vol. E-7, *Documents on South Asia, 1969–1972*.

89. NT, WHT 16–64 between Nixon and Kissinger, December 8, 1971, U.S. Dept. of State, *FRUS, 1969–1976*, vol. E-7, *Documents on South Asia, 1969–1972*.

90. "Brezhnev to Nixon," December 8, 1971, *Détente Years*, 534–35.

91. "Telegram from Vorontsov to the Soviet Foreign Ministry," December 9, 1971, *Détente Years*, 535–36.

92. Henry A. Kissinger, "Memorandum for the President," December 9, 1971, NSC Files, President's Trip Files, Box 492, RNPLM. The memo is initialed "HK" and has a stamp noting, "The President has seen."

93. OVAL 634–12, U.S. Dept. of State, *FRUS, 1969–1976*, vol. E-7, *Documents on South Asia, 1969–1972*.

94. "Nixon, Matskevich, Vorontsov, Kissinger Memcon: Memorandum for the President's File," Washington, December 9, 1971, U.S. Dept. of State, *FRUS, 1969–1976*, vol. 14, *Soviet Union, October 1971–May 1972*, 771.

95. The Soviets were likely protesting the tacit American encouragement that Pakistan receive military aid through third parties, such as Iran and Jordan (U.S. Dept. of State, *FRUS, 1969–1976*, vol. 14, *Soviet Union, October 1971–May 1972*). Kissinger told as much to visiting Pakistani prime minister Bhutto: "First, in the light of all we have done, it is absolutely essential that we are not exposed to Chinese charges that we are not doing enough. Because if that is going to be the charge why should we do anything? I mean we are standing alone against our public opinion, against our whole bureaucracy at the very edge of legality" (Kissinger-Bhutto Telcon, December 12, 1971, no time, HAK Telcons).

96. NT, OVAL 635–8, December 10, 1971, U.S. Dept. of State, *FRUS, 1969–1976*, vol. E-7, *Documents on South Asia, 1969–1972*.

97. "Nixon to Brezhnev," December 10, 1971, U.S. Dept. of State, *FRUS, 1969–1976*, vol. 11, *South Asia Crisis, 1971*, 745–46.

98. *Détente Years*, 538; U.S. Dept. of State, *FRUS, 1961–1963*, vol. 19, *South Asia*, Document 191.

99. "Nixon to Brezhnev," December 10, 1971, U.S. Dept. of State, *FRUS, 1969–1976,* vol. 11, *South Asia Crisis, 1971,* 745–46.

100. "Memcon Huang Hua, Ch'en Ch'u, T'ang Wen'sheng, Kissinger, Bush, Haig and Lord," December 10, 1971, 6:05–7:55 p.m., New York City–East Side, DNSA online.

101. "Kissinger-Vorontsov Telcon," December 11, 1971, ca. 3:00 p.m., *Détente Years,* 539–40. According to the editors of *Détente Years,* the call was actually made "at approximately 8:30 p.m." (*Détente Years,* 539n1).

102. NT, OVAL 637–3 between Nixon and Kissinger, December 12, 1971.

103. Kissinger-Vorontsov Telcon, December 12, 1971, 10:05 a.m., HAK Telcons.

104. "Nixon to Brezhnev," December 12, 1971, *Détente Years,* 543.

105. "Soviet Hotline Message," December 13, 1971, NSC Files, Box 492, RNPLM.

106. William Safire, "On Language: Off the Record," *New York Times,* October 29, 1989, http://query.nytimes.com/gst/fullpage.html?res=950DE6DC1F3CF93AA 15753C1A96F948260&sec=&spon=&pagewanted=all.

107. Stanley Karnow, "Moscow Warned on India: '72 Nixon Visit May Hinge on War Restraint," *Washington Post,* December 15, 1971, A1. The *New York Times* repeated the story and also reported the deployment of the *Enterprise* and Press Secretary Ronald Ziegler's immediate denial of Kissinger's statements—a "hypothetical" scenario, and that the United States was not considering canceling the Soviet summit (see James M. Naughton, "Nixon May Review Trip Unless Soviet Curbs India," *New York Times,* December 15, 1971, 1).

108. Jack Anderson, "The Washington Merry-Go-Round: US, Soviet Vessels in Bay of Bengal," *Washington Post,* December 14, 1971, B15.

109. Rosen, *The Strong Man,* 169.

110. Len Colodny, "Excerpt of an Interview with Admiral Moorer," January 27, 1987, www.nixonera.com/media/audio/transcripts/moorer.asp.

111. The archive at the United Nations never responded to repeated inquiries to locate the text of the draft resolutions, which were not published.

112. "Kissinger-Vorontsov Memcon (U.S.)," December 15, 1971, *Détente Years,* 552–53; "Kissinger-Vorontsov Memcon (U.S.S.R.)," December 15, 1971, ibid., 553–54.

113. Nixon misspoke in the heat of the moment, equating Ambassador Smith with the Middle East instead of SALT.

114. U.S. Dept. of State, *FRUS, 1969–1976,* vol. 11, *South Asia Crisis, 1971,* 837–41.

115. Dobrynin-Kissinger Telcon, January 20, 1972, 5:04 p.m., HAK Telcons.

116. OVAL 652–17, January 20, 1972, U.S. Dept. of State, *FRUS, 1969–1976,* vol. 11, *South Asia Crisis, 1971,* 119–21. The editors of *FRUS, 1969–1976,* vol. 14, *Soviet Union, October 1971–May 1972* failed to identify the telegram from Pegov, although another, partially declassified document published in the *FRUS* volume on South Asia describes Pegov's conversations with Indian officials (see "Kissinger to

Nixon," December 16, 1971, U.S. Dept. of State, *FRUS, 1969–1976,* vol. 11, *South Asia Crisis, 1971,* 843–46, esp. 845).

117. NT, OVAL 639–30 between Nixon, Haldeman, Ehrlichman, and Mitchell, December 21, 1971, courtesy of James Rosen.

118. Ehrlichman, *Witness to Power,* 279.

119. NT, EOB 309–1 between Nixon, Ehrlichman, and Kissinger, December 24, 1971, 12:00–1:37 p.m. Kissinger entered at 12:15 p.m. and departed at 12:45 p.m.

5. Vietnam in U.S.-Soviet Back Channels, November 1971–April 1972

Epigraph: NT, CAB 89–1 between Richard Nixon, Spiro Agnew, William Rogers, Melvin Laird, George Lincoln, John B. Connally, John Mitchell, Richard Helms, Thomas H. Moorer, Ellsworth Bunker, Henry Kissinger, Alexander M. Haig, and Ronald Ziegler, February 2, 1972.

1. Garthoff, *Détente and Confrontation,* 279–94.

2. NT, OVAL 759–5 between Nixon and Kissinger, August 2, 1972.

3. Stephen Randolph, *Powerful and Brutal Weapons* (Cambridge: Harvard University Press, 2004), 30–31. See also Kimball, *Vietnam War File,* 199.

4. The Tet offensive was a military failure for the North Vietnamese, but it was a major shock in U.S. politics (see Ronald Spector, *After Tet: The Bloodiest Year in Vietnam* [New York: Vintage, 1993], 1–25). At a Senior Review Group meeting in June 1971, Kissinger told policymakers: "We got creamed in 1968, or so the public thought. We all know we can't stand another Tet next year. This is the problem we're up against" (H-Files, Senior Review Group Minutes, June 9, 1971, 3:33–4:42 p.m., Box H–112, RNPLM).

5. Although Kissinger had prepared different versions of memoranda for the State Department, it was not until February 2–3, 1972, that he sanitized a letter from Brezhnev to Nixon to omit any discussion of the back-channel discussions on the Middle East. A copy of the sanitized letter can be found at NSC Files, President's Trip Files, Dobrynin/Kissinger 1972, Vol. 9 [Pt. 2], Box 493, RNPLM.

6. NT, OVAL 469–13 between Nixon, Kissinger, and Haldeman, March 18, 1971. U.S. tactical air support, helicopters, and artillery supported the South Vietnamese incursion into Laos at Lam Son 719 (called Dewey Canyon II by the United States). The South Vietnamese got to Tchepone, and South Vietnamese president Nguyen Van Thieu declared the operation a success. Although the South Vietnamese captured a number of weapons caches and disrupted North Vietnamese supply lines, the operation was a public relations nightmare, with ARVN troops evacuating on the skids of American helicopters. The operation was also costly in terms of troops and morale (William K. Nolan, *Into Laos: The Story of Dewey Canyon II/Lam Son 719* [Novato, CA: Presidio, 1986]).

7. Memorandum from Kissinger to President Nixon, Washington, March 20, 1971, NSC Files, Vietnam Subject Files, Vietnam Operations in Laos and Cambodia, Vol. V, Box 82, RNPLM.

8. Minutes of a Senior Review Group Meeting, April 13, 1971, H-Files, SRG

Minutes, Originals, 1971, Box H–112, RNPLM. Similarly, at the end of the month, a National Intelligence Estimate noted: "The approaching US election period, coupled with continued drawdowns of US troop strength in South Vietnam, make it probable that Hanoi will elect to step up its military activity by early 1972. We do not envisage an effort to duplicate in scale or intensity the 1968 Tet offensive" (National Intelligence Estimate 53–71, "South Vietnam: Problems and Prospects 4/29/71," in *Estimative Products on Vietnam: 1948–1975*, CD-ROM, National Intelligence Council, April 2005).

American policymakers were also hearing warnings from abroad predicting a Soviet-supplied North Vietnamese attack, one that could throw a wrench into both Sino-American rapprochement and Soviet-American détente. In July 1971, South Vietnamese president Nguyen Van Thieu told Kissinger and Haig that "the Viet Cong would increase their infiltration until March before launching offensives, per the usual yearly cycle." When Kissinger asked whether the North Vietnamese might strike earlier, Thieu replied that "February might be a good time" (Memorandum of Conversation, July 4, 1971, 10:40 a.m.–12:20 p.m., NSC Files, Country Files–Far East, Vietnam, Saigon Background Docs, Box 103, RNPLM). Sino-American rapprochement was unbeknownst to Thieu at that time. On his October 1971 planning trip to China to lay the groundwork for the Beijing summit, Kissinger also reported, "If the conflict continues, Peking (and Moscow) will not want to see a major offensive—and our reaction—shadowing the summit" (Memorandum from Kissinger to Nixon, "My October China Visit: Discussions of the Issues," November 1971, U.S. Dept. of State, *FRUS, 1969–1976*, vol. 17, *China, 1969–1972*, 545).

9. "Memcon (U.S.)," January 9, 1971, and "Memcon (U.S.S.R.)," January 9, 1971, *Détente Years*, 257–63.

10. "Kissinger-Gromyko Memcon," September 30, 1971, *Détente Years*, 479.

11. For the text of the October 11, 1971, proposal put forward by the White House, see *Department of State Bulletin*, February 21, 1972, 229–30.

12. Henry A. Kissinger, *Ending the Vietnam War*, 228–29. Kissinger reported to President Nixon on November 16, 1971, "The North Vietnamese may be canceling our meeting." After discussing some potential North Vietnamese "pretexts" for canceling the meeting, the president reassured Kissinger: "Giving our proposal was essential. . . . And everything we've done has been essential, Henry." Before turning to discuss the issue of Japanese textiles, Nixon again expressed confidence in Kissinger's assessment of the North Vietnamese: "Your thought that they have got to take a good look at their hole card is well taken. And if the Chinese, or the Russians, or anybody have indicated anything that we've got these signals to, they know damn well they're running some risks here. And, incidentally, they are running risks: If they cancel the meeting we have got to bang 'em a few times" (NT, EOB 295–14, November 16, 1971).

13. NT, OVAL 620–8 between Nixon and Kissinger, November 17, 1971. Haldeman briefly discussed Le Duc Tho's "illness" with the president in NT, OVAL 620–1, November 17, 1971. For additional conversations on the status of the nego-

tiations with the North Vietnamese and the absence of Le Duc Tho, see NT, EOB 294–6, November 18, 1971; NT, EOB 294–22, November 18, 1971; and NT, OVAL 621–18, November 20, 1971. Nixon discussed the possible North Vietnamese postponement of the peace negotiations with Kissinger and Attorney General John Mitchell in NT, EOB 295–15, November 16, 1971.

14. Ibid., EOB 294–22 between Nixon and Kissinger, November 18, 1971.

15. "Kissinger-Dobrynin Memcon (U.S.)," November 18, 1971, *Détente Years*, 520–21.

16. NT, OVAL 621–18, November 20, 1971, italics added.

17. Nixon saw "protective reaction" strikes as both a justification for bombing North Vietnamese areas and as strike opportunity (see, for example, NT, OVAL 462–5, March 5, 1971; and NT, OVAL 574–3, September 17, 1971).

18. Kissinger, *Ending the Vietnam War*, 229. *Ending the Vietnam War* is largely taken from Kissinger's *White House Years* but was expanded.

19. Surprisingly, Ilya Gaiduk has provided little analysis of the Soviet aid to North Vietnam issue during 1971–72 (see Gaiduk, *The Soviet Union and the Vietnam War*, 215). A telegram from the American embassy in Moscow in April 1972 reported that the Soviets readily admitted their support for North Vietnam ("Telegram 3568 American Embassy in Moscow to Secretary of State in Washington DC," April 17, 1972, NSC Files, President's Trip Files, Box 474, RNPLM).

20. "Memo for Congressional Support Officer, OCI," May 15, 1974, "Soviet and Chinese Aid to North Vietnam," http://foia.cia.gov, Number S-6176.

21. NT, WHT 18–66 between Nixon and Kissinger, January 11, 1972.

22. Senior Review Group Minutes, 3:09–4:05 p.m., January 17, 1972, H-Files, Box H–113, SRG Minutes, Originals, 1972–1973, RNPLM.

23. Dobrynin, *In Confidence*, 237. Dobrynin wrote that he returned on December 12, 1971, but this was likely in error. I would argue that he meant January 12, 1972. There are no U.S. telcons or Nixon tapes referencing any meetings or phone calls with Dobrynin from his departure in November 1971 through early January 1972. On January 4, 1972, Vorontsov told Kissinger that Dobrynin would return "between the 10th and 15th [of January 1972]" (Kissinger-Vorontsov Telcon, January 4, 1972, 11:35 a.m., HAK Telcons). Vorontsov later told Kissinger that Dobrynin was "delayed but coming on the 19th [of January]" (Kissinger-Vorontsov Telcon, January 17, 1972, 10:12 a.m., HAK Telcons).

24. NT, OVAL 652–17, January 20, 1972, U.S. Dept. of State, *FRUS, 1969–1976*, vol. 14, *Soviet Union, October 1971–May 1972*, 123. By the beginning of 1972, warnings to the Soviets about a possible North Vietnamese offensive were hardly novel. For example, at a December 22, 1970, Kissinger-Dobrynin meeting discussing deteriorating U.S.-Soviet relations, the national security advisor reported that he told Dobrynin: "If the Soviet Union wanted to use its influence for negotiations, now was the time. This was the best way to prevent a deterioration of US/Soviet relationships. . . . We would simply not sit by while the North Vietnamese were building up for an offensive" (Kissinger-Dobrynin Mem-

con, NSC Files, President's Trip Files, Dobrynin/Kissinger 1970, Vol. 3, Box 490, RNPLM).

25. Memcon, Washington, January 21, 1972, 8:00 p.m.–12:00 a.m., U.S. Dept. of State, *FRUS, 1969–1976*, vol. 14, *Soviet Union, October 1971–May 1972*, 123.

26. Richard Nixon, "Address to the Nation Making Public a Plan for Peace in Vietnam," January 25, 1972, *PPP, 1972*, 100–106.

27. Nixon was present with Kissinger in the Lincoln Sitting Room, which is the reason the conversation was automatically recorded. The tape is the only American record of the conversation. On Nixon's instructions to coordinate with Dobrynin, see "Kissinger-Dobrynin Memcon (U.S.S.R.)," January 25, 1972, *Détente Years*, 569.

28. NT, WHT 19–65 between Kissinger and Dobrynin, January 25, 1972. The audio quality of the tape is poor, especially for a telephone conversation, which could have been caused by competing recording systems at the White House and the Soviet embassy. According to the Nixon tape log for NT, OVAL 655–5, January 25, 1972, "The President delivered his 'Address to the Nation Making Public a Plan for Peace in Vietnam,' between 8:30 pm and an unknown time before 8:55 pm" (Tapes Log WHT 19–65, RNPLM, www.nixonlibrary.gov/forresearchers/find/tapes/finding_aids/tapesubjectlogs/wht019.pdf).

29. "Letter from President Nixon to Leonid Brezhnev," January 25, 1972, U.S. Dept. of State, *FRUS, 1969–1976*, vol. 14, *Soviet Union, October 1971–May 1972*, 139–40.

30. "Kissinger-Dobrynin Memcon (U.S.S.R.)," January 25, 1972, *Détente Years*, 569–71.

31. "Kissinger Dobrynin Memcon (U.S.S.R.)," January 28, 1972, *Détente Years*, 574–79.

32. See, for example, NT, OVAL 464–17 between Nixon and Kissinger, March 9, 1971, in which Kissinger offers his resignation.

33. NT, OVAL 632–11, December 8, 1971.

34. "Kissinger to Rogers Memorandum," January 14, 1972, U.S. Dept. of State, *FRUS, 1969–1976*, vol. 14, *Soviet Union, October 1971–May 1972*, 114.

35. U.S. Dept. of State, *FRUS, 1969–1976*, vol. 14, *Soviet Union, October 1971–May 1972*, 116–17.

36. NT, OVAL 664–6, February 2, 1972.

37. "Kissinger-Dobrynin Memcon," February 4, 1972, *Détente Years*, 580–81.

38. NT, CAB 89–1, February 2, 1972, 10:05 a.m.–12:16 p.m. The loose definition of "protective-reaction" became something of a controversy that cost the career of at least one Air Force general, John D. Lavelle. Lavelle was blamed for allegedly unauthorized protective-reaction strikes that hit nonmilitary targets and killed civilians (Seymour Hersh, "Authorizations: Forced Retirement of a Vietnam-era Air Force General," *New Yorker*, March 26, 2007), www.newyorker.com/magazine/2007/03/26/authorizations. Hersh based his article on Aloysius Casey and Patrick Casey, "Lavelle, Nixon, and the White House Tapes," *Air Force Magazine*,

February 2007. I believe the actual moment of decision is in NT, CAB 89–1, on February 2, 1972, in which Nixon clearly relaxed the interpretation of protective-reaction strikes in the context of countering the predicted North Vietnamese spring offensive.

39. "Brezhnev to Nixon," February 5, 1972, *Détente Years,* 581–82.

40. "Kissinger-Dobrynin Memcon (U.S.)," February 7, 1972, 1:07 p.m., *Détente Years,* 583–84.

41. NT, OVAL 670–13 between Nixon, Kissinger, and Haldeman, February 14, 1972, U.S. Dept. of State, *FRUS, 1969–1976,* vol. 14, *Soviet Union, October 1971–May 1972,* 168–73.

42. NT, OVAL 672–2 between Nixon and Kissinger, February 15, 1972.

43. "Kissinger-Dobrynin Memcon (U.S.)," February 15, 1972, in *Détente Years,* 585–87. Kissinger did not mention Vietnam in his memcon of the meeting. Dobrynin reported that Kissinger said it seemed "unreasonable to expect that solutions [to Vietnam] will be found during discussion of this matter at the Soviet-U.S. summit in Moscow, but just an exchange of views on this issue at the highest level could itself be useful" ("Kissinger-Dobrynin Memcon [U.S.S.R.]," February 15, 1972, *Détente Years,* 588).

44. "Nixon to Brezhnev," February 15, 1972, *Détente Years,* 593–94.

45. Max Frankel, "Nixon Sees Chou in Two Sessions of Policy Talks," *New York Times,* February 23, 1972, 1; Stanley Karnow, "Chinese Press, TV Play up Nixon Visit," *Washington Post,* February 23, 1972, A1.

46. "Brezhnev to Nixon," February 23, 1972, *Détente Years,* 594–95.

47. President's Daily Diary (hereafter cited as PDD), February 27–28, 1972, RNPLM, http://nixon.archives.gov/virtuallibrary/documents/dailydiary.php.

48. Kissinger-Reagan Telcon, February 28, 1972, 10:30 p.m., HAK Telcons.

49. Nixon-Kissinger Telcon, February 28, 1972, 10:55 p.m., HAK Telcons.

50. NT, WHT 20–106, February 28, 1972. The Nixon Tape conversation overlaps with the Kissinger telcon cited previously, which is not as accurate as the tape transcript.

51. "Kissinger-Dobrynin Memcon (U.S.)," March 1, 1972, *Détente Years,* 595.

52. "Kissinger-Dobrynin Memcon (U.S.S.R.)," March 1, 1972, *Détente Years,* 597–602. Dobrynin cabled a meticulous report on the impact of Nixon's China visit on March 8, 1972, ibid., 602–5.

53. Dobrynin, *In Confidence,* 242.

54. "Nixon-Kissinger-Dobrynin Memcon (U.S.S.R.)," *Détente Years,* 612–15.

55. NT, OVAL 695–2, March 28, 1972.

56. "Brezhnev to Nixon," March 27, 1972, *Détente Years,* 629–30.

57. Nixon, *RN,* 586.

58. H. R. Haldeman, "March 30, 1972," *The Haldeman Diaries: Multimedia Edition.*

59. NT, OVAL 697–2, March 30, 1972, U.S. Dept. of State, *FRUS, 1969–1976,* vol. 14, *Soviet Union, October 1971–May 1972,* 234–35. Later than evening, Kis-

singer called the president with a status update on the offensive: "I think, Mr. President, we should watch for another day to see . . . whether it was just a high point or a real offensive. . . . If it is, then we can go after these SAM sites that we just bombed . . . [a]nd take all of them out." Nixon: "Right." Kissinger: "And, in fact, go for it the first pretext that we can do it" (NT, WHT 22–62, March 30, 1972).

60. Dobrynin recollected that Kissinger had told him "that the advancing North Vietnamese troops were 'armed 90 percent with Soviet-made weapons'" (Dobrynin, *In Confidence*, 243).

61. NT, OVAL 697–2, March 30, 1972, U.S. Dept. of State, *FRUS, 1969–1976*, vol. 14, *Soviet Union, October 1971–May 1972*, 234–35, italics added. According to his memcon, Kissinger met with Dobrynin from 1:15 p.m. to 3:00 p.m. and largely discussed the trip to Poland, technical arrangements for the summit, and SALT ("Kissinger-Dobrynin Memcon [U.S.]," March 30, 1972, *Détente Years*, 633–34).

62. The release of the third chronological series of Nixon tapes in 2002 unleashed a torrent of news stories about how Nixon considered the use of nuclear weapons against North Vietnam in response to the Easter Offensive (see, for example, "Nixon Proposed Using A-Bomb in Vietnam War," *New York Times*, March 23, 2002). The most frequently cited conversation is NT, EOB 332–35 between Nixon, Kissinger, and Ziegler, April 25, 1972. Jeffrey Kimball provides a brief extract and states: "Nixon's tone of voice on the tape is both sincere *and* angry. There is every reason to believe and little reason to doubt that at that moment at his hideaway in the Executive Office Building, Nixon was seriously considering the use of a nuclear weapon or seriously floating a trial balloon" (Kimball, *Vietnam War File*, 214, italics in original). The entire discussion of the nuclear option is as follows: Nixon: "Fine, and then, I still think we ought to take the dikes out now." Kissinger: "I think, Mr. President—" Nixon: "Will that drown people?" Kissinger: "That will drown about 200,000 people [unclear]—" Nixon: "Well, no, no, no, no, no, no. I'd rather use a nuclear bomb. Have you got that ready?" Kissinger: "Now, that, I think, would just too much, uh—" Nixon: "A nuclear bomb doesn't bother you?" Kissinger: "In Vietnam, actually, you wouldn't do it anyway" (ibid., 217). As Kimball has it in his transcript, the president angrily admonished his NSC advisor: "I just want you to think big, Henry, for Christ's sakes!" Most accounts omit the presence of Press Secretary Ronald Ziegler. Also, the entire discussion about the nuclear option took all of sixteen seconds, hardly constituting a serious policy discussion. The use of nuclear weapons came up in passing several times in the tapes of April–May 1972, but it was described with immediate caveats (see NT, OVAL 710–4, April 17, 1972; NT, OVAL 713–1, April 19, 1972; and NT, OVAL 726–8, May 19, 1972).

63. NT, OVAL 700–2, April 3, 1972, U.S. Dept. of State, *FRUS, 1969–1976*, vol. 14, *Soviet Union, October 1971–May 1972*, 250–53.

64. Nixon-Kissinger Telcon, April 3, 1972, 6:20 p.m., HAK Telcons.

65. "Kissinger-Dobrynin Memcon (U.S.S.R.)," April 3, 1972, *Détente Years*, 638–41.

66. Ibid. There was no U.S. record of the meeting.

67. Ibid. Dobrynin's report suggests that Kissinger had accurately described the end of the conversation on the linkage between Vietnam and the Berlin treaty.

68. NT, WHT 22–69 between Nixon and Kissinger, April 3, 1972. See also "Nixon-Kissinger Telcon," April 3, 1972, 7:10 p.m., HAK Telcons; and, Kissinger, *WHY*, 1114.

69. "Kissinger-Dobrynin Memcon (U.S.S.R.)," April 6, 1972, *Détente Years*, 642–49.

70. "Kissinger-Dobrynin Memcon (U.S.)," April 6, 1972, *Détente Years*, 641–42.

71. "Washington to Moscow Telegram," April 7, 1972, *Détente Years*, 649–51.

72. Kissinger–Joseph Kraft Telcon, April 9, 1972, 10:15 a.m., HAK Telcons.

73. Nixon-Kissinger Telcon, April 9, 1972, 10:45 a.m., HAK Telcons.

74. Joseph Kraft, "The Russian Role," *Washington Post*, April 11, 1972, A19.

75. Nixon-Kissinger Telcon, April 9, 1972, 10:45 a.m., HAK Telcons. Kissinger's message to Bahr can be found in "Editorial Note," U.S. Dept. of State, *FRUS, 1969–1976*, vol. 40, *Germany and Berlin, 1969–1972*, 994. The following day, Kissinger explicitly explained the linkage between Vietnam and U.S. support for the ratification of the Berlin treaties (see NT, OVAL 705–13 between Nixon and Kissinger, April 10, 1972).

76. Sonnenfeldt to Kissinger, "The Soviets and Vietnam—Our Signals," April 10, 1972, U.S. Dept. of State, *FRUS, 1969–1976*, vol. 14, *Soviet Union, October 1971–May 1972*, 286–90.

77. "Kissinger-Dobrynin Memcon (U.S.)," April 9, 1972, *Détente Years*, 651.

78. "Kissinger-Dobrynin Memcon (U.S.S.R.)," April 9, 1972, *Détente Years*, 653–54.

79. Nixon, *RN*, 589. For Nixon's comments, see *PPP, 1972*, 525–26. For more on the background and aftermath of the signing ceremony, see U.S. Dept. of State, *FRUS, 1969–1976*, vol. E-2, *Documents on Arms Control and Non-Proliferation, 1969–1972*, www.state.gov/r/pa/ho/frus/nixon/e2/83722.htm.

80. "Telegram from Dobrynin to Soviet Foreign Ministry," April 10, 1972, *Détente Years*, 654–55.

81. Julie Nixon Eisenhower, *Pat Nixon: The Untold Story* (New York: Simon and Schuster, 1986), 337.

82. "Nixon-Kissinger-Dobrynin Memcon (U.S.S.R.)," April 10, 1972, *Détente Years*, 654.

83. Nixon, *RN*, 589. The HAK Telcons contain two conversations between Kissinger and Dobrynin on April 10, 1972, although only one has a vague reference to Mrs. Dobrynin and Mrs. Nixon (Kissinger-Dobrynin Telcon, April 10, 1972, 10:10 a.m., HAK Telcons). The other conversation between Kissinger and Dobrynin took place at 12:26 p.m.

84. NT, OVAL 705–13, April 10, 1972. Nixon talked to the White House operator in NT, WHT 22–94, April 10, 1972.

85. NT, WHT 22–95, April 10, 1972. Nixon said: "Pat, for foreign policy reasons we'd like very much if you could see Mrs. [Irina] Dobrynin after your lunch

tomorrow, tomorrow afternoon, about four o'clock or so? Would you be available to do that? Dobrynin's going back to Moscow [on] Friday. She isn't going, but it's just a little move we want to make. She'll just come in and chat about the trip and so forth."

86. NT, WHT 22–97, April 10, 1972.

87. Nixon-Kissinger Telcon, April 10, 1972, 5:25 p.m., HAK Telcons.

88. Nixon Eisenhower, *Pat Nixon*, 335–36.

89. Ibid. I could not locate a Kissinger-Dobrynin telcon after the tea, and *Détente Years* does not mention one.

90. Nixon, *RN*, 589.

91. NT, WHT 22–111, April 11, 1972, 7:41–7:54 p.m.; see also Nixon-Kissinger Telcon, April 11, 1972, 7:30 p.m., HAK Telcons.

92. NT, EOB 330–36, April 12, 1972, U.S. Dept. of State, *FRUS, 1969–1976*, vol. 14, *Soviet Union, October 1971–May 1972*, 300–306.

93. "Kissinger-Dobrynin Memcon (U.S.S.R.)," April 15, 1972, *Détente Years*, 667.

94. "Kissinger-Dobrynin Memcon (U.S.)," April 12, 1972, *Détente Years*, 655–56.

95. Kissinger-Dobrynin Telcon, April 12, 1972, 3:15 p.m., HAK Telcons.

96. "Kissinger-Dobrynin Memcon (U.S.S.R.)," April 12, 1972, *Détente Years*, 656–57.

97. NT, WHT 22–119, April 12, 1972. Kissinger's staff also prepared a telcon for the conversation, although it does not cover the entire conversation (Nixon-Kissinger Telcon, April 12, 1972, 3:22 p.m., HAK Telcons).

98. Wayne Thompson, *To Hanoi and Back: The U.S. Air Force and North Vietnam, 1966–1973* (Washington, DC: Smithsonian Institution Press, 2000), 223, 225–26. Nixon effectively lifted the self-imposed bombing limit that President Lyndon Johnson set on March 31, 1968.

99. *Airpower and the 1972 Spring Invasion*, ed. A. J. C. Lavalle, USAF Southeast Asia Monograph Series, vol. 2, monograph 3 (Washington, DC: Office of Air Force History, 1985), www.afhso.af.mil/shared/media/document/AFD-100922-027.pdf.

100. Ibid. See also Thompson, *To Hanoi and Back*, 225–26. Kissinger called Admiral Moorer "to check . . . to make sure you are going to start to move up to the 18th parallel—the president wanted that," and asked for "no civilian casualties if possible." Moorer noted: "We have to take action so that the Russians don't supply them. I told you about the submarines that are surfacing—they will shake them up" (Kissinger-Moorer Telcon, April 12, 1972, HAK Telcons).

101. "Kissinger-Dobrynin Memcon (U.S.S.R.)," April 13, 1972, *Détente Years*, 659–60. Kissinger discussed his meeting with Dobrynin half an hour later with the president in NT, EOB 329–32, April 13, 1972. Portions are published in an editorial note in U.S. Dept. of State, *FRUS, 1969–1976*, vol. 14, *Soviet Union, October 1971–May 1972*, 314–18.

102. Note delivered to Haig/Howe by Vorontsov, April 14, 1972, NSC Files, President's Trip Files, Dobrynin/Kissinger 1972, Vol. 10, Box 493, RNPLM.

103. "Address to a Joint Meeting of the Canadian Parliament," April 14, 1972, *PPP, 1972*, www.nixonlibraryfoundation.org/clientuploads/directory/archive/1972_pdf_files/1972_0122.pdf.

104. "Editorial Note," U.S. Dept. of State, *FRUS, 1969–1976*, vol. 14, *Soviet Union, October 1971–May 1972*, 318.

105. Nixon, *RN*, 590.

106. "Entry for April 15, 1972," *Haldeman Diary: Multimedia Edition*.

107. Nixon, *RN*, 590–91.

108. NT, EOB 329–42, April 15, 1972, U.S. Dept. of State, *FRUS, 1969–1976*, vol. 14, *Soviet Union, October 1971–May 1972*, 323–36.

109. Oral Note, 5:00 p.m., April 15, 1972, NSC Files, Trip Files, Dobrynin/Kissinger 1972, Vol. 10, Box 493, RNPLM. A handwritten notation on the first page states: "Read by HK to Vorontsov in Map Room, 4–15–72, 5:00 p.m." Dobrynin was out of the embassy but returned later that afternoon.

110. "Telegram from Soviet Embassy in Washington to Moscow," April 15, 1972, *Détente Years*, 663–64.

111. Dobrynin, *In Confidence*, 244.

112. "Kissinger-Dobrynin Memcon (U.S.)," April 15, 1972, *Détente Years*, 664–65.

113. "Kissinger-Dobrynin Memcon (U.S.S.R.)," April 15, 1972, *Détente Years*, 665–68.

114. Nixon-Kissinger Telcon, April 15, 1972, 10:25 p.m., HAK Telcons.

115. Nixon-Kissinger Telcon, April 15, 1972, 11:30 p.m., HAK Telcons. The telcon is incomplete, but the conversation overlaps with the Nixon taping system (NT, WHT 22–131, April 15, 1972, 11:05–11:27 p.m.).

116. "Kissinger-Dobrynin Telcon," April 16, 1972, *Détente Years*, 668–69. The actual message is from a note Col. Richard Kennedy retrieved from the Soviet embassy at 9:30 p.m. (NSC Files, President's Trip Files, Dobrynin/Kissinger 1972, Vol. 10, Box 493, RNPLM).

117. "Memo from Sonnenfeldt to Kissinger," April 16, 1972, NSC Files, President's Trip Files, Dobrynin/Kissinger 1972, Vol. 11, Box 494, RNPLM. The file includes the handwritten message "delivered by Vorontsov to Colonel Kennedy at 1:30 p.m."

118. Nixon-Kissinger Telcon, April 16, 1972, 3:30 p.m., HAK Telcons.

119. Kissinger, *WHY*, 1124; Dobrynin, *In Confidence*, 244–45.

6. Cancellation Crises

First epigraph: NT, WHT 22–131 between Nixon and Kissinger, April 15, 1972. A telcon began in the middle of the conversation and is therefore incomplete (Nixon-Kissinger Telcon, April 15, 1972, 11:30 p.m., HAK Telcons). *Second epigraph:* NT, OVAL 716–4 between Nixon and Kissinger, May 1, 1972, U.S. Dept. of State, *FRUS, 1969–1976*, vol. 14, *Soviet Union, October 1971–May 1972*, 671–76.

1. Nixon conferred with Kissinger about the wording and message of the speech several times on May 8, 1972 (see NT, WHT 24–5; NT, WHT 24–13; and NT WHT 24–16).

2. "Address to the Nation on the Situation in Southeast Asia," May 8, 1972, *PPP, 1972.*

3. Robert B. Semple Jr., "Speaks to Nation: He Gives the Ships of Other Countries 3 Days to Leave," *New York Times,* May 9, 1972, 1.

4. Bernard Gwertzman, "President Urges Soviet to Avoid Confrontation," *New York Times,* May 9, 1972, 1, C19.

5. NT, OVAL 713–1, April 19, 1972, U.S. Dept. of State, *FRUS, 1969–1976,* vol. 14, *Soviet Union, October 1971–May 1972,* 29–30.

6. NT, OVAL 713–1. I transcribed this portion of the conversation, which was not in U.S. Dept. of State, *FRUS, 1969–1976,* vol. 14, *Soviet Union, October 1971–May 1972.*

7. OVAL 713–1, U.S. Dept. of State, *FRUS, 1969–1976,* vol. 14, *Soviet Union, October 1971–May 1972,* 432. See also "Kissinger-Dobrynin Memcon, Dobrynin's Journal," April 13, 1972, *Détente Years,* 660–62; Kissinger-Dobrynin Telcon, 3:45 p.m., April 13, 1972, HAK Telcons.

8. Kissinger, *WHY,* 1155.

9. Ibid., 1125–26.

10. "Dobrynin to Soviet Foreign Ministry," April 19, 1972, *Détente Years,* 675–79.

11. "Nixon to Kissinger," April 20, 1972, 12:03 p.m., U.S. Dept. of State, *FRUS, 1969–1976,* vol. 14, *Soviet Union, October 1971–May 1972,* 449–51, italics in *FRUS.* Nixon described his decision of revised instructions to Kissinger to his chief of staff, H. R. Haldeman. Haldeman wrote that Kissinger "apparently" had plans "to make a long philosophical opening statement," and Nixon disagreed with the approach ("Entry for April 20, 1972," *Haldeman Diaries: Multimedia Edition*). For the actual discussion, see NT, OVAL 714–2, April 20, 1972, U.S. Dept. of State, *FRUS, 1969–1976,* vol. 14, *Soviet Union, October 1971–May 1972,* 451–54. Nixon also informed John Connally that Kissinger was on a secret trip; he described the telegram in NT, OVAL 714–4, April 20, 1972.

12. "Kissinger to Nixon," April 20, 1972, [received 12:16 p.m.], U.S. Dept. of State, *FRUS, 1969–1976,* vol. 14, *Soviet Union, October 1971–May 1972,* 451n4.

13. Kissinger, *WHY,* 1125–26.

14. NT, EOB 332–22, April 25, 1972.

15. "Kissinger, Dobrynin, and Gromyko Memcon," April 20, 1972, 11:00–11:40 p.m. [Moscow], U.S. Dept. of State, *FRUS, 1969–1976,* vol. 14, *Soviet Union, October 1971–May 1972,* 457–63.

16. Kissinger, *WHY,* 1126.

17. "Kissinger to Nixon," April 20, 1972, U.S. Dept. of State, *FRUS, 1969–1976,* vol. 14, *Soviet Union, October 1971–May 1972,* 463–44.

18. Kissinger, *WHY,* 1144.

19. "Group Meeting Memcon," April 21, 1972, noon–4:45 p.m. [Moscow], *FRUS, 1969–1976*, vol. 14, *Soviet Union, October 1971–May 1972*, 474–506. See also *Détente Years*, 681–97, esp. 683–84.

20. "Group Meeting Memcon," April 21, 1972, noon–4:45 p.m. [Moscow], *FRUS, 1969–1976*, vol. 14, *Soviet Union, October 1971–May 1972*, 484.

21. Ibid., 486. Using only the American memcon would reinforce the "decent interval" theory, championed by historians Jeffrey Kimball, William Burr, Jussi Hanhimäki (*Flawed Architect*), and others. These scholars argue that Kissinger suggested to the Soviets and the Chinese that the United States wanted a "decent" or "reasonable" interval between the final exit of U.S. forces from Southeast Asia and a Communist takeover of South Vietnam. It is worth noting, however, that there is a minor, although substantive, difference between the Soviet record of the April 21 meeting and the American record. The Soviet memorandum of conversation confirms Kissinger's first point about the withdrawal of forces but points to a political process rather than a military victory ("Memcon [U.S.S.R.]," April 21, 1972, *Détente Years*, 697–709, esp. 701–2).

22. U.S. Dept. of State, *FRUS, 1969–1976*, vol. 14, *Soviet Union, October 1971–May 1972*, 486.

23. The Viet Cong attacked an army barracks near Pleiku in South Vietnam on February 7, 1965. In retaliation and on the advice of advisors and top legislators, President Johnson ordered the systematic bombing of North Vietnam. The bombing occurred while Kosygin was in Hanoi (Frederick Logevall, *Choosing War: The Lost Chance for Peace and the Escalation of War in Vietnam* [Berkeley: University of California Press, 1999], 324–32).

24. U.S. Dept. of State, *FRUS, 1964–1968*, vol. 14, *Soviet Union, October 1971–May 1972*, 499.

25. *Détente Years*, 695–96.

26. Kissinger, *WHY*, 1145.

27. "Nixon-Haig Telcon," U.S. Dept. of State, *FRUS, 1969–1976*, vol. 14, *Soviet Union, October 1971–May 1972*, 511–13.

28. Kissinger, *WHY*, 1154–55.

29. "Haig to Kissinger," April 22, 1972, 11:08 a.m., U.S. Dept. of State, *FRUS, 1969–1976*, vol. 14, *Soviet Union, October 1971–May 1972*, 554–55.

30. "Haig to Kissinger," April 21, 1972, U.S. Dept. of State, *FRUS, 1969–1976*, vol. 14, *Soviet Union, October 1971–May 1972*, 514–15.

31. "Memcon between Brezhnev, Gromyko, Dobrynin, Aleksandrov-Agentov, Sukhodrev, Samoteykin, Kissinger, Sonnenfeldt, Lord, Negroponte, and Rodman," 11:00 a.m.–4:05 p.m. [Moscow], April 21, 1972, U.S. Dept. of State, *FRUS, 1969–1976*, vol. 14, *Soviet Union, October 1971–May 1972*, 516–44, 522.

32. David Reynolds, *Summits: Six Meetings That Shaped the Twentieth Century* (New York: Basic, 2007), 252–53; Garthoff, *Détente and Confrontation*, 180–83. See also Smith, *Doubletalk*, 228–29.

33. Kissinger, *WHY*, 1149.

34. "Memcon," April 22, 1972, U.S. Dept. of State, *FRUS, 1969–1976*, vol. 14, *Soviet Union, October 1971–May 1972*, 529.

35. Ibid., 532.

36. Gromyko, *Memoirs*, 281.

37. U.S. Dept. of State, *FRUS, 1969–1976*, vol. 14, *Soviet Union, October 1971–May 1972*, 543–44.

38. "Kissinger to Haig," April 22, 1972, [received 4:44 a.m. in Washington], U.S. Dept. of State, *FRUS, 1969–1976*, vol. 14, *Soviet Union, October 1971–May 1972*, 544–46.

39. "Haig to Kissinger," April 22, 1972, 11:08 a.m., U.S. Dept. of State, *FRUS, 1969–1976*, vol. 14, *Soviet Union, October 1971–May 1972*, 554–55.

40. "Entry for April 22, 1972," *Haldeman Diaries: Multimedia Edition*.

41. "Haig to Kissinger," April 22, 1972, 3:00 p.m., U.S. Dept. of State, *FRUS, 1969–1976*, vol. 14, *Soviet Union, October 1971–May 1972*, 559–61.

42. "Haig to Kissinger," April 22, 1972, 4:55 p.m. [Washington], U.S. Dept. of State, *FRUS, 1969–1976*, vol. 14, *Soviet Union, October 1971–May 1972*, 561–63.

43. "Kissinger to Haig," April 22, 1972, [received 5:20 p.m.], U.S. Dept. of State, *FRUS, 1969–1976*, vol. 14, *Soviet Union, October 1971–May 1972*, 565–68.

44. "Memcon of Meeting between Gromyko, Dobrynin, Sukhodrev, Kissinger, Lord and Rodman," April 23, 1972, 10:00 a.m.–1:12 p.m., U.S. Dept. of State, *FRUS, 1969–1976*, vol. 14, *Soviet Union, October 1971–May 1972*, 570–88.

45. "Kissinger to Haig," April 23, 1972, [received 3:54 a.m.], U.S. Dept. of State, *FRUS, 1969–1976*, vol. 14, *Soviet Union, October 1971–May 1972*, 589.

46. "Kissinger to Haig," April 23, 1972, [received 10:12 a.m.], U.S. Dept. of State, *FRUS, 1969–1976*, vol. 14, *Soviet Union, October 1971–May 1972*, 90.

47. "Haig to Kissinger," April 23, 1972, 12:08 p.m., U.S. Dept. of State, *FRUS, 1969–1976*, vol. 14, *Soviet Union, October 1971–May 1972*, 596–97.

48. "Kissinger to Haig," April 23, 1972, no time indicated, U.S. Dept. of State, *FRUS, 1969–1976*, vol. 14, *Soviet Union, October 1971–May 1972*, 598.

49. "Nixon to Kissinger," April 23, 1972, 7:45 p.m., U.S. Dept. of State, *FRUS, 1969–1976*, vol. 14, *Soviet Union, October 1971–May 1972*, 599–603. Nixon's conversations with Haldeman show that the president was very concerned about public relations (see entries for April 23–25, 1972, in *Haldeman Diaries: Multimedia Edition*).

50. "Memcon," April 24, 1972, 11:15 a.m.–1:45 p.m. [Moscow time], U.S. Dept. of State, *FRUS, 1969–1976*, vol. 14, *Soviet Union, October 1971–May 1972*, 605–17. Kissinger describes the meeting in his memoirs (Kissinger, *WHY*, 1151–53).

51. Kissinger maintained that the Soviets had sent him a formal invitation, although he may have actually planted the seeds of the trip in the first place (Kissinger, *WHY*, 1151–53).

52. "Memcon," April 24, 1972, 1:50–3:00 p.m., U.S. Dept. of State, *FRUS, 1969–1976*, vol. 14, *Soviet Union, October 1971–May 1972*, 618–23.

53. Kissinger, *WHY*, 1152–53.

54. Ibid., 1153.

55. "Entry for April 24, 1972," *Haldeman Diaries: Multimedia Edition.*

56. PDD, April 1972, 137–39.

57. NT, EOB 332–22, April 25, 1972.

58. Ibid.

59. NT, EOB 332–35, April 25, 1972.

60. "Nixon to Brezhnev," April 25, 1972, U.S. Dept. of State, *FRUS, 1969–1976,* vol. 14, *Soviet Union, October 1971–May 1972,* 646.

61. Richard M. Nixon, "Address to the Nation on Vietnam," April 26, 1972, 10:00 p.m., *PPP, 1972.*

62. "Memcon (U.S.S.R.)," *Détente Years,* 783–86. There was no American record of the meeting.

63. "New Man in Town," *Time,* March 28, 1969, www.time.com/time/magazine/article/0,9171,839954–1,00.html.

64. The president spent the second half of the week in Key Biscayne and then in Texas, which is why there are no Nixon tapes describing the Kissinger-Dobrynin meeting (April 27–30, 1972, PDD).

65. Peter Osnos, "Outlook Grim for Stopping Foe in North," *Washington Post,* May 1, 1972, A1. Osnos's article was cited in a daily news summary for Kissinger (see "Memo for Mr. Kissinger," May 1, 1972, NSC Files, HAK's Morning News Summary February 1, 1972–June 30, 1972 [1 of 2], Box 349, RNPLM).

66. "Entry for May 1, 1972," *Haldeman Diaries: Multimedia Edition.*

67. William Bundy, *Tangled Web,* 315.

68. "Brezhnev to Nixon," May 1, 1972, NSC Files, President's Trip Files, Dobrynin/Kissinger 1972, Vol. 11, Box 494, RNPLM.

69. Ibid., 2.

70. NT, OVAL 716–2 between Nixon, Rogers, and Kissinger, May 1, 1972.

71. "Lord to Kissinger," May 1, 1972, RG 59, Records of the Policy Planning Staff, Director's Files, 1969–77, Box 340, RNPLM.

72. According to William Bundy, the commander of U.S. forces in Vietnam, General Creighton Abrams, "emphasized that American and Vietnamese airpower could not contain the offensive; additional measures were needed" (see Bundy, *Tangled Web,* 314).

73. NT, OVAL 716–4 between Nixon and Kissinger, May 1, 1972.

74. Luu Van Loi and Nguyen Anh Vu, *Le Duc Tho–Kissinger Negotiations in Paris* (Hanoi: The Gioi, 1995), 216–20.

75. NT, OVAL 717–10 between Nixon and Haig, May 2, 1972.

76. Ibid. Nixon's criticism of Kissinger to Haig on the morning of May 2 repeats the same dissatisfaction Nixon had earlier expressed to Haldeman ("Entry for May 1, 1972," *Haldeman Diaries: Multimedia Edition*).

77. NT, OVAL 717–10 between Nixon, Ziegler, Haldeman, Butterfield, and Haig, May 2, 1972.

78. NT, OVAL 717–19 between Nixon and Haldeman, May 2, 1972. See also "Entry for May 2, 1972," *Haldeman Diaries: Multimedia Edition.*

79. NT, OVAL 717–19.

80. NT, OVAL 717–20 between Nixon and Alexander Haig, May 2, 1972. The conversation could be used in a primer on foreign relations to exemplify several classical theories relating to the Cold War, including the zero-sum game and the domino theory. See also Nixon, *RN,* 600.

81. Haig, *Inner Circles,* 284–85.

82. "Memo from Kissinger to Nixon," May 2, 1972. Included as part of the Document Reader on "NATO, the Warsaw Pact and the Rise of Détente, 1965–1972," CD-ROM, Machiavelli Center for Cold War Studies, September 2002.

83. Kissinger, *WHY,* 1176.

84. Kissinger attributed the divergence of the president's judgments from his own to a "communications cycle and a time-zone difference that left Washington hours behind events" (ibid., 1154).

85. Ibid., 1169, 1175.

86. Nixon, *RN,* 600–601.

87. Isaacson, *Kissinger,* 417, 419. Isaacson wrote: "Hal Sonnenfeldt predicted the Soviets would cancel the summit, John Holdridge predicted the Chinese would freeze relations, John Negroponte predicted the impact of South Vietnamese morale would be dramatic, and the CIA's George Carver said that land supply routes would soon substitute for sea ones. Each was wrong."

88. NT, OVAL 718–1 between Nixon and Haldeman, May 3, 1972.

89. "Memo for Mr. Kissinger," May 3, 1972, NSC Files, HAK's Morning News Summary February 1, 1972–June 30, 1972 [1 of 2], Box 349, RNPLM. The memo cites the *Washington Post,* May 3, 1972, A-14.

90. NT, OVAL 718–1.

91. "Nixon to Brezhnev," May 3, 1972, *Détente Years,* 793–94.

92. NT, OVAL 718–4 between Nixon and Haldeman, May 3, 1972.

93. NT, OVAL 718–9 between Nixon and Kissinger, May 3, 1972.

94. Reeves, *President Nixon,* 472.

95. NT, OVAL 719–22, May 4, 1972, 1:24–1:51 p.m. Before the relevant Nixon tapes had been declassified and released, Jeffrey Kimball accurately described Connally's influence in *Nixon's Vietnam War,* 314.

96. NT, OVAL 720–4 between Nixon and Kissinger, May 5, 1972.

97. Bundy, *Tangled Web,* 316.

98. NT, OVAL 719–9 between Nixon and Kissinger, May 4, 1972.

99. NT, OVAL 720–4.

100. "Dobrynin to Gromyko," May 5, 1972, *Détente Years,* 794–95.

101. "Memcon (U.S.S.R.)," May 5, 1972, *Détente Years,* 796–97.

102. "Brezhnev to Nixon," May 6, 1972, NSC Files, Trip Files, Dobrynin/Kissinger 1972, Vol. 11, Box 494, RNPLM.

103. NT, OVAL 720–19.

104. Kimball, *Nixon's Vietnam War,* 315. Kimball wrote: "At 2:00 p.m. on May 8, after a meeting with the NSC, Nixon gave the execute order for the

operation, which in honor of Nixon's love of football, the military code-named Linebacker."

105. Dobrynin, *In Confidence*, 246–47.

106. "Kissinger-Dobrynin Memcon," May 8, 1972, 8:20–8:55 p.m., NSC Files, Trip Files, Dobrynin/Kissinger 1972, Vol. 11, Box 494, RNPLM.

107. Dobrynin, *In Confidence*, 246–47.

108. In Kissinger's memcon of the meeting, the national security advisor noted: "Dobrynin said he wasn't surprised . . . but it would be much harder to understand in Moscow. . . . If he could explain American conditions in Moscow, it might be easier, but he was far away. He seemed very resigned to a drastic Soviet response" (see "Kissinger-Dobrynin Memcon," May 8, 1972, 8:20–8:55 p.m., NSC Files, Trip Files, Dobrynin/Kissinger 1972, Vol. 11, Box 494, RNPLM; see also Kissinger, *WHY,* 1188).

109. "Nixon to Brezhnev," May 8, 1972, NSC Files, Trip Files, Dobrynin/Kissinger 1972, Vol. 11, Box 494, RNPLM.

110. Garthoff, *Détente and Confrontation,* 117. Kissinger describes the perceived linkage on the part of the Soviets: *WHY,* 1191–92. The record of conversation is Kissinger-Dobrynin Telcon, May 9, 1972, HAK Telcons.

111. Dobrynin, *In Confidence*, 248.

112. Ibid., 247. Dobrynin's memoir account is accurate when compared to a note Dobrynin handed to Kissinger (see "Note from Dobrynin to Kissinger," May 10, 1972, delivered 3:15 p.m. in the White House Map Room, NSC Files, Trip Files, Dobrynin/Kissinger 1972, Vol. 11, Box 494, RNPLM).

113. Dobrynin, *In Confidence,* 247.

114. "Kissinger-Dobrynin Memcon," May 10, 1972, 3:30 p.m., NSC Files, Trip Files, Dobrynin/Kissinger 1972, Vol. 11, Box 494, RNPLM.

115. Kissinger, *WHY,* 1193. For the meeting with Patolichev, see NT, OVAL 723–5, May 11, 1972, and "Meeting Memcon (U.S.)," May 11, 1972, *Détente Years,* 810–11.

116. "Brezhnev to Nixon," May 11, 1972, 4:45 p.m., NSC Files, Trip Files, Dobrynin/Kissinger 1972 , Vol. 11, Box 494, RNPLM.

117. Dobrynin, *In Confidence,* 247.

118. NT, OVAL 723–11, May 11, 1972.

119. "Soviet Position Paper," May 14, 1972, NSC Files, Trip Files, Dobrynin/Kissinger 1972, Vol. 11, Box 494, RNPLM. Although Nixon made his decision and stuck by it, plans were ready if the Soviets had moved to cancel (see "Nixon to Rogers," May 8, 1972, NSC Files, President's Trip Files, President's Moscow Trip May [1972] [Part 3], Box 475, RNPLM). The memo was crossed out and was attached to a contingency statement, if the Soviets should cancel or postpone the summit meeting: "Game Plan for Soviet Cancellation or Postponement," not dated, NSC Files, President's Trip Files, President's Moscow Trip May [1972] [Part 2], Box 475, RNPLM. This game plan was probably prepared on or around May 5, 1972, in light of the text that the president would continue his trips to Austria and Iran (but not

Poland). The plan was for the president to have a stopover for a day in Austria before the Moscow summit to acclimate to the time zone differences (Kissinger, *WHY,* 1204).

120. "Kissinger-Dobrynin Memcon," May 14, 1972, 10:30 a.m., NSC Files, Trip Files, Dobrynin/Kissinger 1972, Vol. 11, Box 494, RNPLM.

121. Aleksandrov-Agentov, *Ot Kollontai,* 228.

122. CIA, "Intelligence Memorandum: Shelest Revisited," July 1, 1972, 2, "The Soviet Estimate: U.S. Analysis of the Soviet Union, 1947–1991," DNSA. It is probable that this report was among those leaked to influential reporters. Raymond Garthoff notes that Jack Anderson and Hedrick Smith "cited classified intelligence reports detailing the Shelest story" (Garthoff, *Détente and Confrontation,* 113n103).

123. Aleksandrov-Agentov, *Ot Kollontai,* 228–30; Shevchenko, *Breaking with Moscow,* 206–16; *The First Directorate;* Shelest, *Spravjniy Sud Istorii,* 688.

124. Dobrynin, *In Confidence,* 248.

125. Shelest, *Spravjniy Sud Istorii,* 688, 377–78.

Conclusion

NT, EOB 382–3 between Nixon, Kissinger, and Haig, December 14, 1972.

1. Shevchenko, *Breaking with Moscow,* 191.

2. Smith, *Doubletalk,* 441.

3. Aleksandrov-Agentov, *Ot Kollontai,* 229.

4. Kissinger, *WHY,* 1223.

5. Ibid., 1222.

6. Aleksandrov-Agentov, *Ot Kollontai,* 229.

7. Kissinger, *WHY,* 1222–29, quote 1227.

8. Aleksandrov-Agentov, *Ot Kollontai,* 229.

9. Arbatov, *The System,* 187.

10. "Entry for March 19, 1971," *Haldeman Diaries: Multimedia Edition.*

11. "Richard M. Nixon: White House Farewell," August 9, 1974, www .historyplace.com/speeches/nixon-farewell.htm.

Bibliography

Archival Sources

Lyndon B. Johnson Library, Austin, TX

National Security File
Vietnam Country File

National Security Archive, George Washington University, Washington, DC

China and the U.S., 1960–1998

Presidential Directives from Truman to Clinton

The Soviet Estimate, U.S. Analysis of the Soviet Union, 1947–1991
U.S. Espionage and Intelligence
U.S. Nuclear Non-Proliferation
U.S. Policy in the Vietnam War, Part I: 1954–1968
U.S. Policy in the Vietnam War, Part II: 1969–1975
Volkogonov Papers (Copy from Library of Congress collection)

Richard Nixon Presidential Library and Museum (RNPLM), Yorba Linda, CA (records formerly at the Nixon Presidential Materials Project, National Archives and Records Administration, College Park, MD)

Henry A. Kissinger (HAK) Office Files
HAK Staff Meeting Transcripts
HAK Trip Files
Henry A. Kissinger Telephone Conversation Transcripts (Telcons) (records available and keyword searchable through the Digital National Security Archive via ProQuest)
    Chronological File
Anatoli Dobrynin File
    Home File
    Jordan File
National Security Council (NSC) Files
    ABM-MIRV

Back-Channel Files
    Briefing Books
Country Files
    Haig Chronological Files
President's Trip Files
Subject Files
National Security Council (NSC) Institutional Files (H-Files)
    Senior Review Group (SRG) Minutes
State Department Lot Files, Record Group 59
    Central Files
    Records of the Policy Planning Staff
White House Central Files
    Staff Members and Office Files
        Office Files of H.R. "Bob" Haldeman
            Haldeman Diaries/Journals
Haldeman Notes
White House Special Files
White House Tapes
Cabinet Room (CAB)
Camp David Hard Wire (CDHW)
Camp David Study (CDS)
Executive Office Building (EOB)
Oval Office (OVAL)
White House Telephone (WHT)

Public Records Office, Kew, United Kingdom

Foreign Office Files (FCO)
Prime Minister's Files (PREM)

Woodrow Wilson Center, Washington, DC

Cold War International History Project

Other Sources

Abuse of Power: The New Nixon Tapes. Edited with introduction by Stanley Kutler. New York: Free Press, 1997.

Aijazuddin, F. S. *From a Head, through a Head, to a Head: The Secret Channel between the U.S. and China through Pakistan.* New York: Oxford USA, 2000.

———. *The White House and Pakistan: Secret Declassified Documents, 1969–1974.* Karachi: Oxford University Press, 2004.

Aleksandrov-Agentov, Andrei Mikhailovich. *Ot Kollontai do Gorbacheva* [Russian]. Moscow: International Relations, 1994.

Ambrose, Stephen. *Nixon: The Education of a Politician, 1913–1962.* Vol. 1. New York: Simon and Schuster, 1987.

———. *Ruin and Recovery, 1973–1990.* Vol. 3. New York: Simon and Schuster, 1992.

———. *The Triumph of a Politician, 1962–1972.* Vol. 2. New York: Simon and Schuster, 1989.

Anderson, Jack. *The Anderson Papers.* With George Clifford. New York: Ballantine, 1974.

Andrade, Dale. *Trial by Fire: The 1972 Easter Offensive.* New York: Hippocrene, 1995.

Andrew, Christopher, and Vasili Mitrokhin. *The Sword and the Shield: The Mitrokhin Archive and the Secret History of the KGB.* New York: Basic, 1999.

Arbatov, Georgi. *The System: An Insider's Life in Soviet Politics.* Introduction by Strobe Talbott. New York: Times Books, 1992.

Asselin, Pierre. *A Bitter Peace: Washington, Hanoi and the Making of the Paris Agreement.* Chapel Hill: University of North Carolina Press, 2002.

Axelrod, Robert. *The Evolution of Cooperation.* New York: Basic, 1984.

Bacon, Edwin, and Mark Sandle, eds. *Brezhnev Reconsidered.* New York: Palgrave, 2002.

Baldwin, David A., ed. *Neorealism and Neoliberalism: The Contemporary Debate.* New York: Columbia University Press, 1993.

Bass, Gary J. *The Blood Telegram: Nixon, Kissinger, and a Forgotten Genocide.* New York: Knopf Doubleday, 2013.

Beam, Jacob. *Multiple Exposure: An American Ambassador's Unique Perspective on East-West Issues.* New York: Norton, 1978.

Berkowitz, Edward D. *Something Happened: A Political and Cultural Overview of the Seventies.* New York: Columbia University Press, 2006.

Berman, Larry. *No Peace, No Honor: Nixon Kissinger and Betrayal in Vietnam.* New York: Simon and Schuster, 2001.

Bower, Mike, and Phil Williams. *Superpower Détente: A Reappraisal.* London: Royal Institute of International Affairs, 1988.

Brandt, Willy. *People and Politics: The Years 1960–1975.* Translated by S. Maxwell Brownjohn. Boston: Little, Brown, 1976.

Brezhnev, Leonid Ilyich. *Memoirs.* Translated by Penny Dole. Oxford, UK: Pergamon, 1982.

Brinkley, Douglas, and Luke Nichter. *The Nixon Tapes.* New York: Houghton Mifflin Harcourt, 2014.

Buchan, Alastair. "The Irony of Henry Kissinger." *International Affairs* 50, no. 3 (July 1974): 367–79.

Bundy, William. *A Tangled Web: The Making of Foreign Policy in the Nixon Presidency.* New York: Hill and Wang, 1998.

Burr, William. "Sino-American Relations, 1969: The Sino-Soviet Border War and Steps Towards Rapprochement." *Cold War History* 1, no. 3 (2001): 73–112.

Burr, William, and Jeffrey Kimball. "Nixon's Secret Nuclear Alert: Vietnam War Diplomacy and the Joint Chiefs of Staff Readiness Test, October 1969." *Cold War History* 3, no. 2 (January 2003): 113–56.

———. *The Secret Alert of 1969, Madman Diplomacy, and the Vietnam War.* Lawrence: University Press of Kansas, 2015.

Burr, William, and Robert A. Wampler. "'With Friends Like These . . .': Kissinger, the Atlantic Alliance and the Abortive 'Year of Europe,' 1973–1974." Paper presented at the International Conference on NATO, the Warsaw Pact, and the Rise of Détente, 1965–1972, Machiavelli Center, Dobbiaco, Italy, September 22, 2002.

Caldwell, Dan. *American-Soviet Relations: From 1947 to the Nixon-Kissinger Grand Design.* Westport, CT: Greenwood, 1981.

Central Intelligence Agency (CIA). Freedom of Information Act (FOIA) website. http://foia.cia.gov.

Chang, Gordon H. *Friends and Enemies: The United States, China, and the Soviet Union, 1948–1972.* Stanford: Stanford University Press, 1990.

Colodny, Len, and Robert Gettlin. *Silent Coup: The Removal of a President.* New York: St. Martin's, 1991.

Connally, John. *In History's Shadow: An American Odyssey.* New York: Hyperion, 1993.

Connolly, Chris. "The American Factor: Sino-American Rapprochement and Chinese Attitudes to the Vietnam War, 1968–1972." *Cold War History* 5, no. 4 (November 2005): 501–27.

Daigle, Craig A. "The Limits of Détente: The United States, the Soviet Union, and the Arab-Israeli Conflict, 1969–1973." Ph.D. diss., George Washington University, 2008.

———. "The Russians Are Going: Sadat, Nixon, and the Soviet Presence in Egypt, 1970–1971." *Middle East Review of International Affairs* 1 (Spring 2004): 1–15.

Dallek, Robert. *Nixon and Kissinger: Partners in Power.* New York: HarperCollins, 2007.

Davidson, Phillip B. *Vietnam at War: The History, 1946–1975.* New York: Oxford University Press, 1991.

Dean, John. *Blind Ambition: The White House Years.* New York: Simon and Schuster, 1976.

Dobrynin, Anatoly. *In Confidence: Moscow's Ambassador to America's Six Cold War Presidents.* Seattle: University of Washington Press, 1995.

———. *Sugubo Doveritel'no: Posol v Vashingtone pri shesti prezidentach CShA, 1962–1986* [Russian]. Moscow: Avtor, 1997. The Russian edition of Dobrynin's memoirs differs slightly from the earlier, English-language version.

Doyle, William. *Inside the Oval Office: The White House Tapes from FDR to Clinton.* New York: Kodansha International, 1999.

Dujardin, Vincent. "Go Between: Belgium and Détente, 1961–1973." *Cold War History* 7, no. 1 (February 2007): 95–116.

Ehrlichman, John. *Witness to Power: The Nixon Years.* New York: Pocket, 1982.

Ethell, Jeffrey, and Alfred Price. *One Day in a Very Long War: May 10, 1972.* New York: Random House, 1989.

Evangelista, Matthew. *Innovation and the Arms Race: How the United States and the Soviet Union Develop New Military Technologies.* Ithaca, NY: Cornell University Press, 1988.

Feldman, Mark. *Poisoning the Press: Richard Nixon, Jack Anderson, and the Rise of Washington's Scandal Culture.* New York: Farrar, Straus and Giroux, 2010.

From: The President: Richard Nixon's Secret Files. Edited by Bruce Oudes. New York: Harper and Row, 1989.

Gaddis, John Lewis. *The Cold War: A New History.* New York: Penguin, 2005.

———. *Strategies of Containment: A Critical Appraisal of Postwar American National Security Policy.* New York: Oxford University Press, 1982.

———. *We Now Know: Rethinking Cold War History.* Oxford: Clarendon, 1997.

Gaiduk, Ilya V. *Confronting Vietnam: Soviet Policy toward the Indochina Conflict, 1954–1963.* Washington, DC: Woodrow Wilson Center Press, 2003.

———. *The Soviet Union and the Vietnam War.* Chicago: I. R. Dee, 1996.

Garment, Leonard. *Crazy Rhythm: My Journey from Brooklyn, Jazz, and Wall Street to Nixon's White House, Watergate, and Beyond.* New York: Random House, 1997.

Garthoff, Raymond. *Détente and Confrontation: U.S.-Soviet Relations from Nixon to Reagan.* Rev. ed. Washington, DC: Brookings Institution Press, 1994.

———. *A Journey through the Cold War: A Memoir of Containment and Coexistence.* Washington, DC: Brookings Institution Press, 2001.

Gelman, Harry. *The Brezhnev Politburo and the Decline of Détente.* Ithaca, NY: Cornell University Press, 1984.

———. *The Rise and Fall of Détente: Causes and Consequences.* Santa Monica, CA: RAND Corporation, 1985.

Geyer, David. "'A Russian Game, a Chinese Game, and an Election Game': Richard Nixon, the Easter Offensive and the Road to the Moscow Summit." Paper presented at the International Conference on NATO, the Warsaw Pact, and the Rise of Détente, 1965–1972, Machiavelli Center, Dobbiaco, Italy, September 28, 2002.

Geyer, David, and Bernd Schaefer, eds. "American Détente and German Ostpolitik, 1969–1972." *Bulletin Supplement.* Washington, DC: German Historical Institute, September 1, 2004.

Graubard, Stephen R. *Kissinger: Portrait of a Mind.* New York: Norton, 1973.

Greenberg, David. *Nixon's Shadow: The History of an Image.* New York: Norton, 2003.

Gromyko, Andrei. *Memoirs.* Translated by Harold Shukman. New York: Doubleday, 1989.

Haig, Alexander. *Inner Circles: How America Changed the World—A Memoir.* With Charles McCarry. New York: Warner, 1992.

Haldeman, H. R. *The Ends of Power.* With Joseph DiMona. New York: Times Books, 1978.

———. *The Haldeman Diaries: Inside the Nixon White House. The Complete Multimedia Edition.* CD-ROM. Santa Monica, CA: Sony Electronic Publishing, 1994.

Hanhimäki, Jussi M. *The Flawed Architect: Henry Kissinger and American Foreign Policy.* New York: Oxford University Press, 2004.

———. "Some More 'Smoking Guns'? The Vietnam War and Kissinger's Summitry with Moscow and Beijing, 1971–73." *SHAFR Newsletter,* December 2001, 40–45.

Haslam, Jonathan. "Collecting and Assembling Pieces of the Jigsaw: Coping with Cold War Archives." *Cold War History* 4, no. 3 (April 2004): 140–52.

Helms, Richard. *A Look over My Shoulders: A Life in the Central Intelligence Agency.* New York: Random House, 2003.

The Henry A. Kissinger Telephone Conversations on World Affairs, 1969–1974. Robert E. Lester project coordinator. Bethesda, MD: UPA collection from LexisNexis, 2005.

Herring, George C. *America's Longest War: The United States and Vietnam, 1950–1975.* New York: McGraw-Hill, 1996.

———. *LBJ and Vietnam: A Different Kind of War.* Austin: University of Texas Press, 1994.

Hersh, Seymour. "Kissinger and Nixon in the White House." *Atlantic Monthly,* May 1982, 35–48.

———. *The Price of Power: Kissinger in the Nixon White House.* New York: Summit, 1983.

Hickman, Martin. *David Matthew Kennedy: Banker, Statesman, Churchman.* Salt Lake City, UT: Deseret, 1987.

Hillenbrand, Martin J. *Fragments of Our Time: Memoirs of a Diplomat.* Athens: University of Georgia Press, 1998.

Hoang Van Hoan. *A Drop in the Ocean: Hoang Van Hoan's Revolutionary Reminiscences.* Beijing: Foreign Language Press, 1986.

Hoff, Joan. *Nixon Reconsidered.* New York: Basic, 1994.

Holland, Max. "Soviet Dezinformatsiya, 1963–1973: Active Measures under Détente." Paper presented at the International Conference on NATO, the Warsaw Pact, and the Rise of Détente, 1965–1972, Machiavelli Center, Dobbiaco, Italy, September 28, 2002.

Hyland, William G. *Mortal Rivals: Superpower Relations from Nixon to Reagan.* New York: Random House, 1987.

Isaacson, Walter. *Kissinger: A Biography.* New York: Simon and Schuster, 1992.

Israelyan, Victor. *On the Battlefields of the Cold War: A Soviet Ambassador's Confession.* University Park: Pennsylvania State University Press, 2003.

Jian, Chen, and David Wilson. "'All under the Heavens Is Great Chaos': Beijing, the Sino-Soviet Border Clashes, and the Turn toward Sino-American Rapprochement." *CWIHP Bulletin,* no. 11 (Winter 1998): 155–75.

Johnson, Robert "KC." "Did Nixon Commit Treason in 1968? What the New LBJ Tapes Reveal." *History News Network,* January 26, 2009. http://hnn.us/articles/60446.html.

Johnson, U. Alexis. *Right Hand of Power: Memoirs of an American Diplomat.* New York: Prentice-Hall, 1984.

Kalb, Marvin, and Bernard Kalb. *Kissinger.* Boston: Little Brown, 1974.

Kalugin, Oleg. *The First Directorate: My 32 Years in Intelligence and Espionage against the West.* With Fen Montaigne. New York: St. Martin's, 1994.

Khan, Roedad, ed. *The American Papers: Secret and Confidential India-Pakistan-Bangladesh Documents 1965–1973.* Karachi: Oxford University Press, 1999.

Kimball, Jeffrey. *Nixon's Vietnam War.* Lawrence: University of Kansas Press, 1998.

———. *The Vietnam War Files: Uncovering the Secret History of Nixon-Era Strategy.* Lawrence: University of Kansas Press, 2004.

Kissinger, Henry A. *Crisis: The Anatomy of Two Major Foreign Policy Crises.* New York: Simon and Schuster, 2003.

———. *Ending the Vietnam War: A History of America's Involvement in and Extrication from the Vietnam War.* New York: Simon and Schuster, 2003.

———. *White House Years.* Boston: Little, Brown, 1979.

———. *Years of Redemption.* Boston: Little, Brown, 1999.

———. *Years of Upheaval.* Boston: Little, Brown, 1982.

The Kissinger Transcripts: The Top-Secret Talks with Beijing & Moscow. Edited by William Burr. New York: New Press, 1998.

Kramer, Mark. "The Soviet-Romanian Split and the Crisis with Czechoslovakia: Context, Reverberations, and Fallout." Paper presented at the International Conference on NATO, the Warsaw Pact, and the Rise of Détente, 1965–1972, Machiavelli Center, Dobbiaco, Italy, September 26–28, 2002.

Kuisong, Yang. "The Sino-Soviet Border Clash of 1969: From Zhenbao Island to Sino–American *Rapprochement.*" *Cold War History* 1, no. 1 (August 2000): 21–52.

Kutler, Stanley. *The Wars of Watergate: The Last Crisis of Richard Nixon.* New York: Knopf, 1990.

Kux, Dennis. *India and The United States: Estranged Democracies 1941–1991.* Washington: NDU Press, 1993.

———. *The United States and Pakistan, 1947–2000, Disenchanted Allies.* Washington and Baltimore: Woodrow Wilson Center Press and Johns Hopkins University Press, 2001.

LaFeber, Walter. *America, Russia, and the Cold War, 1945–1996.* 8th ed. New York: McGraw-Hill, 1997.

Litwak, Robert S. *Détente and the Nixon Doctrine: American Foreign Policy and the Pursuit of Stability, 1969–1976.* Cambridge: Cambridge University Press, 1984.

Logevall, Fredrik, and Andrew Preston, eds. *Nixon in the World: American Foreign Relations, 1969–1977.* New York: Oxford University Press, 2008.

Luu Van Loi, and Nguyen Anh Vu. *Le Duc Tho–Kissinger Negotiations in Paris.* Hanoi: Thé Giói Publishers, 1996.

Machiavelli Center for Cold War Studies. "NATO, the Warsaw Pact and the Rise of Détente, 1965–1972," Document Reader. CD-ROM. Dobbiaco, Italy: September 2002.

Michel, Marshall, III. *Clashes: Air Combat over North Vietnam 1965–1973.* Annapolis: Naval Institute Press, 1997.

Military History Institute of Vietnam. *Victory in Vietnam: The Official History of the People's Army of Vietnam 1954–1975.* Translated by Merle Pribbenow. Lawrence: University Press of Kansas, 2002.

Morgan, Patrick M., and Keith L. Nelson, eds. *Re-Viewing the Cold War: Domestic Factors and Foreign Policy in the East-West Confrontation.* Westport, CT: Praeger, 2000.

Morris, Roger. *Haig: The General's Progress.* New York: Playboy, 1982.

———. *Richard Milhous Nixon: The Rise of an American Politician.* New York: Henry Holt, 1990.

———. *Uncertain Greatness: Henry Kissinger and American Foreign Policy.* New York: Harper and Row, 1977.

Morris, Stephen J. "The Soviet-Chinese-Vietnamese Triangle in the 1970s: The View from Moscow." Cold War International History Project. Working Paper 25, April 1999. www.wilsoncenter.org/sites/default/files/ACFB2E.pdf.

Moss, Richard, and Luke Nichter. "Presidential Scholars and Presidential Recordings." *White House Studies* 8, no. 2 (Fall 2008): 197–202.

Nalty, Bernard. *Air War over South Vietnam, 1968–1975.* Washington, DC: Air Force History and Museums Program, 2000.

National Aeronautics and Space Administration, NASA History Division. *The Partnership: A History of the Apollo-Soyuz Test Project.* NASA SP-4209. Washington, DC: National Aeronautics and Space Administration, Scientific and Technical Information Office, 1978.

National Intelligence Council. *Tracking the Dragon: Selected National Intelligence Estimates on China, 1948–1976.* CD-ROM. Washington DC: U.S. GPO, 2004.

———. *Vietnam Estimative Products, 1945–1975.* Washington, DC: U.S. GPO, 2005. CD-ROM.

Nelson, Keith. *The Making of Détente: Soviet-American Relations in the Shadow of Vietnam.* Baltimore: Johns Hopkins University Press, 1995.

Newhouse, John. *Cold Dawn: The Story of SALT.* New York: Holt, Rinehart and Winston, 1973.

Nichols, John B., and Barrett Tillman. *On Yankee Station: The Naval Air War over Vietnam.* Annapolis: Naval Institute Press, 1987.

Nitze, Paul. *From Hiroshima to Glasnost: At the Center of Decision—A Memoir.* New York: Grove, 1989.

Nixon, Richard M. *In the Arena: A Memoir of Victory, Defeat and Renewal.* New York: Simon and Schuster, 1990.

———. *RN: The Memoirs of Richard Nixon.* New York: Touchstone, 1978.

Nogee, Joseph L., and Robert H. Donaldson. *Soviet Foreign Policy since World War Two.* 4th ed. New York: Pergamon, 1992.

Olson, James S., and Randy Roberts. *Where the Domino Fell: America and Vietnam, 1945–1995.* 3rd ed. St. James, NY: Brandywine, 1999.

Ouimet, Matthew. *The Rise and Fall of the Brezhnev Doctrine in Soviet Foreign Policy.* Chapel Hill: University of North Carolina Press, 2003.

Perlstein, Rick. *Nixonland: The Rise of a President and the Fracturing of America.* New York: Scribner, 2008.

Pipes, Richard. *U.S.-Soviet Relations in the Era of Détente.* Boulder, CO: Westview, 1981.

Porter, Roger. *The U.S.-U.S.S.R. Grain Agreement.* New York: Cambridge University Press, 1984.

Price, Raymond. *With Nixon.* New York: Viking, 1977.

Public Papers of the President: Richard Nixon, 1969–1972. 6 vols. Washington DC: U.S. GPO, 1970–75. Digitized at: www.nixonlibraryfoundation.org/.

Randolph, Stephen A. "A Bigger Game: Nixon, Kissinger and the 1972 Easter Offensive." Ph.D. diss., George Washington University, 2005.

Reeves, Richard. *President Nixon: Alone in the White House.* New York: Simon and Schuster, 2001.

Reston, James. *Lone Star: The Life of John Connally.* New York: Harper and Row, 1989.

Richardson, Elliot. *Reflections of a Radical Moderate.* New York: Pantheon, 1996.

Rosen, James. "Nixon and the Chiefs." *Atlantic Monthly,* April 2002, 53–59.

Rothkopf, David J. *Running the World: The Inside Story of the National Security Council and the Architects of American Power.* New York: Public Affairs, 2005.

Rubinstein, Alvin Z. *The Foreign Policy of the Soviet Union.* 3rd ed. New York: Random House, 1972.

———. *Moscow's Third World Strategy.* Princeton, NJ: Princeton University Press, 1990.

———. *Red Star on the Nile: The Soviet-Egyptian Influence Relationship since the June War.* Princeton, NJ: Princeton University Press, 1977.

———. *Soviet Foreign Policy since World War Two: Imperial and Global.* 4th ed. New York: HarperCollins, 1992.

Ryavic, Karl W. *United States–Soviet Relations.* New York: Longman, 1989.

Safire, William. *Before the Fall: An Inside View of the Pre-Watergate White House.* New York: Doubleday, 1975.

Sagan, Scott D., and Jeremi Suri. "The Madman Nuclear Alert: Secrecy, Signaling, and Safety in October 1969." *International Security* 27, no. 4 (Spring 2003): 150–83.

Sarotte, Mary E. *Dealing with the Devil: East Germany, Détente, and Ostpolitik, 1969–1973.* Chapel Hill: University of North Carolina Press, 2001.

Schulzinger, Robert. *Henry Kissinger: Doctor of Diplomacy.* New York: Columbia University Press, 1991.

Schurmann, Franz. *The Foreign Politics of Richard Nixon: The Grand Design.* Berkeley: Institute of International Studies, 1987.

Seitzinger, Michael V. "Conducting Foreign Relations without Authority: The Logan Act." February 1, 2006. *Congressional Research Report.* www.fas.org/sgp/crs/misc/RL33265.pdf.

Shawcross, William. *Sideshow: Kissinger, Nixon, and the Destruction of Cambodia.* Rev. ed. New York: Simon and Schuster, 1987.

Shelest, Petro. *"The True Judgment of History Still Awaits Us": Memoirs, Diaries, Documents, Materials* [Ukrainian and Russian]. Edited by Juri Shapoval. Kiev: National Academy of Sciences of Ukraine, 2003.

Sherwood, John Darrell. *Fast Movers: Jet Pilots and the Vietnam Experience.* New York: Free Press, 1999.

Shevchenko, Arkady N. *Breaking with Moscow.* New York: Knopf, 1985.

Simon, William. *A Time for Truth.* New York: Reader's Digest Press, 1978.

Sinever, Asaf. "The Nixon Administration and the Cienfuegos Crisis of 1970: Crisis-Management of a Non-Crisis?" *Review of International Studies* 34 (2008): 69–88.

———. *Nixon, Kissinger, and U.S. Foreign Policy Making: The Machinery of Crisis.* Cambridge: Cambridge University Press, 2008.

Sisson, Richard, and Leo E. Rose. *War and Secession: Pakistan, India, and the Creation of Bangladesh.* Berkeley: University of California Press, 1991.

Smith, Gerard. *Disarming Diplomat: The Memoirs of Ambassador Gerard C. Smith, Arms Control Negotiator.* Lanham, MD: Madison Books, 1996.

———. *Doubletalk: The Story of the First Strategic Arms Limitation Talks.* Garden City, NY: Doubleday, 1980.

Sorley, Lewis. *A Better War: The Unexamined Victories and Final Tragedy of America's Last Years in Vietnam.* New York: Harvest, 1999.

Stans, Maurice. *One of the Presidents' Men: Twenty Years with Eisenhower and Nixon.* Washington, DC: Brasseys, 1995.

Stevenson, Richard W. *The Rise and Fall of Détente: Relaxations of Tension in U.S.-Soviet Relations, 1953–1984.* Urbana: University of Illinois Press, 1985.

Summers, Anthony, and Robbyn Swan. *The Arrogance of Power: The Secret World of Richard Nixon.* New York: Viking, 2000.

Suri, Jeremi. "Convergent Responses to Disorder: Cultural Revolution and Détente among the Great Powers during the 1960s." Ph.D. diss., Yale University, 2001.

———. *Henry Kissinger and the American Century.* Cambridge: Harvard University Press, 2007.

———. *Power and Protest: Global Revolution and the Rise of Détente.* Cambridge: Harvard University Press, 2003.

Szulc, Tad. *The Illusion of Peace: Foreign Policy in the Nixon Years.* New York: Viking, 1978.

Terriff, Terry. *The Nixon Administration and the Making of U.S. Nuclear Strategy.* Ithaca, NY: Cornell University Press, 1995.

Thompson, Wayne. *To Hanoi and Back: The U.S Air Force and North Vietnam 1966–1973.* Washington, DC: Smithsonian Institution Press, 2000.

Thornton, Richard C. *The Nixon-Kissinger Years: The Reshaping of American Foreign Policy.* New York: Paragon House, 1989.

Tinguy, Anne de, ed. *The Fall of the Soviet Empire.* Boulder, CO: East European Monographs, 1997.

———. *U.S.-Soviet Relations during the Détente.* Translated by A. P. M. Bradley. Boulder, CO: East European Monographs, 1999.

Truong, Ngo Quang. *The Easter Offensive.* Center for Military History Indochina Monograph series. Washington, DC: Center for Military History, 1979.

Turley, Gerald C. *The Easter Offensive: Vietnam, 1972.* Novato, CA: Presidio, 1985.

United States Department of State. *Foreign Relations of the United States, 1961–1963.* Vol. 19, *South Asia.* Washington, D.C.: U.S. GPO, 1996.

———. *Foreign Relations of the United States, 1964–1968.* Vol. 6, *Vietnam, January–August 1968.* Washington, DC: U.S. GPO, 2002.

———. *Foreign Relations of the United States, 1964–1968.* Vol. 7, *Vietnam, January–August 1968.* Washington, DC: U.S. GPO, 2002.

———. *Foreign Relations of the United States, 1964–1968.* Vol. 14, *Soviet Union.* Washington, DC: U.S. GPO, 2001.

———. *Foreign Relations of the United States, 1964–1968.* Vol. 17, *Eastern Europe.* Washington, DC: U.S. GPO, 1996.

———. *Foreign Relations of the United States, 1964–1968.* Vol. 19, *Arab-Israeli Crisis and War, 1967.* Washington, DC: U.S. GPO, 2004.

———. *Foreign Relations of the United States, 1964–1968.* Vol. 20, *Arab-Israeli Dispute, 1967–1968.* Washington, DC: U.S. GPO, 2000.

———. *Foreign Relations of the United States, 1969–1976.* Vol. 1, *Foundations of Foreign Policy, 1969–1972.* Washington, DC: U.S. GPO, 2003.

———. *Foreign Relations of the United States, 1969–1976.* Vol. 2, *Organization and Management of Foreign Policy, 1969–1976.* Washington, DC: U.S. GPO, 2003.

———. *Foreign Relations of the United States, 1969–1976.* Vol. 5, *United Nations, 1969–1972.* Washington, DC: U.S. GPO, 2004.

———. *Foreign Relations of the United States, 1969–1976.* Vol. 6, *Vietnam, January 1969–July 1970.* Washington, DC: U.S. GPO, 2006.

———. *Foreign Relations of the United States, 1969–1976.* Vol. 11, *South Asia Crisis, 1971.* Washington, DC: U.S. GPO, 2003.

———. *Foreign Relations of the United States, 1969–1976.* Vol. 12, *Soviet Union, January 1969–October 1970.* Washington, DC: U.S. GPO, 2006.

———. *Foreign Relations of the United States, 1969–1976.* Vol. 14, *Soviet Union, October 1971–May 1972.* Washington, DC: U.S. GPO, 2006.

———. *Foreign Relations of the United States, 1969–1976.* Vol. 17, *China, 1969–1972.* Washington, DC: U.S. GPO, 2006.

———. *Foreign Relations of the United States, 1969–1976.* Vol. 24, *Middle East Region and Arabian Peninsula, 1969–1972; Jordan, September 1970.* Washington, DC: U.S. GPO, 2008.

———. *Foreign Relations of the United States, 1969–1976.* Vol. 32, *SALT 1, 1969–1972.* Washington, DC: U.S. GPO, 2010.

———. *Foreign Relations of the United States, 1969–1976.* Vol. 39, *European Security, 1969–1972.* Washington, DC: U.S. GPO, 2008.

———. *Foreign Relations of the United States, 1969–1976.* Vol. 40, *Germany and Berlin, 1969–1972.* Washington, DC: U.S. GPO, 2008.

———. *Foreign Relations of the United States, 1969–1976.* Vol. E-1, *Documents on Global Issues, 1969–1972*. 2005. Online only: www.state.gov/r/pa/ho/frus/nixon/e1/index.htm.

———. *Foreign Relations of the United States, 1969–1976*. Vol. E-2, *Documents on Arms Control and Non-Proliferation, 1969–1972*. 2007. Online only: www.state.gov/r/pa/ho/frus/nixon/e2/index.htm.

———. *Foreign Relations of the United States, 1969–1976*. Vol. E-7, *Documents on South Asia, 1969–1972*. 2005. Online only: www.state.gov/r/pa/ho/frus/nixon/e7/index.htm.

———. *Foreign Relations of the United States, 1969–1976*. Vol. E-10, *Documents on American Republics, 1969–1972*. 2009.

———. *Foreign Relations of the United States, 1969–1976*. Vol. E-13, *Documents on China, 1969–1972*. 2006. Online only: www.state.gov/r/pa/ho/frus/nixon/e13/index.htm.

———. *Soviet-American Relations: The Détente Years, 1969–1972*. Forewords by Henry A. Kissinger and Anatoly Dobrynin. Washington, DC: U.S. GPO, 2007.

Van Atta, Dale. *With Honor: Melvin Laird in War, Peace, and Politics*. Madison: University of Wisconsin Press, 2008.

van der Linden, Frank. *Nixon's Quest for Peace*. Washington, DC: Robert B. Luce, 1972.

Vassiliev, Alexei. *Russian Policy in the Middle East: From Messianism to Pragmatism*. Reading, UK: Ithaca, 1993.

Weihmiller, Gordon R., and Dusko Doder. *U.S.-Soviet Summits: An Account of East-West Diplomacy at the Top, 1955–1985*. Washington, DC: Georgetown University Press, 1986.

Westad, Odd Arne, ed. *Brothers in Arms: The Rise and Fall of the Sino-Soviet Alliance, 1945–1963*. Washington: Woodrow Wilson Center Press, 1998.

———, ed. *The Fall of Détente: Soviet-American Relations during the Carter Years*. Oslo: Scandinavian University Press, 1997.

White, Brian. *Britain, Détente and Changing East-West Relations*. New York: Routledge, 1992.

The White House Tapes: Eavesdropping on the President. Edited by John Prados. New York: New Press, 2003.

Willbanks, James H. *Abandoning Vietnam: How America Left and South Vietnam Lost Its War*. Lawrence: University of Kansas Press, 2004.

Zhai, Qiang. *China and the Vietnam Wars, 1950–1975*. Chapel Hill: University of North Carolina Press, 2000.

Zubok, Vladislav. "Brezhnev Factor in Détente, 1968–1972." International Conference on NATO, the Warsaw Pact, and the Rise of Détente, 1965–1972, Machiavelli Center, Dobbiaco, Italy, September 26–28, 2002.

Index

Kissinger's review and analysis
of, 268–73; Nixon's instructions
regarding Vietnam, 254, 255,
259, 262–63, 264–65; Nixon's
public announcement on Vietnam
following, 274–75; summary of,
294–95; White House public
announcement of and public
relations concerns, 273–74
Moscow Summit: agreements signed at,
61, 103, 297–98; announcement of,
128, 220; Cadillac gift to Brezhnev,
292–93; cancellation crisis (see
Moscow Summit cancellation
crisis); détente and, 300–301;
discussions of Vietnam, 299, 300;
Dobrynin-Kissinger channel and,
214–15, 220; impact of the Sino-
American rapprochement on,
139, 143; imperiled by the North
Vietnamese Easter Offensive, 226,
229, 230, 231–32, 233–37 (see
also Moscow Summit cancellation
crisis); Kissinger's secret trip
to Moscow and (see Moscow,
Kissinger's secret trip to); moving
toward in 1972, 213–15; Nixon-
Brezhnev correspondence on
subjects to be discussed at, 224–
25; Nixon's and Kissinger's use of
triangular diplomacy to obtain,
113–14; Nixon's arrival in Moscow,
297; Polish stopover issue, 220–23;
U.S. Middle East strategy and,
Nixon's and Kissinger's discussion
of, 222–24
Moscow Summit cancellation crisis:
Dobrynin-Kissinger channel and,
233–37, 250–51, 286, 288, 289,
290–93, 294, 295; Kissinger's failed
negotiations with North Vietnam in
May 1972, 250, 276–84; Kissinger's
secret trip to Moscow and, 237–45;

Pat Nixon, Irina Dobrynin, and
the ladies meeting and, 234–37;
Nixon's bombing-mining of North
Vietnam and, 249–51, 284–93;
Nixon's use of public opinion polls
and, 282, 284; the Soviet crisis,
293–94; summary of, 294–95
Moscow Treaty, 78, 103. See also
Eastern treaties
Mujibur Rahman, Sheikh (Mujib), 153,
155, 164, 195
Mukti Bahini, 148, 155, 166
Multiple Independently-targeted
Reentry Vehicles (MIRVs), 62, 68,
71, 74, 92, 95, 100, 108

Nasser, Gamal Abdul, 50
National Command Authority (NCA),
63, 89, 98
National Security Archive, 7, 309, 310
National Security Council (NSC):
back-channel diplomacy and the
centralization of foreign policy by
Nixon and Kissinger, 13, 16–19;
Indo-Pakistani crisis/war of 1971
and, 156; Nixon's consolidation of
control U.S. foreign policy and,
200; Nixon's decision to pursue the
bombing-mining of North Vietnam
in 1972 and, 287–88; Sino-
American rapprochement and, 117;
spying on by the Joint Chiefs of
Staff, xiii–xiv, 151; timeline on the
back-channel discussions regarding
a Soviet-American summit, 127–28
National Security Decision
Memorandum (NSDM) 51, 74
Negroponte, John, 300
Newhouse, John, 5, 67–68, 72, 78,
315n19
New Yorker, 5
New York Times, 21–22, 35, 92, 117,
170, 217, 250

Nothing Less Than War: A New History of America's Entry into World War I
Justus D. Doenecke

Aid under Fire: Nation Building and the Vietnam War
Jessica Elkind

Enemies to Allies: Cold War Germany and American Memory
Brian C. Etheridge

Grounded: The Case for Abolishing the United States Air Force
Robert M. Farley

The American South and the Vietnam War: Belligerence, Protest, and Agony in Dixie
Joseph A. Fry

Obama at War: Congress and the Imperial Presidency
Ryan C. Hendrickson

The Conversion of Senator Arthur H. Vandenberg: From Isolation to International Engagement
Lawrence S. Kaplan

Nixon's Back Channel to Moscow: Confidential Diplomacy and Détente
Richard A. Moss

The Currents of War: A New History of American-Japanese Relations, 1899–1941
Sidney Pash

Eisenhower and Cambodia: Diplomacy, Covert Action, and the Origins of the Second Indochina War
William J. Rust

So Much to Lose: John F. Kennedy and American Policy in Laos
William J. Rust

Foreign Policy at the Periphery: The Shifting Margins of US International Relations since World War II
Edited by Bevan Sewell and Maria Ryan

Lincoln Gordon: Architect of Cold War Foreign Policy
Bruce L. R. Smith